4400 Quotations
for Christian Communicators

4400 Quotations for Christian Communicators

Carroll E. Simcox, Compiler

BAKER BOOK HOUSE
Grand Rapids, Michigan 49516

Copyright © 1991 by Baker Book House Company

ISBN 0-8010-8321-4

Printed in the United States of America

Acknowledgments

Because of the nature of this book as a treasury of quotations from all ages, practically all its contents are drawn from sources in the public domain. Listed below are some works still under copyright from which a considerable number of quotations are taken and permission to quote is in order, with thanks.

The Closing of the American Mind, by Allan Bloom. New York, Simon and Schuster, 1987. Used with permission.

Letters and Papers from Prison, by Dietrich Bonhoeffer. Revised and enlarged edition. Reprinted with permission of Macmillan Publishing Company. Copyright 1953, © 1967, 1971 by SCM Press, Ltd.

The Unquiet Grave, by Cyril Connolly. Published by Harper and Row (now Harper/Collins), New York and London, copyright 1945 by Cyril Connolly. Used with permission of International Creative Management, Inc.

The Little, Brown Book of Anecdotes, edited by Clifton Fadiman. Published by Little, Brown and Company, Boston and Toronto, 1985.

Rudyard Kipling's Verse, Definitive Edition. Contents now in public domain. Doubleday and Company, Garden City, N.Y., 1940.

Making Sense Out of Suffering, by Peter J. Kreeft. Copyright 1986 by Peter J. Kreeft. Ann Arbor, Mich., Servant Publications. Used with permission.

Kung-Fu Meditations. Used with permission from Thor Publishing Company, Ventura, California.

A Grief Observed, by C. S. Lewis. Faber & Faber Ltd., London 1953. Used with Permission.

From MARKINGS by Dag Hammarskjöld, trans., WH Auden. & L Sjöberg Translation Copyright © 1964 by Alfred A. Knopf. Inc. and Faber and Faber, Ltd. Reprinted by permission of the publisher.

Who Needs God, by Harold Kushner. Simon & Schuster, New York, 1989. Used with permission.

Leaves from the Notebook of a Tamed Cynic, by Reinhold Niebuhr. Copyright 1929, 1956 by Reinhold Niebuhr. Foreword copyright 1980 by Harper and Row (Harper/Collins).

Preface

This book is a sequel to *3,000 Quotations on Christian Themes,* and I hope the two books will be companions on many shelves.

Two changes have been made that I think are improvements. In the earlier book the material was organized topically rather than alphabetically, and only the name of the author of each entry was given. Now the order is simply alphabetical, and the name of the book or periodical or other source of each entry is provided.

The fact that a quotation is included doesn't necessarily mean that I wholly or even partly agree with its content (though usually I do). It is included because it strikes me as worthy of reading and marking, even if not inwardly digesting and made an article of faith.

My special thanks to the friends who over the years have known of my collector's mania for apt and lively quotations and have shared their goodies with me. More than a few appear in these two books.

Carroll E. Simcox

A

Abba

Ye have not received the spirit of bondage again to fear; but ye have received the Spirit of adoption, whereby we cry, Abba, Father.   1
Romans 8:15

Because ye are sons, God hath sent forth the Spirit of his Son into your hearts, crying, Abba, Father.   2
Galatians 4:6

A child with strong trust in its parents is encouraged by that very trust to ask all kinds of questions. The disciple who can address God as "Abba" need not fear to use his critical faculties. He can question and reflect and reason without disrespect—as Jesus himself did. It will not diminish the trust or jeopardize the bond. It might do that in a human relationship where the parent is insecure, but with God it leads to maturity. 3
Sister Margaret Magdalen, Jesus, Man of Prayer

It seems from the available testimonies that Jesus constantly addressed God as *abba.... Hitherto only one explanation has been found: abba,* like our "Daddy," is originally a child's word, used however in Jesus' time also as a form of address to their father by grown-up sons and daughters as an expression of politeness generally to older persons deserving of respect. But to use this not particularly manly expression of tenderness . . . as a form of addressing God must have struck Jesus' contemporaries as irreverent and offensively familiar, very much as if we were to address God today as "Dad." For Jesus however this expression is no more lacking in respect than it is when it is used as the child's familiar way of addressing his father. For familiarity does not exclude respect. Reverence remains the basis of his understanding of God. But not its center. Just as a child addresses its earthly father, so according to Jesus should man address his heavenly Father: reverently, ready to obey, but above all securely and confidently.   4
Hans Küng, On Being a Christian

My little Son, who looked with thoughtful eyes
And moved and spoke in quiet grown-up wise,
Having my law the seventh time disobeyed,
I struck him, and dismiss'd
With hard words and unkiss'd,

—His Mother, who was patient, being dead.
Then, fearing lest his grief should hinder sleep,
I visited his bed
But found him slumbering deep
With darken'd eyelids, and their lashes yet
From his late sobbing wet.
And I, with moan,
Kissing away his tears, left others of my own;
For, on a table drawn beside his head,
He had put, within his reach,
A box of counters and a red-veined stone,
A piece of glass abraded by the beach
And six or seven shells,
A bottle with bluebells
And two French copper coins, ranged there with careful art,
To comfort his sad heart.
So when that night I pray'd
To God, I wept, and said:
"Ah, when at last we lie with trancéd breath,
Not vexing Thee in death,
And Thou rememberest of what toys
We made our joys,
How weakly understood
Thy great commanded good,
Then, fatherly not less
Than I whom Thou hast moulded from the clay,
Thou'lt leave Thy wrath, and say,
'I will be sorry for their childishness.'"   5
                                  Coventry Patmore, *The Toys*

Filial fear is childlike love of God, the love that cries *Abba*. When our sense of being God's dear children is strong enough to give us a dread of disappointing him, then—and only then—are we beginning to love God as we ought; beginning to know him as *Abba*.   6
                          C.E.S.*

Ability

Unto one he gave five talents, to another two, and to another one; to each man according to his ability.   7
                          Matthew 25:15

There are diversities of gifts, but the same Spirit.   8
                          1 Corinthians 12:4

The winds and the waves are always on the side of the ablest navigators.   9
                          Edward Gibbon, *The Decline and Fall*
                          of the Roman Empire

*Quotes identified C.E.S. are by the compiler.

Behind an able man there are always other able men.   10
>> Chinese Proverb

Everyone must row with the oars he has.   11
>> English Proverb

Let him sing to the flute who cannot sing to the harp.   12
>> Cicero, *Pro Murena*

Consciousness of our abilities augments them.   13
>> Luc de Clapiers, Marquis de Vauvenargues, *Reflections*

Intelligence is quickness to apprehend as distinct from ability which is capacity to act wisely on the thing apprehended.   14
>> Alfred North Whitehead, *Dialogues of Alfred North Whitehead,* as recorded by Lucien Price

Abnormality

It is defective oysters that produce the pearls.   15
>> Author Unknown

Blessed are the cracked: for they shall let in light.   16
>> David Weeks, *Eccentrics: The Scientific Investigation*

Much Madness is divinest Sense
To a discerning Eye—
Much Sense—the starkest Madness—
'Tis the Majority
In this, as All, prevail—
Assent—and you are sane—
Demur—you're straightway dangerous—
And handled with a Chain.   17
>> Emily Dickinson, "Much madness is divinest sense"

Since the very idea of a normal person is logically a necessary fiction, there being no fixed rule for determining normality, can anybody tell me how either a definitely normal person or a definitely abnormal one can exist—except as a logically necessary fiction?   18
>> C.E.S.

Abortion

Prevention of birth is a precipitation of murder. He also is a man who is about to be one.   19
>> Tertullian, *Apologeticus.* c. A.D. 197

I've noticed that everybody who is for abortion has already been born.   20
>> Ronald Reagan, as a presidential candidate. *New York Times,* 22 September 1980

Dear Abby:

So "Hurting in Fort Worth" and her husband have decided not to have children because "there's so much wrong with the world." And now he insists on an abortion, presumably to "save" the child from all these wrongs.

Yes indeed. That poor child will never see a butterfly. Or a rainbow. A waterfall. A smile. A dog wagging his tail. A tree. The Grand Canyon. Tio. A baseball game. A rose. Grazing sheep. A Raphael painting. The love in a spouse's eyes. "Swan Lake." A parade. A jet stream. A flame in the fireplace. A bicycle. An emerald. A sailboat. A snowflake. A fishing village. A cathedral.

That poor child will never hear a babbling brook. Or rustling leaves. A ball. "Rigoletto." The patter of rain. Another child's laughter. A piano concerto. A hooting owl. The "silence" of a desert. A foghorn. A church organ.

The poor child will never read a poem by Burns. Or a love letter. Tolstoy. A science magazine. Victor Hugo. A name on a boat. A Christmas card. Mark Twain. The Bible.

The poor child will never feel excitement. Or warmth. Love. Anticipation. Awe. The atmosphere of a jazz concert. A cold shower. The satisfaction of a job well done. A friend's handshake. Reverence.

But it seems the parents have never seen, heard, read or felt any of these things either. That's why they're willing to deprive their child of them. Maybe that's the real "wrong in the world."   21

> Gordon Bennett, of Granada Hills, California, in letter to *Dear Abby*, 16 December 1986

Once you pass into the utilitarianism of abortion, where do you go? Why do you kill an unborn child after six months and not old people or criminals or just every second person in the world?   22

> Msgr. Victor Heylen, speech to physicians, Brussels, 1967

Abraham

By faith Abraham, when he was called to go out into a place which he should after receive for an inheritance, obeyed; and he went out, not knowing where he went.   23

> Hebrews 11:8

Abraham was neither a Jew nor a Christian, but he was of the true religion, one resigned unto God, and was not of the number of the idolaters.   24

> The Koran, III

Abraham never "possessed" God; God possessed him.   25

> Karl Barth, *The Epistle to the Romans*

Absence

The Lord watch between thee and me when we are absent one from another. 26

> Genesis 31:49

Absence sharpens love; presence strengthens it.   27

> Thomas Fuller, *Gnomologia*

It takes time for the absent to assume their true place in our thoughts. After death they take on a firmer outline and then cease to change.   28

> Colette (*Sidonie Gabrielle Claudine Colette* 1873–1954), *Earthly Paradise,* "The Captain"

The pain without the peace of death.   29

> Thomas Campbell, *Absence*

The joy of life is variety; the tenderest love requires to be renewed by intervals of absence.   30

> Samuel Johnson, *The Idler* (1758–1760), no. 39

Absence and death are the same—only that in death there is no suffering.   31

> Walter Savage Landor, *Letter to Robert Browning,* c. 1862

Abstinence

Abstain from all appearance of evil.   32

> 1 Thessalonians 5:22

Dearly beloved, I beseech you as strangers and pilgrims, abstain from fleshly lusts, which war against the soul.   33

> 1 Peter 2:11

Abstinence is as easy to me as temperance would be difficult.   34

> Samuel Johnson. Hannah More, *Anecdotes of Johnson*

The man who causes himself pain by not enjoying what is not sinful may be called a sinner.   35

> Talmud, *Nazir*

True mortifications are those which are not known.   36

> François de la Rochefoucauld, *Maxims*

Even devout Christians today seem to have trouble making a case for abstinence of any kind. But surely they must approve such a precept as this: Abstain that others may obtain. Fast that others may feast.   37

> C.E.S.

Acceptance

Now he is dead, wherefore should I fast? can I bring him back again?   38

> 2 Samuel 12:23

Shall we receive good at the hand of God, and shall we not receive evil?   39

> Job 2:10

The cup which my Father hath given me, shall I not drink it?   40

> Jesus in John 18:11

I have to accept the Universe and the English temperament. They are a shiftless lot.   41

> Stephen Mackenna, *Letters*

It just ain't possible to explain some things. It's interesting to wonder on them and do some speculation, but the main thing is you have to accept it—take it for what it is, and get on with your growing.　　　　　　42

　　　　Jim Dodge, *Fub*

I like trees because they seem more resigned to the way they have to live than other creatures do.　　　　　　43

　　　　Willa Cather, *O Pioneers!*

"—Night is drawing nigh—"
For all that has been—Thanks!
To all that shall be—Yes!　　　　　　44

　　　　Dag Hammarskjöld, *Markings*

Acceptance of one's life has nothing to do with resignation: it does not mean running away from the struggle. On the contrary, it means accepting it as it comes, with all the handicaps of heredity, of suffering, of psychological complexes and injustices.　　　　　　45

　　　　Paul Tournier, *The Meaning of Persons*

Margaret Fuller: I accept the universe!
Thomas Carlyle: By God, she'd better!　　　　　　46

　　　　Apocryphal, but probably true

Things cannot always go your way. Learn to accept in silence the minor aggravations, cultivate the gift of taciturnity and consume your own smoke with an extra draught of hard work, so that those about you may not be annoyed with the dust and soot of your complaints.　　　　　　47

　　　　Sir William Osler. Harvey Cushing, *The Life of Sir William Osler*

Accident

Receive the accidents that befall you as good, knowing that nothing happens without God.　　　　　　48

　　　　The Teaching of the Twelve Apostles (The Didache), author
　　　　unknown. A.D. 2d century

It has been said that Providence is the Christian name of Accident and someone else may say that Accident is a nickname of Providence.　　　　　　49

　　　　Nicolas Chamfort, *Maxims and Thoughts*

I never say the universe was an accident. The word *accident* should be erased from the dictionary.　　　　　　50

　　　　Isaac Bashevis Singer, interview in *The New York Times Magazine*,
　　　　3 December 1978

Achievement

Except the Lord build the house, they labor in vain that build it.　　　　　　51

　　　　Psalm 127:1

By their fruits ye shall know them.　　　　　　52

　　　　Jesus in Matthew 7:20

14

How my achievements mock me!   53
> William Shakespeare, *Troilus and Cressida*, IV, ii, 72

To achieve great things we must live as though we were never going to die.   54
> Luc de Clapiers (Marquis de Vauvanargues), *Maxims and Reflections*

The responsibility for our mistakes is ours, but not the credit for our achievements. Man's freedom is freedom to betray God. God may love us—yes—but our response is voluntary.   55
> Dag Hammarskjöld, *Markings*

So much one man can do
That doth both act and know.   56
> Andrew Marvell, *Upon Cromwell's Return from Ireland*

The house praises the carpenter.   57
> Ralph Waldo Emerson, *Journal,* 1836

Few works of merit and importance have been executed either in a garret or a palace.   58
> Edward Gibbon, *Memoirs of My Life*

No man has lived to much purpose unless he has built a house, begotten a son, or written a book.   59
> Italian Proverb

Action

Even a child is known by his doings.   60
> Proverbs 20:11

Let your light so shine before men, that they may see your good works.   61
> Jesus in Matthew 5:16

Whatsoever ye do in word or deed, do all in the name of the Lord Jesus.   62
> Colossians 3:17

Action springs not from thought, but from a readiness for responsibility.   63
> Dietrich Bonhoeffer, *Letters and Papers from Prison*

In our age, the road to holiness necessarily passes through the world of action.   64
> Dag Hammarskjöld, *Markings*

"I am ashamed of my emptiness," said the Word to the Work. "I know how poor I am when I see you," said the Work to the Word.   65
> Rabindranath Tagore, *Stray Birds*

To dispose a soul to action we must disturb its equilibrium.   66
> Eric Hoffer, *The Ordeal of Change*

Every act leaves the world with a deeper or a fainter impress of God.   67
> Alfred North Whitehead, *Religion in the Making*

Act quickly, think slowly.   68
> Greek Proverb

People who know how to act are never preachers.   69

Ralph Waldo Emerson, Journal, 1844

A thought which does not result in an action is nothing much, and an action which does not proceed from a thought is nothing at all.   70

George Bernanos, The Last Essays of George Bernanos, "France
Before the World of Tomorrow"

Too many churchgoers are singing "Standing on the Promises" when all they are doing is sitting on the premises.   71

Author Unknown

Adam

When he opened his eyes, Adam did not ask God: Who are *you?* He asked: Who am *I?*   72

Elie Wiesel, The Oath

The man without a navel still lives in me.   73

Sir Thomas Browne, Religio Medici

Adam ate the apple, and our teeth still ache.   74

Hungarian Proverb

Divine educator; first inventor of science and literature. (*Adam, divinitus edoctus, primus scientiarum et litterarum inventor.*)   75

Author unknown, inscription upon a portrait of Adam in the
Vatican, c. 1550

O Adam, what have you done? (*O Adam, quid fecisti?*)   76

Author Unknown

Adam's naming of the animals in Paradise was his vision of the nature, distinction, and purpose of his own instincts and powers: for *he* was paradise.   77

Coventry Patmore, The Rod, the Root and the Flower, "Aurea Dicta,"
XCI

Before the entrance of the female Eve into the story, it should be just as impossible to call Adam a "male" as it would be to speak or think of a "father" before there was a concept "child." There can't be a "father" without a "child"; no more can there be a "male" without a "female." To call the pre-Eve Adam a "male" is to get ahead of the story, to have moved into a language game that does not and cannot exist at that point.   78

Vernard Eller, The Language of Canaan and the Grammar of
Feminism

In the eyes of science, which at long range can only see things in bulk, the "first" man is, and can only be, a *crowd,* and his infancy is made up of thousands and thousands of years.   79

Pierre Teilhard de Chardin, The Phenomenon of Man

I do not doubt that if the Paradisal man could now appear among us, we should regard him as an utter savage, a creature to be exploited or, at best, patronized. Only one or two, and those the holiest among us, would glance a second time at the naked, shaggy-bearded, slow-spoken creature: but they, after a few minutes, would fall at his feet.   80

C. S. Lewis, *The Problem of Pain*, ch. 5, "The Fall of Man"

Adam and Christ

For as in Adam all die, even so in Christ shall all be made alive.   81

1 Corinthians 15:22

The fall of the first Adam was the end of the beginning; the rise of the second Adam was the beginning of the end.   82

Samuel A. W. Duffield, attributed

When Jesus gave the gift of "Abba" to his disciples he—the second Adam—restored to mankind something that the first Adam had lost. The concept of man's "original" intimacy with God was something rendered by the church fathers in the Greek word *parrhesia*—free speech. It describes the utter freedom of communication that Adam enjoyed with God. Before the fall he was able to converse familiarly with the God who came down to walk with him in the garden in the evenings. Adam was at one with himself, with the creatures around him and with God. The "free speech" of which the fathers speak was a symbolic expression of the perfect adaptation to reality which came from the fact that man was what God intended him to be—himself. He had no guile or deception until the fall, no masks or illusions, no posing or posturing. He had intimate communication with his creator, because he was innocent.   83

Sister Margaret Magdalene, *Jesus, Man of Prayer*

Adam and Eve

Eve always seems closer to us than Adam.   84

Croatian Proverb

The whole point about Adam and Eve (before the fall) is that they would never, but for sin, have been old, so they were never young, never immature or undeveloped. They were created full-grown and perfect.   85

C. S. Lewis, *A Preface to Paradise Lost*

Adjustment

Stop trying to "adjust." Adjust to what? To the general fiction?   86

Thomas Merton, *Conjectures of a Guilty Bystander*

The supple, well-adjusted man is the one who has learned to hop into the meat grinder while humming a hit-parade tune.   87

Marshall Mc Luhan, *The Mechanical Bride*, "Education"

Mahomet made the people believe that he would call a hill to him, and from the top of it offer his prayers for the observers of his law. The people assembled: Mahomet called the hill to come to him again and again; and when the hill stood still, he was never a whit abashed, but said, "If the hill will not come to Mahomet, Mahomet will go to the hill."   88

Francis Bacon, *Essays*, "Of Boldness"

17

One aim of any satisfying religious philosophy is to teach us how to adjust to the inevitable. "Things and actions are what they are," said Bishop Joseph Butler, "and the consequences of them will be what they will be: why then should we desire to be deceived?" Why indeed? Unfortunately unregenerate human nature often does desire to be deceived, as Gautama Buddha and our Lord Himself were made painfully aware.   89

Dom Aelred Graham, Zen Catholicism

I have never known a person worth knowing who was not maladjusted to the world around him, the "general fiction." The closer people become "adjusted" to Jesus as their only master and guide of life and their only criterion of what is worth thinking, saying, and doing—the ultimate Maladjusted Man,—the more maladjusted they appear to everybody else.   90

C.E.S.

Adoption

God has made his children by adoption nearer to himself than the angels. The angels are the friends of Christ; believers are his members.   91

Thomas Watson, The Golden Treasury of Puritan Quotations

Adoration

Adoration says, "What must be the quality of that being whose far-off and momentary coruscations are like this?" One's mind runs up the sunbeam to the sun.   92

C. S. Lewis, Letters to Malcolm: Chiefly on Prayer

It is magnificent to be clothed like the lilies of the field . . . but the supreme glory is to be nothingness in adoration.   93

Søren Kierkegaard, quoted in Antonin Sertillanges, Rectitude

Ascription of praise to God is the utterance of joy and gladness which the excellence tends to excite in us, and may be called a caress of words.   94

Henry Ward Beecher, Proverbs from Plymouth Pulpit

To be with God wondering, that is adoration. To be with God gratefully, that is thanksgiving. To be with God ashamed, that is contrition. To be with God with people and things we care about in our hearts, that is intercession. But the center of it in desire and in design will be the being with God.   95

Arthur Michael Ramsey, Archbishop of Canterbury. Christian World,
"Heart of Prayer," 7 December 1978

Adultery

Drink waters out of thine own cistern, and running waters out of thine own well.   96

Proverbs 5:15

Whosoever looketh on a woman to lust after her hath committed adultery with her already in his heart.   97

Jesus in Matthew 5:28

Adventure

Adventure is hardship aesthetically considered. 98
> Barry Targan, *Kingdoms*

Some cynic from the edge of the crowd insists that humans still can't really fly. But somewhere in some little garage some maniac with a gleam in his eye is scarfing vitamins and mineral supplements, and practicing flapping his arms faster and faster. 99
> Robert Fulghum, *All I Really Need to Know*
> *I Learned in Kindergarten*

Adversary

Agree with thine adversary quickly, whilst thou art in the way with him. 100
> Jesus in Matthew 5:25

Do as adversaries do in law,
Strive mightily, but eat and drink as friends. 101
> William Shakespeare, *The Taming of the Shrew,* I, ii, 278

In dealing with a foolish or stubborn adversary remember your own mood constitutes half the force opposing you. 102
> Austin O'Malley, *Keystones of Thought*

Adversity

If thou faint in the day of adversity, thy strength is small. 103
> Proverbs 24:10

In the day of prosperity be joyful, but in the day of adversity, consider. 104
> Ecclesiastes 7:14

When an elephant is in trouble, a frog will kick him. 105
> Hindu Proverb

The Promised Land always lies on the other side of a wilderness. 106
> Havelock Ellis, The *Dance of Life*

Adversity not only draws people together but brings forth that beautiful inward friendship, just as the cold winter forms ice-figures on the window panes which the warmth of the sun effaces. 107
> Søren Kierkegaard, *Journals*

To rejoice in adversity . . . is to joy in the cross of Christ. 108
> Thomas à Kempis, *The Imitation of Christ*

Prosperity getteth friends, but adversity trieth them. 109
> Nicholas Ling, *Politeuphuia*, 1597

Sweet are the uses of adversity,
Which, like the toad, ugly and venomous,
Wears yet a precious jewel in his head;
And this our life, exempt from public haunt,

Finds tongues in trees, books in the running brooks,
Sermons in stones, and good in everything. [*Duke Senior.*]   110
William Shakespeare, *As You Like It*, II, ii. 12

I never knew a man in my life who could not bear another's misfortunes perfectly like a Christian.   111
Alexander Pope, *Thoughts on Various Subjects*

There are three modes of bearing the ills of life: by indifference, by philosophy, and by religion.   112
Charles Caleb Colton, *Lacon*

Every calamity is a spur and valuable hint.   113
Ralph Waldo Emerson, *The Conduct of Life,* "Fate"

Adversity makes a man wise, not rich.   114
Author Unknown

Adversity makes a man, luck makes monsters.   115
French Proverb

Advice

There is yet one man, Micaiah, the son of Imlah, by whom we may inquire of the Lord: but I hate him, for he doth not prophesy good concerning me, but evil. [*Ahab, King of Israel.*]   116
1 Kings 22:8

Give instruction to a wise man, and he will be yet wiser; teach a just man, and he will increase in learning.   117
Proverbs 9:9

The lips of the righteous feed many.   118
Proverbs 10:21

The poor man's wisdom is despised, and his words are not heard.   119
Ecclesiastes 9:16

If I declare it unto thee, wilt thou not surely put me to death? [*Jeremiah the prophet to Zedekiah the king.*]   120
Jeremiah 38:15

He that heareth, and doeth not, is like a man that, without a foundation, built an house upon the earth.   121
Jesus in Luke 6:49

No one wants advice—only corroboration.   122
John Steinbeck, *The Winter of Our Discontent*

You will always find some Eskimos ready to instruct the Congolese on how to cope with heat waves.   123
Stanislaw J. Lec, *Unkempt Thoughts*

There is little serenity comparable to the serenity of the inexperienced giving advice to the experienced.   124
Anonymous, (*Henry S. Haskins*), *Meditations in Wall Street*

Use me, Lord, oh, use me—in some advisory capacity!   125
>Author unknown, heard in a prayer meeting

Affection

Be kindly affectioned one to another with brotherly love.   126
>Romans 12:10

Talk not of wasted affection! Affection never was wasted!   127
>Henry Wadsworth Longfellow, *Evangeline*

Praise is well, compliment is well, but affection—that is the last and final and most precious reward that any man can win, whether by character or achievement.   128
>Mark Twain, *Speech,* "When in Doubt, Tell the Truth"

Affection without action is like Rachel, beautiful but barren.   129
>John Trapp, *The Golden Treasury of Puritan Quotations*

Affection magnifies trifles.   130
>Leigh Hunt, *Table Talk,* 1851

True affection is a body of enigmas, mysteries and riddles, wherein two so become one that they both become two.   131
>Sir Thomas Browne, *Religio Medici*

'Tis sweet to feel by what fine-spun threads our affections are drawn together.   132
>Laurence Sterne, *A Sentimental Journey*

Affection is a bad adviser.   133
>German Proverb

One must not be mean with affections; what is spent of the funds is renewed in the spending itself. Left untouched for too long they diminish imperceptibly or the lock gets rusty; they are there all right but one cannot make use of them.   134
>Sigmund Freud. *Letter to Martha Bernays,* 18 August 1882

Human nature is so constructed that it gives affection most readily to those who seem least to demand it.   135
>Bertrand Russell, *The Conquest of Happiness*

Affliction

I have chosen thee in the furnace of affliction.   136
>Isaiah 48:10

Wherefore is light given to him that is in misery, and life unto the bitter in soul?   137
>Job 3:20

In all their affliction he was afflicted, and the angel of his presence saved them; in his love and in his mercy he redeemed them; and he bare them, and carried them all the days of old.   138
>Isaiah 63:9

Affliction is not a psychological state: it is a pulverization of the soul by the mechanical brutality of circumstances. 139
> Simone Weil, *Gateway to God*

It is said that in some countries trees will grow, but will bear no fruit, because there is no winter there. 140
> John Bunyan, *The Golden Treasury of Puritan Quotations*

Affliction may be lasting, but it is not everlasting. 141
> Thomas Watson, *ibid.*

There is more evil in a drop of sin than in a sea of affliction. 142
> Ibid.

We often learn more of God under the rod that strikes us than under the staff that comforts us. 143
> Stephen Charnock, *The Golden Treasury of Puritan Quotations*

Afterlife

Have you been shown the gates of Death
or met the janitors of Shadowland? 144
> Job 38:17, *The Jerusalem Bible*

We have no guarantee that the afterlife will be any less exasperating than this one, have we? 145
> Noel Coward, *Blithe Spirit*

Age, Aging

So teach us to number our days that we may apply our hearts unto wisdom. 146
> Psalm 90:12

I am certain there is no greater misfortune than to have a heart that will not grow old. 147
> Benjamin Disraeli. *Letter to Lady Bradford,* 1873

Grow old along with me!
The best is yet to be,
The last of life, for which the first was made:
Our times are in His hand
Who saith "A whole I planned,
Youth shows but half; trust God: see all, nor be afraid!" 148
> Robert Browning, *Rabbi Ben Ezra,* st. 1

I'm growing old! I'm *coming apart!* And it's VERY INTERESTING! 149
> William Saroyan. Interview in *New York Times,* 20 May 1979

Time has laid his hand
Upon my heart, gently not smiting it,
But as the harper lays his open palm
Upon his harp to deaden the vibrations. 150
> Henry Wadsworth Longfellow, *The Golden Legend,* "The Cloisters"

Age, Infancy, and Childhood

I see the sleeping babe, nestling the breast of its mother;
The sleeping mother and babe-hushed,
I study them long and long.   101
> Walt Whitman, *Leaves of Grass,* "Mother and Babe"

A baby, after an exhibition on the pot, with much anger and howling, stretches out its arms with a little cry, as when its pram is passing under the trees, to reveal an immense wonder and love for life,—a Soul.   152
> Cyril Connolly, *The Unquiet Grave*

Among the three or four million cradles now rocking in the land are some which this nation would preserve for ages as sacred things, if we could know which ones they are.   153
> Mark Twain, answering a toast "to the babies," at a banquet in honor of General U. S. Grant, 14 November 1879

A baby is God's opinion that the world should go on.   154
> Carl Sandburg, attributed

A sleeping child gives me the impression of a traveller in a very far country. 155
> Ralph Waldo Emerson, *Journals,* 1839–1841

A baby is an angel whose wings decrease as his legs increase.   156
> French Proverb

I fancy that most of those who think at all have done a great deal of their thinking in the first fourteen years.   157
> C. S. Lewis, *Surprised by Joy*

At the same time came the disciples unto Jesus, saying, Who is the greatest in the kingdom of heaven? And Jesus called a little child unto him, and set him in the midst of them, and said, Verily I say unto you, Except ye be converted, and become as little children, ye shall not enter into the kingdom of heaven. Whosoever, therefore, shall humble himself as this little child, the same is greatest in the kingdom of heaven. 158
> Matthew 18:1–4

There are some of us who in after years say to Fate, "Now deal us your hardest blow, but let us never again suffer as we suffered when we were children."   159
> Olive Schreiner, *The Story of an African Farm*

Children begin by loving their parents. After a time they judge them. Rarely, if ever do they forgive them.   160
> Oscar Wilde, *A Woman of No Importance*

Age, Youth

It is good for a man that he bear the yoke in his youth.   161
> Lamentations 3:27

Youth is almost everything else, but it is hardly ever original.   162
> G. K. Chesterton, *Charles Dickens*

Nobody understands anyone 18, including those who are 18.   163

Jim Bishop, Shrewsbury (NJ) *Daily Register,* "Age of Consent to What?" 26 April 1979

The deepest definition of youth is, Life as yet untouched by tragedy.   164

Alfred North Whitehead, *Adventures of Ideas*

The imagination of a boy is healthy, and the mature imagination of a man is healthy; but there is a space of life between in which the soul is in a ferment, the character undecided, the way of life uncertain, the ambition thick-sighted. . . .   165

John Keats, in preface to *Endymion*

Don't laugh at a youth for his affectations; he is only trying on one face after another until he finds his own.   166

Logan Pearsall Smith, *Afterthoughts*

Man reaches the highest point of lovableness at 12 to 17—to get it back, in a second flowering, at the age of 70 to 90.   167

Isak Dinesen, *Shadows of the Grass*

The young are permanently in a state resembling intoxication; for youth is sweet and they are growing.   168

Aristotle, *Nicomathean Ethics*

It is an illusion that youth is happy, an illusion of those who have lost it.   169

W. Somerset Maugham, *Of Human Bondage*

Age, Middle Age

At middle age the soul should be opening up like a rose, not closing up like a cabbage.   170

John Andrew Holmes, *Wisdom in Small Doses*

Any man worth his salt has by the time he is forty-five accumulated a crown of thorns, and the problem is to learn to wear it over one ear.   171

Christopher Morley, attributed

As you got older, and felt yourself to be at the center of your time, and not at a point in its circumference, as you felt when you were little, you were seized with a sort of shuddering.   172

Thomas Hardy, *Jude the Obscure*

Men, like peaches and pears, grow sweet a little while before they begin to decay.   173

Oliver Wendell Holmes, *The Autocrat of the Breakfast-Table*

Age, Old Age

Cast me not off in the time of old age; forsake me not when my strength faileth.   174

Psalm 71:9

The hoary head is a crown of glory, if it be found in the way of righteousness.   175

Proverbs 16:31

Our brains are seventy-year clocks. The angel of life winds them up once for all, then closes the case, and gives the key into the hands of the angel of the resurrection. 176

Oliver Wendell Holmes, *The Autocrat of the Breakfast-Table*

Old age, calm, expanded, broad with the haughty breath of the universe,
Old age, flowing free with the delicious nearby freedom of death. 177

Walt Whitman, *Leaves of Grass,* "Song of the Open Road"

It is a man's own fault. It is from want of use, if his mind goes torpid in old age. 178

Samuel Johnson. Boswell's *Life,* 9 April 1778

At seventy-seven it is time to be in earnest. 179

Samuel Johnson, *Journey to the Western Islands of Scotland*

When one has reached 81, one likes to sit back and let the world turn by itself, without trying to push it. 180

Sean O'Casey. *New York Times,* 25 September 1960

I agree that the last years of life are the best, if one is a philosopher. 181

George Santayana, *Letters*

A little more tired at close of day,
A little less anxious to have our way;
A little less ready to scold and blame,
A little more care of a brother's name;
And so we are nearing our journey's end,
When time and eternity meet and blend. 182

Rollin John Wells, *Growing Old*

The riders in a race do not stop short when they reach the goal. There is a little finishing canter before coming to a standstill. There is time to hear the kind voice of friends and to say to one's self: "The work is done." 183

Oliver Wendell Holmes, Jr. Speech on his 90th birthday,
Washington, D.C., 8 March 1931

The love we have in our youth is superficial compared to the love that an old man has for his old wife. 184

Will Durant, on his 90th birthday. *New York Times,*
6 November 1975

As a white candle
In a holy place,
So is the beauty
of an agéd face.

As the spent radiance
Of the winter sun,
So is a woman
With her travail done.

Her brood gone from her
And her thoughts as still

As the waters
Under a ruined mill.   185

Joseph Campbell, The Old Woman

Fortunate are those who actually enjoy old age.   186

Jewish Proverb

Father Time in his kindness bestows wrinkles on those who walk with him long enough and do the work God gives them to do well enough. Wrinkles deserve a good press and universally get a bad one. To the best of my knowledge, the only time anybody has ever spoken well of them was on January 20, 1961, when an editorialist for *The London Daily Mail* wrote: "There is a case for keeping wrinkles. They are the long-service stripes earned in the hard campaign of life." These stripes have to be earned. I don't have many of them compared to most people of my age, and I'm rather ashamed that I haven't because evidently I haven't earned them. I must try harder.   187

C.E.S.

Ages, The

How can an age which is so devoid of imagination as ours be truly religious? 188

Reinhold Niebuhr, Leaves from the Notebook of a Tamed Cynic

Every age has a blind eye and sees nothing wrong in practices and institutions which its successors view with just horror.   189

Sir Richard Livingstone, On Education

The Middle Ages had their wars and agonies, but also intense delights. Their gold was dashed with blood; but ours is sprinkled with dust.   190

John Ruskin, Modern Painters

We are children of our age, but children who will never know their mother. 191

Logan Pearsall Smith, Afterthoughts

In every age, even the most enlightened, there is what may justly be called the spirit of the time—a kind of atmosphere that will pass away but which, while it lasts, deceives everybody as to the importance and even the truth of the dominant opinions.   192

Blaise Pascal, Pensées

Oh the times! Oh the manners! (*O tempora! O mores!*)   193

Cicero, Against Catiline

Agnosticism

It is very good for a man to talk about what he does not understand, as long as he understands that he does not understand it.   194

G. K. Chesterton, A Handful of Authors

I do not see much difference between avowing that there is no God and implying that nothing definite for certain can be known about God.   195

John Henry Newman, On the Scope and Nature of University Education

The modern agnostic improves upon the ancient by adding "I don't care" to "I don't know."   196

> Coventry Patmore, *The Rod, the Root and the Flower,*
> "Aurea Dicta," LIV

An agnostic is a person who doesn't know for sure whether there really is a God. That is some people all of the time and all people some of the time.   197

> Frederick Buechner, *Wishful Thinking: A Theological ABC*

They are ill discoverers that think there is no land, when they can see nothing but sea.   198

> Francis Bacon, *The Advancement of Learning*

All great religions, in order to escape absurdity, have to admit a dilution of agnosticism. It is only the savage, whether of the African bush or the American gospel tent, who pretends to know the will and intent of God exactly and completely.   199

> Henry L. Mencken, *Damn! A Book of Calumny*

I do not consider it an insult, but rather a compliment to be called an agnostic. I do not pretend to know where many ignorant men are sure—that is all that agnosticism means.   200

> Clarence Darrow, at the Scopes trial, Dayton, Tenn., 13 July 1925

Aim

The aim, if reached or not, makes great the life:
>   Try to be Shakespeare, leave the rest to fate!   201

> Robert Browning, *Bishop Bloughram's Apology*

How many cares one loses when one decides not to be something but to be somebody.   202

> Gabrielle ("CoCo") Chanel. *This Week*, 21 August 1961

Life is too short to waste
In critic peep or cynic bark,
Quarrel or reprimand:
'Twill soon be dark;
Up! mind thine own aim, and
God speed the mark!   203

> Ralph Waldo Emerson, *Poems*, "To J. W."

All that we do is done with an eye to something else.   204
> Aristotle, *Nichomachean Ethics*

If you would hit the mark, you must aim a little above it;
Every arrow that flies feels the attraction of earth.   205
> Henry Wadsworth Longfellow, *Elegiac Verse*

Aloneness

And Jacob was left alone; and there wrestled a man with him until the breaking of the day.   206
> Genesis 32:24

When Jesus, therefore, perceived that they would come and take him by force, to make him a king, he departed again into a mountain himself alone.   207
> John 6:15

A man alone is either a god or a devil. (*Homo solus, aut deus aut daemon.*) 208
> Latin Proverb

Eagles commonly fly alone; they are crows, daws, and starlings that fly together.   209
> John Webster, *The Duchess of Malfi*

He who from zone to zone
Guides through the boundless sky thy certain flight,
In the long way that I must tread alone
Will guide my steps aright.   210
> William Cullen Bryant, *To a Waterfowl*

Through the wide world he only is alone
Who lives not for another. Come what will,
the generous man has his companions still.   211
> Samuel Rogers, *Human Life*

Altruism

I was eyes to the blind, and feet was I to the lame.   212
> Job in Job 29:15

He that hath pity on the poor lendeth unto the Lord; and that which he hath given will he pay him again.   213
> Proverbs 19:17

Give, and it shall be given unto you.   214
> Jesus in Luke 6:38

The idea of strictly minding our own business is moldy rubbish. Who could be so selfish?   215
> Myrtle Lillian Barker, *I Am Only One*

It is the free man who must win freedom for the slave; it is the wise man who must think for the fool; it is the happy man who must serve the unhappy.   216
> Jean Paul Richter, *Hesperus*

He who wants to do good knocks at the gate; he who loves finds the gate open.   217
> Rabindranath Tagore, *Stray Birds*

The world goes on only because of those who disregard their own existence. 218
> Jewish Proverb

Ambition

Should I forsake my sweetness, and my good fruit, and go to be promoted over the trees?   219
> Judges 9:11

The eye is not satisfied with seeing, nor the ear filled with hearing.   220
      Ecclesiastes 1:8

What shall it profit a man, if he shall gain the whole world, and lose his soul?   221
      Jesus in Mark 8:36

If any man desire to be first, the same shall be last of all, and servant of all.   222
      Jesus in Mark 9:35

I had Ambition, by which sin
   The angels fell;
I climbed, and, step by step, O Lord,
   Ascended into Hell.   223
      W. H. Davies, *Ambition*

He who stands on the tips of his toes cannot be steady.   224
      Chinese Proverb

To plunder, to lie, to show your arse, are three essentials for climbing high.   225
      Aristophanes, *The Knights*

Most people would succeed in small things if they were not troubled by great ambitions.   226
      Henry Wadsworth Longfellow, *Driftwood*

A man who wants to play billiards must have no other ambition. Billiards is all.   227
      E(dward) V(errall) Lucas, *Character and Comedy*

Cromwell was a man in whom ambition had not wholly suppressed, but only suspended, the sentiments of religion.   228
      Edmund Burke, *Letter to a Member of the National Assembly,* 1791

Ambition dares not stoop.   229
      Ben Jonson, *Cynthia's Revels*

The same sun which gilds all nature, and exhilarates the whole creation, does not shine upon disappointed ambition.   230
      Edmund Burke, *Observations on a Publication,* "The Present State of the Nation"

Man strives and God laughs.   231
      Jewish Proverb

Ambition is bondage.   232
      Ibn Gabirol, *Choice of Pearls*

There is a profound causal relation between the height of a man's ambition and the depth of his possible fall.   233
      Dag Hammarskjöld, *Markings*

A glassblower lies here at rest
Who one day burst his noble chest
While trying, in a fit of malice,
To blow a second Crystal Palace.   234
      H. B. Morton, *The Faber Book of Epigrams and Epitaphs*

America

Ours is the only country deliberately founded on a good idea.   235
     Thom Gunn, *Inside U.S.A.*

Americans cannot believe that any intelligent and good person does not at bottom share the Will Rogers Weltanschauung, "I never met a man I didn't like."   236
     Allan Bloom, *The Closing of the American Mind*

America is a passionate idea or it is nothing. America is a human brotherhood or it is chaos.   237
     Max Lerner, *Actions and Passions*

We are a nation of twenty million bathrooms, with a humanist in every tub. 238
     Mary McCarthy, *On the Contrary*

Amusement

When men are rightly occupied, their amusement grows out of their work, as the color-petals out of a fruitful flower; when they are faithfully helpful and compassionate, all their emotions become steady, deep, perpetual, and vivifying to the soul as the natural pulse is to the body.   239
     John Ruskin, *Sesame and Lilies*

The banality of human amusements is the most cogent argument against human immortality.   240
     Author Unknown

Nothing is so perfectly amusement as a total change of ideas.   241
     Laurence Sterne, *Tristram Shandy*

Amusement is the happiness of those who cannot think.   242
     Alexander Pope, *Thoughts on Various Subjects*

Ancestry

Think not to say within yourselves, We have Abraham to our father; for I say unto you that God is able of these stones to raise up children unto Abraham.   243
     Jesus in Matthew 3:9

Our father was Adam, our grandfather dust, our great-grandfather nothing. 244
     William Jenkyn, *The Golden Treasury of Puritan Quotations*

No man can cause more grief than that one clinging to the vices of his ancestors.   245
     William Faulkner, *Intruders in the Dust*

The man who has nothing to boast of but his illustrious ancestors is like a potato—the only good belonging to him is underground.   246
     Thomas Overbury, *Characters*

You should study the Peerage. It's the best thing in fiction the English have ever done.   247
     Oscar Wilde, *A Woman of No Importance*

Our ancestors are a very good kind of folks; but they are the last people I should like to have a visiting acquaintance with. 248
Richard Brinsley Sheridan, *The Rivals*

[Man is descended from] a hairy, quadruped, furnished with a tail . . . probably arboreal in its habits. 249
Charles Darwin, *The Descent of Man*

I am, in point of fact, a particularly haughty and exclusive person, of pre-Adamite ancestral descent. You will understand this when I tell you that I can trace my ancestry back to a protoplasmal primordial atomic globule. [*Pooh-Bah.*] 250
W. S. Gilbert, *The Mikado*

Angels

What is man, that thou art mindful of him? and the son of man, that thou visitest him? for thou hast made him a little lower than the angels, to crown him with glory and honor. 251
Psalm 8:4–5

The chariots of God are twenty thousand, even thousands of angels. 252
Psalm 68:17

Whether the angels play only Bach praising God, I am not quite sure. I am sure, however, that *en famille* they play Mozart. 253
Karl Barth, recalled on his death, 9 December 1968

Angels can fly because they take themselves lightly. 254
G. K. Chesterton, *Orthodoxy*

But all God's angels come to us disguised:
Sorrow and sickness, poverty and death,
One after other lift their frowning masks,
And we behold the Seraph's face beneath,
All radiant with the glory and the calm
Of having looked upon the front of God. 255
James Russell Lowell, *On the Death of a Friend's Child*

In Scripture the visitation of an angel is always alarming; it has to begin by saying "Fear not." The Victorian angel looks as if it were going to say, "There, there." 256
C. S. Lewis, *The Screwtape Letters*, author's preface to 1962 edition

Every man hath a good and a bad angel attending on him in particular, all his life long. 257
Robert Burton, *The Anatomy of Melancholy*

What's impossible to all humanity may be possible to the metaphysics and physiology of angels. 258
Joseph Glanvill, *The Vanity of Dogmatizing*, 1661

"The chariots of God are twenty thousand, even thousands of angels" (Ps. 68:17). I once read the story of a man and wife who had lived together most unhappily for years and were about to split, when one cold, winter evening a forlorn, lost dog scratched at their door and invited his way into their home, and into their hearts. Neither had ever had a pet before. This one took over their hearth, their hearts, and their lives. He unit-

31

ed them as they had never been united before. But it was not the dog that did it; it was the Lord who had sent his angel as he is so frequently reported in the Bible to have done. The dog was one of God's angelic charioteers. Angels come in all shapes and sizes, sorts, and conditions. And there are in fact very many more than twenty thousand of them.   259

C.E.S.

Anger

He that is slow to anger appeaseth strife.   260
Proverbs 15:18

Anger resteth in the bosom of fools.   261
Ecclesiastes 7:9

Whosoever is angry with his brother without a cause shall be in danger of judgment.   262
Jesus in Matthew 5:22

Be ye angry, and sin not; let not the sun go down upon your wrath.   263
Ephesians 4:26

How much more grievous are the consequences of anger than the causes of it!   264
Marcus Aurelius, *Meditations*

Hate is a kind of "passive suffering," but indignation is a kind of joy.   265
William Butler Yeats, *Letters*

The world needs anger. The world often continues to let evil flourish because it is not angry enough.   266
Bede Jarrett, *The House of Gold*

When I am angry I can write, pray, and preach well, for then my whole temperament is quickened, my understanding sharpened, and all mundane vexations and temptations depart.   267
Martin Luther, *Table Talk*

Anger should not be destroyed but sanctified.   268
William Jenkyn, *The Golden Treasury of Plymouth Quotations*

A man that does not know how to be angry does not know how to be good. 269
Henry Ward Beecher, *Proverbs from Plymouth Pulpit*

Two things a man should never be angry at: what he can help, and what he cannot help.   270
Thomas Fuller, *History of the Holy War*

If you are patient in one moment of anger, you will escape a hundred days of sorrow.   271
Chinese Proverb

Of the Seven Deadly Sins, anger is possibly the most fun. To lick your wounds, to smack your lips over grievances long past, to roll over your tongue the prospect of bitter confrontations still to come, to savor the last toothsome morsel both of the pain you are given and the pain you are giving back—in many ways it is a feast fit for a king. The chief drawback is that what you are wolfing down is yourself. The skeleton at the feast is you.   272

Frederick Buechner, *Wishful Thinking: A Theological ABC*

Anglicanism

The constant temptation of Anglicans is to take their church too seriously and their God not seriously enough—to be too ecclesiological and not theological enough. This may be no less true of other fields in Christ's vineyard, but Anglicanism is the only church home I know from living inside it.   273

C.E.S.

Animals

A righteous man regardeth the life of his beast.   274

Proverbs 12:10

Thou shalt not muzzle the ox when he treadeth out the corn.   275

Deuteronomy 25:4

And there was a certain beggar named Lazarus, which was laid at [the rich man's] gate, full of sores, And desiring to be fed with the crumbs which fell from the rich man's table; moreover the dogs came and licked his sores.   276

Luke 16:20–21

When I play with my cat, who knows if I am not a pastime to her more than she is to me?   277

Michel de Montaigne, *Essays,* Bk. II, ch. 12

An animal's eyes have the power to speak a great language.   278

Martin Buber, *I and Thou*

I think I could turn and live with the animals, they are so placid
    and self-contained. . . .
They do not lie awake in the dark and weep for their sins,
They do not make me sick discussing their duty to God,
Not one is dissatisfied, not one is demented with the mania of owning things,
Not one kneels to another, nor to his kind that lived thousands of years ago,
Not one is respectable or unhappy over the whole earth.   279

Walt Whitman, *Leaves of Grass,* "Song of Myself"

When a man wants to murder a tiger he calls it sport; when the tiger wants to murder him he calls it ferocity.   280

George Bernard Shaw, *The Revolutionist's Handbook*

All animals, except man, know that the principal business of life is to enjoy it—and they do enjoy it as much as man and other circumstances will allow.   281

Samuel Butler, *The Way of All Flesh*

Though I am far from denying that to this day the counsels of Divine Goodness regarding dumb creatures are, for us, involved in deep obscurity, yet we see nevertheless that Scripture foretells for them a "glorious liberty," and we are assured that the compassion of Heaven, to which we owe so much, will not be wanting to them. 282

John Keble, *Lectures on Poetry*

The bleat, the bark, bellow and roar
Are waves that beat on Heaven's shore.   283
> William Blake, *Auguries of Innocence*

Just read such a nice little bit about Luther. When he'd finished his commentary on the verse in Romans about "all creation travailing together, etc." he turned to his little dog and said exultantly, "Thou too shalt have a little golden tale!"   284
> Evelyn Underhill, *Letter to G. F.,* 8 January 1936

Christian theologians, many of them, confine Christianity to the human form of life. It does not seem to me correct. It lacks the essential universalization that I associate with Jesus.   285
> Albert Schweitzer, *Out of My Life and Thought*

Driving to the airport early this morning I saw the corpse of a dog lying by the road. Instantly, without thought, I prayed, "Dear Lord, receive in mercy this poor creature of yours, and give it life and canine joy in the Land of the living." Was I crazy? Or right? Or both?   286
> C.E.S., 14 October 1986

Anonymity

When thou doest alms, let not thy left hand know what thy right hand doeth.   287
> Jesus in Matthew 6:3

Mark how my fame rings out from zone to zone,
A·thousand critics shouting, "He's unknown!"   288
> Ambrose Bierce, *Couplet*

I'm Nobody! Who are you?
Are you—Nobody—too?
Then there's a pair of us!
Don't tell! They'd advertise—you know!

How dreary—to be—Somebody!
How public—like a Frog—
To tell one's name—the livelong June—
To an admiring bog.   289
> Emily Dickinson, "I'm Nobody! Who are you?"

Anti-Semitism

Anti-Semitism is the socialism of fools.   290
> August Bebel, *Anti-Semitism and Social Democracy*

It is not possible for Christians to take part in anti-Semitism. We are Semites spiritually.   291
> Pope Pius XI, in address to Belgian pilgrims, December 1938

Since my little daughter is only half Jewish, would it be all right if she went into the pool only up to her waist? 292

> Groucho Marx, in letter to a country club after it had barred his daughter as Jewish; quoted in obituary in *New York Times,* 20 August 1977

The Jews are not hated because they have evil qualities; evil qualities are sought for them, because they are hated. 293

> Max Nordau. Quoted in Leo Rosten, *Treasury of Jewish Quotations*

Anxiety

Be not anxious about tomorrow, for tomorrow will be anxious for itself. 294

> Jesus in Matthew 6:34

Anxiety is the income tax of civilization. 295

> Author Unknown

Anxiety is love's greatest killer, because it is like the stranglehold of the drowning. 296

> Anaïs Nin, *The Diary of Anaïs Nin*

One cannot remove anxiety by arguing it away. 297

> Paul Tillich, *The Courage to Be*

Anxiety shouts in the headlines, laughs nervously at cocktail parties, nags from advertisements, speaks suavely in the boardroom, whines from the stage, clatters from the Wall Street ticker, jokes with fake youthfulness on the golf course and whispers in privacy each day before the shaving mirror and the dressing table. 298

> *Time,* 31 March 1961

The natural mode of twentieth-century man is anxiety. 299

> Norman Mailer, *The Naked and the Dead*

Stupidity is without anxiety. 300

> Johann Wolfgang von Goethe. Quoted in Eckermann, *Conversations with Goethe*

Appearance

The Lord seeth not as man seeth, for man looketh on the outward appearance, but the Lord looketh on the heart. 301

> 1 Samuel 16:7

Why take ye thought for raiment? 302

> Jesus in Matthew 6:28

He is not a Jew, which is one outwardly. 303

> Romans 2:28

The most winning woman I ever knew was hanged for poisoning three little children for their insurance money. [*Sherlock Holmes.*] 304

> Arthur Conan Doyle, *The Sign of Four*

The tragedy of our time is that we are eye centered, so appearance besotted. 305

> Jessamyn West, *Love Is Not What You Think*

Art

The ultimate justification of the work of art is to help the spectator to become a work of art himself. 306
Bernard Berenson, *Essays in Appreciation*

This is the eternal origin of art: that a human being confronts a form that wants to become a work through him. 307
Martin Buber, *I and Thou*

The basis of art is truth, both in manner and in mode. The person who aims after art in his work aims after truth, in an imaginative sense, no more and no less. 308
Flannery O'Connor, *Mystery and Manners*

Art is the communication of ecstasy. 309
Peter Ouspensky, *A New Model of the Universe*

If you see the Laocoön again, just notice whether you do not think that the father's head may have been a model for later representations of Christ. Last time I saw this classical man of sorrows it impressed me deeply and kept me thinking for a long time. 310
Dietrich Bonhoeffer, *Letters and Papers from Prison*

All art constantly aspires toward the condition of music. 311
Walter Pater, *Studies in the Literature of the Renaissance*

A great artist is like a fig tree whose roots run a hundred feet underground, in search of tea leaves, cinders and old boots. 312
Cyril Connolly, *The Unquiet Grave*

Art is our chief means of breaking bread with the dead. 313
W. H. Auden. *New York Times,* 7 August 1971

You use a glass mirror to see your face: you use works of art to see your soul. 314
George Bernard Shaw, *Back to Methuselah*

Art does not reproduce the visible; rather, it makes visible. 315
Paul Klee, *The Inward Vision*

Aspiration

Lead me to the rock that is higher than I. 316
Psalm 61:2

We are all in the gutter, but some of us are looking at the stars. 317
Oscar Wilde, *The Picture of Dorian Gray*

An aspiration is a joy forever, a possession as solid as a landed estate, a fortune which we can never exhaust and which gives us year by year a revenue of pleasurable activity. 318
Robert Louis Stevenson, *Virginibus Puerisque*

What I aspired to be,
And was not, comforts me:
A brute I might have been, but would not sink i' the scale! 319
Robert Browning, *Rabbi Ben Ezra*

Men would be angels, angels would be gods. 320
>> Alexander Pope, *An Essay on Man*

To love the beautiful, to desire the good, to do the best. 321
>> Moses Mendelssohn (1729–1786), his motto

Build thee more stately mansions, O my soul,
>> As the swift seasons roll!
>> Leave thy low-vaulted past!

Let each new temple, nobler than the last,
Shut thee from heaven with a dome more vast,
>> Till thou at last art free,

Leaving thine outgrown shell by life's unresting sea! 322
>> Oliver Wendell Holmes, *The Chambered Nautilus*

Assistance

They fought from heaven; the stars in their courses fought against Sisera. 323
>> Judges 5:20

Curse ye Meroz, said the angel of the Lord, curse ye bitterly the inhabitants thereof; because they came not to the help of the Lord, to the help of the Lord against the mighty. 324
>> Judges 5:23

Vain is the help of man. 325
>> Psalm 60:11

If I can stop one Heart from breaking
I shall not live in vain
If I can ease one Life the Aching
Or cool one Pain,
Or help one fainting Robin
Unto his Nest again—
I shall not live in Vain. 326
>> Emily Dickinson, "If I can stop one heart from breaking"

The aid we can give each other is only incidental, lateral, and sympathetic. 327
>> Ralph Waldo Emerson, *Journal,* 1836

In about the same degree as you are helpful, you will be happy. 328
>> Karl Reiland. *New York Herald Tribune,* 6 November 1961

Association

And it came to pass, as Jesus sat at meat in the house, behold, many publicans and sinners came and sat down with him and his disciples. And when the Pharisees saw it, they said unto his disciples, Why eateth your master with publicans and sinners? But when Jesus heard that he said unto them, They that be whole need not a physician, but they that are sick. 329
>> Matthew 9:10–12

The Sun visits cesspools without being defiled. 330

> Diogenes the Cynic, quoted in Diogenes Laertes, *Lives and Opinions of Eminent Philosophers*

Assurance

From that time many of his disciples went back, and walked no more with him. Then said Jesus unto the twelve, Will ye also go away? Then Simon Peter answered him, Lord, to whom shall we go? thou hast the words of eternal life, and [we] are sure that thou art that Christ, the Son of the living God. 331

> John 6:66–69

I know whom I have believed, and am persuaded that he is able to keep that which I have committed unto him against that day. 332

> 2 Timothy 1:12

Assurance made David divinely fearless, and divinely careless. 333

> Thomas Brooks, *The Golden Treasury of Puritan Quotations*

I am wholly His; I am peculiarly His; I am universally His; I am eternally His. 334

> Ibid.

Assurance is glory in the bud, it is the suburbs of paradise. 335

> Ibid.

The assured Christian is more motion than notion, more work than word, more life than lip, more hand than tongue. 336

> Ibid.

The Christian must trust in a withdrawing God. 337

> William Gurnall, *The Golden Treasury of Puritan Quotations*

I wish I was as cocksure of anything as Tom Macauley is of everything. 338

> William Lamb, Viscount Melbourne. From *Melbourne's Papers*, edited by L. V. Saunders

Atheism

The fool hath said in his heart, There is no God. 339

> Psalm 14:1

My people is foolish, they have not known me. 340

> Jeremiah 4:22

Strangers from the covenants of promise, having no hope, and without God in the world. 341

> Ephesians 2:12

The world knoweth us not, because it knew him not. 342

> 1 John 3:1

Men may have atheistical hearts without atheistical heads. 343

> Stephen Charnock, *The Golden Treasury of Puritan Quotations*

We shall say without hesitation that the atheist who is moved by love is moved by the spirit of God; and the atheist who lives by love is saved by his faith in the God whose existence (under that name) he denies. 344

William Temple, *Christus Veritas*

The worst moment for the atheist is when he is really thankful and has nobody to thank. 345

Dante Gabriel Rossetti, attributed

One can be an atheist in a Protestant or Catholic way: the first argues God out of court, the second fights against him for dear life. 346

Salvador de Madariana, *Anarchy or Hierarchy*

Atheism is rather in the lip than in the heart of man. 347

Francis Bacon, *Essays*, "Of Atheism"

Forth from his dark and lonely hiding place
(Portentous sight) the owlet Atheism,
Sailing on obscene wings athwart the noon,
Drops his blue-fringèd lips, and holds them close,
And hooting at the glorious sun in heaven,
   Cries out, "Where is it?" 348

Samuel Taylor Coleridge, *Fears in Solitude*

Note the greater part of our atheists and you will see that they are atheists from a kind of rage, rage at not being able to believe that there is a God. They are the personal enemies of God. They have invested Nothingness with substance and personality, and their No-God is an Anti-God. 349

Miguel de Unamuno, *Tragic Sense of Life*

Atomic Age

We have grasped the mystery of the atom and rejected the Sermon on the Mount. 350

General Omar Bradley, in an Armistice Day address, 1948

The Atomic Age is here to stay—but are we? 351

Bennett Cerf, *Observer*, "Sayings of the Week," 12 February 1950

Now we are all sons of bitches. 352

Kenneth Bainbridge, *The Decision to Drop the Bomb*. After the first atomic attack, of which he was in charge

It is an atomic bomb. It is the harnessing of the basic power of the universe. 353

Harry S. Truman, in an announcement about the bombing of Hiroshima, 28 July 1945

Nature is neutral. Man has wrested from nature the power to make the world a desert or to make the deserts bloom. There is no evil in atoms; only in men's souls. 354

Adlai E. Stevenson. Address, Hartford, Conn., 18 September 1952

It is impossible, except for theologians, to conceive of a world-wide scandal or a universe-wide scandal; the proof of this is the way people have settled down to living with nuclear fission, radiation poisoning, satellites, and space rockets.   355
                    Mary McCarthy, *On the Contrary*

Authority

The ox knoweth his owner, and the ass, his master's crib: but Israel does not know; my people doth not consider.   356
          Isaiah 1:3

Shall the clay say to him that fashioneth it, What makest thou?   357
          Isaiah 45:9

To sit on my right hand, and on my left, is not mine to give, but it shall be given to them for whom it is prepared of my Father.   358
          Jesus in Matthew 20:23

Thou couldst have no power at all against me, except it were given thee from above.   359
          Jesus in John 19:11

Nothing that somebody else says is true will be of any use to any of us in an hour of trial. Nothing will hold us as an anchor in a stormy sea save that little bit of the truth of God which we have made our very own. The very Greek word for "authority" is *exousia,* namely, "out of that which is one's very own." But what we have made our own will hold us.   360
          Leslie Weatherhead, *The Christian Agnostic*

Whoever in discussion adduces authority uses not intellect but rather memory.   361
          Leonardo da Vinci, *The Notebooks*

He that takes up conclusions on the trust of authors . . . loses his labor, and does not know anything, but only believeth.   362
          Thomas Hobbes, *The Leviathan*

Every great advance in natural knowledge has involved the absolute rejection of authority.   363
          Thomas Henry Huxley, *Lay Sermons*

Authority intoxicates
And makes mere sots of magistrates;
The fumes of it invade the brain,
And make men giddy, proud, and vain.   364
          Samuel Butler, *Remains*

Authority without wisdom is like a heavy axe without an edge, fitter to bruise than polish.   365
          Anne Bradstreet, *Meditations Divine and Moral*

    . . . but man, proud man,
Drest in a little brief authority,
Most ignorant of what he's most assured,
His glassy essence, like an angry ape,

40

Plays such fantastic tricks before high heaven
As make the angels weep . . . [Isabella]   366
> William Shakespeare, *Measure for Measure*, II, ii, 117

The donkey of the Mullah has a more pleasing bray.   367
> Arabic Proverb

Awe

I have seen God face to face, and my life is preserved.   368
> Genesis 32:30

Then said I, Woe is me! for I am undone, because I am a man of unclean lips, and I dwell in the midst of a people of unclean lips; for mine eyes have seen the King, the Lord of hosts.   369
> Isaiah 6:5

Fear ye not me? saith the Lord: Will ye not tremble at my presence?   370
> Jeremiah 5:22

What manner of man is this, that even the winds and the sea obey him?   371
> Matthew 8:27

I was in the Spirit on the Lord's day, and heard behind me a great voice, as of a trumpet, saying, I am Alpha and Omega, the first and the last. . . . And when I saw him, I fell at his feet as dead.   372
> Revelation 1:10, 11, 18

The tremor of awe is the best in man.   373
> Johann Wolfgang von Goethe. Quoted in *The Journals of André Gide*

When the people lack a proper sense of awe, then some awful visitation will descend upon them.   374
> Lao-tzu, *Tao te ching*

The eternal silence of these infinite spaces fills me with dread.   375
> Blaise Pascal, *Pensées*

Two things fill the mind with ever-increasing wonder and awe, the more often and the more seriously reflection concentrates upon them: the starry heaven above me and the moral law within me.   376
> Immanuel Kant, *Critique of Practical Reason*, conclusion

B

Babies

See Age, Infancy, and Childhood

Barbarism

The barbarous people showed us no little kindness: for they kindled a fire, and received us, every one, because of the present rain, and because of the cold.   377
> Acts 28:2

Beauty

Give unto the Lord the glory due unto his name; worship the Lord in the beauty of holiness.   378
> Psalm 29:2

Let the beauty of the Lord our God be upon us; and establish thou the work of our hands upon us; yea, the work of our hands establish thou it.   379
> Psalm 90:17

Thine eyes shall see the king in his beauty; they shall behold the land that is very far off.   380
> Isaiah 33:17

He hath made every thing beautiful in his time.   381
> Ecclesiastes 3:11

Consider the lilies of the field, how they grow; they toil not, neither do they spin, and yet I say unto you, that even Solomon in all his glory was not arrayed like one of these.   382
> Jesus in Matthew 6:28–29

Beauty be not caused: It Is.
Chase it, and it ceases.
Chase it not, and it abides.
Overtake the creases
In the meadow when the wind
Runs his fingers thru' it:

Beauty will see to it
That you never do it. 383
> Emily Dickinson, "Beauty be not caused: It Is"

Beauty is the index of a larger fact than wisdom. 384
> Oliver Wendell Holmes, *The Autocrat of the Breakfast-Table*

Truth is the strong compost in which beauty may sometimes germinate. 385
> Christopher Morley, *Inward Ho!*

Snakes are beautiful, but not to us. 386
> Thomas Merton, *No Man Is an Island*

Though we travel the world over to find the beautiful we must carry it with us whether we find it or not. 387
> Ralph Waldo Emerson, *Essays,* "Art"

Beauty is the purgation of superfluities. 388
> Michelangelo. Quoted in Emerson, *The Conduct of Life,* "Beauty"

The passion excited by beauty is nearer to a species of melancholy than to jollity and mirth. 389
> Edmund Burke, *On the Sublime and Beautiful*

The beauty of the world is Christ's tender smile coming to us through matter. 390
> Simone Weil, *Waiting on God*

Beauty for some provides escape,
Who gain a happiness in eyeing
The gorgeous buttocks of the ape
Or autumn sunsets exquisitely dying. 391
> Aldous Huxley, *The Ninth Philosopher's Song*

There is no excellent beauty that hath not some strangeness in the proportion. 392
> Francis Bacon, *Essays,* "Of Beauty"

Too late I loved you, O Beauty ever ancient and ever new! Too late I loved you! And, behold, you were within me, and I out of myself, and there I searched for you. 393
> St. Augustine, *Confessions*

Beauty is the only finality here below. 394
> Simone Weil, *Waiting on God*

Beginnings

When I begin, I will also make an end. 395
> 1 Samuel 3:12

New wine must be put into new bottles. 396
> Jesus in Mark 2:22

Begin to weave and God will give the thread. 397
> German Proverb

"We must do something" is the unanimous refrain. "You begin" is the deadening reply. 398

> Walter Dwight, *The Saving Sense*

Nothing, of course, begins at the time you think it did. 399

> Lillian Hellman, *An Unfinished Woman*

God always gives a greater blessing to humble beginnings than to those that start with the chiming of bells. 400

> St. Vincent de Paul, *Life and Works*, vol. iii

Being

See also Existence

To be or not to be is *not* the question. The vital question is *how* to be and *how* not to be. 401

> Abraham Heschel, *The Wisdom of Abraham Heschel*

Being is the great explainer. 402

> Henry David Thoreau, *Journal*, 26 February 1841

The Courage to Be. 403

> Paul Tillich, title of book

Being and Becoming

Beloved, now are we the sons of God, and it doth not yet appear what we shall be, but we know that, when he shall appear, we shall be like him; for we shall see him as he is. 404

> 1 John 3:2

When we are doing nothing in particular, it is then that we are living through all our being; and when we cease to add to our growth it is only that we may ripen and possess ourselves. 405

> Henri Frédéric Amiel, *Journal*, 17 December 1854

Being Ourselves

At times we are as different from ourselves as we are from others. 406

> François de la Rochefoucald, *Maxims*

Before Rebbe Zusia died, he said: "When I shall face the celestial tribunal, I shall not be asked why I was not Abraham, Jacob or Moses. I shall be asked why I was not Zusia." 407

> Elie Wiesel, *Souls on Fire*

Belief

Thou shalt find him, if thou seek him with all thy heart and with all thy soul. 408

> Deuteronomy 4:29

If ye will not believe, surely ye shall not be established. 409
Isaiah 7:9

He that believeth shall not make haste. 410
Isaiah 28:16

Whatsoever ye shall ask in prayer, believing, ye shall receive. 411
Jesus in Matthew 21:22

Lord, I believe; help thou mine unbelief. 412
Mark 9:24

He that believeth not the Son shall not see life; but the wrath of God abideth on him. 413
Jesus in John 3:36

A man must not swallow more beliefs than he can digest. 414
Havelock Ellis, *The Dance of Life*

The most important convictions in religion cannot really be *reached* on the word of another. 415
Leslie Weatherhead, *The Christian Agnostic*

Everything possible to be believed is an image of truth. 416
William Blake, *Proverbs of Hell*

He that will believe only what he can fully comprehend must have a very long head or a very short creed. 417
Charles Caleb Colton, *Lacon*

I find myself taking more and more as literal fact what I used in my youth to admire and love as poetry. 418
F. H. Bradley, *Essays on Truth and Reality*

I am confident that if a single ray of light reaches a man from Christ, penetrates into his being and influences his way of living, he is further along the road to true belief in him than if he gives his unreflecting assent to a multitude of orthodox propositions which have no perceptible effect upon his conduct. 419
J. H. Oldham, *Life Is Commitment*

Belief which produces something real is called faith. 420
Simone Weil, *Gateway to God*

I do not seek to understand that I may believe, but I believe that I may understand. For this I believe, that unless I first believe, I shall not understand. 421
St. Anselm of Canterbury, *Proslogion*

We either see the evidence of God everywhere, or nowhere. 422
Paul Davies, *God and the New Physics*

Bereavement

Ah, why should we wear black for the guests of God? 423
John Ruskin, attributed

Birds sing after a storm; why shouldn't people feel as free to delight in whatever remains to them? 424

Rose Kennedy, *Times to Remember*

The death of a good man is like the putting out of a wax perfumed candle: he recompenses the loss of light with the sweet odor he leaves behind him. 425

Owen Felltham, *Resolves*

If, as I can't help suspecting, the dead also feel the pains of separation (and this may be one of their purgatorial sufferings), then for both lovers, and for all pairs of lovers without exception, bereavement is a universal and integral part of our experience of love. 426

C. S. Lewis, *A Grief Observed*

Bible

Thy word is a lamp unto my feet, and a light unto my path. 427

Psalm 119:105

If ye believe not his writings, how shall ye believe my words? 428

Jesus in John 5:47

All scripture is given by inspiration of God. 429

2 Timothy 3:16

Blessed Lord, who hast caused all holy Scriptures to be written for our learning; Grant that we may in such wise hear them, read, mark, learn, and inwardly digest them, that by patience and comfort of thy holy Word, we may embrace, and ever hold fast, the blessed hope of everlasting life, which thou hast given us in our Saviour Jesus Christ. 430

Book of Common Prayer, Collect for the Second Sunday in Advent

The Bible is a letter from our Fatherland. 431

St. Augustine, *Commentary on Psalm 64*

The Spirit of God rides most triumphantly in his own chariot. 432

Thomas Manton, *The Golden Treasury of Puritan Quotations*

The Lord has more truth yet to break forth out of his holy Word. 433

John Robinson, Ibid.

The Bible is a stream in which the elephant may swim and the lamb may wade. 434

Pope Gregory the Great, attributed

One has either got to be a Jew or stop reading the Bible. The Bible cannot make sense to anybody who is not "spiritually a Semite." 435

Thomas Merton, *Conjectures of a Guilty Bystander*

To read the Bible as literature is like reading *Moby Dick* as a whaling manual or *The Brothers Karamazov* for its punctuation. 436

Frederick Buechner, *Wishful Thinking: A Theological ABC*

We are not to make the Torah into God himself, nor the Bible into a "paper pope." The Bible is only the result of the Word of God. 437

Jacques Ellul, *Living Faith*

On her deathbed, Gertrude Stein is said to have asked, "What is the answer?" Then, after a long silence, "What is the question?" Don't start looking in the Bible for the answers it gives. Start by listening for the questions it asks.   438

> Frederick Buechner, *Wishful Thinking: A Theological ABC*

Strange, after having passed the whole of my life in gliding about the dancing floors of philosophy, and abandoning myself to all the orgies of the intellect, and dallying with systems without ever being satisfied—I have suddenly arrived at the same point of view as Uncle Tom, taking my stand on the Bible and kneeling beside my black brother in prayer in the same act of devotion.   439

> Henrich Heine. Quoted in *The Crown Treasury of Relevant Quotations,* edited by Edward E. Murphy

You can learn more about human nature by reading the Bible than by living in New York.   440

> William Lyon Phelps, quoted in *New York Times,* 19 October 1952

When you eat fish, you don't eat the bones. You eat the flesh. Take the Bible like that.   441

> Robert R. Moton, President, Tuskegee Institute. *New York Post,* 17 May 1964

Bigotry

They shall put you out of the synagogues: yea, the time cometh, that whosoever killeth you will think that he doeth God service.   442

> John 16:2

Bigotry may be rightly defined as the anger of men who have no opinions.   443

> G. K. Chesterton, *Heretics*

Men never do evil so completely and cheerfully as when they do it from religious conviction.   444

> Blaise Pascal, *Pensées*

Bigotry murders Religion, to frighten fools with her ghost.   445

> Charles Caleb Colton, *Lacon*

I cannot tolerate bigots. They are all so obstinate, so opinionated.   446

> Senator Joseph McCarthy, attributed

We are least open to precise knowledge concerning the things we are most vehement about.   447

> Eric Hoffer, *The Passionate State of Mind*

Birth

Before I formed thee in the belly I knew thee.   448

> Jeremiah 1:5

A woman loses a child even in having a child. All creation is separation. Birth is as solemn a parting as death.   449

> G. K. Chesterton, *Orthodoxy*

In the medical sense now, birth is not the beginning but just a developmental transition. 450

Barbara Yuncker, "The Riddle of Birth." *New York Post,* 23 May 1969

The birth and death of the leaves are the rapid whirl of the eddy whose wider circles move slowly among stars. 451

Rabindranath Tagore, *Stray Birds,* XCII

My mother groan'd! my father wept.
Into the dangerous world I leapt:
Helpless, naked, piping loud,
Like a fiend hid in a cloud. 452

William Blake, *Infant Sorrow*

It is natural to die as to be born, and to a little infant perhaps the one is as painful as the other. 453

Francis Bacon, *Essays*

Blacks

It is the function of speech to free men from the bondage of irrational fears. 454

Justice Louis D. Brandeis, *Whitney v. California,* 1927

Black is beautiful. 455

Civil Rights Slogan

If you will protest courageously, and yet with dignity and Christian love, when the history books are written in future generations, the historians will have to pause and say, "There lived a great people—a black people—who injected new meaning and dignity into the veins of civilization." 456

Martin Luther King, Jr., address at Montgomery, Alabama,
31 December 1955

I want to be the white man's brother, not his brother-in-law. 457

Martin Luther King, Jr., quoted in *New York Herald American,*
10 September 1962

It's hard being black. You ever been black? I was black once—when I was poor. 458

Larry Holmes, heavyweight boxing champion. Quoted in Joyce Carol
Oates, *On Boxing*

Something is dismally wrong with an America in which a white prostitute can buy a house where a black businessman can't. 459

The Rev. Theodore M. Hesburgh, U. S. Civil Rights Commission
hearing, 1970

The Negro is superior to the white race. If the latter do not forget their pride of race and color, and amalgamate with the purer and richer blood of the blacks, they will die out and wither away in unprolific skinniness. 460

Henry Ward Beecher. Speech, New York City, 1866

It is not healthy when a nation lives within a nation, as colored Americans are living inside America. A nation cannot live confident of its tomorrow if its refugees are among its own citizens. 461

Pearl S. Buck, *What America Means to Me*

49

Blasphemy

Thou shalt not take the name of the Lord thy God in vain.   462
> Exodus 20:7

Jerusalem is ruined, and Judah is fallen: because their tongue and their doings are against the Lord.   463
> Isaiah 3:8

I will ascend above the heights of the clouds; I will be like the Most High.   464
> Isaiah 14:14

Whosoever shall speak a word against the Son of man, it shall be forgiven him; but unto him that blasphemeth against the Holy Ghost, it shall not be forgiven.   465
> Jesus in Luke 12:10

Genuine blasphemy, genuine in spirit and not merely verbal, is the product of partial belief, and is as impossible to the complete atheist as to the complete Christian.   466
> T. S. Eliot, *Baudelaire*

Blasphemy itself could not survive religion; if anyone doubts that, let him try to blaspheme Odin.   467
> G. K. Chesterton, quoted in *Daily News,* 25 June 1904

Blessings

As thy days . . . so shall thy strength be.   468
> Deuteronomy 33:25

The Lord bless thee, and keep thee: the Lord make his face shine upon thee, and be gracious unto thee; The Lord lift up his countenance upon thee, and give thee peace.   469
> Numbers 6:24–26

Grace be with you, mercy, and peace.   470
> 2 John 3

Those blessings are sweetest that are won with prayers and worn with thanks.   471
> Thomas Goodwin, *The Golden Treasury of Puritan Quotations*

Bless me in this life with but peace of conscience, command of my affections, the love of Thyself and my dearest friends, and I shall be happy enough to pity Caesar.   472
> Sir Thomas Browne, *Religio Medici*

Blessed are the valiant that have lived in the Lord.   473
> Thomas Carlyle, concerning Oliver Cromwell's *Letters and Opinions*

Ah, bless the Lord, O my soul! Bless him for wildness, for crows that will not alight within gunshot! and bless him for hens, too, that croak and cackle in the yard.   474
> Henry David Thoreau, *Journal,* 12 January 1855

Did you never run for shelter in a storm, and find fruit which you expected not? Did you never go to God for safeguard, driven by outward storms, and there find unexpected fruit? 475

John Owen, *The Golden Treasury of Puritan Quotations*

This is something that I cherish. Once in a friend's home I came across this blessing, and took it down in shorthand. It is something I like to live with: "Oh Thou, who dwellest in so many homes, possess Thyself of this. Bless the life that is sheltered here. Grant that trust and peace and comfort and usefulness may go out from this home forever." 476

Claudia ("Lady Bird") Johnson, interview. CBS TV 12 August 1964

May you have warm words on a cold evening and a full moon in a dark night. 477

Irish Blessing

The Christ in me salutes the Christ in you. 478

Author Unknown

May the Babe of Bethlehem be yours to tend:
May the Boy of Nazareth be yours for friend:
May the Man of Galilee his healing send:
May the Christ of Calvary his courage lend:
May the Risen Lord his presence send:
And his holy angels defend you at the end. 479

Author unknown. "Pilgrim's Prayer," found in Oberammergau, Germany

Blindness

The Lord openeth the eyes of the blind. 480

Psalm 146:8

Jesus said, For judgment I am come into this world, that they which see not might see; and that they which see might be made blind. And some of the Pharisees which were with him heard these words, and said unto him, Are we blind also? Jesus said unto them, If ye were blind, ye should have no sin; but now ye say, We see. Therefore your sin remaineth. 481

John 9:39–41

It is one thing to be blind, and another to be in darkness. 482

Coventry Patmore, *The Rod, the Root and the Flower*

Why should I not submit with complacency to this loss of sight, which seems only withdrawn from the body without to increase the sight of the mind within? 483

John Milton, Letter to Emeric Bigot, 24 March 1658

From all blindness of heart; from pride, vain-glory, and hypocrisy; from envy, hatred, and malice, and from all uncharitableness, *Good Lord, deliver us.* 484

Book of Common Prayer, *The Litany*

Blood

The voice of thy brother's blood crieth unto me from the ground.   485
>Genesis 4:10

The best blood will sometimes get into a fool or a mosquito.   486
>Austin O'Malley, *Keystones of Thought*

The blood of man should never be shed but to redeem the blood of man. It is well shed for our family, for our friends, for our God, for our country, for our kind. The rest is vanity; the rest is crime.   487
>Edmund Burke, *Letters on a Regicide Peace*, 1797

Body

Dust thou art, and unto dust shalt thou return.   488
>Genesis 3:19

I am fearfully and wonderfully made.   489
>Psalm 139:14

There is no riches . . . above a sound body.   490
>Ecclesiasticus 30:16, *The Jerusalem Bible*

The body is not for fornication, but for the Lord.   491
>1 Corinthians 6:13

It is sown in corruption; it is raised in incorruption.   492
>I Corinthians 15:42

I have sinned against my brother the ass.   493
>St. Francis of Assisi, to his body; his dying words.

A landscape can sing about God, a body about Spirit.   494
>Dag Hammarskjöld, *Markings*

[The body is] a cell state in which every cell is a citizen.   495
>Rudolf Virchow, *Cellular Pathology*

"The human form divine." It is *actually* divine; for the Body is the home of God, and an image of Him, though the Devil may be its present tenant.   496
>Coventry Patmore, *The Rod, the Root and the Flower*

I hope you are more comfy and free from pain. Sometimes I think the resurrection of the body, unless much improved in construction, a mistake!   497
>Evelyn Underhill, *The Letters of Evelyn Underhill*

In 1846 John Quincy Adams suffered a stroke and, although he returned to Congress the following year, his health was clearly failing. Daniel Webster described his last meeting with Adams: "Someone, a friend of his, came in and made particular inquiry of his health. Adams answered, 'I inhabit a weak, frail, decayed tenement, battered by the winds and broken in upon by the storms, and, from all I can learn, the landlord does not intend to repair.'"   498
>Clifton Fadiman, *The Little, Brown Book of Anecdotes*

The head sublime, the heart pathos, the genitals beauty, the hands and feet proportion. 499

William Blake, *Proverbs of Hell*

The body is a big sagacity, a plurality with one sense, a war and a peace, a flock and a shepherd. 500

Friedrich Wilhelm Nietzsche, *Thus Spake Zarathustra*

Our own physical body possesses a wisdom which we who inhabit the body lack. We give it orders which make no sense. 501

Henry Miller, *A Devil in Paradise*

There is nothing so humiliating as to know what a controlling influence the intestines have on the thoughts and ways of man. 502

John Lancaster Spalding, *Glimpses of Truth*

The body remembers past pleasures and on being made aware of them floods the mind with sweetness. 503

Cyril Connolly, *The Unquiet Grave*

Bondage

Ye have not received the spirit of bondage again to fear; but ye have received the Spirit of adoption, whereby we cry, Abba, Father. 504

Romans 8:15

Golden fetters hurt as cruelly as iron ones. 505

Minna Antrim, *Naked Truth and Veiled Allusions*

There is no real bondage but what is either *from* or *for* sin. 506

Vavasor Powell, *The Golden Treasury of Puritan Quotations*

A man is in bondage to whatever he cannot part with that is less than himself. 507

George MacDonald, *Unspoken Sermons, Second Series,* "The Way"

Books

Oh, that my words were now written! oh, that they were printed in a book! 508

Job 19:23

Of making many books there is no end. 509

Ecclesiastes 12:12

How much will some officious men give to preserve an old book, of which perchance only a single copy exists, while a wise God is already giving, and will still give, infinitely more to get it destroyed! 510

Henry David Thoreau, *Journal,* 18 August 1841

Some books are to be tasted, others to be swallowed, some few to be chewed and digested. 511

Francis Bacon, *Essays,* "Of Studies"

To produce a mighty book you must choose a mighty theme. No great and enduring volume can ever be written on the flea, though be many that have tried it. 512

Herman Melville, *Moby Dick*

There are a million times too many books being written *about* this or that, and a corresponding dearth of books being written *of* this or that. And here I am getting ready to write another book *about!*   513

C.E.S

Brains

There never was a man with a big brain, except Christ, who was not despotic somewhere.   514

Henry Ward Beecher, *Proverbs from Plymouth Pulpit*

Brains are no substitute for judgment.   515

Dean Acheson, in letter to Harry S. Truman, 3 May 1961

Brokenness

The sacrifices of God are a broken spirit; a broken and a contrite heart, O God, thou wilt not despise.   516

Psalm 51:17

God can heal a broken heart, but he has to have all the pieces.   517

Author Unknown

Brotherhood

Did not he that made me in the womb make him?   518

Job 31:15

Why do we deal treacherously, every man against his brother?   519

Malachi 2:10

He that loveth not his brother abideth in death.   520

1 John 3:14

Horrible in [God's] sight is brotherliness that is unaccompanied by fear and trembling, and forgets that men can be brothers only in God.   521

Karl Barth, *The Epistle to the Romans*

Brotherhood is not so wild a dream as those, who profit by postponing it, pretend.   522

Eric Sevareid, *Not So Wild a Dream*

A low capacity for getting along with those near us often goes hand in hand with a high receptivity to the idea of the brotherhood of man.   523

Eric Hoffer, *The Ordeal of Change*

A "fraternity" is the antithesis of fraternity. The first (that is, in order of organization) is predicated on the idea of exclusion; the second (that is, the abstract thing) is based on a feeling of total equality.   524

E. B. White, *One Man's Meat*

Business

A false balance is an abomination to the Lord; but a just weight is his delight.   525
> Proverbs 11:1

Seest thou a man diligent in his business? He shall stand before kings.   526
> Proverbs 22:29

The kingdom of heaven is like unto a merchant man, seeking goodly pearls. 527
> Jesus in Matthew 13:45

Business, especially big business, is now organized like an army. It is, as some would say, a sort of mild militarism without bloodshed; as I should say, a militarism without the military virtues.   528
> G. K. Chesterton, *The Thing: Why I Am a Catholic*

There is no glory so bright but the veil of business can hide it effectually.   529
> Henry David Thoreau, *Journals,* 21 July 1851

C

Candor

Let me alone, and let me speak, and let come on me what will.　　　530
>Job 13:13

Open rebuke is better than secret love.　　　531
>Proverbs 27:5

A time to keep silence, and a time to speak.　　　532
>Ecclesiastes 3:7

If I yet pleased men, I should not be the servant of Christ.　　　533
>Galatians 1:10

How furious it makes people to tell them of the things which belong to their peace!　　　534
>Logan Pearsall Smith, *Afterthoughts*

If people would dare to speak to one another unreservedly, there would be a good deal less sorrow in the world a hundred years hence.　　　535
>Samuel Butler, *The Way of all Flesh*

Frankness consists of having your back bitten right to your face.　　　536
>Ogden Nash, *Hush, Here They Come*

The art of life is to show your hand. There is no diplomacy like candor. You may lose by it now and then, but it will be a loss well gained if you do. Nothing is so boring as to have to keep up a deception.　　　537
>E. V. Lucas, in *Words of Wisdom,* compiled and edited by William Safire and Leonard Safir

Cant

Cant is moral assumption without moral feeling.　　　538
>Van Wyck Brookes, *The Opinions of Oliver Alston*

My dear friend, clear your *mind* of cant. You may *talk* as other people do; you may say to a man, "Sir, I am your most humble servant." But you are *not* his most humble servant.　　　539
>Samuel Johnson. Boswell's *Life,* 1783

Capitalism

The invective which the United States Chamber of Commerce hurls at communism is but 3-per-cent abuse compared to the 100-per-cent vitriol the Catholic and Lutheran churches heaped upon the early capitalists. Capitalism had to struggle for over two hundred years before it became a respectable word at church suppers.　　540

Max Dimont, *Jews, God, and History*

The trouble with socialism is socialism. The trouble with capitalism is capitalists.　　541

Author Unknown

Is it not remarkable that the greatest atrocities of life—I think of the capitalistic system and the war—can justify themselves on purely moral principles? The devil may also make use of morality.　　542

Karl Barth, *The Word of God and the Word of Man*

Capital is only the fruit of labor, and could never have existed had not labor first existed.　　543

Abraham Lincoln. *First Annual Message to Congress,*
8 December 1861

The basic law of capitalism is you or I, not both you and I.　　544

Karl Liebknecht. *Speech before the Fourth Socialist Young People's Conference,* Stuttgart, 1907

Cares, Caring

Is it nothing to you all ye that pass by? Behold, and see if there be any sorrow like unto my sorrow, which is done unto me, wherewith the Lord hath afflicted me in the day of his fierce anger.　　545

Lamentations 1:12

Then all the Greeks took Sosthenes, the chief ruler of the synagogue, and beat him before the judgment seat. And Gallio cared for none of these things.　　546

Acts 18:17

It is a bad thing for a man to talk too much about his cares to anybody. Cares are very much like pimples: if you let them alone they will dry up and disappear.　　547

Henry Ward Beecher, *Proverbs from Plymouth Pulpit*

You can create only if you care.　　548

George Orwell, *A Collection of Essays,* "Charles Darwin"

Not caring is hurtful. Jesus put it well by saying that he who is not for him is against him.　　549

Karl Menninger, *The Crime of Punishment*

Christianity has taught us to care. Caring is the greatest thing—caring matters most. My faith is not enough—it comes and goes. I have it about some things and not about others. So we make up and supplement each other. We give and others give to us.　　550

Friedrich von Hügel, *Letters to a Niece*

I know you feel insecure, don't know what to say, don't know what to do. But please believe me, if you care, you can't go wrong. Just admit that you are. That is really for what we search. We may ask for whys and wherefores, but we don't really expect answers. Don't run away—wait—all I want to know is that there will be someone to hold my hand when I need it, I am afraid. Death may get to be a routine for you, but it is new to me. You may not see me as unique, but I've never died before. To me, once is pretty unique!

You whisper about my youth, but when one is dying, is he really so young any more? I have lots I wish we could talk about. . . .

If only we could be honest, both admit of our fears, touch one another. If you really care, would you lose so much of your precious professionalism if you even cried with me? Just person to person? Then it might not be so hard to die—in a hospital—with friends close by.   551

> Anonymous, a young student nurse dying of cancer. Published in
> *The American Journal of Nursing,* February 1970

Certainty

How long halt ye between two opinions?   552
> 1 Kings 18:21

Boast not thyself of to morrow, for thou knowest not what a day may bring forth.   553
> Proverbs 27:1

If the trumpet giveth an uncertain sound, who shall prepare himself to the battle?   554
> 1 Corinthians 14:8

People who want absolute certainty, even about things in this present life, seem to be hiding from their own insecurities.   555
> Morton Kelsey, *Afterlife*

Ah, what a dusty answer gets the soul
When hot for certainties in this our life!   556
> George Meredith, *Modern Love*

Certainty generally is illusion, and repose is not the destiny of man.   557
> Oliver Wendell Holmes, Jr., *The Path of the Law*

If a man will begin with certainties, he shall end in doubts; but if he will be content with doubts, he will end in certainties.   558
> Francis Bacon, *The Advancement of Learning*

What men really want is not knowledge but certainty.   559
> Bertrand Russell, quoted by G. M. Carstairs in *Listener,* 30 July 1964

Change

Now there arose up a new king over Egypt, who knew not Joseph.   560
> Exodus 1:8

New wine must be put into new bottles.   561
> Jesus in Mark 2:22

The fashion of this world passeth away.	562
    1 Corinthians 7:31

Old things are passed away; behold, all things are become new.	563
    2 Corinthians 5:17

Jesus Christ the same yesterday, and today, and for ever.	564
    Hebrews 13:8

Things do not change; we change.	565
    Henry David Thoreau, *Walden*

Let everyone try and find that as a result of daily prayer he adds something new to his life, something with which nothing can be compared.	566
    Mohandas K. Gandhi, quoted in *Words of Wisdom,* compiled and
    edited by William Safire and Leonard Safir

We all know how Adam said to Eve: "My dear, we live in a period of transition."	567
    Vida D. Scudder, *The Privilege of Age*

Times change, and we are changed in them. (*Tempora mutantur, et nos mutamur in illis.*)	568
    Author unknown. Commonly attributed to the Emperor Lothar
    (795–855) in the form "All things change, and we are changed in
    them"

Tomorrow to fresh woods, and pastures new.	569
    John Milton, *Lycidas,* closing line.

When it is not necessary to change, it is necessary not to change.	570
    Lucius Cary, Viscount Falkland. Speech concerning episcopacy,
    1641

To change and to improve are two different things.	571
    German Proverb

I say, beware of all enterprises that require new clothes, but not rather a new wearer of clothes.	572
    Henry David Thoreau, *Walden*

Nothing is ever restored.	573
    Alfred North Whitehead, *Adventures of Ideas*

Character

Unstable as water, thou shalt not excel. [*Jacob to Reuben.*]	574
    Genesis 49:4

As the man is, so is his strength.	575
    Judges 8:21

What, is thy servant a dog, that he should do this great thing? [*Hazael to Elisha.*]	576
    2 Kings 8:13

Dost thou still retain thine integrity? curse God, and die. [*Job's wife to Job.*] 577
    Job 2:9

Let not mercy and truth forsake thee: bind them about thy neck.   578
        Proverbs 3:3

Even a child is known by his doings.   579
        Proverbs 20:11

Ye are the salt of the earth.   580
        Jesus in Matthew 5:13

We then that are strong ought to bear the infirmities of the weak.   581
        Romans 15:1

Only in the case of complete innocency, as that of a child's, is life more beautiful in repose than in activity. Character is created by a balance of tensions, and is more lovely even when the balance is imperfect than in a state of complete relaxation.   582
        Reinhold Niebuhr, *Leaves from the Notebook of a Tamed Cynic*

There are three Johns: 1, the real John, known only to his Maker; 2, John's ideal John, never the real one, and often very unlike him; 3, Thomas's ideal John, never the real John, nor John's John, but often very unlike either.   583
        Oliver Wendell Holmes, *The Autocrat of the Breakfast-Table*

A good man cannot be corrupted by the tavern nor a bad one reformed by the synagogue.   584
        Yiddish proverb

Good old Watson! You are the one fixed point in a changing age. [*Sherlock Holmes.*]   585
        Arthur Conan Doyle, *His Last Bow*

While a good man is always hard to find, he is easy to recognize.   586
        Sydney J. Harris, *Pieces of Eight*

A man's character never changes radically from youth to old age. What happens is that circumstances bring out characteristics which had not been obvious to the superficial observer.   587
        Hesketh Pearson, *Dickens*

Keep in mind that the true measure of an individual is how he treats a person who can do him absolutely no good.   588
        Ann Landers. Quoted in *Words of Wisdom*, compiled and edited by
        William Safire and Leonard Safir

The aura of victory that surrounds a man of good will, the sweetness of soul which emanates from him—a flavor of cranberries and cloudberries, a touch of frost and fiery skies.   589
        Dag Hammarskjöld, *Markings*

Charity

Thou shalt not harden thine heart, nor shut thine hand from thy poor brother.   590
        Deuteronomy 15:7

When the ear heard me, then it blessed me; and when the eye saw me, it gave witness to me, Because I delivered the poor that cried, and the fatherless, and him that had none to help him. The blessing of him that was ready to perish came upon me; and I caused the widow's heart to sing for joy. . . . I was eyes to the blind, and feet was I to the lame. I was a father to the poor; and the cause which I knew not I searched out. 591

Job 29:11–13, 16

Blessed is he that considereth the poor: the Lord will deliver him in time of trouble. 592

Psalm 41:1

If thou wilt be perfect, go and sell that thou hast, and give to the poor, and thou shalt have treasure in heaven; and come and follow me. 593

Jesus in Matthew 19:21

Inasmuch as ye have done it to the least of these my brethren, ye have done it unto me. 594

Jesus in Matthew 25:40

And though I bestow all my goods to feed the poor, and though I give my body to be burned, and have not charity, it profiteth me nothing. 595

1 Corinthians 13:3

I love Robertson, and I won't talk of his book. 596

Samuel Johnson. Boswell's *Life,* 1768

Don't look at a torn dress. 597

Malagasy Proverb

Charity should link us together by the very thing which divides us. 598

Antonin G. Sertillanges, *Rectitude*

Charity that is always beginning at home stays there. 599

Austin O'Malley, *Keystones of Thought*

Despise not a small wound, a poor kinsman, or an humble enemy. 600

English Proverb

Here lies Estella, who transported a large fortune to Heaven in acts of charity, and has gone hither to enjoy it. 601

Author unknown. Quoted in Loring, *Epitaphs Quaint, Curious and Elegant*

The rule for all of us is perfectly simple. Do not waste time bothering whether you "love" your neighbor; act as if you did. 602

C. S. Lewis, *Mere Christianity*

The true nature of charity: not a sterile fear of doing wrong but a vigorous determination that all of us together shall break open the doors of life. 603

Pierre Teilhard de Chardin, *Hymn of the Universe*

A strong argument for the religion of Christ is this—that offenses against charity are about the only ones which men on their deathbed can be made—not to understand—but to feel—as crimes. 604

Edgar Allan Poe, *Marginalia*

The desire of power in excess caused the angels to fall, but in charity there is no excess; neither angel nor man can come in danger of it.   605

> Francis Bacon, *Essays*, "Of Goodness and Goodness of Nature"

Nobody yet has come up with the final definition of charity, but Bishop Charles Gore said that charity is "reading statistics with compassion." A good note toward that final definition.   606

> C.E.S.

Charm

Charm is a glow within a person that casts a most becoming light upon others.   607

> John Mason Brown. *Vogue,* 15 November 1956

Charm walks on art-gum soles. It is gentle, but it can pack a wallop like a bag of wet cement. Charm has a magical quality that defrosts, disarms, delights and fascinates. It is not a sudden gush of sweetness that can be turned off and on like a faucet. It is woven subtly into the fabric of a personality, like a silver thread. It glistens. It shines, and wears well. For months. For years. Forever.   608

> Ann Landers. *Syndicated column,* 31 January 1980

Chastisement

Happy is the man whom God correcteth.   609

> Job 5:17

Despise not the chastening of the Lord, neither be weary of his correction.   610

> Proverbs 3:11

Whom the Lord loveth he chasteneth, and scourgeth every son whom he receiveth.   611

> Hebrews 12:6

Better to be pruned to grow than cut up to burn.   612

> John Trapp, *The Golden Treasury of Puritan Quotations*

Chastity

Dearly beloved, I beseech you as strangers and pilgrims, abstain from fleshly lusts, which war against the soul.   613

> 1 Peter 2:11

Christians have never said, so far as I am aware, *why* chastity (and more especially virginity) possesses a spiritual value. This is a serious lacuna, and one that keeps away a great many souls from Christ.   614

> Simone Weil, *Letter to a Priest*

Chastity is a wealth that comes from abundance of love.   615

> Rabindranath Tagore, *Stray Birds*

Chastity is a perpetual acquaintance with the All.   616

> Henry David Thoreau, *Journals,* 8 February 1857

We Christians regard a stain upon our chastity as more dreadful than any punishment, or even than death itself.   617

Tertullian, *Apologeticus.* 2d cent.

Cheer

And when the disciples saw him walking on the sea, they were troubled, saying, It is a spirit; and they cried out for fear. But straightway Jesus spake unto them, saying, Be of good cheer; it is I; be not afraid.   618

Matthew 14:26–27

I have tried too in my time to be a philosopher; but I don't know how; cheerfulness was always breaking in.   619

Oliver Edwards. Quoted in James Boswell, *Life of Johnson,*
17 April 1778

I have found myself dubbed "the gloomy dean," in contrast with certain more popular ecclesiastics who, because they can always conscientiously shout with the largest crowd, are naturally cheerful deans.   620

William R. Inge, *The Church and the Age*

What is the odds so long as the fire of soul is kindled at the taper of conviviality, and the wing of friendship never moults a feather! [*Dick Swiveller.*]   621

Charles Dickens, *The Old Curiosity Shop*

Be of good cheer. And remember, my dear friends, what a wise man said—"A merry heart doeth good like a medicine, but a broken spirit drieth the bones."   622

Adlai E. Stevenson, in his concession speech after losing the
presidential election, 1956

Childhood

See Age, Infancy, and Childhood

Childishness

Childishness follows us all the days of our life. If anybody seems wise it is only because his follies are in keeping with his age and circumstances.   623

François de la Rochefoucauld, *Maxims*

Childlikeness

Man is a born child; his power is the power of growth.   624

Rabindranath Tagore, *Stray Birds*

God waits for man to regain his childhood in wisdom.   625

Ibid.

Look for me in the nurseries of heaven.   626

Francis Thompson, *To My Godchild.* Inscribed on Thompson's
tombstone

When I grow up I want to be a little boy.   627

Joseph Heller, *Something Happened*

"To become as little children." Everyone bows his head in silence when this utterance is repeated. But no one truly believes it. And parents will always be the last to believe. 628

Henry Miller, *The Books in My Life*

A childlike man is not a man whose development has been arrested; on the contrary, he is a man who has given himself a chance of continuing to develop long after most adults have muffled themselves in the cocoon of middle-aged habits and convention. 629

Aldous Huxley, *Music at Night*

Children

See also Age, Infancy, and Childhood

Out of the mouths of babes and sucklings hast thou ordained strength. 630

Psalm 8:2

Respect the child. Be not too much his parent. Trespass not on his solitude. 631

Ralph Waldo Emerson. Quoted in *Words of Wisdom,* compiled and edited by William Safire and Leonard Safir

Viewing the child solely as an immature person is a way of escaping confronting him. 632

Clark Moustakas, *Creativity and Conformity*

The scars left from the child's defeat in the fight against irrational authority are to be found at the bottom of every neurosis. 633

Erich Fromm, *Man for Himself*

Even the happiest child has moments when he wishes his parents were dead. 634

Allen Fromme. *New York Times,* 2 October 1960

Children are born optimists, and we slowly educate them out of their heresy. 635

Louise Imogen Guiney, *Goose-Quill Papers*

We should not make light of the troubles of children. They are worse than our own, because we can see the end of our trouble and they can never see any end. 636

William Middleton. Quoted by W. B. Yeats in *Autobiography*

I love these little people; and it is not a slight thing when they, who are so fresh from God, love us. 637

Charles Dickens, *The Old Curiosity Shop*

People with bad consciences always fear the judgment of children. 638

Mary McCarthy, *On the Contrary*

Christ

See Jesus Christ

Christians, Christianity

The disciples were called Christians first at Antioch. 639

Acts 11:26

By this shall all men know that ye are my disciples, if ye have love one to another.   640

Jesus in John 13:35

The Spirit itself beareth witness with our spirit, that we are the children of God: And if children, then heirs; heirs of God, and joint-heirs with Christ; if so be that we suffer with him, that we may be also glorified together.   641

Romans 8:16–17

Ye are the body of Christ.   642

1 Corinthians 12:27

If any man suffer as a Christian, let him not be ashamed.   643

1 Peter 4:16

The world knoweth us not, because it knew him not.   644

1 John 3:1

In order to see Christianity, one must forget almost all the Christians.   645

Henry Frédéric Amiel, *Journal,* 30 August 1872

Christianity has died many times and risen again; for it had a god who knew his way out of the grave.   646

G. K. Chesterton, *George Bernard Shaw*

Christianity taught men that love is worth more than intelligence.   647

Jacques Maritain, *I Believe*

Christianity is strange: it bids man to recognize that he is vile, and even abominable, and bids him want to be like God.   648

Blaise Pascal, *Pensées*

He who begins by loving Christianity better than Truth will proceed by loving his own sect or church better than Christianity, and end by loving himself better than all.   649

Samuel Taylor Coleridge, *Aids to Reflection: Moral and Religious Aphorisms*

The essence of Christianity is extremely simple: in Christ God appears as our lover, who asks our free permission to impregnate us with his eternal life, and faith is our "yes" to his proposal.   650

Peter J. Kreeft, *Love is Stronger than Death*

Nothing is more aggressive and illogical than aggressive Christianity.   651

Gerald Vann, *The Heart of Man*

It doesn't take much of a man to make a Christian, but it takes all of him that there is.   652

Author Unknown

It is one of the great advantages (or disadvantages) of Christianity that in the last resort it has no arguments; it can do nothing but say, in the phrase which the Church claims that she has the only right to borrow from her Lord: "I am."   653

Charles Williams, *He Came Down From Heaven*

They would have been equally horrified at hearing the Christian religion doubted, and at seeing it practised. 654

> Samuel Butler, *The Way of All Flesh*, ch. 15, describing the congregation at Battersby-on-the-Hill

I go about with a Bible in one hand and a newspaper in the other. The two go well together, for the concentrated study of the newspaper is the Christian's duty as this age draws to its close. 655

> Christabel Pankhurst, speech at Albert Hall, London, September 1928

You are to follow no man further than he follows Christ. 656

> John Collins, *The Golden Treasury of Puritan Quotations*

The weak Christian is willing to live and patient to die; but the strong, patient to live and willing to die. 657

> John Boys, *The Golden Treasury of Puritan Quotations*

Catholicism and Protestantism are both obsolescent phases in the evolution of the Christian religion. 658

> William R. Inge. Quoted in Manchester *Guardian*, 4 March 1954

Religion would frame a just man; Christ would make a whole man. Religion would save a man; Christ would make him worth saving. 659

> Henry Ward Beecher, *Proverbs from Plymouth Pulpit*

We are all *revenants;* all living Christians are dead pagans walking about. 660

> G. K. Chesterton, *Orthodoxy*

Christianity begins where religion ends—with the Resurrection. 661

> Author Unknown

There are only two kinds of people in the modern world who know what they are after. One, quite frankly, is the Communist. The other, equally frankly, is the convinced Christian. . . . The rest of the world are amiable nonentities. 662

> Geoffrey Fisher, Archbishop of Canterbury. Recalled on his death, 14 September 1972

What! at peace with the Father, and at war with his children? It cannot be. 663

> John Flavel, of Christian divisions. *The Golden Treasury of Puritan Quotations*

Gospel duties are to be performed with a Gospel temper. 664

> Stephen Charnock, *The Golden Treasury of Puritan Quotations*

The Christian religion begins with the word "Follow!" and ends with the word "Go!" 665

> Author Unknown

Church

Thou art Peter, and upon this rock I will build my church; and the gates of hell shall not prevail against it. 666

> Jesus in Matthew 16:18

Mine house shall be called an house of prayer for all people. 667

> Isaiah 56:7

We, being many, are one body in Christ, and every one members one of another. 668

Romans 12:5

[The Church is] the communion of saints seeking forgiveness, of the lost who are saved, of the dead who are alive. 669

Karl Barth, *The Epistle to the Romans*

Wherever God erects a house of prayer,
The Devil always builds a chapel there;
And 'twill be found upon examination
the latter has the largest congregation. 670

Daniel Defoe, *The True-Born Englishman*

The Church exists for those outside. 671

William Temple, attributed

I believe in the Church, One, Holy, Catholic, and Apostolic, and I regret that it nowhere exists. 672

Ibid.

When we belong to the Church we belong to something which is outside all of us; which is outside everything you talk about, outside the Cardinals and the Pope. They belong to it, but it does not belong to them. If we all fell dead suddenly, the Church would still somehow exist in God. 673

G. K. Chesterton, *The Ball and the Cross*

The place of the Church is not to change society, but to change men and women who will then do the changing of society. 674

Daniel A. Poling, quoted in his obituary in *New York Times*,
8 February 1968

Query, Whether churches are not dormitories of the living as well as of the dead? 675

Jonathan Swift, *Thoughts on Various Subjects, Moral and Diverting*

We do not want churches. They will teach us to quarrel about God. 676

Chief Joseph, of the Nez Percé. Quoted in Dee Brown, *Bury My Heart at Wounded Knee*

The Church comes out of Christ's side in the sleep of his death. 677

William Jenkyn, *The Golden Treasury of Puritan Quotations*

We read not that Christ ever exercised force but once, and that was to drive profane ones out of his Temple, and not to force them in. 678

John Milton, *The Golden Treasury of Puritan Quotations*

O be not too quick to bury the Church before she is dead. 679

John Flavel, *The Golden Treasury of Puritan Quotations*

Nowhere does the unpredictable, the unusual, excite such confusion as in that settled institution—the church. 680

David Grayson, *The Friendly Road*

Those who are content with the church are just those who have not imagination enough to be Christians. 681

Charles Horton Cooley, *Life and the Student*

Some will have to cease thinking of the Church as a memorial association for a deceased clergyman called Christ.   682

> Stephen F. Bayne, Executive Officer of the Anglican Communion, at the Anglican Congress, Toronto, 19 August 1963

The work of the church in the world is not to teach the mysteries of life so much as to persuade the soul to that arduous degree of purity at which God himself becomes her teacher. The work of the church ends where the knowledge of God begins. 683

> Coventry Patmore, *The Rod, the Root and the Flower*

What we accomplish in the way of church unity ought to be accepted with humility and not hailed with pride. We are not creating. We are merely catching up with creation.   684

> Reinhold Niebuhr, *Leaves from the Notebook of a Tamed Cynic*

Circumstances

Our Lord did not try to alter circumstances. He submitted to them. They shaped his life and eventually brought him to Calvary. I believe we miss opportunities and lovely secrets our Lord is waiting to teach us by not taking what comes.   685

> Mother Maribel CSMV, quoted by Sister Janet CSMV in *Mother Maribel of Wantage*

Circumstances break men's bones; it has never been shown that they break men's optimism.   686

> G. K. Chesterton, *Charles Dickens*

Cities

And when he was come near, he beheld the city, and wept over it, saying, If thou hadst known, even thou, at least in this thy day, the things which belong unto thy peace! but now they are hid from thine eyes.   687

> Jesus in Luke 19:41–42

For [Abraham] looked for a city which hath foundations, whose builder and maker is God.   688

> Hebrews 11:10

For here we have no continuing city, but we seek one to come.   689

> Hebrews 13:14

And I John saw the holy city, new Jerusalem, coming down from God out of heaven, prepared as a bride adorned for her husband.   690

> Revelation 21:2

A great city is that which has the greatest men and women,
If it be but a few ragged huts it is still the greatest city in the whole world. 691

> Walt Whitman, *Leaves of Grass,* "Song of the Broad-Axe"

Fields and trees teach me nothing, but the people in a city do. [*Socrates.*]   692

> Plato, *Phaedrus*

With all history to contradict me, it is hardly worthwhile to speak of city life as entailing "spiritual loss" because it is out of touch with Nature. It is in touch with humanity, and humanity is Nature's heaviest asset.   693
Agnes Repplier, *Times and Tendencies*

Civilization

The civilized man is a more experienced and wiser savage.   694
Henry David Thoreau, *Walden*

Civilization is a method of living, an attitude of equal respect for all men.   695
Jane Addams, lecture in Honolulu, 1933

No society can be considered civilized unless tenderness is viewed as an integral part of manliness, and not alien to it.   696
Sydney J. Harris, *Clearing the Ground*

Civilization is the making of civil persons.   697
John Ruskin, *The Crown of Wild Olive*

Past civilizations have been destroyed by barbarians from without, but we are doing this job ourselves.   698
Malcolm Muggeridge, in speech at Edinburgh International Festival, 24 August 1969

Every civilization is, among other things, an arrangement for domesticating the passions and setting them to do useful work.   699
Aldous Huxley, *Collected Essays*

The civilized are those who get more out of life than the uncivilized, and for this the uncivilized have not forgiven them.   700
Cyril Connolly, *The Unquiet Grave*

When a civilization is overripe it turns rotten and begins to stink. You can read all about it in Romans 1:18–32.   701
C.E.S.

Class

My brothers, do not try to combine faith in Jesus Christ, our glorified Lord, with the making of distinctions between classes of people.   702
James 2:1, *The Jerusalem Bible*

The danger is not that a particular class is unfit to govern. Every class is unfit to govern.   703
Lord Action, in letter to Mandell Creighton, 5 April 1887

When Adam dalf and Eve span
Who was thanne a gentil man?   704
John Ball (?–1381), *Sermon to rebels at Blackheath*

I never could believe that Providence had sent a few men into the world, ready booted and spurred to ride, and millions ready saddled and bridled to be ridden. 705
Richard Rumbold (c. 1622–1685), on the scaffold

Clergy

They shall teach my people the difference between the holy and profane. 706
Ezekiel 44:23

The priest's lips should keep knowledge 707
Malachi 2:7

They which preach the gospel should live of the gospel. 708
1 Corinthians 9:14

People expect the clergy to have the grace of a swan, the friendliness of a sparrow, the strength of an eagle and the night hours of an owl—and some people expect such a bird to live on the food of a canary. 709
Edward Jeffrey, *Observer*, "Sayings of the Week," 14 June 1964

It is the clergy's task to feed the sheep—not to entertain the goats. 710
Donald Coggan, Archbishop of Canterbury. *Convictions*

It is not a priest's business to impose his own ideas, but to aid the workings of grace. 711
Abbé Huvelin, *Some Spiritual Guides of the Seventeenth Century*

The people may admire him for the eloquence of his sermons, but they will love him for the eloquence of his beneficent acts. 712
James Cardinal Gibbons, *The Ambassador of Christ*

Had an interesting lunch sitting next to the Archbishop [of Canterbury] on Wed. He pleased me greatly by saying the only really important thing for Clergy was to make a Retreat every year: and then told me a tale of an utterly lonely, poverty-stricken one in an utterly irresponsive village, with an ill wife and no servants, who rang his own Church bell daily, said his offices and made his meditation and never lost heart; and then added quietly, "*That* is the true evidence of the Supernatural." Nice, don't you think? 713
Evelyn Underhill, *The Letters of Evelyn Underhill*

Cleverness

To be clever enough to get all that money, one must be stupid enough to want it. 714
G. K. Chesterton, *Wisdom of Father Brown, "The Purple Wig"*

A little touch of cleverness is not bad, and let us not have too much simplicity. 715
St. Teresa of Avila, quoted in Rodolphe Hoornaert, *St. Teresa in Her Writings*

Cleverness opens no gates to truths that matter. 716
Owen Chadwick, *Newman*

In psychology, in sociology, above all in education, we are learning to do a great many clever things. Unless we are much mistaken the next great step will be to learn not to do them. 717
G. K. Chesterton, *Varied Types*

Very clever, but his brains go to his head.   718

> Margot Asquith, speaking of F. E. Smith, 1st Earl of Birkenhead. Quoted in *The Little, Brown Book of Anecdotes*, compiled by Clifton Fadiman

The proper motto is not "Be good, sweet maid, and let who can be clever," but "Be good, sweet maid, and don't forget that this involves being as clever as you can."   719

> C. S. Lewis, *Mere Christianity*

Comfort

As he that taketh away a garment in cold weather, and as vinegar upon nitre, so is he that singeth songs to an heavy heart.   720

> Proverbs 25:20

Thy rod and thy staff they comfort me.   721

> Psalm 23:4

As one whom his mother comforteth, so will I comfort you.   722

> Isaiah 66:13

Blessed are they that mourn: for they shall be comforted.   723

> Jesus in Matthew 5:4

Blessed be God, even the Father of our Lord Jesus Christ, the Father of mercies, and the God of all comfort; Who comforteth us in all our tribulation, that we may be able to comfort them which are in any trouble, by the comfort wherewith we ourselves are comforted of God.   724

> 2 Corinthians 1:3–4

Ye cannot expect to be baith grand and comfortable.   725

> James Barrie, *The Little Minister*

Love comforteth like sunshine after rain.   726

> William Shakespeare, *Venus and Adonis,* 1. 799

That it may please thee to strengthen such as do stand; and to comfort and help the weak-hearted; and to raise up those who fall; and finally to beat down Satan under our feet; *We beseech thee to hear us, good Lord.*   727

> Book of Common Prayer, *The Litany*

Commandments

The law of the Lord is perfect . . . making wise the simple.   728

> Psalm 19:7

Great peace have they which love thy law.   729

> Psalm 119:165

Whosoever shall do and teach them, the same shall be called great in the kingdom of heaven.   730

> Jesus in Matthew 5:19

The law was given by Moses, but grace and truth came by Jesus Christ.   731
John 1:17

A new commandment I give unto you, That ye love one another; as I have loved you, that ye also love one another.   732
Jesus in John 13:34

The letter killeth, but the spirit giveth life.   733
2 Corinthians 3:6

The law was our schoolmaster to bring us unto Christ, that we might be justified by faith.   734
Galatians 3:24

The Ten Commandments, which have been found substantially common to mankind, were merely military commands; a code of regimental orders, issued to protect a certain ark across a certain desert. Anarchy was evil because it endangered the sanctity. And only when they made a holy day for God did they find that they had made a holiday for men.   735
G. K. Chesterton, *Orthodoxy*

I stand by the Ten Commandments. They are bully.   736
Theodore Roosevelt, attributed

The commandments have made as many good martyrs as the creed.   737
Author Unknown

Begin where we will, we are pretty sure in a short space to be mumbling our ten commandments.   738
Ralph Waldo Emerson, *Essays,* "Prudence"

Communion of Saints

Seeing we also are compassed about with so great a cloud of witnesses, let us lay aside every weight, and the sin which doth so easily beset us, and let us run with patience the race that is set before us, Looking unto Jesus the author and finisher of our faith; who for the joy that was set before him endured the cross, despising the shame, and is set down at the right hand of the throne of God.   739
Hebrews 12:1–2

These are they which came out of great tribulation, and have washed their robes, and made them white in the blood of the Lamb. Therefore are they before the throne of God, and serve him day and night in his temple: and he that sitteth on the throne shall dwell among them. They shall hunger no more, neither thirst any more; neither shall the sun light on them, nor any heat. For the Lamb which is in the midst of the throne shall feed them, and shall lead them unto living fountains of waters: and God shall wipe away all tears from their eyes.   740
Revelation 7:14–17

The closer we are to God, the closer we are to those who are close to Him. We can understand others only by loving Him Who understands them from within the depths of their own being. Otherwise we know them only by the surmises that are formed within the mirror of our own soul.   741
Thomas Merton, *No Man Is an Island*

There is a land of the living and a land of the dead and the bridge is love, the only survival, the only meaning.   742

> Thornton Wilder, *The Bridge of San Luis Rey,* closing line

The great ones of earth have been those who have struggled to share their solitude. The sign of their success has lain in the conviction of others that they are less solitary because of these struggles. The way of this sharing has been love.   743

> Jessamyn West, *Love Is Not What You Think*

Found myself, surprised myself, with a prayer on my lips, a prayer to Plotinus that I might translate him: I am certain it would be as well to pray to him as to pray to St. Augustine or St. Patrick, but I think Plotinus would not be pleased with this my prayer: it would seem to him a worldly thing, still. It is very strange to me as I write this to feel that perhaps very truly he looks down upon me writing: at least that is what the Catholic Church means with her "communion of the Saints and Intercession of the Saints": can they really believe that the Once Human, now ravished in the Beatific Vision, do look down upon the upper room of No. 1, Goldhurst Terrace, Finchley Road, where the Wax Lady waits at the door? Amazing the things one can believe when one is called *homo*.   744

> Stephen Mackenna, *Journal,* 11 December 1907

God forbid that in a higher state of existence she should cease to think of me, to long to comfort me, she who loved me more than words can tell.   745

> St. Augustine, *Confessions,* of his mother

The Communion of Saints works by divine empathy. We know and love others in the body *as God does:* not from without but from within; not by looking at others' lives but by *living* them; not by sympathy but by empathy. God is right now living in all the cells of the body of His Son. When we share this ubiquity of the Head, we share it from within. The consequences of this idea are mind-boggling.   746

> Peter J. Kreeft, *Everything You Ever Wanted to Know About Heaven—But Never Dreamed of Asking*

Compassion

Thou shalt not harden thine heart, nor shut thine hand from thy poor brother.   747

> Deuteronomy 15:7

Remember that thou wast a bondman in the land of Egypt, and the Lord thy God redeemed thee.   748

> Deuteronomy 15:15

This day thou shalt bear no tidings, because the king's son is dead.   749

> 2 Samuel 18:20

As a father pitieth his children, so the Lord pitieth them that fear him.   750

> Psalm 103:13

For I was an hungred, and ye gave me meat: I was thirsty, and ye gave me drink: I was a stranger, and ye took me in; Naked, and ye clothed me; I was sick, and ye visited me; I was in prison, and ye came unto me.   751

> Jesus in Matthew 25:35–36

No tears in the writer, no tears in the reader.   752
> Robert Frost, *Collected Poems*, Preface

Want of tenderness is want of parts, and is no less a proof of stupidity than depravity.   753
> Samuel Johnson, Boswell's *Life*, 170

The bowels of compassion: a wonderful old phrase. They ought to be kept open.   754
> Norman Douglas, *South Wind*

God is absent from the world, except in the existence in this world of those in whom his love is alive. Therefore they ought to be in the world through compassion. Their compassion is the visible presence of God here below.   755
> Simone Weil, *Gateway to God*

Great Spirit, grant that I may not criticize my neighbor until I have walked a mile in his moccasins.   756
> Native American Prayer

Compassion alone stands apart from the continuous traffic between good and evil proceeding within us.   757
> Eric Hoffer. Quoted in *Christian Science Monitor*, 22 April 1980

I cannot but think that he who finds a certain proportion of pain and evil inseparably woven up in the life of the very worms, will bear his own share with more courage and submission.   758
> Thomas Henry Huxley, *On the Educational Value of the Natural History Sciences*

It is considered an absolute necessity these days for writers to have compassion. Compassion is a word that sounds good in anybody's mouth and which no book jacket can do without. It is a quality which one can put his finger on in any exact critical sense, so it is always safe for anybody to use. Usually I think what is meant by it is that the writer excuses all human weaknesses because human weakness is human. The kind of hazy compassion demanded of the writer makes it difficult for him to be anti-anything.   759
> Flannery O'Connor, *Mystery and Manners*

Conceit

Seest thou a man wise in his own conceit? there is more hope of a fool than of him.   760
> Proverbs 26:12

He that trusteth in his own heart is a fool.   761
> Proverbs 28:26

Woe unto them that are wise in their own eyes.   762
> Isaiah 5:21

But thou didst trust in thine own beauty.   763
> Ezekiel 16:15

Every one that exalteth himself shall be abased; and he that humbleth himself shall be exalted. 764

Jesus in Luke 18:14

Be not wise in your own conceits. 765

Romans 12:16

Conceit is God's gift to little men. 766

Bruce Barton, *Coronet,* September 1958

He was like a cock who thought the sun had risen to hear him crow. 767

George Eliot, *Adam Bede*

What is the first business of philosophy? To part with self-conceit. For it is impossible for any one to begin to learn what he thinks that he already knows. 768

Epictetus, *Discourses,* 2, 17

Conduct

Take heed to thyself, and keep thy soul diligently, lest thou forget the things which thine eyes have seen. 769

Deuteronomy 4:9

The steps of a good man are ordered by the Lord, and he delighteth in his way. 770

Psalm 37:23

What doth the Lord require of thee, but to do justly, and to love mercy, and to walk humbly with thy God? 771

Micah 6:8

Do all the good you can,
In all the ways you can,
In all places you can,
At all times you can,
To all the people you can,
As long as ever you can. 772

John Wesley, *Rules of Conduct*

Conduct is three-fourths of our life and its largest concern. 773

Matthew Arnold, *Literature and Life*

Right conduct can never, except by some rare accident, be promoted by ignorance or hindered by knowledge. 774

Bertrand Russell, *Marriage and Morals*

It may be [that] a good working guide to conduct might be framed in this ideal of living to the fullest here and now: it is likely that the soul seeking admission among the bodiless immortals in another world would be elected at once on the strength of having kept itself from death in days here below. 775

Stephen Mackenna, *Journal*

Confession

I must say to myself that I ruined myself, and that nobody great or small can be ruined except by his own hand.   776
Oscar Wilde, *De profundis*

Conflict

Think not that I am come to send peace on earth; I came not to send peace, but a sword. For I am come to set a man at variance against his father, and the daughter against her mother, and the daughter-in-law against her mother-in-law. And a man's foes shall be they of his own household.   777
Jesus in Matthew 10:34–36

All human conflict is ultimately theological.   778
Henry Edward Cardinal Manning, quoted by Hilaire Belloc, *Cruise of the Nona*

All men have in them an instinct for conflict: at least, all healthy men.   779
Hilaire Belloc, *The Silence of the Sea*

No doubt there are other important things in life besides conflict, but there are not many other things so inevitably interesting. The very saints interest us most when we think of them as engaged in a conflict with the Devil.   780
Robert Lynd, *The Blue Lion*

The opposite is beneficial; from things that differ comes the fairest attunement; all things are born through strife.   781
Heraclitus (c. 540–c. 480 B.C.), *On the Universe*, fragment 46

Conscience

Thou knowest all the wickedness which thine heart is privy to.   782
1 Kings 2:44

The wicked flee when no man pursueth.   783
Proverbs 28:1

Whether it be right in the sight of God to hearken unto you more than unto God, judge ye.   784
Acts 4:19

A conscience is something that hurts us when everything else feels terrific. 785
Author Unknown

We learn to recognize a mere blunting of the conscience in that incapacity for indignation which is not to be confounded with the gentleness of charity or the reserve of humility.   786
Henri Frédéric Amiel, *Journal*, 29 December 1871

There is another man within me that's angry with me, rebukes, commands, and dastards me.   787
Sir Thomas Browne, *Religio Medici*

There is a conscience in man; therefore there is a God in heaven.   788
Ezekiel Hopkins, *The Golden Treasury of Puritan Quotations*

I cannot and will not cut my conscience to fit this year's fashions.   789
> Lillian Hellman, in a letter to John S. Wood, Chairman of the House Committee on un-American Activities, 1952

Conscience is the face of the soul.   790
> Thomas Merton, *No Man Is an Island*

Conscience is the perfect interpreter of life.   791
> Karl Barth, *The Word of God and the Word of Man*

Conscience is thoroughly well-bred and soon leaves off talking to those who do not wish to hear it.   792
> Samuel Butler, *Note-Books*

To make conscience tolerable, love should be thrown around it. Conscience is the frame of character, and love is the covering of it.   793
> Henry Ward Beecher, *Proverbs from Plymouth Pulpit*

Conscience, the domestic chaplain.   794
> John Trapp, *The Golden Treasury of Puritan Quotations*

Contempt

He that condemneth small things shall fall little by little.   795
> Ecclesiasticus 19:1, *The Jerusalem Bible*

I say unto you, That whosoever is angry with his brother without a cause shall be in danger of the judgment; and whosoever shall say to his brother, Raca, shall be in danger of the council; but whosoever shall say, Thou fool, shall be in danger of hell fire.   796
> Jesus in Matthew 5:22

God hath not called us unto uncleanness, but unto holiness. He therefore that despiseth, despiseth not man, but God, who hath also given us his Holy Spirit.   797
> 1 Thessalonians 4:7–8

Only the contemptible are afraid of being treated with contempt.   798
> François de la Rochefoucauld, *Maxims*

Many men can bear adversity, but few contempt.   799
> Thomas Fuller, *Gnomologia*

Contempt is egotism in ill humor.   800
> Samuel Taylor Coleridge, *Omniana*

Who can refute a sneer?   801
> William Paley, *Principles of Moral and Political Philosophy*

Contentment

Better is little with the fear of the Lord than great treasure and trouble therewith.   802
> Proverbs 15:16

The eye is not satisfied with seeing, nor the ear with hearing.   803
> Ecclesiastes 1:8

I have learned, in whatsoever state I am, therewith to be content.   804
> Philippians 4:11

Godliness with contentment is great gain.   805
> 1 Timothy 6:6

Better is a dinner with herbs where love is, than a stalled ox and hatred
therewith.   806
> Proverbs 15:17

Contentment has been worn as a crown by no end of sleepy heads.   807
> Anonymous (Henry S. Haskins), *Meditations in Wall Street*

The toad beneath the harrow knows
Exactly where each tooth-point goes;
The butterfly upon the road
Preaches contentment to that toad.   808
> Rudyard Kipling, *Pagett M.P.*

The secret of contentment is the realization that life is a gift, not a right.   809
> Author Unknown

You can't have everything. Where would you put it?   810
> Author Unknown

Conversation

The test of a man is in his conversation.   811
> Ecclesiasticus 27:6, *The Jerusalem Bible*

Don't let small talk fill up the time and the silence except as a medium for bearing
unexpressed messages between two people who are attuned to each other.   812
> Dag Hammarskjöld, *Markings*

That is the happiest conversation where there is no competition, no vanity, but a
calm quiet interchange of sentiments.   813
> Samuel Johnson. Boswell's *Life,* 14 April 1775

Debate is masculine; conversation is feminine.   814
> A. Bronson Alcott, *Concord Days*

You smiled and talked to me of nothing and I felt that for this I had waited
long.   815
> Rabindranath Tagore, *Stray Birds*

Conversion

Thy people shall be my people, and thy God my God.   816
> Ruth 1:16

And the Lord said, Simon, Simon, behold, Satan hath desired to have you, that he
may sift you as wheat: But I have prayed for thee, that thy faith fail not: and when thou
art converted, strengthen thy brethren.   817
> Luke 22:31–32

Every story of a conversion is the story of a blessed defeat.   818
> C. S. Lewis, in Preface to Joy Davidson, *Smoke on the Mountain*

Dear Lord, make all bad people good, and all good people nice.   819
   Author unknown, reportedly a little girl

You are converted when you are changed from wanting what *you* want *for* yourself to wanting what *God* wants *from* yourself.   820
   C.E.S.

Corruption

His sons walked not in his ways, but turned aside after lucre.   821
   1 Samuel 8:3

Who can bring a clean thing out of an unclean? not one.   822
   Job 14:4

There is none that doeth good, no, not one.   823
   Psalm 14:3

All that honored her despise her, because they have seen her nakedness.   824
   Lamentations 1:8

Ye have turned judgment into gall, and the fruit of righteousness into hemlock.   825
   Amos 6:12

Save yourselves from this untoward generation.   826
   Acts 2:40

Lilies that fester smell worse than weeds.   827
   William Shakespeare, *Sonnets,* 94

No man ever became thoroughly bad all at once. (*Nemo repente fuit turpissimus.*)   828
   Juvenal, *Satires*

The first gold star a child gets in school for the mere performance of a needful task is its first lesson in graft.   829
   Philip Wylie, *Generation of Vipers*

Everything is good as it leaves the hands of the Author of things; everything degenerates in the hands of man.   830
   Jean-Jacques Rousseau, *Emile,* opening sentence

Courage

Be strong, and quit yourselves like men.   831
   1 Samuel 4:9

Is not this the blood of the men who went in jeopardy of their lives?   832
   2 Samuel 23:17

The Lord is the strength of my life; of whom then shall I be afraid?   833
   Psalm 27:1

Fear none of those things which thou shalt suffer.   834
   Jesus in Revelation 2:10

By faith he forsook Egypt, not fearing the king . . . for he endured, as seeing him who is invisible.   835

> Hebrews 11:27

Courage is the price that life exacts for granting peace.   836

> Amelia Earhart Putnam, *Courage*

The strong cannot be brave. Only the weak can be brave; and yet again, as in practice, only those who can be brave can be trusted, in time of doubt, to be strong. 837

> G. K. Chesterton, *Heretics*

Courage is resistance to fear—mastery of fear —not absence of fear. Except a creature be part coward, it is not a compliment to say it is brave; it is merely a loose application of the word. Consider the flea!—incomparably the bravest of all the creatures of God, if ignorance of fear were courage. Whether you are asleep or awake he will attack you, caring nothing for the fact that in bulk and strength you are to him as are the massed armies of the world to a sucking child; he lives both day and night in the very lap of peril and the immediate presence of death, and yet is no more afraid than is the man who walks the streets of a city that was threatened by an earthquake ten centuries before. When we speak of Clive, Nelson, and Putnam as men who "didn't know what fear was," we ought always to add the flea—and put him at the head of the procession.   838

> Mark Twain, *Pudd'nhead Wilson's Calendar*

Creation

In the beginning God created the heaven and the earth.   839

> Genesis 1:1

God created man in his own image, in the image of God created he him; male and female created he them.   840

> Genesis 1:27

And God saw every thing he had made, and, behold, it was very good.   841

> Genesis 1:31

Who hath made man's mouth? or who maketh the dumb, or deaf, or the seeing, or the blind? have not I the Lord?   842

> Exodus 4:11

He spake, and it was done; he commanded, and it stood fast.   843

> Psalm 33:9

We are the clay, and thou our potter.   844

> Isaiah 64:8

Every house is builded by some man; but he that hath built all things is God.   845

> Hebrews 3:4

Hast thou not poured me out as milk, and curdled me like cheese?   846

> Job 10:10

The account of the Creation in Genesis is prophecy, not history. We are now in the beginning of the Sixth Day. Woman is being created out of Man. 847

Coventry Patmore, *The Rod, the Root and the Flower*

The ordinary progressive position is that this is a bad universe, but will certainly get better. I say it is certainly a good universe, even if it gets worse. 848

G. K. Chesterton, *The Apostle and the Wild Duck*

A man looking at a hippopotamus may sometimes be tempted to regard a hippopotamus as an enormous mistake; but he is also bound to confess that a fortunate inferiority prevents him from making such mistakes. 849

G. K. Chesterton, *Charles Dickens*

The pride of the peacock is the glory of God.
The lust of the goat is the bounty of God.
The wrath of the lion is the wisdom of God.
The nakedness of woman is the work of God. 850

William Blake, *Proverbs of Hell*

Creation itself seems to be delegation through and through. He will do nothing simply of Himself which can be done by creatures. I suppose this is because He is a giver. And He has nothing to give but Himself. And to give Himself is to do His deeds—in a sense, on varying levels to be Himself—through the things He has made. 851

C. S. Lewis, *Letters to Malcolm: Chiefly on Prayer*

The poet enters into himself in order to create. The contemplative enters into God in order to be created. 852

Thomas Merton, *New Seeds of Contemplation*

When for you the most obvious fact about yourself is your createdness, God becomes for you both the most immediate and the most ultimate obviosity: for all that you are is simply a sign of the Creator. The creature is a sign and a proof of the Creator, but more than a proof, more even than a sign: an *expression* of God, in the way that a poem is an expression of a poet. If you see yourself as a rather bad poem, don't blame the Poet. 853

C.E.S.

Creativity

They [creative people] deal with what all men know and they make it new. 854

Alfred North Whitehead, *Religion in the Making*

It is the stretched soul that makes music, and souls are stretched by the pull of opposites—opposite bents, tastes, yearnings, loyalties. Where there is no polarity—where energies flow smoothly in one direction—there will be much doing but no music. 855

Eric Hoffer, *Reflections on the Human Condition*

The essence of the creative act is to see the familiar as strange. 856

Author unknown. *Kaiser News,* no. 3, 1967

The invention of IQ did a great disservice to creativity in education. . . . Individuality, personality, are too precious to be meddled with by amateur psychiatrists whose patterns for a "wholesome personality" are probably their own.   857

> Joel H. Hildebrand, Emeritus Professor of Chemistry, University of California. *New York Times,* 16 June 1964

Could *Hamlet* have been written by a committee, or the *Mona Lisa* painted by a club? Could the New Testament have been composed as a conference report? Creative ideas do not spring from groups. They spring from individuals. The divine spark leaps from the finger of God to the finger of Adam.   858

> A. Whitney Griswold, President of Yale. Baccalaureate address, 8 June 1957

I have a bit of FIAT in my soul,
And can myself create my little world.   859

> Thomas Lovell Beddoes, *Death's Jest Book*

Creatures

And God remembered Noah, and every living thing, and all the cattle that was with him in the ark: and God made the wind to pass over the earth, and the waters asswaged.   860

> Genesis 8:1

For we are only creatures: our *role* must be that of patient to agent, female to male, mirror to light, echo to voice. Our highest activity must be response, not initiative.   861

> C. S. Lewis, *The Problem of Pain*

Forgive us all our trespasses,
Little creatures, everywhere!   862

> James Stephens, *Little Things*

We know that every created, temporal thing—of uncreated, infinite things we have no knowledge—bears its eternal existence in itself as unborn, eternal future, and seeks to give it that birth which can never take place in time.   863

> Karl Barth, *The Epistle to the Romans*

God made all the creatures and gave them our love and our fear,
To give sign, we and they are his children, one family here.   864

> Robert Browning, *Saul*

The deepest experience of the [human] creator is feminine, for it is experience of receiving and bearing.   865

> Rainer Maria Rilke, *Letters of Rainer Maria Rilke 1892–1910*

If a created being has no rights which the Creator is bound to respect, there is an end to all moral relations between them.   866

> Oliver Wendell Holmes. *Life and Letters of Oliver Wendell Holmes,* Vol. I, by John T. Morse, Jr.

Every existing thing is equally upheld in its existence by God's creative love. The friends of God would love him to the point of merging their love into his with regard to all things here below.   867

> Simone Weil, *Waiting on God*

Creeds

Once one believes in a creed, one is proud of its complexity, as scientists are proud of the complexity of science. It shows how rich it is in discoveries. If it is right at all, it is a compliment to say that it is elaborately right. A stick might fit a hole or a stone a hollow by accident. But a key and a lock are both complex. And if a key fits a lock, you know it is the right key.   868
> G. K. Chesterton, *Orthodoxy*

I do not believe in any creed, but I use certain creeds to express, to conserve, and to deepen my belief in God.   869
> William Temple, *Nature, Man and God*

Crime

Men do not despise a thief, if he steal to satisfy his soul when he is hungry.   870
> Proverbs 6:30

He that pursueth evil pursueth it to his own death.   871
> Proverbs 11:19

The thief cometh not, but for to steal, and to kill, and to destroy.   872
> Jesus in John 10:10

The greater the man, the greater the crime.   873
> Author Unknown

The faculties for getting people into jail seem to be simple. We want some organizations for keeping people out.   874
> Charles Dudley Warner, *Backlog Studies*

The study of crime begins with the study of oneself.   875
> Henry Miller, *The Air-Conditioned Nightmare*

The greatest crimes are caused by surfeit, not by want. Men do not become tyrants in order that they may not suffer cold.   876
> Aristotle, *Politics*

The casuists of the Roman church, who gain, by confession, great opportunities of knowing human nature, have generally determined that what it is a crime to do, it is a crime to think.   877
> Samuel Johnson. *The Rambler,* 14 April 1750

Commit a crime, and the earth is made of glass. Commit a crime, and it seems as if a coat of snow fell on the ground, such as reveals in the woods the track of every partridge and fox and squirrel and mole.   878
> Ralph Waldo Emerson, *Compensation*

No one can live without crime. (*Nemo sine crimine vivit.*)   879
> Latin Proverb

Criticism

Ye are forgers of lies, ye are all physicians of no value.   880
> Job 13:4

Reprove not a scorner lest he hate thee: rebuke a wise man, and he will love thee. 881

Proverbs 9:8

What embitters the world is not excess of criticism but absence of self-criticism. 882

G. K. Chesterton, *Sidelights on New London and Newer New York*

They have vilified me, they have crucified me, yes, they have even criticized me. 883

Richard J. Daley. *Quotations from Mayor Daley,* compiled by Peter Yessne

Few people are wise enough to prefer useful criticism to the sort of praise which is their undoing. 884

François de la Rochefoucauld, *Maxims*

The temptation is tremendous to say that you like what you think you ought to like and don't like what you think you oughtn't to like. 885

Arnold Bennett. *Arnold Bennett: The Evening Standard Years,* edited by Andrew Mylett

Criticism is easier than craftsmanship. 886

Zeuxis, Greek painter, 5th cent. B.C. Quoted in Pliny, *Natural History*

I have always very much despised the artificial canons of criticism. When I have read a work in prose or poetry, or seen a painting, a statue, etc., I have only asked myself whether it gives me pleasure, whether it is animating, interesting, attaching? If it is, it is good for these reasons. 887

Thomas Jefferson, in letter to William Wirt, 1816

I have never found, in a long experience of politics, that criticism is ever inhibited by ignorance. 888

Harold MacMillan. *Wall Street Journal,* 13 August 1963

They have a right to censure that have a heart to help. 889

William Penn, *Some Fruits of Solitude*

Cross

Whosoever will come after me, let him deny himself, and take up his cross, and follow me. 890

Jesus in Mark 8:34

Ye shall weep and lament, but the world shall rejoice. 891

Jesus in John 16:20

The language of the cross may be illogical to those who are not on the way to salvation, but those of us who are on the way see it as God's power to save. 892

1 Corinthians 1:18, *The Jerusalem Bible*

The Cross is the ground plan of the universe. 893

Evelyn Underhill, *Mysticism*

Hitler could die and return to life again fifty times, but I still would not look on him as the Son of God. And if the Gospel omitted all mention of Christ's resurrection, faith would be easier for me. The Cross by itself suffices me.   894

Simone Weil, *Gateway to God*

To repel one's cross is to make it heavier.   895

Henri Frédéric Amiel, *Journal,* 30 December 1850

In one manner or the other it still remains true that, even in the view of the mere biologist, the human epic resembles nothing so much as a way of the Cross.   896

Pierre Teilhard de Chardin, closing words of *The Phenomenon of Man,* written in Rome, 28 October, 1948

The Christian is not asked to swoon in the shadow, but to climb in the light of the Cross.   897

Pierre Teilhard de Chardin, *The Divine Milieu*

On many occasions Jesus let people know that living this life and preparing for the next one is serious business. He warned them against mistreating anyone or refusing to take the way of God seriously. Jesus did not promise people a Pollyannaish afterlife any more than he suggested that his followers in this life would find their path strewn with roses and approval. The way of the cross which he demonstrated is hard, but it is the way of transformation, of finding the lost parts of ourselves, as well as the lost souls in this world.   898

Morton T. Kelsey, *Afterlife*

If you bear the cross gladly, it will bear you.   899

Thomas à Kempis, *Imitation of Christ*

Cruelty

And David said unto Gad, I am in a great strait: let us fall now into the hand of the Lord; for his mercies are great: and let me not fall into the hand of man.   900

2 Samuel 24:14

The merciful man doeth good to his own soul: but he that is cruel troubleth his own flesh.   901

Proverbs 11:17

The tender mercies of the wicked are cruel.   902

Proverbs 12:10

I was an hungred, and ye gave me no meat: I was thirsty, and ye gave me no drink.   903

Jesus in Matthew 25:42

Wild animals never kill for sport. Man is the only one to whom the torture and death of his fellow creatures is amusing to himself.   904

James Anthony Froude, *Oceana*

Cruelty is a still more appalling crime than lust. Moreover, lust satisfies itself as readily by murder as it does by sexual intercourse.   905

Simone Weil, *Gateway to God*

I would not enter on my list of friends
(Tho grac'd with polish'd manners and fine sense,
Yet wanting sensibility) the man
Who needlessly sets foot upon a worm.   906
> William Cowper, *The Task*

Opinions which justify cruelty are inspired by cruel impulses.   907
> Bertrand Russell, *Unpopular Opinions*

Cruelty is, perhaps, the worst kind of sin. Intellectual cruelty certainly is the worst kind of cruelty.   908
> G. K. Chesterton, *All Things Considered*

Cruelty is a tyrant that is always attended by fear.   909
> English Proverb

Custom

Custom is the plague of wise men and the idol of fools.   910
> Thomas Fuller, *Gnomologia*

There is a deep meaning in all old customs.   911
> J. C. F. Schiller, *Marie Stuart,* i.

What custom hath endeared
We part with sadly, though we prize it not.   912
> Joanna Baillie, *Basil,* i.

Custom doth make dotards of us all.   913
> Thomas Carlyle, *Sartor Resartus*

When a thing is done again and again, it seems to proceed from a deliberate judgment of reason. Accordingly, custom has the force of a law, abolishes law, and is the interpreter of law.   914
> St. Thomas Aquinas, *Summa Theologica,* Q. 97, art. 3

Custom is the principal magistrate of man's life.   915
> Francis Bacon, *Essays,* "Of Custom and Education"

Wherever in Christendom King Custom rules, King Jesus has been deposed and is under house arrest.   916
> C.E.S.

Cynicism

The sword devoureth one as well as another.   917
> 2 Samuel 11:25

Vanity of vanities . . . all is vanity.   918
> Ecclesiastes 1:2

He that increaseth knowledge increaseth sorrow.   919
> Ecclesiastes 1:18

Money answereth all things.   920
> Ecclesiastes 10:19

Can there any good thing come out of Nazareth? 921
John 1:46

Cynicism is humor in ill-health. 922
H. G. Wells, *Short Stories,* "The Last Trump"

Cynicism is intellectual dandyism. 923
George Meredith, *The Egoist*

The cynic is one who never sees a good quality in a man, and never fails to see a bad one. He is the human owl, vigilant in darkness, and blind to light, mousing for vermin, and never seeing noble game. 924
Henry Ward Beecher, *Proverbs from Plymouth Pulpit*

The difference between the pessimist and the cynic is that the pessimist is unhappy in his cynicism and the cynic is happy in his pessimism. 925
C.E.S.

D

Daily Living

This is the day which the Lord hath made; we will rejoice and be glad in it. 926

Psalm 118:24

I die daily. 927

1 Corinthians 15:31

Give us this day our daily bread. 928

Jesus in Matthew 6:11

Day by day,

Dear Lord, of Thee three things I pray:

To see Thee more clearly,

Love Thee more dearly,

Follow Thee more nearly,

Day by day. *Amen.* 929

St. Richard of Chichester, adapted

Is not every meanest day the confluence of two eternities? 930

Thomas Carlyle, *The French Revolution*

I have always felt that the moment when you first wake up in the morning is the most wonderful of the 24 hours. No matter how weary or dreary you feel, you possess the certainty that absolutely anything may happen. And the fact that it practically always *doesn't,* matters not one jot. The possibility is always there. 931

Monica Baldwin, *I Leap Over the Wall*

New every morning is the love

Our wakening and uprising prove;

Through sleep and darkness safely brought,

Restored to life, and power, and thought.

New mercies, each returning day,

Hover around us while we pray;

New perils past, new sins forgiven,

New thoughts of God, new hopes of heaven.

Old friends, old scenes, will lovelier be,
As more of heaven in each we see;
Some softening gleam of love and prayer
Shall dawn on every cross and care.

The trivial round, the common task,
Will furnish all we ought to ask;
Room to deny ourselves—a road
To bring us daily nearer God.

Only, O Lord, in thy dear love,
Fit us for perfect rest above;
And help us this and every day
To live more nearly as we pray.   932
                              John Keble, *The Christian Year*

Death, The Dead, Dying

Let me die the death of the righteous, and let my last end be like his! [*Balaam.*] 933
                    Numbers 23:10

But now he is dead, wherefore should I fast? can I bring him back again? [*David, of his son.*]   934
                    2 Samuel 12:23

There the wicked cease from troubling, and the weary be at rest.   935
                    Job 3:17

The worm shall feed sweetly on him; he shall be no more remembered. [*him: the wicked.*]   936
                    Job 24:20

In death there is no remembrance of thee; in the grave who shall give thee thanks?   937
                    Psalm 6:5

Yea, though I walk through the valley of the shadow of death, I will fear no evil: for thou art with me.   938
                    Psalm 23:4

They that are far from thee shall perish.   939
                    Psalm 73:27

That which befalleth the sons of men befalleth beasts.   940
                    Ecclesiastes 3:19

There be some standing here, which shall not taste of death, till they see the Son of man coming in his kingdom.   941
                    Matthew 16:28

If a man keep my saying, he shall never see death.   942
                    John 8:51

The last enemy that shall be destroyed is death.   943
                    1 Corinthians 15:26

We brought nothing into this world, and it is certain we can carry nothing out. 944
1 Timothy 6:7

Blessed are the dead which die in the Lord from henceforth. 945
Revelation 14:13

There shall be **no more death**, neither sorrow, nor crying, neither shall there be any more pain: for the former things are passed away. 946
Revelation 21:4

The dead don't die. They look on and help. 947
D. H. Lawrence, *The Letters of D. H. Lawrence*

Ever notice that everybody wants to go to heaven and nobody wants to die? 948
Author Unknown

Detroit isn't the only place where the Maker can recall his product on a moment's notice. 949
Ann Landers. *Syndicated column,* 8 April 1983

In the midst of life we are in death. 950
Book of Common Prayer, *Burial of the Dead*

When we are dead to ourselves, the death of the body is only the consummation of the work of grace. 951
François de Fenelon, *Christian Perfection*

When God wants you to die, he will show you how to do it easily. 952
Henry Ward Beecher, *Proverbs from Plymouth Pulpit*

Life levels all men; death reveals the eminent. 953
Bernard Shaw, *Maxims for Revolutionaries*

One night some short weeks ago, for the first time in her not always happy life, Marilyn Monroe's soul sat down alone to a quiet supper from which it did not rise. 954
Clifford Odets, "To Whom It May Concern: Marilyn Monroe." *Show,* October 1962

You must overcome death by finding God in it. 955
Pierre Teilhard de Chardin, *The Divine Milieu*

You never realize death until you realize love. 956
Katharine Butler Hathaway, *The Journals and Letters of the Little Locksmith*

Neither the sun nor death can be looked at steadily. 957
François de la Rochefoucauld, *Maxims*

Death is the sound of distant thunder at a picnic. 958
W. H. Auden, *The Dyer's Hand*

Certainly there is no happiness within this circle of flesh, nor is it in the optics of these eyes to behold felicity; the first day of our Jubilee is death. 959
Sir Thomas Browne, *Religio Medici*

Put out the lamp when thou wishest. I shall know thy darkness and shall love it. 960
Rabindranath Tagore, *Stray Birds*

The world does not leak because death is not a crack. 961

Ibid.

Death cannot harm me because it is a stingless bee: its stinger is lodged in Christ. 962

Peter J. Kreeft, *Love is Stronger Than Death*

I died as a mineral and became a plant.
I died as a plant and rose to animal.
I died as animal and I was man.
Why should I fear? What was I less by dying? . . .
I must pass on: all except God perish. 963

Jalaluddin Rumi (1207–1273), quoted in *Anthology of Islamic Literature,* edited by Hames Kritzeck

"There is no death," she said. "No, my dear lady, but there are funerals." 964

Peter de Vries, *Comfort Me with Apples*

Life! we've been long together
Through pleasant and through cloudy weather;
'Tis hard to part when friends are dear—
Perhaps will cost a sigh, a tear;
Then steal away, give little warning,
   Choose thine own time;
Say not good-night,—but in some brighter clime
   Bid me good-morning. 965

Anna Letitia Barbauld, *Ode to Life*

We sometimes congratulate ourselves at the moment of waking from a troubled dream; it may be so the moment after death. 966

Nathaniel Hawthorne, *Journal,* 25 October 1835

Come, lovely and soothing death,
Undulate round the world, serenely arriving, arriving,
In the day, in the night, to all, to each,
Sooner or later, delicate death. 967

Walt Whitman, *Leaves of Grass,* "When Lilacs Last in the Dooryard Bloom'd"

A dying man needs to die as a sleepy man needs to sleep, and there comes a time when it is wrong, as well as useless, to resist. 968

Stewart Alsop, *Stay of Execution;* on his losing fight against cancer

Those who have the strength and the love to sit with a dying patient *in the silence that goes beyond words* will know that this moment is neither frightening nor painful, but a peaceful cessation of the functioning of the body. 969

Elisabeth Kübler-Ross, *On Death and Dying*

The hardest thing of all—to die *rightly*—an exam nobody is spared—and how many pass it? And you? You pray for strength to meet the test—but also for leniency on the part of the Examiner. 970

Dag Hammarskjöld, *Markings*

Death is a radical reorganization of life—the only total revolution any of us will ever pass through.   971
                    C.E.S.

Debt

And forgive us our debts, as we forgive our debtors.   972
                    Jesus in Matthew 6:12

I am debtor both to the Greeks and to the barbarians: both to the wise, and to the unwise.   973
                    Romans 1:14

Owe no man anything but to love one another.   974
                    Romans 13:8

Interest works night and day, in fair weather and in foul. It gnaws at a man's substance with invisible teeth.   975
                    Henry Ward Beecher, *Proverbs from Plymouth Pulpit*

Let us live in as small a circle as we will; we are either debtors or creditors before we have had time to look around.   976
                    Johann Wolfgang von Goethe, *Elective Affinities*

Decadence

To be wrong, and to be carefully wrong, that is the definition of decadence.   977
                    G. K. Chesterton, *A Miscellany of Men*

The difference between our decadence and the Russians' is that while theirs is brutal, ours is apathetic.   978
                    James Thurber, *Observer*, "Sayings of the Week," 5 February 1961

Ill fares the land, to hastening ills a prey,
Where wealth accumulates, and men decay.   979
                    Oliver Goldsmith, *The Deserted Village*

Deceit

Bread of deceit is sweet to a man; but afterwards his mouth shall be filled with gravel.   980
                    Proverbs 20:17

And Jacob said unto his father, I am Esau thy firstborn.   981
                    Genesis 27:19

Let no man deceive himself.   982
                    1 Corinthians 3:18

Beware lest any man spoil you through philosophy and vain deceit.   983
                    Colossians 2:8

Oh, what a tangled web we weave,
When first we practice to deceive.   984
                    Sir Walter Scott, *Lochinvar*

Dost thou hate to be deceived? Do not deceive another. 985

St. John Chrysostom, *Homily 13*

From all inordinate and sinful affections; and from all the deceits of the world, the flesh and the devil, *Good Lord, deliver us.* 986

Book of Common Prayer, *The Litany*

You can fool some of the people all of the time, and all of the people some of the time, but you cannot fool all of the people all of the time. 987

Abraham Lincoln, attributed, but not to be found in any of his published papers.

We get together and talk, and say we think and feel and believe in such a way, and yet what we really think and feel and believe we never say at all. 988

Thomas Wolfe, *Of Time and the River*

Deeds

See Action

Defeat

Knowest thou not yet that Egypt is destroyed? [*Pharaoh's servants to Pharaoh.*] 989

Exodus 10:7

How should one chase a thousand, and two put ten thousand to flight, except their Rock had sold them, and the Lord had shut them up? 990

Deuteronomy 32:30

How are the mighty fallen, and the weapons of war perished! 991

2 Samuel 1:27

They cried, but there was none to save them; even unto the Lord, but he answered them not. 992

Psalm 18:41

The flight shall perish from the swift, and the strong shall not strengthen his force, neither shall the mighty deliver himself. 993

Amos 2:14

The light of a candle shall shine no more at all in thee. 994

Revelation 18:23

It is defeat that turns bone to flint; it is defeat that turns gristle to muscle; it is defeat that makes men invincible. 995

Henry Ward Beecher, *Proverbs from Plymouth Pulpit*

Every step of progress the world has made has been from scaffold to scaffold, and from stake to stake. 996

Wendell Phillips. Speech on women's rights, 1851

How you handle defeat is not something to be taken lightly. You've got to think it through. Defeat is an art form. You've got to accept it, and you've got to go on. And once you do that, it's not bad.   997

> Walter F. Mondale. Quoted in *Words of Wisdom,* compiled and
> edited by William Safire and Leonard Safir

Democracy

Democracy is a charming form of government, full of variety and disorder, and dispensing a sort of equality to equals and unequals alike.   998

> Plato, *The Republic*

I should be very sorry to find myself on board a ship in which the voices of the cook and of the loblolly boys counted for as much as those of the officers upon a question of steering, or reefing topsails; or where the "great heart" of the crew was called upon to settle the ship's course.   999

> Thomas Henry Huxley, *On the Natural Inequality of Man,* 1890

I believe in democracy because it releases the energies of every human being.   1000

> Woodrow Wilson. Speech in New York, 4 September 1912

All lawful authority comes from God to the people.   1001

> Constitution of the Irish Free State, preamble, 1922

It would be folly to argue that the people cannot make political mistakes. They can and do make grave mistakes. They know it, they pay the penalty, but compared with the mistakes which have been made by every kind of autocracy they are unimportant.   1002

> Calvin Coolidge. Speech in Evanston, Ill., 21 January 1923

Democracy gives every man the right to be his own oppressor.   1003

> James Russell Lowell, *The Biglow Papers*

Even though counting heads is not the ideal way to govern, it is better than breaking them.   1004

> Learned Hand. Speech to Federal Bar Association, 8 March 1932

So Two Cheers for Democracy: one because it admits variety and two because it permits criticism. Two cheers are quite enough: there is no occasion to give three. Only Love, the Beloved Republic, deserves that.   1005

> E. M. Forster, *Two Cheers for Democracy*

Democracy cannot be saved by supermen, but only by the unswerving devotion and goodness of millions of little men.   1006

> Adlai E. Stevenson, speech, 1955

Desire

The desire accomplished is sweet to the soul.   1007

> Proverbs 13:19

Better is the sight of the eyes than the wandering of the desire.   1008

> Ecclesiastes 6:9

The world passeth away, and the lust thereof: but he that doeth the will of God abideth forever.   1009

             1 John 2:17

Our best havings are wantings.   1010

             C. S. Lewis, *Letters*

We are half-hearted creatures, fooling about with drink and sex and ambition when infinite joy is offered us, like the ignorant child who wants to go on making mud pies in a slum because he cannot imagine what is meant by an offer of a holiday at the sea. We are far too easily pleased.   1011

             C. S. Lewis, *The Weight of Glory*

First deserve, and then desire.   1012

             English Proverb

God plants no yearning in the human soul that he does not intend to satisfy.   1013

             Henry Ward Beecher, *Proverbs from Plymouth Pulpit*

Life is a progress from want to want, not from enjoyment to enjoyment.   1014

             Samuel Johnson. Boswell's *Life,* 1776

Do not desire to be what you are, but to be very well what you are.   1015

             St. Francis de Sales, *Letters to Persons in the World*

What you have become is the price you paid to get what you used to want. 1016

             Mignon McLaughlin, *The Neurotic's Notebook*

There are two tragedies in life. One is not to get your heart's desire. The other is to get it.   1017

             Bernard Shaw, *Man and Superman*

I like to go to Marshall Field's in Chicago just to see how many things there are in the world that I do not want.   1018

             Mother Mary Madeleva CSC, *My First Seventy Years*

It was spring, but it was summer I wanted,
The warm days, and the great outdoors.

It was summer, but it was fall I wanted,
The colorful leaves, and the cool, dry air.

It was spring, but it was winter I wanted,
The beautiful snow, and the joy of the holiday season.

I was a child, but it was adulthood I wanted,
The freedom, and the respect.

I was 20, but it was 30 I wanted,
to be mature, and sophisticated.

I was middle-aged, but it was 20 I wanted,
The youth, and the free spirit.

I was retired, but it was middle age I wanted,
The presence of mind, without limitations.

My life was over,
But I never got what I wanted.   1019
> Jason Lehman, *Present Tense*. Written at age 14. Quoted in "Dear
> Abby," syndicated column, 14 February 1989

Despair

Would God that we had died in the land of Egypt!   1020
> Numbers 14:2

Would to God that we had been content, and dwelt on the other side of
the Jordan!   1021
> Joshua 7:7

God is departed from me, and answereth me no more, neither by prophets, nor by
dreams.   1022
> 1 Samuel 28:15

Let the day perish wherein I was born.   1023
> Job 3:3

Where, and who is he?   1024
> Job 9:24

There is none that doeth good, no, not one.   1025
> Psalm 14:3

My God, my God, why hast thou forsaken me?   1026
> Psalm 22:1

I am forgotten as a dead man out of mind: I am like a broken vessel.   1027
> Psalm 31:12

Vanity of vanities; all is vanity.   1028
> Ecclesiastes 1:2

The harvest is past, the summer is ended, and we are not saved.   1029
> Jeremiah 8:20

O earth, earth, earth, hear the word of the Lord.   1030
> Jeremiah 22:29

Despair does not lie in being weary of suffering, but in being weary of joy.   1031
> G. K. Chesterton, *The Everlasting Man*.

Despair is the absolute extreme of self-love. It is reached when a man deliberately
turns his back on all help from anyone else in order to taste the rotten luxury of knowing himself to be lost.   1032
> Thomas Merton, *Seeds of Contemplation*

Despair is vinegar from the wine of hope.   1033
> Austin O'Malley, *Keystones of Thought*

Chew my terbacker
And spit my juice:
Want to go to Heaven
But it ain't no use.   1034
> Ray Wood, *Mother Goose in the Ozarks*

In despair there are the most intense enjoyments, especially when one is very acutely conscious of the hopelessness of one's position.   1035

> Fyodor Dostoyevski, *Notes from the Underground*

In a real dark night of the soul it is always three o'clock in the morning, day after day.   1036

> F. Scott Fitzgerald, *The Crack-Up*

Where there is no hope there can be no endeavor.   1037

> Samuel Johnson, *The Rambler*

Safe Despair it is that raves—
Agony is frugal:
Puts itself severe away
For its own perusal.   1038

> Emily Dickinson, *Poems,* "Safe Despair it is that raves"

Destiny

It was not you that sent me hither, but God.   1039

> Genesis 45:8

Such as are for death, to death; and such as are for the sword, to the sword; and such as are for the famine, to the famine; and such as are for the captivity, to the captivity.   1040

> Jeremiah 15:2

As the clay is in the potter's hand, so are ye in mine hand, O house of Israel. 1041

> Jeremiah 18:6

Men heap together the mistakes of their lives and call the monster Destiny. 1042

> Author Unknown

Destiny, n. A tyrant's authority for crime and a fool's excuse for failure.   1043

> Ambrose Bierce, *The Devil's Dictionary*

We are not permitted to choose the frame of our destiny, but what we put into it is ours.   1044

> Dag Hammarskjöld, *Markings*

It is a mistake to look too far ahead. Only one link of the chain of destiny can be handled at a time.   1045

> Sir Winston Churchill. Speech, House of Commons, 27 February 1945

Destiny grants us our wishes, but in its own way, in order to give us something beyond our wishes.   1046

> Johann Wolfgang von Goethe, *Elective Affinities*

Man's destiny lies half within himself, half without. To advance in either half at the expense of the other is literally insane.   1047

> Philip Wylie, *Generation of Vipers*

Detachment

"Detachment" consists, not in casting aside all natural loves and goods, but in the possession of a love so good and so great that all others, though they may and do acquire increase through the presence of a greater love and good, which explains and justifies them, seem nothing in comparison. 1010

Coventry Patmore, *The Rod, the Root and the Flower*

Devil (Satan)

Now there was a day when the sons of God came to present themselves before the Lord, and Satan came also among them. And the Lord said unto Satan, Whence comest thou? Then Satan answered the Lord, and said, From going to and fro in the earth, and from walking up and down in it. 1049

Job 1:6–7

Then was Jesus led up by the Spirit into the wilderness to be tempted by the devil. 1050

Matthew 4:1

Then Peter took him, and began to rebuke him, saying, Be it far from thee, Lord: this shall not be unto thee. But he turned, and said unto Peter, Get thee behind me, Satan: thou art an offence unto me: for thou savourest not the things that be of God, but those that be of men. 1051

Jesus in Matthew 16:22–23

I beheld Satan as lightning fall from heaven. 1052

Jesus in Luke 10:18

Ye are of your father the devil, and the lusts of your father ye will do. He was a murderer from the beginning, and abode not in the truth, because there is no truth in him. When he speaketh a lie, he speaketh of his own: for he is a liar, and the father of it. 1053

Jesus in John 8:44

Can a devil open the eyes of the blind? 1054

John 10:21

Lest I should be exalted above measure through the abundance of the revelations, there was given to me a thorn in the flesh, the messenger of Satan to buffet me, lest I should be exalted above measure. 1055

2 Corinthians 12:7

Resist the devil, and he will flee from you. 1056

James 4:7

Be sober, be vigilant; because your adversary the devil, as a roaring lion, walketh about, seeking whom he may devour. 1057

1 Peter 5:8

The devil is no fool. He can get people feeling about heaven the way they ought to feel about hell. He can make them fear the means of grace the way they do not fear sin. And he does so not by light but by obscurity, not by realities but by shadows; not by clarity and substance, but by dreams and the creatures of psychosis. And men are so

poor in intellect that a few cold chills down their spine will be enough to keep them from ever finding out the truth about anything. 1058
> Thomas Merton, *The Seven Storey Mountain*

The Devil is God's ape. (*Diabolus est Dei simia.*) 1059
> English proverb, borrowed from the Latin;
> traced to Tertullian, c. 200.

The Devil has two manners of shapes or forms, wherein he disguises himself; he either appears in the shape of a serpent, to affright and kill; or else in the form of a silly sheep, to lie and deceive; these are his two court colors. 1060
> Martin Luther, *Table-Talk*

The devil can cite Scripture for his purpose. 1061
> William Shakespeare, *The Merchant of Venice,* I, iii, 99.

Grant that he may have power and strength to have victory, and to triumph, against the devil, the world, and the flesh. 1062
> Book of Common Prayer, *The Ministration of Holy Baptism*

It is so stupid of modern civilization to have given up believing in the devil when he is the only explanation of it. 1063
> Ronald Knox, quoted in Evelyn Waugh, *Ronald Knox*

His laws are easy, and his gentle sway
Makes it exceeding pleasant to obey. 1064
> Daniel Defoe, *The True-born Englishman*

And when I saw my devil, I found him serious, thorough, profound, solemn: he was the spirit of gravity—through him all things fall. 1065
> Friedrich Wilhelm Nietzsche, *Thus Spake Zarathustra*

A perfidious and astute charmer who manages to insinuate himself into us by way of the senses, of fantasy, of concupiscence, of utopian logic, of disorderly social contracts. 1066
> Pope Paul VI, in address to papal audience, November 1972

The devil is called "the prince of the power of the air." Infected air is drawn into the lungs without pain, and we get a disease before we feel it. 1067
> Thomas Manton, *The Golden Treasury of Puritan Quotations*

The devil is a great student of divinity. 1068
> William Gurnall, *The Golden Treasury of Puritan Quotations*

Devotion

Serve the Lord thy God with all thy heart and with all thy soul. 1069
> Deuteronomy 10:12

Whither thou goest, I will go; and where thou lodgest, I will lodge: thy people shall be my people, and thy God, my God. 1070
> Ruth 1:16

If ye seek him, he will be found of you. 1071
> 2 Chronicles 15:2

I will not give sleep to mine eyes, or slumber to my eyelids, Until I find out a place for the Lord. 1072
>Psalm 132:4–5

Whosoever he be of you that forsaketh not all that he hath, he cannot be my disciple. 1073
>Jesus in Luke 14:33

I am the good shepherd: the good shepherd giveth his life for the sheep. 1074
>Jesus in John 10:11

I am ready not to be bound only, but also to die at Jerusalem for the name of the Lord Jesus. 1075
>Acts 21:13

We have continually to test the reality of our devotion to Him by our practical devotion to one another. 1076
>Robert Hugh Benson, *The Friendship of Christ*

Charity and devotion differ no more from each other than the flame from the fire. 1077
>St. Francis de Sales, *Introduction to the Devout Life*

God waits to win back his own flowers, as gifts from man's hands. 1078
>Rabindranath Tagore, *Stray Birds*

A man cannot make a pair of shoes rightly unless he do it in a devout manner. 1079
>Thomas Carlyle, Letter to Thomas Erskine, date unknown

The devotion of the moth for the star,
   Of the night for the morrow,
The devotion to something afar
   From the sphere of our sorrow. 1080
>Percy Bysshe Shelley, *To—One Word Is Too Often Profaned*

Difficulties

Difficulty, my brethren, is the nurse of greatness—a harsh nurse, who roughly rocks her foster children into strength and athletic proportion. 1081
>William Cullen Bryant. Speech of welcome to Lajos Kossuth, 15 December 1851

To the stars through bolts and bars. (*Per ardua per astra.*) 1082
>Mulvany family motto. Quoted in Rider Haggard, *The People of the Mist*

A man's worst difficulties begin when he is able to do what he likes. 1083
>Thomas Henry Huxley, *Aphorisms and Reflections*

Ten thousand difficulties do not make one doubt. 1084
>John Henry Newman, *Apologia Pro Vita Sua*

When you encounter difficulties and contradictions, do not try to break them, but bend them with gentleness and time. 1085
>St. Francis de Sales, *Spiritual Meditations*

"Though with great difficulty I am got hither, yet now I do not repent me of all the trouble I have been at to arrive where I am. My sword, I give to him that shall succeed me in my pilgrimage, and my courage and skill to him that can get it. My marks and scars I carry with me, that I have fought his battles, who will now be my rewarder. . . ." So he passed over, and the trumpets sounded for him on the other side. [*Mr. Valiant-for-Truth.*]   1086

John Bunyan, The Pilgrim's Progress

Diligence

He that goeth forth and weepeth, bearing precious seed, shall doubtless come again rejoicing, bringing his sheaves with him.   1087

Psalm 126:6

Go to the ant, thou sluggard; consider her ways, and be wise.   1088

Proverbs 6:6

Seest thou a man diligent in his business? He shall stand before kings.   1089

Proverbs 22:29

Seek, and ye shall find.   1090

Jesus in Matthew 7:7

No man, having put his hand to the plough, and looking back, is fit for the kingdom of God.   1091

Jesus in Luke 9:62

Be ye stedfast, unmoveable, always abounding in the work of the Lord.   1092

1 Corinthians 15:58

He which soweth bountifully shall reap also bountifully.   1093

2 Corinthians 9:6

Study to show thyself approved unto God, a workman that needeth not to be ashamed.   1094

2 Timothy 2:15

He who limps is still walking.   1095

Stanislaw J. Lec, Unkempt Thoughts

To travel hopefully is a better thing than to arrive, and the true success is to labor.   1096

Robert Louis Stevenson, Virginibus Puerisque

Life has not taught me to expect nothing, but she has taught me not to expect success to be the inevitable result of my endeavors. She taught me to seek sustenance from the endeavor itself, but to leave the result to God.   1097

Alan Paton, Saturday Review, "The Challenge of Fear,"
9 September 1967

Disappointment

Behold it with thine eyes: for thou shalt not go over this Jordan.   1098

Deuteronomy 3:27

When I looked for good, then evil came unto me; and when I waited for light, there came darkness. 1099

Job 30:26

He looked that it should bring forth grapes, and it brought forth wild grapes. 1100

Isaiah 5:2

He looked for judgment, but behold oppression; for righteousness, but behold a cry. 1101

Isaiah 5:7

How is the gold become dim! 1102

Lamentations 4:1

What, could ye not watch with me one hour? 1103

Jesus in Matthew 26:40

Disappointment should be cremated, not embalmed. 1104

Anonymous (Henry S. Haskins), *Meditations in Wall Street*

If the good people in their wisdom shall see fit to keep me in the background, I am too familiar with disappointment to be much chagrined. 1105

Abraham Lincoln, announcing his candidacy for the Illinois
Legislature, 1832

Blessed is he who expects nothing, for he shall never be disappointed. 1106

Alexander Pope. Letter to John Gay, 6 October 1727

Discipleship

My son, if you aspire to serve the Lord,
prepare yourself for an ordeal. 1107

Ecclesiasticus 2:1, *The Jerusalem Bible*

Follow me, and I will make you fishers of men. 1108

Jesus in Matthew 4:19

I send you forth as sheep in the midst of wolves; be ye therefore wise as serpents, and harmless as doves. 1109

Jesus in Matthew 10:16

Whosoever will come after me, let him deny himself, and take up his cross, and follow me. 1110

Jesus in Mark 8:34

Go ye into all the world, and preach the gospel to every creature. 1111

Jesus in Mark 16:15

Have not I chosen you twelve, and one of you is a devil? 1112

Jesus in John 6:70

By this shall all men know that ye are my disciples, if ye have love one to another. 1113

Jesus in John 13:35

His cry (is) not Forward, but Follow. 1114

William Guthrie, *The Golden Treasury of Puritan Quotations*

The true teacher defends his pupils against his own personal influence. He inspires self-trust. He guides their eyes from himself to the spirit that quickens him. He will have no disciple. 1115

A. Bronson Alcott, *Orphic Sayings From The Dial* [July 1840], "The Teacher"

No true disciple of mine will ever be a Ruskinian; he will follow, not me, but the instincts of his own soul, and the guidance of its Creator. 1116

John Ruskin, *Essays,* "St. Mark's Rest"

Discipline

As a man chasteneth his son, so the Lord thy God chasteneth thee. 1117

Deuteronomy 8:5

Let the righteous smite me: it shall be a kindness. 1118

Psalm 141:5

He that refuseth instruction despiseth his own soul. 1119

Proverbs 15:32

As many as I love, I rebuke and chasten. 1120

Jesus in Revelation 3:19

The man that designs his son to honor and to triumphs, to consular dignities, and presidencies of councils, loves to see him pale with study, or panting with labor, hardened with sufferings, or eminent by dangers. 1121

Jeremy Taylor, *The Rule and Exercises of Holy Dying,* I. 1651

Life is always a discipline, for the lower animals as well as for men; it is so dangerous that only by submitting to some form of discipline can we become equipped to live in any true sense at all. 1122

Havelock Ellis, *On Life and Sex: Essays of Love and Virtue*

It is not the whip that makes men, but the lure of things that are worthy to be loved. 1123

Woodrow Wilson, address, Cleveland, 12 May 1906

Liberty is a beloved discipline. 1124

George Caspar Homans, *The Human Group*

Doubt

Is the Lord among us, or not? 1125

Exodus 17:7

If the Lord be with us, why then is all this befallen us? 1126

Judges 6:13

Art thou he that should come, or do we look for another? 1127

Matthew 11:3

O thou of little faith, wherefore didst thou doubt? 1128

Jesus in Matthew 14:31

Except I shall see in his hands the print of the nails, and put my finger into the print of the nails, and thrust my hand into his side, I will not believe.　　1129
　　　　John 20:25

He that wavereth is like a wave of the sea driven with the wind.　　1130
　　　　James 1:6

Materialists and madmen never have doubts.　　1131
　　　　G. K. Chesterton, *Orthodoxy*

The doubting mind sees many ghosts.　　1132
　　　　Chinese Proverb

Cleave ever to the sunnier side of doubt.　　1133
　　　　Alfred, Lord Tennyson, *The Ancient Sage*

Doubt is part of all religion. All the religious thinkers were doubters.　　1134
　　　　Isaac Bashevis Singer. *New York Times,* 3 December 1978

Religion isn't yours firsthand until you doubt it right down to the ground.　1135
　　　　Francis B. Sayre, Dean of National Cathedral, Washington, D.C.
　　　　Life, 2 April 1965

Doubts are the ants in the pants of faith. They keep it awake and moving.　　1136
　　　　Frederick Buechner, *Wishful Thinking: A Theological ABC*

Drink

I have drunk neither wine nor strong drink, but have poured out my soul before the Lord.　　1137
　　　　1 Samuel 1:15

The drunkard and the glutton shall come to poverty.　　1138
　　　　Proverbs 23:21

Woe unto them that rise up early in the morning, that they may follow strong drink.　　1139
　　　　Isaiah 5:11

Be not drunk with wine, wherein is excess, but be filled with the Spirit.　　1140
　　　　Ephesians 5:18

It is meet before we partake of food to bless the Maker of all things, and to sing while we drink.　　1141
　　　　Clement of Alexandria, *Paedagogus,* c. 190

Long quaffing maketh a short life.　　1142
　　　　John Lyly, *Euphues,* 1579

That I call immoderation is that beside or beyond that order of good things for which God hath given us the use of drink.　　1143
　　　　Jeremy Taylor, *The Rule and Exercises of Holy Living,* 1630

I always naturally hated drinking, and yet I have often drunk, with disgust at the time, attended by great sickness the next day, only because I then considered drinking as a necessary qualification for a fine gentleman, and a man of pleasure.　　1144
　　　　Lord Chesterfield. Letter to his son, 27 March 1747

Drinking a little too much is drinking a great deal too much.   1145

> German Proverb

Through booze I met two Chief Justices, 50 world champs, six Presidents and Di Maggio and Babe Ruth.   1146

> Author Unknown

Alcohol isn't a spectator sport. Eventually the whole family gets to play.   1147

> Joyce Rebeta Burditt, *The Cracker Family*

If alcoholism is a disease, then it is the only disease that is bottled and sold, and it is the only disease that is contracted by the will of man. It is the only disease that requires a license to propagate it and the only disease that requires outlets to spread it. It is the only disease that produces revenues for the government and the only disease that provokes crime. It is the only disease without a germ or a virus. It might be that it's not a disease after all.   1148

> John D. Burroughs, of Overland Park, Kansas, in a letter to
> *USA Today,* 30 December 1987

When you stop drinking, you have to start dealing with this marvelous personality that started you drinking in the first place.   1149

> Jimmy Breslin, *Table Money*

Drinking does not drown your problems, it only irrigates them.   1150

> Author Unknown

Drugs

If God can be found through any drug, God is not worthy of being God.   1151

> Mehere Baba. *Quote,* 17 September 1967

If drugs are the answer, what's the question?   1152

> Author Unknown

Opiate, n. An unlocked door in the prison of Identity. It leads into the jail yard.   1153

> Ambrose Bierce, *The Devil's Dictionary*

What is dangerous about the tranquilizers is that whatever peace of mind they bring is a packaged peace of mind. Where you buy a pill and buy peace with it, you get conditioned to cheap solutions instead of deep ones.   1154

> Max Lerner, *The Unfinished Country*

One's condition on marijuana is always existential. One can feel the importance of each moment and how it is changing one. One feels one's being, one becomes aware of the enormous apparatus of nothingness—the hum of a hi-fi set, the emptiness of a pointless interruption, one becomes aware of the war between each of us, how the nothingness of each of us seeks to attack the being of others, how our being in turn is attacked by the nothingness of others.   1155

> Norman Mailer, *Writers at Work, Third Series,*
> edited by George Plimpton

Dust to Dust

I farm the dust of my ancestors, though the chemist's analysis may not detect it. I go forth to redeem the meadows they have become. I compel them to take refuge in turnips.   1156

Henry David Thoreau, *Journals,* 4 March 1852

Unto Almighty God we commend the soul of our [*brother*] departed, and we commit [*his*] body to the ground; earth to earth, ashes to ashes, dust to dust; in sure and certain hope of the Resurrection unto eternal life, through our Lord Jesus Christ. . . .   1157

Book of Common Prayer, *The Order for the Burial of the Dead*

Duty

What doth the Lord thy God require of thee, but to fear the Lord thy God, to walk in all his ways, and to love him, and to serve the Lord thy God with all thy heart and with all thy soul.   1158

Deuteronomy 10:12

Fear God, and keep his commandments: for this is the whole duty of man. 1159

Ecclesiastes 12:13

Say not, I am a child: for thou shalt go to all that I shall send thee, and whatsoever I command thee thou shalt speak.   1160

Jeremiah 1:7

He hath showed thee, O man, what is good; and what doth the Lord require of thee, but to do justly, and to love mercy, and to walk humbly with thy God?   1161

Micah 6:8

Wist ye not that I must be about my Father's business?   1162

Jesus in Luke 2:49

This is the work of God, that ye believe on him whom he hath sent.   1163

Jesus in John 6:29

I must work the works of him that sent me, while it is day.   1164

Jesus in John 9:4

"Do the Duty which lies nearest thee," which thou knowest to be a Duty! Thy second Duty will already have become clearer.   1165

Thomas Carlyle, *Sartor Resartus*

The rule of joy and the law of duty seem to me all one.   1166

Oliver Wendell Holmes, Jr. Speech at Bar Association dinner, Boston, 1900

Duty is ours and events are God's.   1167

Angelina Grimké, *The Anti-Slavery Banner,* "Appeal to the Christian Women of the South," September 1836

Never to tire, never to grow cold; to be patient, sympathetic, tender; to look for the budding flower and the opening heart; to hope always, like God; to love always—this is duty.   1168

Henri Frédéric Amiel, *Journal,* 27 May 1849

New occasions teach new duties. 1169

James Russell Lowell, *The Present Crisis*

You have not done enough, you have never done enough, so long as it is still possible that you have something to contribute. This is the answer when you are groaning under what you consider a burden and an uncertainty prolonged ad infinitum. 1170

Dag Hammarskjöld, *Markings*

Duty does not have to be dull. Love can make it beautiful and fill it with life. 1171

Thomas Merton, *The Sign of Jonas*

Perhaps, after all, our first duty to our neighbor, in order of appearance, is to protect him from ourselves. 1172

C.E.S.

E

Early Christianity

The disciples were called Christians first in Antioch.   1173
Acts 11:26

King Agrippa, believest thou the prophets? I know that thou believest. Then Agrippa said unto Paul, Almost thou persuadest me to be a Christian.   1174
Acts 26:27–28

Let none of you suffer as a murderer, or as a thief, or as an evildoer, or as a busybody in other men's matters. Yet if any man suffer as a Christian, let him not be ashamed; but let him glorify God on this behalf.   1175
1 Peter 4:15–16

Feeling was ripe for a mythology loaded with pathos.   1176
George Santayana, *The Life of Reason*

In the first century A.D., the Pharisees were the most numerous [of the Jewish sects], the Sadducees the most powerful, the Essenes the most devout, and the Christians the most intolerant.   1177
Max Dimont, *Jews, God and History*

If you will here stop and ask yourselves why you are not as pious as the primitive Christians were, your own heart will tell you that it is neither through ignorance nor inability but purely because you never thoroughly intended it.   1178
William Law, *A Serious Call to a Devout and Holy Life*

Earth

All the earth is mine.   1179
Exodus 19:5

The earth is the Lord's, and the fulness thereof; the world, and they that dwell therein.   1180
Psalm 24:1

One generation passeth away, and another generation cometh: but the earth abideth forever.   1181
Ecclesiastes 1:4

He hath established it, he created it not in vain, he formed it to be inhabited. 1182
Isaiah 45:18

Speak to the earth, and it shall teach thee. 1183
Job 12:8

I came to your shore as a stranger, I lived in your house as a guest, and I leave your door as a friend, my earth. 1184
Rabindranath Tagore, *Stray Birds*

Earth provides enough to satisfy every man's need, but not every man's greed. 1185
Mohandas K. Gandhi, quoted in E. F. Schumacher, *Small Is Beautiful*

Now there is one outstanding important fact regarding Spaceship Earth, and that is that no instruction book came with it. 1186
R. Buckminster Fuller, quoted in *New York Times*, 8 August 1971

The poetry of earth is never dead. 1187
John Keats, *On the Grasshopper and the Cricket*

Rhea, the Earth, was the mother of the gods, and it is only by inspired knowledge of our own nature, the earth, which is seen, that we can know anything of the Divine, which is unseen. "The natural first, afterwards the supernatural." 1188
Coventry Patmore, *The Rod, the Root and the Flower*

With a sincere regard for the learned of the Church, I demonstrate by means of philosophy that the earth is round, and is inhabited on all sides; that it is insignificantly small, and is borne through the stars. 1189
Johann Kepler, *Astronomica nova*, 1609

All our pomp the earth covers. 1190
George Herbert, *Outlandish Proverbs*

On this little shell how few are the spots where man can live and flourish! Even under those mild climates which seem to breathe peace and happiness, the poison of slavery, the fury of despotism, and the rage of superstition are all combined against man. 1191
St. John de Crèvecoeur, *Letters from an American Farmer*, 1782

Earth, with her thousand voices, praises God. 1192
Samuel Taylor Coleridge, *Hymn Before Sunrise*

Let me enjoy the earth no less
Because the all-enacting Might
That fashions forth its loveliness
Had other aims than my delight. 1193
Thomas Hardy, *Time's Laughingstocks and Other Verses*, "Let Me Enjoy"

That we are bound to the earth does not mean that we cannot grow; on the contrary, it is the *sine qua non* of growth. No noble, well-grown tree ever disowned its dark roots, for it grows not only upwards but downwards as well. 1194
Carl Gustav Jung, *Psychological Reflections*, edited by Jolande Jacobi and R. F. Hull

The earth is a Paradise, the only one that we will ever know. We will realize it the moment we open our eyes. We don't have to make it a Paradise—it *is* one. We have only to make ourselves fit to inhabit it.   1195

> Henry Miller, *The Air-Conditioned Nightmare*

Eating

Tell me what you eat and I will tell you what you are.   1196

> Anthelme Brillat-Savarin, *Physiologie du Goût,* Aphorisms

Eating is one of the lowest actions of our lives; it is common to us with mere animals; yet we see that the piety of all ages of the world has turned this ordinary action of an animal life into a piety to God, by making every meal to begin and end with devotion.   1197

> William Law, *A Serious Call to a Devout and Holy Life*

... don't you know,
I promised, if you'd watch dinner out,
We'd see truth dawn together?—truth that peeps
Over the glass's edge when dinner's done,
And body gets its sop and holds its noise
And leaves soul free a little. . . .   1198

> Robert Browning, *Bishop Bloughram's Apology*

By suppers more have been killed than Galen ever cured.   1199

> George Herbert, *Jacula Prudentum*

Strange to see how a good dinner and feasting reconciles everybody.   1200

> Samuel Pepys, *Diary,* 9 November 1665

"Kissing don't last; cookery do!"   1201

> George Meredith, *The Ordeal of Richard Feverel*

It takes some skill to spoil a breakfast—even the English can't do it.   1202

> John Kenneth Galbraith, *Ambassador's Journal,* 1969

Never eat more than you can lift.   1203

> "Miss Piggy." Robert Byrne, *The 637 Best Things Anybody Ever Said*

Economics

Economics is about the cost of our appetites.   1204

> George F. Will. *Newsweek,* 23 February 1976

Economists need to be reminded regularly that the idea of growth for its own sake is precisely the philosophy of the cancer cell.   1205

> Sydney J. Harris, *Pieces of Eight*

Everybody is always in favor of general economy and particular expenditures.   1206

> Anthony Eden. *Observer,* "Sayings of the Week," 17 June 1956

Annual income twenty pounds, annual expenditure nineteen nineteen six, result happiness. Annual income twenty pounds, annual expenditure twenty pound ought and six, result misery.[*Mr. Micawber.*]   1207
>   Charles Dickens, *David Copperfield*

With the exception of the instinct of self-preservation, the propensity for emulation is probably the strongest and most alert and persistent of the economic motives proper.   1208
>   Thorstein Veblen, *The Theory of the Leisure Class*

Instead of doing anything about economics the moralists fulminate against the murder of unborn children and the selfishness of modern young people (in the practice of birth prevention). As somebody said: "The drains are smelling—let's have a day of intercession." And as another said: "The economic depression is a good thing—it is sent to try us."   1209
>   Eric Gill. Quoted in Donald Attwater, *Modern Christian Revolutionaries*

Eden

Who loves a garden still his Eden keeps,
Perennial pleasures plants, and wholesome harvests reaps.   1210
>   A. Bronson Alcott, *Tablets*

Eden meant ignorant immortality. After Eden comes informed mortality.   1211
>   Martin E. Marty, *A Cry of Absence*

Eden is that old-fashioned House
We dwell in every day
Without suspecting our abode
Until we drive away.   1212
>   Emily Dickinson, "Eden is that old-fashioned house"

Education

And thou shalt teach them diligently unto thy children, and shalt talk of them when thou sittest in thine house, and when thou walkest by the way, and when thou liest down, and when thou risest up.   1213
>   Deuteronomy 6:7

Teach them the good way wherein they should walk.   1214
>   1 Kings 8:36

Fools despise wisdom and instruction.   1215
>   Proverbs 1:7

Train up a child in the way he should go, and when he is old, he will not depart from it.   1216
>   Proverbs 22:6

Precept must be upon precept, precept upon precept; line upon line, line upon line; here a little, and there a little.   1217
>   Isaiah 28:10

All thy children shall be taught of the Lord; and great shall be the peace of thy children.   1218

        Isaiah 54:13

Beware lest any man spoil you through philosophy and vain deceit.   1219

        Colossians 2:8

Education is to get where you can start to learn.   1220

        George Aiken. Quoted in *New York Times,* 29 January 1967

Education is an admirable thing, but it is well to remember from time to time that nothing that is worth knowing can be taught.   1221

        Oscar Wilde, *The Critic as Artist*

What does education often do? It makes a straight-out ditch of a free, meandering brook.   1222

        Henry David Thoreau, *Journals,* 1850

Can't somebody just want to learn the poems of Pushkin because he loves them?   1223

        Karel van Het Reve, on "education for relevance." *New York Times,* 21 May 1976

Socrates gave no diplomas or degrees, and would have subjected any true disciple who demanded one to a disconcerting catechism on the nature of true knowledge.   1224

        George M. Trevelyan, *History of England*

The task of the modern educator is not to cut down jungles but to irrigate deserts.   1225

        C. S. Lewis, *The Abolition of Man*

A child's education should begin at least a hundred years before he is born. 1226

        Oliver Wendell Holmes, *The Autocrat of the Breakfast-Table*

The moment men begin to care for education more than for religion they begin to care more for ambition than for education. It is no longer a world in which all souls are equal before heaven, but a world in which each is bent on achieving unequal advantage over the other.   1227

        G. K. Chesterton, *The Common Man*

A good education is the next best thing to a pushy mother.   1228

        Charles Schulz, "Peanuts," 5 October 1976

Four years was enough at Harvard. I still had a lot to learn, but had been given the liberating notion that now I could teach myself.   1229

        John Updike. Quoted in *Life,* September 1986

The aim of education is the knowledge not of facts but of values.   1230

        William R. Inge, *The Church in the World*

Education is what survives when what has been learned has been forgotten.   1231

        B. F. Skinner. *New Scientist,* 23 May 1964

A whale ship was my Yale College and my Harvard.   1232

        Herman Melville, *Moby Dick*

Election, The Elect

The elect are whosoever will, and the nonelect are whosoever won't. 1233
Henry Ward Beecher, *Proverbs from Plymouth Pulpit*

When God elects us, it is not because we are handsome. 1234
John Calvin, attributed

We know there is a sun in heaven, yet we cannot see what matter it is made of, but perceive it only by the beams, light and heat. Election is a sun, the eyes of eagles cannot see it; yet we may find it in the heat of vocation . . . in the beams of good works. 1235
Thomas Adams, *The Golden Treasury of Puritan Quotations*

Elijah

The greatest merit of the Prophet Elijah is that when he fought the kings and crushed the idols, the people did not react as to a miracle but instead cried: God is our God. 1236
Rebbe Barukh of Medzebozh. Quoted in Elie Wiesel, *Souls on Fire*

Emotion

We boil at different degrees. 1237
Ralph Waldo Emerson, *Society and Solitude*, "Eloquence"

An emotional element is present in every rational act. 1238
Paul Tillich, *Systematic Theology*

Emotions should be servants, not masters—or at least not tyrants. 1239
Robert Hugh Benson, *The Sentimentalists*

It is as healthy to enjoy sentiment as to enjoy jam. 1240
G. K. Chesterton, *Generally Speaking*

Emotion is the chief source of all-becoming-conscious. There can be no transforming of darkness into light and of apathy into movement without emotion. 1241
Carl Gustav Jung, *A Jung Anthology*, "Psychological Reflections"

Intellect is to emotion as our clothes are to our bodies: we could not very well have civilized life without clothes, but we would be in a poor way if we had only clothes without bodies. 1242
Alfred North Whitehead. *Dialogues of Alfred North Whitehead,* as recorded by Lucien Price

It is not our exalted feelings, it is our sentiments that build the necessary home. 1243
Elizabeth Bowen, *The Death of the Heart*

We have hearts within,
Warm, live, improvident, indecent hearts. 1244
Elizabeth Barrett Browning, *Aurora Leigh*

Nothing vivifies, and nothing kills, like the emotions. 1245
Joseph Roux, *Meditations of a Parish Priest*

Empires and Dictatorships

Empires die of indigestion, dictatorships of swelled heads. 1246

William R. Inge, *A Rustic Moralist*

Encouragement

Fear ye not, stand still, and see the salvation of the Lord, which he will show you today; for the Egyptians whom ye have seen today, ye shall see them again no more for ever. 1247

Exodus 14:13

And David was greatly distressed: for the people spake of stoning him, because the soul of all the people was grieved, every man for his sons and for his daughters. But David encouraged himself in the Lord his God. 1248

1 Samuel 30:6

The Alcott family finances were very low, but they placed great hopes on Bronson Alcott's latest lecture tour. When he arrived home one night in February, the family gathered around to welcome him, offer him food and drink, and rejoice in his homecoming. Then a little silence fell, and it was daughter May who asked the question in all their minds. "Did they pay you?" Slowly Bronson Alcott drew out his pocketbook and displayed its contents—a single dollar. "Another year I shall do better," he said. There was a stunned hush in the group around him. Then Mrs. Alcott flung her arms around his neck and said stoutly, "I call that doing very well." 1249

The Little, Brown Book of Anecdotes, edited by Clifton Fadiman

End

If in this life only we have hope in Christ, we are of all men most miserable. But now is Christ risen from the dead, and become the firstfruits of them that slept. For since by man came death, by man came also the resurrection of the dead. For as in Adam all die, even so in Christ shall all be made alive. But every man in his own order: Christ the firstfruits; afterward they that are Christ's at his coming. Then cometh the end, when he shall have delivered up the kingdom to God, even the Father; when he shall have put down all rule and all authority and power. For he must reign, till he hath put all enemies under his feet. The last enemy that shall be destroyed is death. 1250

1 Corinthians 15:19–26

I am sure that he who began a good work in you will bring it to completion at the day of Jesus Christ. 1251

Philippians 1:6, *Revised Standard Version*

God alone can finish. 1252

John Ruskin, *Modern Painters*

See ever so far, there is limitless space outside of that,

Count ever so much, there is limitless time around that.

My rendezvous is appointed, it is certain,

The Lord will be there and wait till I come on perfect terms,
The great Camerado, the lover true for whom I pine will be there.   1253
>> Walt Whitman, *Song of Myself*

Nothing in our progressive world is truly intelligible until it has reached its end.   1254
>> Pierre Teilhard de Chardin, *Christianity and Evolution*

We do not know the play. We do not even know whether we are in Act I or Act V. . . . That it has a meaning we may be sure, but we cannot see it. When it is over, we may be told. We are led to expect that the Author will have something to say to each of us on the part that each of us has played. The playing it well is what matters infinitely.   1255
>> C. S. Lewis, *The World's Last Night*

Whatever you do, do carefully, and look to the end. *(Quidquid agas, prudenter agas, et respice finem.)*   1256
>> Author unknown, *Gesta Romanorum*, 103

Ends and Means

Great ends never look at means, but produce them spontaneously.   1257
>> William Blake, *Annotations to Lavater*, no. 526

Enemies

His hand will be against every man, and every man's hand against him. [*him: Ishmael.*]   1258
>> Genesis 16:12

Who is this uncircumcised Philistine, that he should defy the armies of the living God?   1259
>> 1 Samuel 17:26

If a man find his enemy, will he let him go well away?   1260
>> 1 Samuel 24:19

Thou preparest a table before me in the presence of mine enemies: thou anointest my head with oil; my cup runneth over.   1261
>> Psalm 23:5

They that hate me without a cause are more than the hairs of mine head.   1262
>> Psalm 69:4

Ye have heard that it hath been said, Thou shalt love thy neighbor, and hate thine enemy. But I say unto you, Love your enemies, bless them that curse you, do good to them that hate you, and pray for them which despitefully use you, and persecute you; That ye may be the children of your Father which is in heaven; for he maketh his sun to rise on the evil and on the good, and sendeth rain on the just and on the unjust.   1263
>> Jesus in Matthew 5:43–45

It is better that my enemy see good in me than that I see bad in him.   1264
>> Jewish Proverb

Friends may come and go, but enemies accumulate.   1265

> Author Unknown

None but myself ever did me any harm.   1266

> Napoleon Bonaparte. Remark at St. Helena, 6 April 1817

Pay attention to your enemies, for they are the first to discover your mistakes. 1267

> Antisthenes (5th–4th c. B.C.) Quoted in Diogenes Laertius, *Lives and Opinions of Eminent Philosophers*

Never ascribe to an opponent motives meaner than your own.   1268

> Sir James M. Barrie. Rectorial address, St. Andrews, 3 May 1922

If we could read the secret history of our enemies, we should find in each man's life sorrow and suffering enough to disarm all hostility.   1269

> Henry Wadsworth Longfellow, *Driftwood*, "Table Talk"

Enjoyment of God

The mere words "enjoyment of God" make sense only to those who already enjoy God; the vast majority of us seem to enjoy the vast majority of things vastly more than we enjoy God. (In fact, it is only God *in* these things that we enjoy, but we do not recognize that.)   1270

> Peter J. Kreeft, *Everything You Ever Wanted to Know About Heaven—But Never Dreamed of Asking*

Envy

Envy is the consuming desire to have everybody else as unsuccessful as you are.   1271

> Frederick Buechner, *Wishful Thinking: A Theological ABC*

Epigrams

The most ardent love is rather epigrammatic than lyrical. The Saints, above all St. Augustine, abound in epigrams.   1272

> Coventry Patmore, *The Rod, the Root and the Flower*

Epitaphs

My friend, judge not me,
Thou seest I judge not thee.
Betwixt the saddle and the ground,
Mercy I asked, and mercy found.   1273

> Author unknown, for a man killed by falling from his horse. William Camden, *Remains Concerning Britain*

When I die, my epitaph, or whatever you call those signs on tombstones, is going to read, "I joked about every prominent man of my time, but I never met a man I didn't like." I am proud of that. I can hardly wait to die so it can be carved.

117

And when you come around to my grave you'll probably find me sitting there proudly reading it.   1274

> Will Rogers. Quoted in Bennett Cerf, *Shake Well Before Using.* Cerf notes: "Will Rogers got what he wanted. He also got the enduring love of his fellow citizens."

Here lies one whose name was writ in water.   1275

> John Keats, epitaph for himself. He, too, got the epitaph he wanted.

The body of Benjamin Franklin, printer (like the cover of an old book, its contents torn out and stript of its lettering and gilding), lies here, food for worms; but the work shall not be lost, for it will (as he believed) appear once more in a new and more elegant edition, revised and corrected by the Author.   1276

> Benjamin Franklin, epitaph for himself, written when he was 22.

Oh, write of me, not "Died in bitter pains,"
But "Emigrated to another star!"   1277

> Helen Hunt Jackson, *Emigravit*

Amavimus. Amamus. Amabimus. (We have loved. We love. We shall love.)   1278

> Author unknown, for a husband and wife buried side by side

He lies below, correct in cypress wood,
And entertains the most exclusive worms.   1279

> Dorothy Parker, *Epitaph for a very rich man*

Here lie I, Martin Elginbrodde:
Hae mercy o' my soul, Lord God;
As I wad do, were I Lord God,
And ye were Martin Elginbrodde.   1280

> George MacDonald, *David Elginbrod*

Under the wide and starry sky,
Dig my grave and let me lie.
Glad did I live and gladly die,
    And I laid me down with a will.

This be the verse you grave for me:
Here he lies where he longed to be;
Home is the sailor, home from the sea,
    And the hunter home from the hill.   1281

> Robert Louis Stevenson, *Underwoods,* "Requiem"

Bland, passionate, and deeply religious, she was second cousin to the Earl of Leitrim, and of such are the kingdom of heaven.   1282

> Author unknown, epitaph for an unnamed eighteenth-century lady. Quoted in Gilbert Murray, *Stoic, Christian, and Humanist*

I would be happy if I knew that on my tombstone could be written these words: "This man was an absolute fool. None of the disastrous things that he reluctantly predicted ever came to pass!"   1283

> Lewis Mumford, *My Works and Days*

Warm summer sun, shine brightly here;
Warm southern wind, blow softly here;

Green sod above, lie light, lie light—
Good-night, dear heart, good-night, good-night.   1284
> Mark Twain, epitaph for his daughter

Unawed by opinion—Unseduced by flattery—Undismayed by disaster—He con-
fronted life with antique courage—And death with Christian hope.   1285
> Author unknown. Epitaph of James Petigru, Charleston, South
> Carolina, *ob.* 1863

What I gave, I have; what I spent, I had; what I kept, I lost.   1286
> Old epitaph, not identifiable

Equality

One law shall be to him that is home-born, and unto the stranger that sojourneth
among you.   1287
> Exodus 12:49

The rich and poor meet together: the Lord is the maker of them all.   1288
> Proverbs 22:2

That which befalleth the sons of men befalleth beasts.   1289
> Ecclesiastes 3:19

The race is not to the swift, nor the battle to the strong, neither yet bread to the
wise, nor yet riches to men of understanding, nor yet favor to men of skill; but time
and chance happeneth to them all.   1290
> Ecclesiastes 9:11

As with the people, so with the priest; as with the servant, so with his master; as
with the maid, so with her mistress; as with the buyer, so with the seller; as with the
lender, so with the borrower; as with the taker of usury, so with the giver of usury to
him.   1291
> Isaiah 24:2

There is no difference between the Jew and the Greek: for the same Lord over all is
rich unto all that call upon him.   1292
> Romans 10:12

We shall all stand before the judgment seat of Christ.   1293
> Romans 14:10

All men, among themselves, are by nature equal. The inequality we now discern
hath its spring from the civil law.   1294
> Thomas Hobbes, *Philosophical Rudiments Concerning Government
> and Society*

Your levellers wish to level down as far as themselves, but they cannot bear level-
ling up to themselves.   1295
> Samuel Johnson. Boswell's *Life,* 1763

We hold these truths to be self-evident: that all men are created equal; that they are
endowed by their creator with certain inalienable rights; that among these are life, liberty, and the pursuit of happiness.   1296
> Thomas Jefferson, *The Declaration of Independence,* 1776

Men of culture are the true apostles of equality.   1297
Matthew Arnold, *Culture and Anarchy*

I am just as good as you are, and a damned sight better.   1298
American Saying

The only real equality is in the cemetery.   1299
German Proverb

Naked I came into the world, naked I shall go out of it! And a very good thing too, for it reminds me that I am naked under my shirt, whatever its color.   1300
E. M. Forster, *Two Cheers for Democracy*

It was the contemplation of God that created men who were equal, for it was in God that they were equal.   1301
Antoine de Sait-Exupéry, *Flight to Arras,* tr. Lewis Galantière

Error

Ye do err, not knowing the scriptures, nor the power of God.   1302
Jesus in Matthew 22:29

Who can understand his errors? cleanse thou me from secret faults.   1303
Psalm 19:12

An error is the more dangerous for the truth it contains.   1304
Henri Frédéric Amiel, *Journal,* 26 December 1852

There is no error so monstrous that it fails to find defenders among the ablest men. Imagine a congress of such eminent celebrities as More, Bacon, Grotius, Pascal, Cromwell, Bossuet, Montesquieu, Jefferson, Napoleon, Pitt, etc. The result would be an Encyclopedia of Errors.   1305
Lord Acton, in letter to Mary Gladstone, 24 April 1881

Truth, crushed to earth, shall rise again;
   Th' eternal years of God are hers;
But Error, wounded, writhes in pain,
    And dies among his worshippers.   1306
William Cullen Bryant, *The Battlefield*

There is no such source of error as the pursuit of absolute truth.   1307
Samuel Butler, *Note-Books*

Who has enough credit in this world to pay for his mistakes?   1308
Edward Dahlberg, *Reasons of the Heart*

If you shut your door to all errors, truth will be shut out.   1309
Rabindranath Tagore, *Stray Birds*

Eternal Life

See also Immortality

Thou wilt not leave my soul in hell; neither wilt thou suffer thy Holy One to see corruption.   1310
Psalm 16:10

He that loseth his life for my sake shall find it.   1311
                    Jesus in Matthew 10:39

There be some standing here, which shall not taste of death, till they see the Son of man coming in his kingdom.   1312
                    Jesus in Matthew 16:28

If thou wilt enter into life, keep the commandments.   1313
                    Jesus in Matthew 19:17

And as Moses lifted up the serpent in the wilderness even so must the Son of man be lifted up: That whosoever believeth in him should not perish, but have eternal life. For God so loved the world, that he gave his only begotten Son, that whosoever believeth in him should not perish, but have everlasting life.   1314
                    Jesus in John 3:14–16

Whosoever drinketh of this water shall thirst again: But whosoever drinketh of the water that I shall give him shall never thirst.   1315
                    Jesus in John 4:13–14

I am the living bread which came down from heaven: if any man eat of this bread, he shall live forever.   1316
                    Jesus in John 6:51

I am the resurrection and the life: he that believeth in me, though he were dead yet shall he live: And whosoever liveth and believeth in me shall never die.   1317
                    Jesus in John 11:25–26

The wages of sin is death; but the gift of God is eternal life through Jesus Christ our Lord.   1318
                    Romans 6:23

Lay hold on eternal life, whereunto thou also are called.   1319
                    1 Timothy 6:12

God hath given to us eternal life, and this life is in his Son.   1320
                    1 John 5:11

Eternal life is the possession of endless life, completely and all at once. (*Interminabilis vitae simul et perfecta possessio.*)   1321
                    Boethius (480?–?524), *The Consolation of Philosophy*

The poor idea of living forever, all that commonplace minds grasp at for eternal life—is mere concomitant shadow. When a man is one with God, what should he do but live forever?   1322
                    George MacDonald, *Unspoken Sermons, Second Series,* "This Way"

The seas are quiet when the winds give o'er;
So calm are we when passions are no more.
For then we know how vain it was to boast
Of fleeting things, so certain to be lost.
Clouds of affection from our younger eyes
Conceal that emptiness which age descries.
The soul's dark cottage, batter'd and decay'd,
Lets in new light through chinks that Time has made;

Stronger by weakness, wiser, men become
As they draw near to their eternal home.
Leaving the old, both worlds at once they view
That stand upon the threshold of the new. 1323
> Edmund Waller (1606–1687), from *Last Verses*

Eternity

But thou, O Lord, shalt endure forever. 1324
> Psalm 102:12

Holy, holy, holy, Lord God Almighty, which was, and is, and is to come. 1325
> Revelation 4:8

God's "eternity" . . . is a powerful, active simultaneity with all times. 1326
> Hans Küng, *Does God Exist?*

Eternity is in love with the productions of time. 1327
> William Blake, *Proverbs of Hell*

It is eternity now. I am in the midst of it. It is about me as the sunshine; I am in it as the butterfly is in the light-laden air. Nothing has to come; it is now. Now is eternity; now is the immortal life. 1328
> Richard Jefferies, *The Story of My Heart*

All that is not eternal is eternally out of date. 1329
> C. S. Lewis, *The Four Loves*

The created world is but a small parenthesis in eternity. 1330
> Sir Thomas Browne, *Christian Morals*

Eternity gives nothing back of what one leaves out of the minutes. 1331
> Friedrich von Schiller, *Resignation*

Eternity! thou pleasing, dreadful thought! 1332
> Joseph Addison, *Cato*

To see a world in a grain of sand
And a heaven in a wild flower,
Hold infinity in the palm of your hand
And eternity in an hour. 1333
> William Blake, *Auguries of Innocence*

Eternity looks grander and kinder if time grows meaner and more hostile. 1334
> Thomas Carlyle

I leave eternity to Thee; for what is man that he should live out the lifetime of his God? 1335
> Herman Melville, *Moby Dick*

To have a sense of the eternal in life is a short flight for the soul. To have had it, is the soul's vitality. 1336
> George Meredith, *Diana of the Crossways*

We can have but a little sense of what an eternal duration is; it swallows up all thought and imagination: if we set ourselves to think upon it, we are presently lost.   1337

> Jonathan Edwards, *Sinners in Zion Tenderly Warned,* 1740

Eternity to the godly is a day that has no sunset; eternity to the wicked is a night that has no sunrise.   1338

> Thomas Watson, *The Golden Treasury of Puritan Quotations*

Evil

The imagination of man's heart is evil from his youth.   1339
> Genesis 8:21

Keep me from evil, that it may not grieve me!   1340
> I Chronicles 4:10, the prayer of Jabez

The triumphing of the wicked is short, and the joy of the hypocrite but for a moment.   1341
> Job 20:5

To depart from evil is understanding.   1342
> Job 28:28

Ye that love the Lord, hate evil.   1343
> Psalm 97:10

Stolen waters are sweet, and bread eaten in secret is pleasant.   1344
> Proverbs 9:17

Woe to them that devise iniquity, and work evil upon their beds!   1345
> Micah 2:1

Lead us not into temptation, but deliver us from evil.   1346
> Jesus in Matthew 6:13

No man is clever enough to know all the evil he has done.   1347
> François de la Rochefoucauld, *Maxims*

There is some soul of goodness in things evil,
Would men observingly distil it out.   1348
> William Shakespeare, *Henry the Fourth,* IV, i, 4

The death of a bee, assassinated by his queen, is charged with as much meaning as the massacres of Dachau.   1349
> R. Abellio, quoted in Jacques Lacarriere, *The Gnostics*

Evil is wrought by want of Thought,
As well as want of Heart.   1350
> Thomas Hood, *The Lady's Dream*

All simplifications of religious dogma are shipwrecked upon the rock of the problem of evil.   1351
> Alfred North Whitehead, *Religion in the Making*

The only thing necessary for the triumph of evil is for good men to do nothing. 1352

Edmund Burke. Letter to William Smith, 9 January 1795

Only among people who think no evil can evil monstrously flourish. 1353

Logan Pearsall Smith, Afterthoughts

Evil is simply all that which contributes to the world's entropy. 1354

Jacques Lacarriere, The Gnostics

Evil is not wholly evil; it is misplaced good. 1355

Samuel Alexander, Space, Time and Deity

We are no more responsible for the evil thoughts that pass through our minds than a scarecrow for the birds that pass over the seedplot he has to guard. The sole responsibility in each case is to prevent them from settling. 1356

John Churton Collins, Maxims and Reflections

Evolution

It is an error to imagine that evolution signifies a constant tendency to increased perfection. That process undoubtedly involves a constant remodeling of the organism in adaptation to new conditions; but it depends on the nature of those conditions whether the direction of the modification effected shall be upward or downward. 1357

Thomas Henry Huxley, The Struggle for Existence in Human Society

Evolution is a fact, not a theory. 1358

Carl Sagan, Cosmos

Man is a product of nearly three billion years of evolution, in whose person the evolutionary process has at last become conscious of itself and its possibilities. Whether he likes it or not, he is responsible for the whole further evolution of this planet. 1359

Julian Huxley, The London Observer, 31 March 1963

The changes which God causes in his lower creatures are almost always from worse to better, while the changes that God allows man to make in himself are very often the other way. 1360

John Ruskin, Lectures on Architecture and Painting

I am very proud of these bright-eyed, furry, four-footed or feathered progenitors, and not at all ashamed of my cousins, the tigers and apes and peacocks. 1361

Logan Pearsall Smith, Trivia

Out of the dusk a shadow,
    Then a spark;
Out of the clouds a silence,
    Then a lark;
Out of the heart a rapture,
    Then a pain;
Out of the dead, cold ashes
    Life again. 1362

John Banister Tabb, Evolution

"The unfit die—the fit both live and thrive."
Alas, who say so? They that do survive. 1363
> Sarah Cleghorn, *The Survival of the Fittest*

Darwinian man, though well behaved,
At best is only a monkey shaved! 1364
> W. S. Gilbert, *Princess Ida*

Example

If I then, your Lord and Master, have washed your feet; ye also ought to wash one another's feet. For I have given you an example, that ye should do as I have done to you. 1365
> Jesus in John 13:14–15

Be ye followers of me, even as I also am of Christ. 1366
> 1 Corinthians 11:1

Example is not the main thing in influencing others. It is the only thing. 1367
> Albert Schweitzer, recalled at his death, 4 December 1965

The example of Alexander's chastity has not made so many continent as that of his drunkenness has made intemperate. 1368
> Blaise Pascal, *Pensées*

None preaches better than the ant, and she says nothing. 1369
> Benjamin Franklin. *Poor Richard's Almanack,* July 1736

Old Testament examples are New Testament instructions. 1370
> John Owen, *The Golden Treasury of Puritan Quotations*

Few things are harder to put up with than the annoyance of a good example. 1371
> Mark Twain, *Pudd'nhead Wilson's Calendar*

What thou wouldst not have thy neighbor do unto himself, do thou not unto thyself. 1372
> C.E.S.

Existence

We exist because God is good. 1373
> St. Augustine, *De doctrina christiana*

Mere existence is so much better than nothing that one would rather exist in pain than not exist. 1374
> Samuel Johnson. Boswell's *Life,* 15 April 1778

Whatever has lived becomes necessary food for new existence. And the Arab who builds himself a hut out of the marble fragments of a Palmyra temple is really more of a philosopher than all the guardians of museums at London, Munich, or Paris. 1375
> Anatole France, *The Crime of Sylvestre Bonnard*

Everything, in some extremely attenuated extension of itself, has existed from the very first. 1376
> Pierre Teilhard de Chardin, *The Phenomenon of Man*

That I exist is a perpetual surprise which is life. 1377
   Rabindranath Tagore, *Stray Birds*

Experience

Remember the days of old, consider the years of many generations: ask thy father, and he will show thee; the elders, and they will tell thee. 1378
   Deuteronomy 32:7

With the ancient is wisdom; and in length of days understanding. 1379
   Job 12:12

I understand more than the ancients, because I keep thy precepts. 1380
   Psalm 119:100

Thou hast not remembered the days of thy youth, when thou wast naked and bare. 1381
   Ezekiel 16:22

Whether he be a sinner or no, I know not: one thing I know, that, whereas I was blind, now I see. 1382
   John 9:25

I was thinking that we all learn by experience, but some of us have to go to summer school. 1383
   Peter de Vries, *Tunnel of Love*

I am a part of all that I have met. 1384
   Alfred, Lord Tennyson, *Ulysses*

We cannot afford to forget any experience, however painful. 1385
   Dag Hammarskjöld, *Markings*

Experience is usually what you get when you are trying to find something else. 1386
   The Milwaukee Journal, 13 October 1976

Experience is a good teacher, but she sends in terrific bills. 1387
   Minna Antrim, *Naked Truth and Veiled Allusions*

F

Faces

Nature gives you the face you have at 20: it is up to you to merit the face you have at 50.   1388

> Gabrielle ("CoCo") Chanel. *Ladies Home Journal,* September 1956

A minister has enough temptations to vanity without bearing the moral hazard of a handsome face.   1389

> Reinhold Niebuhr, *Leaves from the Notebook of a Tamed Cynic*

What effect does the sight of an extraordinarily beautiful person have upon you? I mean the very *first.* Is it not an effect of sadness? Analyze it, and perhaps you will find yourself involuntarily thinking of *death.*   1390

> Lafcadio Hearn. *Lafcadio Hearn: Life and Letters,* edited by Elizabeth Bisland

Every human face is a very special door to paradise, which cannot possibly be confused with any other, and through which there will never enter but one soul.   1391

> Léon Bloy. Quoted in *God and Man,* compiled by Victor Gollancz

Men who have been famous for their looks have never been famous for anything else.   1392

> Arthur Ponsonby, *Casual Observations*

The Methodists have acquired a face; the Quakers, a face; the nuns, a face.   1393

> Ralph Waldo Emerson, *English Traits*

As a beauty I am not a star,
There are others more handsome by far,
But my face, I don't mind it,
For I am behind it;
It's the people in front get the jar.   1394

> Author unknown, commonly ascribed to Woodrow Wilson, who was fond of quoting it.

All I know about Fanny Kelly is what Charles Lamb said about her face in a letter to Mrs. Wordsworth: "Fanny Kelly's divine plain face." Some faces are divinely plain, and these are all plainly divine.   1395

> C.E.S.

Facts

Whatever weaknesses, miscalculations, and guilt there is in what precedes the facts, God is in the facts themselves.   1396

Dietrich Bonhoeffer, *Letters and Papers from Prison*,
23 January 1944

A fact, it seems to me, is a great thing—a sentence printed, if not by God, at least by the devil.   1397

Thomas Carlyle, in letter to Ralph Waldo Emerson, 1836

Truth in her dress finds facts too tight. In fiction she moves with ease.   1398

Rabindranath Tagore, *Stray Birds*

Oh, don't tell me of facts—I never believe facts; you know Canning said nothing was so fallacious as facts, except figures.   1399

Sydney Smith, *Table Talk*

Ugly facts are a challenge to beautify them.   1400

Anonymous (Henry S. Haskins), *Meditations in Wall Street*

All generous minds have a horror of what are commonly called "facts." They are the brute beasts of the intellectual domain.   1401

Oliver Wendell Holmes, *The Autocrat of the Breakfast-Table*

Consciousness of a fact is not knowing it; if it were, the fish would know more of the sea than the geographers and the naturalists.   1402

George Bernard Shaw, *Back to Methuselah*

One has never heard of soft facts, only of hard. Yet it is just because there are such soft facts as eyeballs and fingertips that the hard are manifested.   1403

Alan W. Watts, *Nature, Man and Woman*

The fatal futility of Fact.   1404

Henry James, *The Spoils of Poynton*

"Now what I want is, Facts. . . . Facts alone are wanted in life." [*Mr. Gradgrind.*]   1405

Charles Dickens, *Hard Times*

Sit down before fact as a little child, be prepared to give up every preconceived notion, follow humbly wherever and to whatever abyss nature leads, or you shall learn nothing.   1406

Thomas Henry Huxley, in letter to Charles Kingsley,
23 September 1860

Fable is, generally speaking, far more accurate than fact, for fable describes a man as he was to his own age, fact describes him as he is to a handful of inconsiderable antiquarians many centuries later.   1407

G. K. Chesterton, *Varied Types*

Failure

If thou doest not well, sin lieth at the door.   1408

Genesis 4:7

He that trusteth in his riches shall fall.   1409
        Proverbs 11:28

Pride goeth before destruction, and an haughty spirit before a fall.   1410
        Proverbs 16:18

Even the youths shall faint and be weary, and the young men shall utterly fall: but they that wait upon the Lord shall renew their strength: they shall mount up with wings as eagles; they shall run, and not be weary; and they shall walk, and not faint.   1411
        Isaiah 40:30–31

No good thing is failure and no evil thing is success.   1412
        Author Unknown

The secret of success in life is known only to those who have not succeeded. 1413
        John Churton Collins, *Maxims and Reflections*

Some people spend their lives failing and never notice.   1414
        Judith Rossner, *Attachments*

Good people are good because they've come to wisdom through failure. We get very little wisdom from success, you know.   1415
        William Saroyan. *New York Herald-American,* 23 August 1961

I've often thought with Nixon that if he'd made the football team his life would have been different.   1416
        Adela Rogers St. John. *Los Angeles Times,* 13 October 1974

Whoever heard of a successful saint? Isn't the saint, rightly defined, a faithful failure?   1417
        C.E.S.

Faith

Is anything too hard for the Lord?   1418
        Genesis 18:14

Speak ye unto the rock before their eyes; and it shall give forth his water. 1419
        Numbers 20:8

He will not fail thee, neither forsake thee: fear not, neither be dismayed. 1420
        Deuteronomy 31:8

Thou comest to me with a sword, and with a spear, and with a shield: but I come to thee in the name of the Lord of hosts.   1421
        1 Samuel 17:45

Thou art my lamp, O Lord.   1422
        2 Samuel 22:29

If thou seek him, he will be found of thee. [*David, to Solomon.*]   1423
        1 Chronicles 28:9

Though he slay me, yet will I trust in him.   1424
        Job 13:15

Those that wait upon the Lord, they shall inherit the earth.   1425
   Psalm 37:9

In quietness and confidence shall be your strength.   1426
   Isaiah 30:15

Our God whom we serve is able to deliver us from the burning fiery furnace.   1427
   Daniel 3:17

Speak the word only and my servant shall be healed.   1428
   Matthew 8:8

Why are ye fearful, O ye of little faith?   1429
   Jesus in Matthew 8:26

According to your faith be it unto you.   1430
   Jesus in Matthew 9:29

Father, into thy hands I commend my spirit.   1431
   Jesus in Luke 23:46

Blessed are they that have not seen, and yet have believed.   1432
   Jesus in John 20:29

The just shall live by faith.   1433
   Romans 1:17

We know that in everything God works for good with those who love him.   1434
   Romans 8:28, *Revised Standard Version*

Him that is weak in faith receive ye, but not to doubtful disputations.   1435
   Romans 14:1

Whatsoever is not of faith is sin.   1436
   Romans 14:23

Faith should not stand in the wisdom of men, but in the power of God.   1437
   1 Corinthians 2:5

Though I have all faith, so that I could remove mountains, and have not charity, I am nothing.   1438
   1 Corinthians 13:2

If Christ be not raised, your faith is vain; ye are yet in your sins.   1439
   1 Corinthians 15:17

By faith ye stand.   1440
   2 Corinthians 1:24

We walk by faith, not by sight.   1441
   2 Corinthians 5:7

By grace are ye saved through faith.   1442
   Ephesians 2:8

I have fought a good fight, I have finished my course, I have kept the faith.   1443
   2 Timothy 4:7

Faith is the substance of things hoped for, the evidence of things not seen. 1444
Hebrews 11:1

Without faith it is impossible to please him. 1445
Hebrews 11:6

Faith apart from works is dead. 1446
James 2:26, *Revised Standard Version*

Add to your faith virtue; and to virtue knowledge. 1447
2 Peter 1:5

He that overcometh shall inherit all things. 1448
Revelation 21:7

You can do very little with faith, but you can do nothing without it. 1449
Samuel Butler, *Note-Books*

Faith is love taking the form of aspiration. 1450
William Ellery Channing, *Works*

Faith is trust. By faith I mean a trust in God's unknown, unfelt, untried goodness and mercy. 1451
Martin Luther. Quoted in Joseph Sittler, *Gravity & Grace*

I believe in the sun, even if it does not shine.
I believe in love, even if I do not feel it.
I believe in God, even if I do not see him. 1452
Hans Küng, *On Being a Christian*

It is love that makes faith, not faith love. 1453
John Henry Newman, *Parochial and Plain Sermons*

I swear I will never henceforth have to do with the faith that tells the best.
I will have to do only with that faith that leaves the best untold. 1454
Walt Whitman, *A Song of the Rolling Earth*

Faith is simply the welcome of the one who says "Here I am." And taking that as our starting point, we can be on our way. 1455
Jacques Ellul, *Living Faith*

Faith is always at a disadvantage; it is a perpetually defeated thing which survives all its conquerors. 1456
G. K. Chesterton, *G. F. Watts*

I have not lost faith in God. I have moments of anger and protest. Sometimes I've been closer to him for that reason. 1457
Elie Wiesel, on writing about the Holocaust. Quoted in Joseph Berger, *Witness to Evil*

The realities of faith lie outside the realm of psychology. 1458
Carl Gustav Jung, *Transformation Symbolism in the Mass*

That man is perfect in faith who can come to God in the utter dearth of his feelings and desires, without a glow or an aspiration, with the weight of low thoughts, failures, neglects, and wandering forgetfulness, and say to Him, "Thou art my refuge." 1459
George MacDonald, *Unspoken Sermons, First Series,* "The Child in the Midst"

The faith that stands on authority is not faith. 1460

Ralph Waldo Emerson, *Essays,* "The Over-Soul"

Respiration and inspiration correspond to the life of faith. 1461

Coventry Patmore, *The Rod, the Root and the Flower,* "Aphorisms and Extracts"

Faith is the light of the flame of love. 1462

Ibid.

The only argument against losing faith is that you also lose hope—and usually charity. 1463

G. K. Chesterton. *Hearst's Magazine,* January 1913

Faith outruns reason, and love far outruns understanding. 1464

C.E.S.

The honorific "Defender of the Faith" expresses a false and fraudulent idea. The Faith needs no defense other than one—living for it and by it and dying in it. And that is not a defense but a triumphant assertion and manifestation of it. 1465

C.E.S.

Fall of Man, The

There exists a "deifugal" force. Otherwise all would be God. 1466

Simone Weil, *Criteria of Wisdom,* "Decreation"

If you take a pack of cards as it comes from the maker and shuffle it for a few minutes, all trace of the original order disappears. The order will never come back no matter how long you shuffle. Shuffling is the only thing which nature cannot undo. 1467

Arthur Eddington, *Nature of the Physical World.*

Life is a maze in which we take the wrong turning before we have learnt to walk. 1468

Cyril Connolly, *The Unquiet Grave*

A fallen man *is* very like a fallen angel. 1469

C. S. Lewis, Preface to *"Paradise Lost"*

Eden is on no map, and Adam's fall fits no historical calendar. Moses is no nearer to the Fall than we are, because he lived three thousand years before our time. The Fall refers not to some datable, aboriginal calamity in the historical past of humanity, but to a dimension of human experience which is always present—namely, that we who have been created for fellowship with God repudiate it continually; and that the whole of mankind does this along with us. Every man is his own "Adam," and all men are solidarily "Adam." Thus, Paradise before the Fall, the *status perfectionis,* is not a period of history, but our "memory" of a divinely intended quality of life, given to us along with our consciousness of guilt. 1470

John S. Whale, *Christian Doctrine*

We are ensnared by the wisdom of the serpent; we are set free by the foolishness of God. 1471

St. Augustine, *De doctrina christiana*

Fallibility

Babe Ruth struck out 1,330 times.   1472
>   Author Unknown. Graffito in New York City, 1977

Fame

Saul hath slain his thousands, and David his ten thousands.   1473
>   1 Samuel 21:11

I am forgotten as a dead man out of mind: I am like a broken vessel. 1474
>   Psalm 31:12

His name shall endure for ever: his name shall be continued as long as the
sun.   1475
>   Psalm 72:17

The seed of evildoers shall never be renowned.   1476
>   Isaiah 14:20

I will make you a name and a praise among all people of the earth, when I turn
back your captivity before your eyes.   1477
>   Zephaniah 3:20

A city that is set on a hill cannot be hid.   1478
>   Jesus in Matthew 5:14

Fame sometimes has created something out of nothing.   1479
>   Thomas Fuller, *The Holy State and the Profane State*

Fame usually comes to those who are thinking about something else, very rarely to
those who say to themselves, "Go to now, let us be a celebrated individual!" 1480
>   Oliver Wendell Holmes, *The Autocrat of the Breakfast-Table*

If parts allure thee, think how Bacon shined,
The wisest, brightest, meanest of mankind!
Or ravished with the whistling of a name,
See Cromwell damned to everlasting fame!   1481
>   Alexander Pope, *An Essay on Man,* IV, 1. 281

Fame is the stepmother of death and ambition the excrement of glory. 1482
>   Pietro Aretino, in letter to Lionardo Parpaglioni, 2 December 1537

Blessed is he whose fame does not outshine his truth.   1483
>   Rabindranath Tagore, *Stray Birds*

Einstein—the greatest Jew since Jesus. I have no doubt that Einstein's fame will
still be remembered and revered when Lloyd George, Foch and William Hohenzollern
share with Charlie Chaplin that ineluctable oblivion which awaits the uncreative
mind.   1484
>   J. B. S. Haldane, *Daedalus or Science of the Future*

Fame is the spur that the clear spirit doth raise
(That last infirmity of noble mind)
To scorn delights, and live laborious days;
But the fair guerdon when we hope to find,

133

And think to burst out into sudden blaze,
Comes the blind Fury with th' abhorred shears,
And slits the thin-spun life. 1485
John Milton, *Lycidas*

Family

He that troubleth his own house shall inherit the wind. 1486
Proverbs 11:29

He that loveth father or mother more than me is not worthy of me: and he that loveth son or daughter more than me is not worthy of me. 1487
Matthew 10:37

To make a happy fire-side clime
To weans and wife,
That's the true pathos and sublime
Of human life. 1488
Robert Burns, *To Dr. Blaiklock*

Govern a family as you would cook a small fish—very gently. 1489
Chinese Proverb

He that loves not his wife and children feeds a lioness at home and broods a nest of sorrows. 1490
Jeremy Taylor, *Sermons*, "Married Love"

There's no family but there's a whore or a knave of it. 1491
James Howell, *Proverbs*, 1659

Fond as we are of our loved ones, there comes at times during their absence an unexplainable peace. 1492
Anne Shaw, *But Such Is Life*

A friend loves you for your intelligence, a mistress for your charm, but your family's love is unreasoning; you were born into it and are of its flesh and blood. Nevertheless it can irritate you more than any group of people in the world. 1493
André Maurois, *The Art of Living*

Fasting

I humbled my soul with fasting. 1494
Psalm 35:13

When they fast, I will not hear their cry. 1495
Jeremiah 14:12

Then was Jesus led up of the spirit into the wilderness to be tempted of the devil. And when he had fasted forty days and forty nights, he was afterward an hungred. 1496
Matthew 4:1–2

When you fast, do not look dismal, like the hypocrites, for they disfigure their faces that their fasting may be seen by men. Truly, I say to you, they have received their reward. But when you fast, anoint your head and wash your face, that your fasting may

not be seen by men but by your Father who is in secret; and your Father who sees in secret will reward you. 1497
> Jesus in Matthew 6:16–17, *Revised Standard Version*

Our dear saint (Francis de Sales) disapproved of immoderate fasting. He used to say that the spirit could not endure the body when overfed, but that, if underfed, the body could not endure the spirit. 1498
> Jean Pierre Camus, *The Spirit of St. Francis de Sales*

He who fasts but does no good saves his bread but loses his soul. 1499
> English Proverb

And join with thee calm Peace and Quiet,
Spare Fast, that oft with gods doth diet. 1500
> John Milton, *Il Penseroso*

Fasting is better than prayer. 1501
> St. Clement of Rome, *Second Epistle to the Corinthians*

Fasting today makes the food good tomorrow. 1502
> German Proverb

Fate

I do not believe in a fate that falls on men however they act; but I do believe in a fate that falls on them unless they act. 1503
> G. K. Chesterton, *Generally Speaking*

Fate is not an eagle, it creeps like a rat. 1504
> Elizabeth Bowen, *The House in Paris*

Whatever limits us, we call fate. 1505
> Ralph Waldo Emerson, *The Conduct of Life,* "Fate"

Failure or success seem to have been allotted to men by their stars. But they retain the power of wriggling, of fighting with their star or against it, and in the whole universe the only really interesting movement is this struggle. 1506
> E. M. Forster, *Abinger Harvest*

The Moving Finger writes; and having writ,
Moves on: nor all your piety nor wit
  Shall lure it back to cancel half a line,
Nor all your tears wash out a word of it. 1507
> Omar Khayyám, *Rabáiyát,* translated by Edward Fitzgerald, 2d ed.

Fate leads the willing, and drags along the reluctant. 1508
> Seneca, *Letters to Lucilius*

If by fate anyone means the will or power of God, let him keep his meaning but mend his language: for fate commonly means a necessary process which will have its way apart from the will of God and of men. 1509
> St. Augustine, *The City of God*

Fate is a name for facts not yet passed under the fire of thought; for causes which are unpenetrated. 1510
> Ralph Waldo Emerson, *Fate*

What is written is written.   1511

    Arab Proverb

We talk about fate as if it were something visited upon us; we forget that we create our fate every day we live. And by fate I mean the woes that beset us, which are merely the effects of causes which are not nearly as mysterious as we pretend. Most of the ills we suffer from are directly traceable to our own behavior.   1512

    Henry Miller, *A Devil in Paradise*

I was thinking of my patients, and how the worst moment for them was when they discovered they were masters of their own fate. It was not a matter of bad or good luck. When they could no longer blame fate, they were in despair.   1513

    Anaïs Nin, *The Diaries of Anaïs Nin*

Fathers

See also Parents

What man is there of you, whom if his son ask bread, will he give him a stone?   1514

    Jesus in Matthew 7:9

One father is more than a hundred schoolmasters.   1515

    George Herbert, *Outlandish Proverbs*

It is a wise father that knows his own child.   1516

    William Shakespeare, *The Merchant of Venice,* II, ii, 83

What a father says to his children is not heard by the world, but it will be heard by posterity.   1517

    Jean Paul Richter, *Levana,* Preface

One father takes better care of ten children than ten children take care of one father.   1518

    German Proverb

A father is a banker provided by nature.   1519

    French Proverb

You don't have to deserve your mother's love. You have to deserve your father's. He's more particular.   1520

    Robert Frost, in interview. *Writers at Work, Second Series*

A father is very miserable who has no other hold on his children's affection than the need they have of his assistance, if that can be called affection.   1521

    Michel de Montaigne, *Essays*

An angry father is most cruel toward himself.   1522

    Publilius Syrus, *Sententiae,* 1st cent. B.C.

Don't be a lion in your own house.   1523

    Czech Proverb

Fear

Fear not, for I am with thee, and will bless thee, and multiply thy seed. [*God to Isaac.*]   1524
>Genesis 26:24

Ye shall flee when none pursueth you.   1525
>Leviticus 26:17

Yea, though I walk through the valley of the shadow of death, I will fear no evil: for thou art with me.   1526
>Psalm 23:4

The Lord is my light and my salvation; whom shall I fear? the Lord is the strength of my life: of whom shall I be afraid?   1527
>Psalm 27:1

In God I have put my trust; I will not fear what flesh can do unto me.   1528
>Psalm 56:4

Thou shalt not be afraid for the terror by night; nor for the arrow that flieth by day.   1529
>Psalm 91:5

The wicked flee when no man pursueth.   1530
>Proverbs 28:1

Why are ye fearful, O ye of little faith?   1531
>Jesus in Matthew 8:26

Fear not them which kill the body, but are not able to kill the soul.   1532
>Jesus in Matthew 10:28

The Lord is my helper, and I will not fear what man shall do unto me.   1533
>Hebrews 13:6

Perfect love casteth out fear.   1534
>1 John 4:18

Perfect love, we know, casteth out fear. But so do several other things—ignorance, alcohol, passion, presumption, and stupidity.   1535
>C. S. Lewis, *The World's Last Night*

The man who has ceased to fear has ceased to care.   1536
>F. H. Bradley, *Aphorisms*

The fiercest people are not those who are bold, but those who are frightened.   1537
>Sydney J. Harris, *Clearing the Ground*

Only in a hut built for a moment can one live without fears.   1538
>Kamo No Chomei (1153–1216), *An Account of My Hut*

Our help is in the name of the Lord, but our fears are in the name of man. 1539
>William Greenhill, *The Golden Treasury of Puritan Quotations*

A good scare is worth more to a man than good advice.   1540
>Edgar Watson Howe, *Country Town Sayings*

137

Fear is the main source of superstition, and one of the main sources of cruelty.   1541

> Bertrand Russell, *Unpopular Essays,* "An Outline of Intellectual Rubbish"

Some of your hurts you have cured,
  And the sharpest you still have survived;
But what torments of grief you endured
    From evils which never arrived.   1542

> Ralph Waldo Emerson, *Quatrains,* "Borrowings"

Imagine a little child awakening in the middle of the night and the mother coming into the room to hear the child say, "I'm scared."

The mother says, "There's nothing to be frightened about. There's really no bear in the closet. There's nothing under your bed."

But of course the indeterminate fear is the most irremovable fear, so the child says, "I know, but I'm still scared."

The mother does not answer the fright of the child. A wise mother says, "Don't be frightened, I'm here." That's not an answer to the child's fear, but it is a reply.

To the problem of evil there is, I think, no answer. But there are replies.   1543

> Joseph Sittler, *Gravity & Grace*

He has not learned the lesson of life who does not every day surmount a fear.   1544

> Ralph Waldo Emerson, *Essays,* "Courage"

Fear of God

O that there were such an heart in them that they would fear me, and keep all my commandments always, that it might be well with them, and with their children forever!   1545

> Deuteronomy 5:29

The fear of the Lord, that is wisdom.   1546

> Job 28:28

The secret of the Lord is with them that fear him.   1547

> Psalm 25:14

When he slew them, then they sought him: and they returned and enquired early after God.   1548

> Psalm 78:34

God is greatly to be feared in the assembly of the saints.   1549

> Psalm 89:7

The fear of the Lord is the beginning of knowledge.   1550

> Proverbs 1:7

The fear of the Lord is a fountain of life.   1551

> Proverbs 14:27

His mercy is on them that fear him from generation to generation.   1552

> Luke 1:50

The fear of the Lord is honour, and glory, and gladness, and a crown of joy. The fear of the Lord maketh a merry heart, and giveth joy, and gladness, and a long life. 1553
Ecclesiasticus 1:11–12, *The Jerusalem Bible*

Whosoever among you feareth God, to you is the word of this salvation sent. 1554
Acts 13:26

The devils also believe, and tremble. 1555
James 2:19

Fear God. Honor the king. 1556
1 Peter 2:17

It is only the fear of God that can deliver us from the fear of man. 1557
John Witherspoon

The only sure way to keep fear out of living is to keep a respectful fear of God in our lives, which means to maintain a reverent attitude toward His place and influence in the scheme of things. This brand of fear is a healthy ingredient, a deterrent to want, a spur to courage and confidence, an insurance against loss, a source of comfort and understanding at any age. 1558
Eugene Asa Carr, *Freedom from Fear*

There is a difference between fearing God and being afraid of him. To fear God is to stand in awe of him; to be afraid of God is to run away from him. 1559
C.E.S.

Fellowship

Behold, how good and how pleasant it is for brethren to dwell together in unity! 1560
Psalm 133:1

Have we not all one father? hath not one God created us? 1561
Malachi 2:10

Whosoever shall do the will of my Father which is in heaven, the same is my brother, and sister, and mother. 1562
Jesus in Matthew 12:50

Where two or three are gathered together in my name, there am I in the midst of them. 1563
Jesus in Matthew 18:20

Have salt in yourselves, and have peace one with another. 1564
Jesus in Mark 9:50

I am the vine, ye are the branches. 1565
Jesus in John 15:5

We, being many, are one body in Christ, and every one members one of another. 1566
Romans 12:5

Ye are no more strangers and foreigners, but fellow citizens with the saints. 1567
Ephesians 2:19

If we walk in the light, as he is in the light, we have fellowship one with another.   1568

1 John 1:7

Blest be the tie that binds
   Our hearts in Christian love:
The fellowship of kindred minds
   Is like to that above.

Before our Father's throne
   We pour our ardent prayers:
Our fears, our hopes, our aims are one,
   Our comforts and our cares.

We share our mutual woes,
   Our mutual burdens bear,
And often for each other flows
   The sympathizing tear.

When we at death must part,
   Not like the world's, our pain;
But one in Christ, and one in heart,
   We part to meet again.   1569

John Fawcett, hymn, 1782

Fellowship is Heaven, and lack of fellowship is Hell; fellowship is life, and lack of fellowship is death; and the deeds that we do upon the earth, it is for fellowship's sake that we do them.   1570

William Morris, *The Dream of John Ball,* 1888

To be social is to be forgiving.   1571

Robert Frost, *New Hampshire,* "The Star-Splitter"

Feminism

See also Women

A free race cannot be born of slave mothers.   1572

Margaret Sanger, *Women and the New Race*

George Sand smokes, wears male attire, wishes to be addressed as *Mon frère;* perhaps, if she found those who were as brothers indeed, she would not care whether she was a brother or a sister.   1573

Margaret Fuller, *The Dial,* "The Great Lawsuit, Man versus man, Woman versus woman," July 1843

Many have imagined that feminine politics would be merely pacifist or humanitarian or sentimental. The real danger of feminine politics is too much love of a masculine policy.   1574

G. K. Chesterton, *The Return of Don Quixote*

Feminism is the most revolutionary idea there has ever been. Equality for women demands a change in the human psyche more profound than anything Marx dreamed of. It means valuing parenthood as much as we value banking.   1575

Polly Toynbee. *Guardian,* 19 January 1987

Final Analysis

In the final analysis there is no final analysis.   1576
>Sydney J. Harris, *Pieces of Eight*

Flattery

Meddle not with him that flattereth with his lips.   1577
>Proverbs 20:19

A man that flattereth his neighbor spreadeth a net for his feet.   1578
>Proverbs 29:5

It is better to hear the rebuke of the wise than for a man to hear the song of
fools.   1579
>Ecclesiastes 7:5

Woe unto you, when all men shall speak well of you!   1580
>Jesus in Luke 6:26

Flattery is all right—if you don't inhale.   1581
>Adlai E. Stevenson. Speech, 1 February 1961

Flatterers look like friends, as wolves like dogs.   1582
>George Chapman, *The Conspiracy of Byron*

Flattery sits in the parlor when plain dealing is kicked out of doors.   1583
>Thomas Fuller, *Gnomologia*

He who knows how to flatter also knows how to slander.   1584
>Napoleon Bonaparte, *Maxims*, 1804–15

Flowers

Consider the lilies of the field, how they grow; they toil not, neither do they spin:
And yet I say unto you, that even Solomon in all his glory was not arrayed like one of
these.   1585
>Jesus in Matthew 6:28–29

"We, the rustling leaves, have a voice that answers the storms, but who are you, the
silent?"
"I am a mere flower."   1586
>Rabindranath Tagore, *Stray Birds*

The leaf becomes flower when it loves. The flower becomes fruit when it
worships.   1587
>Ibid.

Flowers are the sweetest things that God ever made, and forgot to put a soul
into.   1588
>Henry Ward Beecher, *Life Thoughts*

Flower in the crannied wall,
I pluck you out of the crannies;—
Hold you here, root and all, in my hand,
Little flower—but *if* I could understand

What you are, root and all, and all in all,
I should know what God and man is. 1589
                    Alfred, Lord Tennyson, *Flower in the Crannied Wall*

Fools

The fool hath said in his heart, There is no God. 1590
                    Psalm 14:1

Fools despise wisdom and instruction. 1591
                    Proverbs 1:7

A wise man feareth, and departeth from evil: but the fool rageth, and is confident. 1592
                    Proverbs 14:16

The father of a fool hath no joy. 1593
                    Proverbs 17:21

Even a fool, when he holdeth his peace, is counted wise. 1594
                    Proverbs 17:28

Every fool will be meddling. 1595
                    Proverbs 20:3

As a dog returneth to his vomit, so a fool returneth to his folly. 1596
                    Proverbs 26:11

A fool's voice is known by multitude of words. 1597
                    Ecclesiastes 5:3

The fool foldeth his hands together, and eateth his own flesh. 1598
                    Ecclesiastes 4:5

"Thou fool, this night thy soul shall be required of thee: then whose shall those things be, which thou hast provided?" 1599
                    Jesus in Luke 12:20

An empty head is not really empty; it is stuffed with rubbish. Hence the difficulty of forcing anything into an empty head. 1600
                    Eric Hoffer, *Reflections on the Human Condition*

A fool is a man who has never tried an experiment in his life. 1601
                    Erasmus Darwin, in letter to Sophy Roxton, 9 March 1892

What's a' your jargon o' your schools,
Your Latin names for horns and stools;
If honest Nature made you fools,
    What sairs your grammar? 1602
                    Robert Burns, *First Epistle to J. Lapraik*

A fool will laugh even when he is drowning. 1603
                    English Proverb

A fool and his money are some party. 1604
                    Author unknown. A very modern revision of the much older
                    proverb: "A fool and his money are soon parted."

A fool sees not the same tree that a wise man sees. 1605
> William Blake, *The Marriage of Heaven and Hell*

Every man is a damned fool for at least five minutes every day. Wisdom consists in not exceeding the limit. 1606
> Elbert Hubbard, *Roycroft Dictionary and Book of Epigrams*

There are two kinds of fools in the world: damned fools and what Paul calls "fools for Christ's sake" (1 Cor. 4:10). 1607
> Frederick Buechner, *Wishful Thinking: A Theological ABC*

Fortunately for themselves and the world, nearly all men are cowards and dare not act on what they believe. Nearly all our disasters come of a few fools having the "courage of their convictions." 1608
> Coventry Patmore, *The Rod, the Root and the Flower*

Fools for Christ

Mindful of the fact that you live in an agricultural country, I presume you know what an ass is. We read in the New Testament that our blessed Lord rode on an ass in triumph into the city of Jerusalem. Today the Lord rides on another ass: I myself. 1609
> Richard Cardinal Cushing, preaching in the slums of Lima, Peru.
> *Time*, 21 July 1964

Force

Not hammer-strokes, but dance of the water sings the pebbles into perfection. 1610
> Rabindranath Tagore, *Stray Birds*

Where might is master, justice is servant. 1611
> German Proverb

When a fact can be demonstrated, force is unnecessary; when it cannot be demonstrated, force is infamous. 1612
> Robert G. Ingersoll, *Prose-Poems and Selections*

There is no real force without justice. 1613
> Napoleon Bonaparte, *Maxims,* 1804–15

Forgiveness

Hearken thou to the supplication of thy servant, and of thy people Israel, when they shall pray toward this place: and hear thou in heaven thy dwelling place: and when thou hearest, forgive. 1614
> 1 Kings 8:30

When the Lord saw that they had humbled themselves, the word of the Lord came to Shemaiah, saying, They have humbled themselves: therefore I will not destroy them. 1615
> 2 Chronicles 12:7

Remember not the sins of my youth. 1616
> Psalm 25:7

He remembered that they were but flesh; a wind that passeth away, and cometh not again.   1617

Psalm 78:39

Hatred stirreth up strifes; but love covereth all sins.   1618

Proverbs 10:12

Thou hast played the harlot with many lovers; yet return again to me, saith the Lord.   1619

Jeremiah 3:1

I will forgive their iniquity, and I will remember their sin no more.   1620

Jeremiah 31:34

I will restore to you the years that the locust hath eaten, the cankerworm, and the caterpillar, and the palmerworm, my great army which I sent among you.   1621

Joel 2:25

He retaineth not his anger forever, because he delighteth in mercy.   1622

Micah 7:18

Whosoever shall smite thee on the right cheek, turn to him the other also. 1623

Jesus in Matthew 5:39

Pray for them which despitefully use you, and persecute you.   1624

Jesus in Matthew 5:44

Forgive us our debts, as we forgive our debtors.   1625

Jesus in Matthew 6:12

Be of good cheer: thy sins be forgiven thee.   1626

Jesus in Matthew 9:2

Forgive, and ye shall be forgiven.   1627

Jesus in Luke 6:37

To whom little is forgiven, the same loveth little.   1628

Jesus in Luke 7:47

Father, forgive them; for they know not what they do.   1629

Jesus in Luke 23:34

Through this man is preached unto you the forgiveness of sins.   1630

Acts 13:38

Bless them which persecute you: bless, and curse not.   1631

Romans 12:14

Let all bitterness, and wrath, and anger, and clamor, and evil speaking, be put away from you, with all malice: And be ye kind one to another, tenderhearted, forgiving one another, even as God for Christ's sake hath forgiven you.   1632

Ephesians 4:31–32

Life is an adventure in forgiveness.   1633

Norman Cousins. *Saturday Review,* 15 April 1978

Forgiveness presupposes remembering.   1634

Paul Tillich, *The Eternal Now*

Miss (Clara) Barton, who never bore grudges, was once reminded by a friend of a wrong done to her some years earlier. "Don't you remember?" asked her friend. "No," replied Clara firmly. "I distinctly remember forgetting that."   1635

> The Little, Brown Book of Anecdotes, edited and compiled by Clifton Fadiman.

Since nothing we intend is ever faultless, and nothing we attempt is ever without error, and nothing we achieve without some measure of finitude and fallibility we call humanness, we are saved by forgiveness.   1636

> David Augsburger, Caring Enough to Forgive

It is easier to forgive an enemy than a friend.   1637

> William Blake, Jerusalem

All human activity is a cry for forgiveness.   1638

> Karl Barth, The Epistle to the Romans

Every person should have a special cemetery lot in which to bury the faults of friends and loved ones.   1639

> Author Unknown

"To forgive oneself"—? No, that doesn't work: we have to be forgiven. But we can believe this is possible only if we ourselves can forgive.   1640

> Dag Hammarskjöld, Markings

To forgive is to set a prisoner free and discover the prisoner was YOU.   1641

> Author Unknown

Forgiveness is the fragrance a violet sheds on the heel that has crushed it.   1642

> Mark Twain

Wherever God pardons sin, He subdues it. "He will have compassion on us, he will subdue our iniquity" (Micah 7:19). Where men's persons are justified, their lusts are mortified. There is in sin a commanding and a condemning power. The condemning power of sin is taken away. We know our sins are forgiven when they are subdued.   1643

> Thomas Watson, The Golden Treasury of Puritan Quotations

What we talked about will have to remain a secret between him and me. I spoke to him as a brother whom I have pardoned and who has my complete trust.   1644

> Pope John Paul II, after visiting in prison Mehmet Ali Agca, who had wounded him in an assassination attempt in 1981. Time, 9 January 1984

For both parties, forgiveness means the freedom again to be at peace inside their own skins and to be glad in each other's presence.   1645

> Frederick Buechner, Wishful Thinking: A Theological ABC

Freedom

Moses and Aaron went in and told Pharaoh, Thus saith the Lord God of Israel, let my people go.   1646

> Exodus 5:1

145

It had been better for us to serve the Egyptians, than that we should die in the wilderness.   1647
    Exodus 14:12

Proclaim liberty throughout all the land unto all the inhabitants thereof.   1648
    Leviticus 25:10

The small and great are there; and the servant is free from his master.   1649
    Job 3:19

He bringeth out those which are bound with chains.   1650
    Psalm 68:6

Ye shall know the truth, and the truth shall make you free.   1651
    Jesus in John 8:32

If the Son therefore shall make you free, ye shall be free indeed.   1652
    Jesus in John 8:36

Where the Spirit of the Lord is, there is liberty.   1653
    2 Corinthians 3:17

Christ hath made us free.   1654
    Galatians 5:1

Use not liberty for an occasion of the flesh.   1655
    Galatians 5:13

Since the Exodus, Freedom has always spoken with a Hebrew accent.   1656
    Heinrich Heine, *Germany to Luther*

No one can be perfectly free till all are free; no one can be perfectly moral till all are moral; no one can be perfectly happy till all are happy.   1657
    Herbert Spencer, *Social Statics*

We are free when our actions emanate from our total personality, when they express it, when they resemble it in the indefinable way a work of art sometimes does the artist.   1658
    Henri Bergson, *Essay on the immediate gifts of the conscience*

The waterfall sings, "I find my song when I find my freedom."   1659
    Rabindranath Tagore, *Stray Birds*

We have confused the free with the free and easy.   1660
    Adlai E. Stevenson, *Putting First Things First*

O Freedom, what liberties are taken in thy name!   1661
    Daniel George, *The Perpetual Pessimist*

There is always more than one way to go, and we are forced to be free—we are free against our will—and have the audacity to choose, rarely knowing how or why.   1662
    Abraham Heschel, *The Wisdom of Abraham Heschel*

Freedom and slavery are mental states.   1663
    Mohandas K. Gandhi, *Non-Violence in Peace and War*

The liberty of others extends mine to infinity.   1664
    Author Unknown. Graffito during French student revolt, 1968

I was not born to be free—I was born to adore and obey. 1665
> C. S. Lewis, quoted in *C. S. Lewis at the Breakfast Table and Other Reminiscences,* edited by James T. Como

There can be no real freedom without freedom to fail. 1666
> Eric Hoffer, *The Ordeal of Change*

No man is good enough to govern another man without that other's consent. 1667
> Abraham Lincoln. Speech at Peoria, Ill., 16 October 1854

It is by the goodness of God that in our country we have those three unspeakably precious things: freedom of speech, freedom of conscience, and the prudence never to practice either of them. 1668
> Mark Twain, *Pudd'nhead Wilson's New Calendar*

Where the mind is without fear and the head is held high;
Where knowledge is free;
Where the world has not been broken up into fragments of narrow domestic
  walls;
Where words come out from the depth of truth;
Where tireless striving stretches its arms toward perfection;
Where the clear stream of reason has not lost its way into the dreary desert sand
  of dead habit;
Where the mind is led forward by thee into ever-widening thought and action—
Into the heaven of freedom, my Father, let my country awake. 1669
> Rabindranath Tagore, *Gitanjali*

Friendship

Intreat me not to leave thee, or to return from following after thee: for whither thou goest, I will go; and where thou lodgest, I will lodge: thy people shall be my people, and thy God my God: Where thou diest, will I die, and there will I be buried: the Lord do so to me, and more also, if ought but death part thee and me. 1670
> Ruth 1:16–17

The soul of Jonathan was knit with the soul of David, and Jonathan loved him as his own soul. 1671
> 1 Samuel 18:1

My friends scorn me: but mine eye poureth out tears unto God. 1672
> Job 16:20

For it was not an enemy that reproached me; then I could have borne it: neither was it he that hated me that did magnify himself against me; then I would have hid myself from him: But it was thou, a man mine equal, my guide, and mine acquaintance. We took sweet counsel together, and walked unto the house of God in company. 1673
> Psalm 55:12–14

A friend loveth at all times, and a brother is born for adversity. 1674
> Proverbs 17:17

Thine own friend, and thy father's friend, forsake not. 1675
> Proverbs 27:10

Woe to him that is alone when he falleth; for he hath not another to help him up. 1676

Ecclesiastes 4:10

Greater love hath no man than this, that a man lay down his life for his friends. 1677

Jesus in John 15:13

I have called you friends; for all things that I have heard of my Father I have made known unto you. 1678

Jesus in John 15:15

Salute one another with an holy kiss. 1679

Romans 16:16

A man, sir, should keep his friendships in constant repair. 1680

Samuel Johnson. Boswell's *Life,* 1755

A friend is one who comes in when the rest of the world goes out. 1681

Author Unknown

The man who treasures his friends is usually solid gold himself. 1682

Marjorie Holmes, *Love and Laughter*

Friendship needs no words—it is solitude delivered from the anguish of loneliness. 1683

Dag Hammarskjöld, *Markings*

Friendships begin with liking or gratitude—roots that can be pulled up. 1684

George Eliot, *Daniel Deronda*

Friendship is a single soul dwelling in two bodies. 1685

Aristotle. Quoted in Diogenes Laertius, *Lives and Opinions of Eminent Philosophers*

Thou art to me a delicious torment. 1686

Ralph Waldo Emerson, *Essays,* "Friendship"

The friendships which last are those wherein each friend respects the other's dignity to the point of not really wanting anything from him. 1687

Cyril Connolly, *The Unquiet Grave*

In a good friendship people sip rather than gulp one another. 1688

C.E.S.

Future

What God is about to do he showeth unto Pharaoh. 1689

Genesis 41:28

Boast not thyself of the morrow; for thou knowest not what a day may bring forth. 1690

Proverbs 27:1

Take therefore no thought for the morrow: for the morrow shall take thought for the things of itself. 1691

Jesus in Matthew 6:34

Ye ought to say, If the Lord will, we shall live, and do this, or that. 1692
James 4:15

The handwriting on the wall may be a forgery. 1693
Ralph Hodgson. *New York Times,* 22 October 1972

The future isn't what it used to be. 1694
Author unknown, variously ascribed

The future is something which everyone reaches at the same rate of 60 minutes an hour, whatever he does, whoever he be. 1695
C. S. Lewis. Recalled at his death, 22 November 1963

Take from me the hope that I can change the future and you will send me mad. 1696
Israel Zangwill, *The Melting Pot*

The veil that hides the face of the future is woven by the hand of mercy. 1697
Author Unknown

G

Gardens

And the Lord God took the man, and put him into the garden of Eden to dress it
and to keep it.   1698
> Genesis 2:15

When Jesus had spoken these words, he went forth with his disciples over the
brook Cedron, where was a garden, into which he entered, and his disciples.   1699
> John 18:1

Now in the place where he was crucified there was a garden; and in the garden a
new sepulchre, wherein was never man yet laid.   1700
> John 19:41

The kiss of the sun for pardon,
   The song of the birds for mirth,
One is nearer God's Heart in a garden
   Than anywhere else on earth.   1701
> Dorothy Frances Gurney, *God's Garden*

God the first garden made, and the first city Cain.   1702
> Abraham Cowley, *The Garden,* 1664

Generosity

Every man shall give as he is able, according to the blessing of the Lord thy God
which he hath given thee.   1703
> Deuteronomy 16:17

Let her glean even among the sheaves, and reproach her not.   1704
> Ruth 2:15

Send portions unto them for whom nothing is prepared.   1705
> Nehemiah 8:10

The righteous showeth mercy, and giveth.   1706
> Psalm 37:21

He that watereth shall be watered also himself.   1707
> Proverbs 11:25

Give to him that asketh thee, and from him that would borrow of thee turn thou not away. 1708
> Jesus in Matthew 5:42

Freely ye have received, freely give. 1709
> Jesus in Matthew 10:8

Silver and gold have I none; but such as I have give I thee. 1710
> Acts 3:6

It is more blessed to give than to receive. 1711
> Jesus in Acts 20:35

Generosity is the flower of justice. 1712
> Nathaniel Hawthorne, *American Notebooks,* 19 December 1850

Be just before you're generous. 1713
> Richard Brinsley Sheridan, *The School for Scandal*

The world is beholden to generous mistakes for the greatest part of the good that is done in it. 1714
> George Savile, Lord Halifax, *Political, Moral, and Miscellaneous Reflections*

It is better that a man should tyrannize over his bank balance than over his fellow citizen. 1715
> John Maynard Keynes, *General Theory of Employment*

People who think they're generous to a fault usually think that's their only fault. 1716
> Sydney J. Harris, *On the Contrary*

We'd all like a reputation for generosity, and we'd all like to buy it cheap. 1717
> Mignon McLaughlin, *The Neurotic's Notebook*

Gentility

I can make a lord, but only God Almighty can make a gentleman. 1718
> King James I of England, attributed

A gentleman has all the qualities of a saint except saintliness. 1719
> Hugh Kingsmill. Quoted in Michael Holroyd, *Hugh Kingsmill*

It is impossible to be a gentleman and not an abolitionist. For a gentleman is one who is fulfilled with all nobleness, and imparts it; is the natural defender and raiser of the weak and helpless. 1720
> Ralph Waldo Emerson, *Journals,* 1838

There is no such thing as being a gentleman in important moments; it is at unimportant moments that a man is a gentleman. 1721
> G. K. Chesterton, *A Handful of Authors*

It is almost a definition of a gentleman to say that he is one who never inflicts pain. 1722
> John Henry Newman, *The Idea of a University*

Gentleness

Nothing appeases an enraged elephant so much as the sight of a little lamb. 1723
St. Francis de Sales, *Introduction to the Devout Life*

Nothing is so strong as gentleness, and nothing is so gentle as real strength 1724
Ralph W. Sockman. *New York Mirror*, 8 June 1952

Giftedness

A gift of any kind is a considerable responsibility. It is a mystery in itself, gratuitous and wholly undeserved, something whose real uses will probably always be hidden from us. 1725
Flannery O'Connor, *Mystery and Manners*

Gifts, Giving

Every good gift and every perfect gift is from above, and cometh down from the Father of lights. 1726
James 1:17

He that giveth unto the poor shall not lack. 1727
Proverbs 28:27

There are three kinds of giving: grudge giving, duty giving, and thanksgiving. Grudge giving says, "I hate to," duty giving says, "I ought to," thanksgiving says, "I want to." The first comes from constraint, the second comes from a sense of obligation, the third from a full heart. Nothing much is conveyed in grudge giving since "the gift without the giver is bare." Something more happens in duty giving but there is no song in it. Thanksgiving is an open gate into the love of God. 1728
Robert N. Rodenmayer, *Thanks Be to God*

The woodcutter's axe begged for its handle from the tree. The tree gave it. 1729
Rabindranath Tagore, *Stray Birds*

A gift with a kind countenance is a double present. 1730
Thomas Fuller, *Gnomologia*

There is a sublime thieving in all giving. Someone gives us all he has and we are his. 1731
Eric Hoffer, *The Passionate State of Mind*

Glory

Let them that love him be as the sun when he goeth forth in his might. 1732
Judges 5:31

He [David] died in a good old age, full of days, riches, and honor. 1733
1 Chronicles 29:28

In thy light shall we see light. 1734
Psalm 36:9

In God is my salvation and my glory. 1735
Psalm 62:7

Not unto us, O Lord, not unto us, but unto thy name give glory.   1736
    Psalm 115:1

The wise shall inherit glory: but shame shall be the promotion of fools.   1737
    Proverbs 3:35

For men to search their own glory is not glory.   1738
    Proverbs 25:27

We preach not ourselves, but Christ Jesus the Lord; and ourselves your servants for Jesus' sake. For God, who commanded the light to shine out of darkness, hath shined in our hearts, to give the light of the knowledge of the glory of God in the face of Jesus Christ.   1739
    2 Corinthians 4:5–6

If ye be reproached for the name of Christ, happy are ye; for the spirit of glory and of God resteth upon you.   1740
    1 Peter 4:14

Glory is largely a theatrical concept. There is no striving for glory without a vivid awareness of an audience.   1741
    Eric Hoffer, *The True Believer*

The paths of glory lead but to the grave, but so do all other paths.   1742
    George F. Will. *Newsweek,* 27 June 1977

The desire of glory is the last infirmity cast off even by the wise.   1743
    Tacitus, *Histories*

May God deny you peace, but give you glory!   1744
    Miguel de Unamuno, *Tragic Sense of Life,* closing words

That the glory of this world is appearance leaves the world more glorious, if we feel it is a show of some fuller splendor.   1745
    F. H. Bradley, *Principles of Logic*

Gluttony

A glutton is a man who raids the icebox for a cure for spiritual malnutrition.   1746
    Frederick Buechner, *Wishful Thinking: A Theological ABC*

God

And Moses said unto God, Behold, when I come unto the children of Israel, and shall say unto them, The God of your fathers hath sent me unto you, and they shall say to me, What is his name? what shall I say unto them? And God said unto Moses, I AM THAT I AM: and he said, Thus shalt thou say unto the children of Israel, I AM hath sent me unto you.   1747
    Exodus 3:13–14

If the concept of God has any validity or any use, it can only be to make us larger, freer, and more loving. If God cannot do this, then it is time we got rid of Him. 1748
    James Baldwin. *The New Yorker,* 7 November 1962, "Down at the Cross"

God is beyond in the midst of our life. 1749
> Dietrich Bonhoeffer, *Letters and Papers from Prison*

What is the prose for God? 1750
> Harley Granville-Parker, *Waste*

The Lord God is subtle, but malicious he is not. (*Raffiniert ist der Herr Gott, aber Boshaft ist er nicht.*) 1751
> Albert Einstein, quip carved above the fireplace of Fine Hall, the
> Mathematical Institute of Princeton University

What do people mean when they say, "I'm not afraid of God because I know He is good"? Have they never been to a dentist? 1752
> C. S. Lewis, *A Grief Observed*

Ah, I wish I knew God's private address. 1753
> Stanislaw J. Lec, *Unkempt Thoughts*

Even bein' God ain't a bed of roses. 1754
> Mark Connelly, *The Green Pastures*

It is visible *that* God is, it is invisible *what* He is. 1755
> Stephen Charnock, *The Golden Treasury of Puritan Quotations*

God is a sea of infinite substance. 1756
> St. John of Damascus, *Concerning the Orthodox Faith*

God is an unutterable sigh, lying in the depths of the heart. 1757
> Sebastian Franck, a mystical visionary of the Reformation, quoted in
> Hans Küng, *Does God Exist?*

God is indeed a jealous God—
He cannot bear to see
That we had rather not with Him
But with each other play. 1758
> Emily Dickinson, "God is indeed a jealous God"

In making up the character of God, the old theologians failed to mention that He is of infinite cheerfulness. The omission has caused the world much tribulation. 1759
> Michael Monahan, *Palms of Papyrus*

You think about people, but God thinks about you. 1760
> Leo Tolstoy, *Last Diaries*

God and His Creation

See Creation, Creatures

God and Man

I would fain be to the Eternal Goodness what his own hand is to a man. 1761
> Author unknown, *Theologia Germanica*

God made no tools for himself, he needs none; he created himself a partner in the dialogue of time, one who is capable of holding converse with him. 1762
> Martin Buber, *Hasidism*

Man is not an innocent bystander in the cosmic drama. There is in us more kinship with the divine than we are able to believe. The souls of men are candles of the Lord, lit on the cosmic way, rather than fireworks produced by the combustion of nature's explosive compositions, and every soul is indispensable to Him. Man is needed, he is a hand of God.   1763

Abraham Heschel, *The Wisdom of Heschel*

God is God and man is not human. The strength of the one does not necessarily apply to the other. God cannot help but be, but find, but win. Man cannot help but lose, but seek, but die, but live his death.   1764

Elie Wiesel, *The Oath*

God and humanity are like two lovers who have missed their rendezvous. Each is there before the time, but each at a different place, and they wait and wait and wait.   1765

Simone Weil, *Paths of Meditation,* "The Things of the World"

Those who will not become God's sons become His tools.   1766

C. S. Lewis, Preface to *"Paradise Lost"*

Sheer joy is his [God's], and this demands companionship.   1767

St. Thomas Aquinas, *Theological Texts*

"Let God do it all," someone will say; but if man folds his hands, God will go to sleep.   1768

Miguel de Unamuno, *Tragic Sense of Life*

God loves man's lamplight better than his own great stars.   1769

Rabindranath Tagore, *Stray Birds*

You think about people, but God thinks about you.   1770

Leo Tolstoy, *Last Diaries*

God and Miracle

He who says "God" says "miracle."   1771

Karl Barth, *The Epistle to the Romans*

God and We

He puts a little of His love into us and that is how we love one another. When you teach a child writing, you hold its hand while it forms the letters: that is, it forms the letters because you are forming them. We love and reason because God loves and reasons and holds our hand while we do it.   1772

C. S. Lewis, *Mere Christianity*

God designed the human machine to run on Himself.   1773

Ibid.

If God were a Kantian who would not have us till we came to Him from the purest and best motives, who could be saved?   1774

C. S. Lewis, *The Problem of Pain*

God is not finished with me yet.   1775

Jesse Jackson, to Democratic National Convention, 1984

The only time God cannot use us is if we make ourselves unavailable.   1776
Emily Gardiner Neal, *The Healing Ministry*

It is not my business to think about myself. My business is to think about God. It is for God to think about me.   1777
Simone Weil, *Waiting for God*

God utters me like a word containing a partial thought of himself.   1778
Thomas Merton, *New Seeds of Contemplation*

God has his own secret stairway into every heart.   1779
Author Unknown

It is the greatness and heart of the Christian message that God, as manifest in the Christ on the Cross, totally participates in the death of a child, in the condemnation of the criminal, in the disintegration of a mind, in starvation and famine, and even in the human rejection of Himself. There is no human condition into which the divine presence does not penetrate.   1780
Paul Tillich, *The Eternal Now*

When all the strings of my life will be tuned, my Master, then at every touch of thine will come out the music of love.   1781
Rabindranath Tagore, *Stray Birds*

It always strikes me, and it is very peculiar, that when we see the image of indescribable and unutterable desolation—of loneliness, of poverty and misery, the end of all things, or their extreme—then rises in our mind the thought of God.   1782
Vincent van Gogh, *Dear Theo: An Autobiography of Vincent van Gogh*

God likes to be pestered by human beings about their needs.   1783
Morton Kelsey, *Afterlife*

God has no grandchildren; either you know him first-hand or you do not know him at all.   1784
Author Unknown

God's Anger

Wilt thou be angry with us forever? wilt thou draw out thine anger to all generations?   1785
Psalm 85:5

He will not always chide: neither will he keep his anger forever.   1786
Psalm 103:9

God's Caring

"If any one slays Cain, vengeance shall be taken on him sevenfold." And the Lord put a mark on Cain, lest any who came upon him should kill him.   1787
Genesis 4:15, *Revised Standard Version*

Thou shalt not muzzle the ox when he treadeth out the corn.   1788
Deuteronomy 25:4. The command is to allow the working ox to eat of the corn.

There is no God, other than you, who cares for every thing.   1789
Wisdom of Solomon 12:13, The Jerusalem Bible

God's Character

God is not nice. He is not an uncle. God is an earthquake.   1790
Abraham Heschel. Quoted in Peter J. Kreeft, *Love Is Stronger than Death*

God's Comforts

As one whom his mother comforteth, so will I comfort you.   1791
Isaiah 66:13

Thy rod and thy staff they comfort me.   1792
Psalm 23:4

Thy statutes have been my songs in the house of my pilgrimage.   1793
Psalm 119:54

When thou passest through the waters, I will be with thee; and through the rivers, they shall not overflow thee: when thou walkest through the fire, thou shalt not be burned.   1794
Isaiah 43:2

Blessed are they that mourn: for they shall be comforted.   1795
Jesus in Matthew 5:4

I will not leave you comfortless: I will come to you.   1796
Jesus in John 14:18

Blessed be God, even the Father of our Lord Jesus Christ, the Father of mercies, and the God of all comfort, who comforteth us in all our tribulation, that we may be able to comfort them which are in any trouble, by the comfort wherewith we ourselves are comforted of God.   1797
2 Corinthians 1:3–4

God's comforts are for the comforters. His mercies are for the merciful. His consolations are for the consolers. His love is for all, but only those who love in the pattern of Christ's loving can know, appreciate, and enjoy it for what it is.   1798
C.E.S.

God's Coming

He shall come down like rain upon the mown grass: as showers that water the earth.   1799
Psalm 72:6

Have you not heard his silent steps? He comes, comes, ever comes.
Every moment and every age, every day and every night, he comes, comes, ever comes.
Many a song have I sung in many a mood of mind, but all their notes have always proclaimed, "He comes, comes, ever comes."
In the fragrant days of sunny April through the forest path he comes, comes, ever comes.

158

In the rainy gloom of July nights on the thundering chariots of clouds he
comes, comes, ever comes.
In sorrow after sorrow it is his steps that press upon my heart, and it is the golden
touch of his footfall that makes my joy to shine.   1800
Rabindranath Tagore, *Gitanjali*

God's Complaint

Hear, O heavens, and give ear, O earth: for the Lord hath spoken: I have nourished
and brought up children, and they have rebelled against me. The ox knoweth his owner, and the ass his master's crib: but Israel doth not know, my people doth not
consider.   1801
Isaiah 1:2–3

My people have committed two evils: they have forsaken me the fountain of living
waters, and hewed them out cisterns, broken cisterns, that hold no water.   1802
Jeremiah 2:13

God's Concern

When Chesterton was still a schoolboy, he wrote about a book he had read: "What I
like about this novelist is that he takes such trouble about his minor characters." To
the eye of faith it is a matter for unceasing wonder, love and praise how the divine
Author takes such trouble about his minor characters, human and other. As I have
seen written somewhere: "Even the sparrow is a cheeky little somebody to
Him."   1803
C. E. S., *Learning to Believe*

God's Corrections

Whom the Lord loveth he correcteth; even as a father the son in whom he
delighteth.   1804
Proverbs 3:12

God says to man, "I heal you, therefore I hurt; love you, therefore punish." 1805
Rabindranath Tagore, *Stray Birds*

God's Encounter

We shall never encounter God in the moment when that encounter takes place. It's
always afterward that we can say, "So that strange situation, that impression, that
unexplainable event was God."   1806
Jacques Ellul, *Living Faith*

God's Goodness

Thou art not a God that hath pleasure in wickedness.   1807
Psalm 5:4

Surely goodness and mercy shall follow me all the days of my life: and I will dwell
in the house of the Lord forever.   1808
Psalm 23:6

The earth is full of the goodness of the Lord. 1809
Psalm 33:5

He maketh his sun to rise on the evil and on the good, and sendeth rain on the just and on the unjust. 1810
Jesus in Matthew 5:45

Why callest thou me good? There is none good but one, that is, God. 1811
Jesus in Matthew 19:17

The goodness of God leadeth thee to repentance. 1812
Romans 2:4

To most of us it would be very good if God were a rascal. 1813
Author Unknown

When all thy mercies, O my God,
    My rising soul surveys,
Transported with the view, I'm lost
    In wonder, love, and praise. 1814
Joseph Addison, hymn

God is good, He is goodness itself. Goodness is not a measuring rod applicable to everything, including God Himself: it is but another name for God Himself. When the rich young man came to Jesus and addressed Him as "good Master," He answered, "Why callest thou me good? None is good but one, that is God." Goodness is simply God Himself, and the command to be good is His loving will. 1815
Romano Guardini, *The Last Things*

God's Greatness

The nations are as a drop of the bucket, and are counted as the small dust of the balance: behold, he taketh up the isles as a very little thing. 1816
Isaiah 40:15

As the marsh-hen secretly builds on the watery sod,
Behold I will build me a nest on the greatness of God:
I will fly in the greatness of God as the marsh hen flies
In the freedom that fills all the space 'twixt the marsh and the skies:
By so many roots as the marsh grass sends in the sod
I will heartily lay me a-hold on the greatness of God:
Oh, like to the greatness of God is the greatness within
The range of the marshes, the liberal marshes of Glynn. 1817
Sidney Lanier, *The Marshes of Glynn*

God's Happiness

What makes God happy? Seeing a poor devil find a treasure and give it back. 1818
Yiddish Proverb

God's Iconoclasm

Images of the Holy easily become holy images—sacrosanct. My idea of God is not a divine idea. It has to be shattered from time to time. He shatters it Himself. He is the great iconoclast. Could we not almost say that this shattering is one of the marks of His presence?   1010

> C. S. Lewis, *A Grief Observed*

God's Inscrutability

O the depth of the riches both of the wisdom and knowledge of God! how unsearchable are his judgments, and his ways past finding out!   1820

> Romans 11:33

For us God is eternal discovery and eternal growth. The more we think we understand Him, the more He reveals Himself as otherwise. The more we think we hold Him, the further He withdraws, drawing us into the depths of Himself.   1821

> Pierre Teilhard de Chardin, *The Divine Milieu*

Why dost thou prate of God? Whatever thou sayest of him is untrue.   1822

> Meister Eckhart. Quoted in Aldous Huxley, *The Perennial Philosophy*

God's Judgments

Shall not the Judge of all the earth do right?   1823

> Genesis 18:25

The fear of the Lord is clean, enduring for ever; the judgments of the Lord are true and righteous altogether.   1824

> Psalm 19:9

Thy righteousness is like the great mountains; thy judgments are a great deep. . . . the children of men put their trust under the shadow of thy wings.   1825

> Psalm 36:6–7

God differs so fundamentally from an earthly judge that He is concerned not with what men do but with what, in their inmost hearts, they *are*.   1826

> Cyril Alington, *The Life Everlasting*

God's Love

Can a woman forget her sucking child, that she should not have compassion on the son of her womb? yea, they may forget, yet will I not forget thee.   1827

> Isaiah 49:15

Let us fall into the hands of the Lord, not into the hands of men; for as his majesty is, so is his mercy.   1828

> Ecclesiasticus 2:22, *The Jerusalem Bible*

God's love is like a river springing up in the Divine Substance and flowing endlessly through his creation, filling all things with life and goodness and strength.   1829

> Thomas Merton, *New Seeds of Contemplation*

161

This much is certain, that we have no theological right to set any sort of limits to the lovingkindness of God which has appeared in Jesus Christ.　　　1830
Karl Barth, *The Humanity of God*

God's Mercy

I have looked upon my people, because their cry is come unto me.　　　1831
1 Samuel 9:16

My mercy shall not depart away from him.　　　1832
2 Samuel 7:15

Thou art a God ready to pardon.　　　1833
Nehemiah 9:17

Thou, O Lord, art a God full of compassion, and gracious, longsuffering, and plenteous in mercy and truth.　　　1834
Psalm 86:15

His mercy is everlasting.　　　1835
Psalm 100:5

As the heaven is high above the earth, so great is his mercy toward them that fear him.　　　1836
Psalm 103:11

His mercy is on them that fear him from generation to generation.　　　1837
Luke 1:50

I will have mercy on whom I will have mercy, and I will have compassion on whom I will have compassion.　　　1838
Romans 9:15

God gives his wrath by weight, and without weight his mercy.　　　1839
George Herbert, *Jacula Prudentum*

There's a wideness in God's mercy
　Like the wideness of the sea;
There's a kindness in his justice,
　Which is more than liberty.
There is welcome for the sinner,
　And more graces for the good;
There is mercy with the Saviour;
　There is healing in his blood.　　　1840
Frederick William Faber, hymn

God's Nature

The nature of God is a circle whose center is everywhere and whose circumference is nowhere.　　　1841
Author unknown, perhaps from a lost treatise of Empedocles

God according to the Persons is Eternal Work, but according to the Essence and Its perpetual stillness He is Eternal Rest.　　　1842
Jan van Ruysbroeck, *Concerning the Seven Steps of Love*

God's Order

All things began in order, so shall they end, and so shall they begin again, according to the ordainer of order and mystical mathematics of the city of heaven.   1843
Sir Thomas Browne, *The Garden of Cyrus*

God's Personality

Imagine an artist whose inspiration was ceaseless and continually followed by realization. A Shakespeare or a Beethoven constantly at his best. All we can do to form an idea of God's personality should be in that direction, removing limitations all the time. That is prayer and that is adoration!   1844
Ernest Dimnet, *What We Live By*

God's Power

And God said, Let there be light: and there was light.   1845
Genesis 1:3

Is anything too hard for the Lord?   1846
Genesis 18:14

Fear ye not, stand still, and see the salvation of the Lord, which he will show you today.   1847
Exodus 14:13

The Lord brought us forth out of Egypt with a mighty hand, and with an outstretched arm.   1848
Deuteronomy 26:8

The Lord killeth, and maketh alive: he bringeth down to the grave, and bringeth up.   1849
1 Samuel 2:6

He maketh sore, and bindeth up: he woundeth, and his hands make whole. 1850
Job 5:18

He spake, and it was done; he commanded, and it stood fast.   1851
Psalm 33:9

As the clay is in the potter's hand, so are ye in mine hand, O house of Israel. 1852
Jeremiah 18:6

God is able of these stones to raise up children unto Abraham.   1853
Matthew 3:9

For thine is the kingdom, and the power, and the glory, for ever.   1854
Jesus in Matthew 6:13

Father, all things are possible unto thee.   1855
Jesus in Mark 14:36

The Son can do nothing of himself, but what he seeth the Father do.   1856
Jesus in John 5:19

If it be of God, ye cannot overthrow it; lest haply ye be found even to fight against God.   1857

    Acts 5:39

His Omnipotence means power to do all that is intrinsically possible, not to do the intrinsically impossible. You may attribute miracles to Him, but not nonsense. 1858

    C. S. Lewis, *The Problem of Pain*

God's great power is in the gentle breeze, not in the storm.   1859

    Rabindranath Tagore, *Stray Birds*

God is powerless, except for the equitable distribution of the good. He can do nothing else. But that is enough.   1860

    Simone Weil, *Gateway to God*

Energy is Eternal Delight.   1861

    William Blake, *Proverbs of Hell*

All public power proceeds from God.   1862

    Pope Leo XIII, *Immortale Dei*

God's Presence

And the Spirit of God moved upon the face of the waters.   1863

    Genesis 1:2

Surely the Lord is in this place; and I knew it not.   1864

    Genesis 28:16

I will walk among you, and will be your God, and ye shall be my people.   1865

    Leviticus 26:12

We have seen this day that God doth talk with man, and he liveth.   1866

    Deuteronomy 5:24

The Lord thy God is among you, a mighty God and terrible.   1867

    Deuteronomy 7:21

The Lord your God, he is God in heaven above, and in earth beneath.   1868

    Joshua 2:11

Imagine an artist whose inspiration was ceaseless and continually followed by realization. A Shakespeare or a Beethoven constantly at his best. All we can do to form an idea of God's personality should be in that direction, removing limitations all the time. That is prayer and that is adoration!   1869

    Ernest Dimnet, *What We Live By*. (I suggest further that there is no better way than this of forming an idea of God's power. *C.E.S.*)

Upon whom doth not his light arise?   1870

    Job 25:3

He that planted the ear, shall he not hear? He that formed the eye, shall he not see?   1871

    Psalm 94:9

The eyes of the Lord are in every place, beholding the evil and the good.   1872

    Proverbs 15:3

My spirit remaineth among you: fear ye not.   1873
        Haggai 2:5

Ye are the temple of the living God.   1874
        2 Corinthians 6:16

The Lord is at hand.   1875
        Philippians 4:5

God be in my head, and in my understanding;
God be in mine eyes and in my looking;
God be in my mouth, and in my speaking;
God be in my heart, and in my thinking;
God be at mine end, and at my departing.   1876
        Author unknown. *Sarum Primer,* 1558

I need Thy presence every passing hour;
What but Thy grace can foil the tempter's power?
Who, like Thyself, my guide and stay can be?
Through cloud and sunshine, Lord, abide with me.   1877
        Henry Francis Lyte, hymn, "Abide with Me"

Does God seem far away? Guess who moved.   1878
        Author Unknown

To some there is revealed a sacrament greater than that of the Real Presence, a sacrament of the Manifest Presence, which is, and is more than, the sum of all the Sacraments.   1879
        Coventry Patmore, *The Rod, the Root and the Flower*

God's Providence

And he said, I am Joseph your brother, whom ye sold into Egypt. Now therefore be not grieved, nor angry with yourselves, that ye sold me hither: for God did send me before you to preserve life.   1880
        Genesis 45:4–5

Who provideth for the raven his food? when his young ones cry unto God, they wander for lack of meat.   1881
        Job 38:41

If God so clothe the grass of the field, which today is, and tomorrow is cast into the oven, shall he not much more clothe you, O ye of little faith?   1882
        Jesus in Matthew 6:30

God who gives the wounds gives the salve.   1883
        Spanish Proverb

If you leap into a well, Providence is not bound to fetch you out.   1884
        Thomas Fuller, *Gnomologia*

Judge not the Lord by feeble sense,
    But trust him for his grace;

> Behind a frowning providence
>> He hides a smiling face.   1885
>>> William Cowper, hymn, "God Moves in a Mysterious Way"

> Providence is the perpetuity and continuity of creation.   1886
>> Richard Sibbes, *The Golden Treasury of Puritan Quotations*

> Some Providences, like Hebrew letters, must be read backwards. 1887
>> John Flavel, *Ibid.*

> There is a Power whose care
> Teaches thy way along the pathless coast—
> The desert and illimitable air—
> Lone wandering, but not lost.   1888
>> William Cullen Bryant, *To a Waterfowl*

> God will provide—if only God would provide until he provides. 1889
>> Yiddish Proverb

Providence has a wild, rough, incalculable road to its end, and it is of no use to try to whitewash its huge, mixed instrumentalities, or to dress up that terrific benefactor in a clean shirt and white neckcloth of a student in divinity.   1890
> Ralph Waldo Emerson, *The Conduct of Life*

God's Secrets

Where wast thou when I laid the foundations of the earth? declare, if thou hast understanding.   1891
> Job 38:4

The secret of the Lord is with them that fear him; and he will show them his covenant.   1892
> Psalm 25:14

My substance was not hid from thee, when I was made in secret, and curiously wrought in the lowest parts of the earth.   1893
> Psalm 139:15

> The Almighty has His own purposes.   1894
>> Abraham Lincoln, *Second Inaugural Address,* 4 March 1865

As there is a foolish wisdom, so there is a wise ignorance in not prying into God's ark, not inquiring into things not revealed. I would fain know all that I need, and all that I may: I leave God's secrets to Himself. It is happy for me that God makes me of His court though not of His council.   1895
> Joseph Hall, *The Golden Treasury of Puritan Quotations*

God's Silence

> God's silence ripens man's thoughts into speech.   1896
>> Rabindranath Tagore, *Stray Birds*

> O Sabbath rest by Galilee!
>> O calm of hills above,
> Where Jesus knelt to share with Thee

The silence of eternity
Interpreted by love!   1897
John Greenleaf Whittier, hymn, "Dear Lord and Father of Mankind"

God's Talk

God language is fundamentally functional—not propositional.   1898
Joseph Sittler, *Gravity and Grace*

Talk of God that does not, in the last resort, *emerge from silence and lead again into silence* does not know with whom it is dealing.   1899
Hans Küng, *Does God Exist?*

I have heard students talking about the attributes of God in a way that made me feel ashamed. They knew everything "about" God, except that he was listening to them. They showed no signs of shame. They were theological students.   1900
Eugen Rosenstock-Huessy. Quoted in J. H. Oldham, *Life Is Commitment*

God's Thoughts and Ways

For my thoughts are not your thoughts, neither are your ways my ways, saith the Lord.   1901
Isaiah 55:8

God's View of the March of Time

Those who quote that fine passage which says that in God's sight a thousand years are as yesterday when it is past and as a watch in the night, do not realize the full force of the meaning. To God a thousand years are not only a watch but an exciting watch. For God time goes at a gallop, as it does to a man reading a good tale.   1902
G. K. Chesterton. Introduction to Charles Dickens, *Nicholas Nickleby*

God's Whispers

And behold, the Lord passed by, and a great and strong wind rent the mountains, and brake in pieces the rocks before the Lord; but the Lord was not in the wind: and after the wind an earthquake; but the Lord was not in the earthquake: and after the earthquake a fire; but the Lord was not in the fire: and after the fire a still small voice.   1903
1 Kings 19:11–12

Breathe through the heats of our desire
    Thy coolness and thy balm:
Let sense be dumb, let flesh retire;
Speak through the earthquake, wind, and fire,
O still small voice of calm!   1904
John Greenleaf Whittier, hymn, "Dear Lord and Father of Mankind"

Ores you'll find there, wood and cattle; water-transit sure and steady
    (That should keep the railway-rates down), coal and iron at your doors.

God took care to hide that country till He judged His people ready,
    Then He chose me for His Whisper, and I've found it, and it's yours!

Yes, your "Never-never country"—yes, your "edge of cultivation"
    And "no sense in going further"—till I crossed the range to see.
God forgive me! No, *I* didn't. It's God's present to our nation.
    Anybody might have found it, but—His Whisper came to Me!   1905
        Rudyard Kipling, *The Explorer,* closing stanzas

I have learnt the simple meanings of thy whispers in flowers and sunshine—teach
me to know thy words in pain and death.   1906
        Rabindranath Tagore, *Stray Birds*

God's Will

It is the Lord: let him do what seemeth him good.   1907
    1 Samuel 3:18

Thy will be done in earth, as it is in heaven.   1908
    Jesus in Matthew 6:10

Not my will, but thine, be done.   1909
    Jesus in Luke 22:42

The world passeth away, and the lust thereof: but he that doeth the will of God
abideth forever.   1910
    1 John 2:14

Man cannot *not* do God's will. Even the wicked obey him. If their negation has any
strength, it is his. Fortunately for them, they are not aware of it. If they were, they
would die of spite.   1911
        Rebbe Israel of Bizhim. Quoted in Elie Wiesel, *Souls on Fire*

Brother Francis, are you so sorry because the brothers defied the will of God, or
because they defied *your* will?   1912
        Brother Elias, to St. Francis of Assisi. Quoted in Reinhold Niebuhr,
        Justice and Mercy

A possibility is a hint from God.   1913
        Søren Kierkegaard, quoted in *The New Book of Christian
        Quotations,* edited by Tony Castle

I just want to do God's will. And He's allowed me to go to the mountain. And I've
looked over, and I've seen the promised land . . . So I'm happy tonight. I'm not worried
about anything. I'm not fearing any man.   1914
        Martin Luther King, Jr. Speech at Birmingham, Alabama,
        3 April 1968, the evening before his assassination.

He who works for sweetness and light united, works to make reason and the will of
God prevail.   1915
        Matthew Arnold, *Culture and Anarchy*

God's Word

The word is very nigh unto thee, in thy mouth, and in thy heart.   1916
    Deuteronomy 30:14

They shall run to and fro to seek the word of the Lord, and shall not find it. 1917
Amos 8:12

In the beginning was the Word, and the Word was with God, and the Word was God. 1918
John 1:1

My doctrine is not mine, but his that sent me. 1919
Jesus in John 7:16

Let the word of Christ dwell in you richly in all wisdom; teaching and admonishing one another in psalms and hymns and spiritual songs, singing with grace in your hearts to the Lord. 1920
Colossians 3:16

The word of God is quick, and powerful, and sharper than any two-edged sword, piercing even to the dividing asunder of soul and spirit, and of the joints and marrow, and is a discerner of the thoughts and intents of the heart. 1921
Hebrews 4:12

The grass withereth, and the flower thereof falleth away: But the word of the Lord endureth forever. 1922
1 Peter 1:24–25

"The Word became flesh and dwelt among us" (John 1:14). What do we mean when we refer to the Word of God? Primarily we do not mean Scripture; there was a Word of God before there was any Bible. The Hebrew term for word, *davar,* does not primarily mean something we say or write; it means that the creative force of God himself goes out of himself to do something.

There developed a body of literature written by a people who had been made a people by that force, and their writings are called the Word of God. The ultimate meaning of Word is not a document; but the documents were preserved by the ancient Hebrews and the early church because they testified, they bore witness, to the force of the Word. The people had experienced it, and they were transformed by it. 1923
Joseph Sittler, *Gravity & Grace*

God in His Creating

God finds himself by creating. 1924
Rabindranath Tagore, *Stray Birds*

Let me feel this world as thy love taking form, then my love can help it. 1925
Ibid.

Is it not certain that the Creator yawns in earthquake and thunder and other popular displays, but toils in rounding the delicate spiral of a shell? 1926
William Butler Yeats, *Autobiography*

God has plans which mortals don't understand. He rests in the womb when the new baby forms. Whispers the life dream to infinitesimal cells. It is God who lies under the thoughts of man. He is cartilege. Memory. 1927
Ellease Southerland, *Let the Lion Eat Straw*

All things have come out of nothingness and are carried onwards to infinity. Who can follow these astonishing processes? The author of these wonders understands them; no one else can.

God is in the lowest effects as well as the highest causes, for he is become a worm that he may nourish the weak.   1928

William Blake, *The Marginalia,* "Annotations to Lavater"

Godliness

I am my Father's child, not his counselor.   1929

Gerhard Tersteegen, attributed

I live and love in God's peculiar light.   1930

Michelangelo Buonarrati, *Sonnet*

Good and Evil

See, I have set before thee this day life and good, and death and evil.   1931

Deuteronomy 30:15

Give therefore thy servant an understanding heart to judge thy people, that I may discern between good and bad.   1932

1 Kings 3:9

When I looked for good, then evil came unto me: and when I waited for light, there came darkness.   1933

Job 30:26

The eyes of the Lord are in every place, beholding the evil and the good.   1934

Proverbs 15:3

Woe unto them that call evil good, and good evil.   1935

Isaiah 5:20

Seek good, and not evil, that ye may live.   1936

Amos 5:14

He maketh his sun to rise on the evil and on the good, and sendeth rain on the just and on the unjust.   1937

Jesus in Matthew 5:45

Every good tree bringeth forth good fruit; but a corrupt tree bringeth forth evil fruit.   1938

Jesus in Matthew 7:17

Be not overcome of evil, but overcome evil with good.   1939

Romans 12:21

Goodness is, so to speak, itself; badness is only spoiled goodness.   1940

C. S. Lewis, *Mere Christianity*

When the people of the world all know beauty as beauty,
There arises the recognition of ugliness.
When they all know the good as good,
There arises the recognition of evil.   1941

Lao-tzu, *The Way of Lao-tzu*

There is no odor so bad as that which arises from goodness tainted. It is human, it is divine, carrion.   1942

    Henry David Thoreau, *Walden*

There is so much good in the worst of us,
And so much bad in the best of us,
That it hardly becomes any of us
To talk about the rest of us.   1943

    Author unknown, variously attributed

No man better knows what good is than he who hath endured evil.   1944

    John Ray, *English Proverbs,* 1670

As it is said of the greatest liar that he tells more truth than falsehood, so it may be said of the worst man that he does more good than evil.   1945

    Samuel Johnson. Boswell's *Life,* 3 April 1778

I always said to people that society consists of two forces fighting one another, good and evil. There's talent on both sides, but there's more talent on the side of evil. Make no mistake. They hire the best brains, the best people.   1946

    Alex Rose, New York Liberal Party Leader. Obituary in
    New York Post, 28 December 1976

Good Friday

Christmas and Easter can be subjects for poetry. But Good Friday, like Auschwitz, cannot.   1947

    W. H. Auden, *A Certain World*

Goodness

Thou art not a God that hath pleasure in wickedness.   1948

    Psalm 5:4

Mark the perfect man, and behold the upright: for the end of that man is peace.   1949

    Psalm 37:37

Whatever good thing any man doeth, the same shall he receive of the Lord. 1950

    Ephesians 6:8

Goodness is not felicity, but the road thither.   1951

    Thomas Overbury, *News from Any Whence*

No good deed goes unpunished.   1952

    Clare Boothe Luce. Quoted in Wilfred Ward, *Clare Boothe Luce*

It is amazing how complete is the delusion that beauty is goodness.   1953

    Leo Tolstoy. Quoted in *365 Quotes, Maxims & Proverbs Calendar
    1990,* compiled by Debby Roth

Goodness is uneventful. It does not flash, it glows.   1954

    David Grayson (Ray Stannard Baker), *Adventures in Contentment*

Good men are not those who now and then do a good act, but men who join one good act to another. 1955

Henry Ward Beecher, *Proverbs from Plymouth Pulpit*

A man is only as good as what he loves. 1956

Saul Bellow, *Seize the Day*

May the good God pardon all good men. 1957

Elizabeth Barrett Browning, *Aurora Leigh*

Loving-kindness is the better part of goodness. It lends grace to the sterner qualities of which this consists. 1958

W. Somerset Maugham, *The Summing Up*

Good people are good because they've come to wisdom through failure. 1959

William Saroyan, in *New York Journal American,* 23 August 1961

An act of goodness, the least act of true goodness, is indeed the best proof of the existence of God. 1960

Jacques Maritain, *Approaches to God*

Most people who contemplate the life of Jesus consider that what they see in him is a superhuman goodness. They are wrong. What they see in him is a *completely human* goodness. Because they've never seen it in anybody else (for it has never been in anybody else) they don't know it when they see it in him. How could they? 1961

C.E.S.

Gospel

Repent ye, and believe the gospel. 1962

Jesus in Mark 1:15

Whosoever shall lose his life for my sake and the gospel's, the same shall save it. 1963

Jesus in Mark 8:35

The gospel must first be published among all nations. 1964

Jesus in Mark 13:10

Go ye into all the world, and preach the gospel to every creature. 1965

Jesus in Mark 16:15

Man shall not live by bread alone, but by every word of God. 1966

Jesus in Luke 4:4

He hath anointed me to preach the gospel to the poor. 1967

Jesus in Luke 4:18

Blessed are they that hear the word of God, and keep it. 1968

Jesus in Luke 11:28

I am not ashamed of the gospel of Christ: for it is the power of God unto salvation to every one that believeth. 1969

Romans 1:16

How beautiful are the feet of them that preach the gospel of peace. 1970

Romans 10:15

The Church conquered, not because of the Christians, but in spite of them—by the power of the Gospels. 1971

> Rudolph Sohm, *Outlines of Church History*

The music of the Gospel leads us home. 1972

> Frederick William Faber, *Oratory Hymns*, "The Pilgrims of the Night"

The news that spread around the Mediterranean like wildfire was not "love your neighbor" but "now is Christ risen!" Both are good, but the second is good *news*. 1973

> Peter J. Kreeft, *Everything You Ever Wanted to Know About Heaven—But Never Dreamed of Asking*

The Gospel faithfully preached meddles with everything else on earth. 1974

> Henry Ward Beecher, *Proverbs from Plymouth Pulpit*

Crash programs and promise of instant cures belong to Batten, Barton, Durstin, and Osborne—not to Matthew, Mark, Luke, and John. 1975

> Ernest T. Campbell, *Locked in a Room with Open Doors*

Gossip

Thou shalt not go up and down as a talebearer among thy people. 1976

> Leviticus 19:16

A whisperer separateth chief friends. 1977

> Proverbs 16:28

The words of a talebearer are as wounds. 1978

> Proverbs 18:8

Where no wood is, there the fire goeth out: so where there is no talebearer, the strife ceaseth. 1979

> Proverbs 26:20

Hast thou heard a word against thy neighbor? Let it die within thee, trusting that it will not burst thee. 1980

> Ecclesiasticus 19:10, *The Jerusalem Bible*

If all knew what others say of them, there would not be four friends upon earth. 1981

> Blaise Pascal, *Pensées*

Little people like to talk about what the great are doing. 1982

> German Proverb

Whoever gossips to you will gossip of you. 1983

> Spanish Proverb

Government

Provide out of all the people able men, such as fear God, men of truth, hating covetousness. 1984

> Exodus 18:21

The God of Israel said, the Rock of Israel spake to me, He that ruleth over men must be just, ruling in the fear of God. And he shall be as the light of the morning . . . even a morning without clouds; as the tender grass springing out of the earth by clear shining after rain.   1985

> 2 Samuel 23:3–4

Blessed is the nation whose God is the Lord.   1986

> Psalm 33:12

It is better to trust in the Lord than to put confidence in princes.   1987

> Psalm 118:9

By me kings reign, and princes decree justice. By me princes rule, and nobles, even all the judges of the earth. (*me: wisdom.*)   1988

> Proverbs 8:15–16

Righteousness exalteth a nation: but sin is a reproach to any people.   1989

> Proverbs 14:34

When the righteous are in authority, the people rejoice: but when the wicked beareth rule, the people mourn.   1990

> Proverbs 29:2

Woe unto them that decree unrighteous decrees.   1991

> Isaiah 10:1

If a kingdom be divided against itself, that kingdom cannot stand.   1992

> Jesus in Mark 3:24

Whether it be right in the sight of God to hearken unto you more than unto God, judge ye.   1993

> Acts 4:19

Let every soul be subject unto the higher powers. For there is no power but of God: the powers that be are ordained of God.   1994

> Romans 13:1

Fear God. Honor the king.   1995

> 1 Peter 2:17

The constitution of a country should not violate the constitutions of its people.   1996

> Stanislaw J. Lec, *Unkempt Thoughts*

A government which robs Peter to pay Paul can always depend on the support of Paul.   1997

> Bernard Shaw. Quoted in Robert Byrne, *The 637 Best Things Anybody Ever Said*

Government by the people is possible, but highly improbable.   1998

> J. William Fulbright, *Fund for the Republic* pamphlet, 1963

The worst thing in the world, next to anarchy, is government.   1999

> Henry Ward Beecher, *Proverbs from Plymouth Pulpit*

A government big enough to give you everything you want is a government big enough to take away everything you have.   2000

> Gerald Ford. Address to Congress, 12 August 1974

When there is a lack of honor in government, the morals of the whole people are poisoned. 2001

> Herbert Hoover, recalled on eve of his 90th birthday.
> *New York Times,* 9 August 1964

The natural progress of things is for liberty to yield and government to gain ground. 2002

> Thomas Jefferson, in letter to Carrington, 1788

To govern means to rectify. 2003

> Confucius, *Analects*

Government is a sign of the divine grace, of the mercy of God, who has no pleasure in murdering, killing, and strangling. If God left all things to go which way they would, as among the Turks and other nations, without good government, we should quickly dispatch one another out of this world. 2004

> Martin Luther, *Table Talk*

If men be good, government cannot be bad. 2005

> William Penn, *Some Fruits of Solitude*

What I must not do, the government must not do. 2006

> Author Unknown

Grace

For the Lord God is a sun and shield: the Lord will give grace and glory: no good thing will he withhold from them that walk uprightly. 2007

> Psalm 84:11

The law was given by Moses, but grace and truth came by Jesus Christ. 2008

> John 1:17

My grace is sufficient for thee: for my strength is made perfect in weakness. 2009

> 2 Corinthians 12:9

By grace are ye saved through faith. 2010

> Ephesians 2:8

Grace is young glory. 2011

> Alexander Peden, *The Golden Treasury of Puritan Quotations*

And why not grace? Why not God's grace, hey? . . . We walk upon it, we breathe it; we live and die by it; it makes the nails and axles of the universe; and a puppy in pyjamas prefers self-conceit! 2012

> Robert Louis Stevenson. Quoted in A. E. Taylor, *The Faith of a Moralist*

Remember, grace is pouring in on you *all the time* and it is not conditioned by the fact that your eyes are shut. 2013

> Evelyn Underhill, *The Letters of Evelyn Underhill*

Heaven goes by favor. If it went by merit, you would stay out and your dog would go in. 2014

> Mark Twain, *Pudd'nhead Wilson's Calendar*

Nature fulfilled by grace is not less natural, but is supernaturally natural. 2015
Coventry Patmore, *The Rod, the Root and the Flower*

The gracious in heart are always spacious in mind. The spacious in mind are not always gracious in heart. 2016
C.E.S.

Gratitude

Remember this day, in which ye came out from Egypt, out of the house of bondage. 2017
Exodus 13:3

Blessed be the Lord, because he hath heard the voice of my supplications. 2018
Psalm 28:6

He that is mighty hath done to me great things: and holy is his name. 2019
Luke 1:49

Thanks be to God, which giveth us the victory through our Lord Jesus Christ. 2020
1 Corinthians 15:57

Every creature of God is good, and nothing to be refused, if it be received with thanksgiving. 2021
1 Timothy 4:4

Gratitude is from the same root word as "grace," which signifies the free and boundless mercy of God. Thanksgiving is from the same root as "think," so that to think is to thank. 2022
Willis P. King, *Pulpit Preaching*

Gratitude is the rosemary of the heart. 2023
Minna Antrim, *Naked Truth and Veiled Allusions*

Gratitude is a necessity of all life; it is love looking at the past as faith is love intending the future, and hope is the motion of the shy consciousness of love in the present self; and gratitude, like love, is its own sufficiency. 2024
Charles Williams, *He Came Down From Heaven*

Gratitude is a fruit of great cultivation; you do not find it among gross people. 2025
Samuel Johnson. Boswell's *Journal of a Tour of the Hebrides,*
20 September 1773

William Kingston, the man born without arms, came to see me of his own accord. Some time since he received a clear sense of the favor of God. 2026
John Wesley, *Journal,* 31 August 1790

No metaphysician ever felt the deficiency of language so much as the grateful. 2027
Charles Caleb Colton, *Lacon*

Lambs have the grace to suck kneeling. 2028
Chinese Proverb

Great and Small

We find great things are made of little things,
And little things go lessening till at last
Comes God behind them.   2029
Robert Browning, Mr. Sludge, the Medium

A great man stands on God. A small man stands on a great one.   2030
Ralph Waldo Emerson, *Journals,* 1839

Great engines turn on small pivots.   2031
English Proverb

All things bright and beautiful,
   All creatures great and small,
All things wise and wonderful,
   The Lord God made them all.   2032
Cecil Frances Alexander, *Hymns for Little Children*

A small leak will sink a great ship.   2033
Thomas Fuller, *Gnomologia*

Greatness

Great men are not always wise: neither do the aged understand judgment.   2034
Job 32:9

Whosoever shall do and teach them, the same shall be called great in the kingdom of heaven. (*them: commandments.*)   2035
Jesus in Matthew 5:19

He that is least among you all, the same shall be great.   2036
Jesus in Luke 9:48

He who stays not in his own littleness loses his greatness.   2037
St. Francis de Sales, *Letters to Persons in Religion*

Men did not love Rome because she was great. She was great because men loved her.   2038
G. K. Chesterton, *Charles Dickens*

If I am a great man, then a good many of the great men of history are frauds.   2039
Andrew Bonar Law, said to Sir Max Aitken during the Ulster crisis.
The Penguin Book of Modern Quotations

The great man is he who does not lose his child's heart.   2040
Mencius, *Works*

The glory of great men must always be measured against the means they have used to acquire it.   2041
François de la Rochefoucald, *Maxims*

My greatness depends upon *reality's* greatness.   2042
Peter J. Kreeft, *Everything You Ever Wanted to Know About Heaven—But Never Dreamed of Asking*

177

Desire of greatness is a godlike sin. 2043

John Dryden, *Essay on Satire*

In *King Lear* (III, vii) there is a man who is such a minor character that Shakespeare has not given him even a name: he is merely "First Servant." All the characters around him—Regan, Cornwall, and Edmund—have fine long-term plans. They think they know how the story is going to end, and they are quite wrong. The servant has no such delusions. He has no notion how the play is going to go. But he understands the present scene. He sees an abomination (the blinding of old Gloucester) taking place. And he will not stand it. His sword is out and pointed at his master's breast in a moment: then Regan stabs him dead from behind. That is the whole part: eight lines all told. But if it were real life and not a play, that is the part it would be best to have acted. 2044

C. S. Lewis, *The World's Last Night*

Gathered at the Passover feast, the disciples were keenly aware that someone needed to wash the others' feet. The problem was that the only people who washed feet were the least. So there they sat, feet caked with dirt. It was such a sore point that they were not even going to talk about it. No one wanted to be considered the least. Then Jesus took a towel and basin and redefined greatness. 2045

Richard C. Foster, *The Celebration of Discipline*

Greed

There shall cleave nought of the cursed thing to thine hand. 2046

Deuteronomy 13:17

Will ye even sell your brethren? 2047

Nehemiah 5:8

Better is a little with righteousness than great revenues without right. 2048

Proverbs 16:8

Hell and destruction are never full; so the eyes of man are never satisfied. 2049

Proverbs 27:20

He that maketh haste to be rich shall not be innocent. 2050

Proverbs 28:20

Woe to those who add house to house
and join field to field
until everything belongs to them
and they are the sole inhabitants of the land. 2051

Isaiah 5:8, *The Jerusalem Bible*

Beware of covetousness. 2052

Jesus in Luke 12:15

Having food and raiment let us be therewith content. 2053

1 Timothy 6:8

The love of money is the root of all evil. 2054

1 Timothy 6:10

Big mouthfuls often choke.   2055
>Italian Proverb

It is not greedy to enjoy a good dinner, anymore than it is greedy to enjoy a good concert. But I do think there is something greedy about trying to enjoy the dinner and the concert at the same time.   2056
>G. K. Chesterton, *Generally Speaking*

Grief

If I am bereaved of my children, I am bereaved.   2057
>Genesis 43:14

Would God I had died for thee, O Absalom, my son, my son!   2058
>2 Samuel 18:33

The Lord is nigh unto them that are of a broken heart; and saveth such as be of a contrite spirit.   2059
>Psalm 34:18

They that sow in tears shall reap in joy. He that goeth forth and weepeth, bearing precious seed, shall doubtless come again with rejoicing, bringing his sheaves with him.   2060
>Psalm 126:5–6

Weep not for me, but weep for yourselves, and for your children.   2061
>Jesus in Luke 23:28

We must learn to grieve. Perhaps that is the supreme wisdom.   2062
>Miguel de Unamuno, *Tragic Sense of Life*

It is only one's own dead who matter.   2063
>E. M. Forster, *A Passage to India*

Between grief and nothing I will take grief.   2064
>William Faulkner, *The Wild Palms*

Grief is a species of idleness.   2065
>Samuel Johnson, to Mrs. Thrale. Boswell's *Life,* 17 March 1773

Social scientists who study grief say that the death of a spouse is the "worst" emotional experience and the death of a child the second worst. There are no second worsts.   2066
>Martin E. Marty, *The Christian Century,* July 1–8, 1987

Grief has a natural eloquence belonging to it, and breaks out in more moving sentiments than can be supplied by the finest imagination.   2067
>Joseph Addison, *The Spectator,* 5 June 1712

Grief is itself a medicine.   2068
>William Cowper, *Charity*

Grief is the agony of an instant; the indulgence of grief the blunder of a life. 2069
>Benjamin Disraeli, *Vivian Grey*

Those who have known grief seldom seem sad.   2070
>Benjamin Disraeli, *Endymion*

Growing Up

Forgetting the injustices and seeming injustices which one has suffered from one's parents during childhood and youth must be the major part of any maturing process. 2071
Peter Taylor, *A Summons to Memphis*

When it comes time to do your own life, you either perpetuate your childhood or you stand on it and finally kick it out from under. 2072
Rosellen Brown, *Civil Wars*

No one over thirty-five is worth meeting who has not something to teach us—something more than we could learn by ourselves, from a book. 2073
Cyril Connolly, *The Unquiet Grave*

Growth

Can the rush grow up without mire? can the flag grow without water? 2074
Job 8:11

He shall be like a tree planted by the rivers of water, that bringeth forth his fruit in his season; his leaf also shall not wither; and whatsoever he doeth shall prosper. (*He: the godly man.*) 2075
Psalm 1:3

The righteous shall flourish like the palm tree: he shall grow like a cedar in Lebanon. 2076
Psalm 92:12

A little one shall become a thousand, and a small one a strong nation. 2077
Isaiah 60:22

For the earth bringeth forth fruit of herself; first the blade, then the ear, after that the full corn in the ear. 2078
Jesus in Mark 4:28

And Jesus increased in wisdom and stature, and in favor with God and man. 2079
Luke 2:52

I have planted, Apollos watered; but God gave the increase. So then neither is he that planteth any thing, neither he that watereth; but God that giveth the increase. 2080
1 Corinthians 3:6–7

Man is a born child, his power is the power of growth. 2081
Rabindranath Tagore, *Stray Birds*

Why stay we on earth except to grow? 2082
Robert Browning, *Cleon*

Men never grow up to manhood as an acorn grows up into an oak-tree. Men come to it by re-births in every faculty, again, and again, and again. 2083
Henry Ward Beecher, *Proverbs from Plymouth Pulpit*

Every man's road in life is marked by the graves of his personal likings. 2084
Alexander Smith, *Dreamthorp*

180

The pains of being a Christian are all growing pains, and growing pains beset only the growing. 2085
> C.E.S.

Guidance

The Lord went before them by day in a pillar of a cloud, to lead them the way; and by night in a pillar of fire, to give them light. 2086
> Exodus 13:21

If I have found grace in thy sight, show me now thy way, that I may know thee. 2087
> Exodus 33:13

Thou art my lamp, O Lord. 2088
> 2 Samuel 22:29

He leadeth me besidqe the still waters. 2089
> Psalm 23:2

The meek will he guide in judgment: and the meek will he teach his way. 2090
> Psalm 25:9

Teach me thy way, O Lord, and I will walk in thy truth. 2091
> Psalm 86:11

Thy word is a lamp unto my feet, and a light unto my path. 2092
> Psalm 119:105

The words of the wise are as goads. 2093
> Ecclesiastes 12:11

The Lord shall be unto thee an everlasting light. 2094
> Isaiah 60:19

I am the light of the world. 2095
> Jesus in John 8:12

God leads every soul by a separate path. 2096
> St. John of the Cross, *Living Flame of Love*

O Lord, guide us aright, for we are verra, verra determined! 2097
> Author unknown, A Scottish preacher

We need to learn to set our course by the stars and not by every passing ship. 2098
> General Omar Bradley, attributed

Scared squirrels stand still
To hear the guidance within;
So should scared people. 2099
> Beverley L. Jolousek. *The Living Church,* "Inner Wisdom,"
> 15 October 1972

He that is down needs fear no fall,
    He that is low no pride.
He that is humble ever shall
    Have God to be his guide. 2100
> John Bunyan, *The Pilgrim's Progress,* "Shepherd Boy's Song"

Guilt

Who told thee that thou wast naked?   2101
        Genesis 3:11

If I be wicked, woe unto me.   2102
        Job 10:15

Our sins testify against us.   2103
        Isaiah 59:12

Though thou wash thee with nitre, and take thee much soap, yet thine iniquity is marked before me.   2104
        Jeremiah 2:22

He that is without sin among you, let him first cast a stone.   2105
        Jesus in John 8:7

Psychologists are the sworn enemies of guilt.   2106
        Allan Bloom, *The Closing of the American Mind*

Look into any man's heart you please, and you will always find, in every one, at least one black spot which he has to keep concealed.   2107
        Henrik Ibsen, *Pillars of Society*

The many men, so beautiful!
And they all dead did lie:
And a thousand, thousand slimy things
Lived on, and so did I.   2108
        Samuel Taylor Coleridge, *The Rime of the Ancient Mariner*

Guilt is what civilizes.   2109
        Philip Lopate, *Confessions of Summer*

You can get used to anything if you have to, even to feeling perpetually guilty.   2110
        Golda Meir, on her inattention to her children. *My Life*

H

Habit

Can the Ethiopian change his skin, or the leopard his spots? then ye may also do good, that are accustomed to do evil.   2111
> Jeremiah 13:23

Wash you, make you clean; put away the evil of your doings from before mine eyes; cease to do evil; learn to do well; seek judgment, relieve the oppressed, judge the fatherless, plead for the widow.   2112
> Isaiah 1:16–17

To fall into habit is to begin to cease to be.   2113
> Miguel de Unamuno, *Tragic Sense of Life*

Man grows used to everything, the scoundrel!   2114
> Fyodor Dostoyevski, *Crime and Punishment*

Happiness

Let all those that put their trust in thee rejoice: let them ever shout for joy.   2115
> Psalm 5:11

Weeping may endure for a night, but joy cometh in the morning.   2116
> Psalm 30:5

Be glad in the Lord.   2117
> Psalm 32:11

Happy is that people whose God is the Lord.   2118
> Psalm 144:15

A merry heart maketh a cheerful countenance.   2119
> Proverbs 15:13

A time to weep, and a time to laugh; a time to mourn, and a time to dance.   2120
> Ecclesiastes 3:4

If ye know these things, happy are ye if ye do them.   2121
> Jesus in John 13:17

Happiness is not a reward—it is a consequence.   2122
> Robert G. Ingersoll, *The Christian Religion*

To enjoy true happiness we must travel to a very far country, and even out of ourselves; for the pearl we seek is not to be found in the Indian but in the Empyrean Ocean.   2123
> Sir Thomas Browne, *Religio Medici*

A lifetime of happiness! No man alive could bear it: it would be hell on earth.   2124
> Bernard Shaw, *Man and Superman*

The moments of happiness we enjoy take us by surprise. It is not that we seize them, but that they seize us.   2125
> Ashley Montagu, *The American Way of Life*

It is the very pursuit of happiness that thwarts happiness.   2126
> Viktor E. Frankl, *The Unconscious God*

Of all forms of caution, caution in love is perhaps the most fatal to true happiness.   2127
> Bertrand Russell, *Conquest of Happiness*

The truth is that a lost empire, lost power and lost wealth provide perfect circumstances for living happily and contentedly in our enchanted island.   2128
> Malcolm Muggeridge, on British culture. *London Observer*, 11 August 1968

That all who are happy are equally happy is not true. A peasant and a philosopher may be equally *satisfied,* but not equally *happy. Happiness* consists in the multiplicity of agreeable consciousness.   2129
> Samuel Johnson. Boswell's *Life,* 9 February 1766

Happiness is a sort of atmosphere you can live in sometimes when you're lucky. Joy is a light that fills you with faith and hope and love.   2130
> Adela Rogers St. John, *Some Are Born Great*

When a man is happy he does not hear the clock strike.   2131
> German Proverb

Hate

They that hate me without a cause are more than the hairs of mine head.   2132
> Psalm 69:4

He that despiseth his neighbor sinneth.   2133
> Proverbs 14:21

A time to love, and a time to hate.   2134
> Ecclesiastes 3:8

Do good to them that hate you.   2135
> Jesus in Matthew 5:44

The poison of asps is under their lips.   2136
> Romans 3:13

He that saith he is in the light, and hateth his brother, is in darkness even until now.   2137
> 1 John 2:9

Whosoever hateth his brother is a murderer.   2138
     1 John 3:15

All men naturally hate each other.   2139
     Blaise Pascal, *Pensées*

Most of the time we hate most truly people we have never met.   2140
     Eric Hoffer, *Reflections on the Human Condition*

People usually hate what they do not understand.   2141
     Moses ibn Ezra, *Shirat Yisrael*

Hate is a prolonged form of suicide.   2142
     Douglas V. Steere, *Dimensions of Prayer*

I tell you there is such a thing as creative hate!   2143
     Willa Cather, *The Song of the Lark*

Healing

God heals, and the doctor takes the fees.   2144
     Benjamin Franklin, *Poor Richard's Almanack*

Health

He maketh sore, and bindeth up: he woundeth, and his hands make whole. 2145
     Job 5:18

The voice of joy and health is in the dwellings of the righteous.   2146
     Psalm 118:15, the version of the Psalter in the *Book of Common Prayer*

Heal me, O Lord, and I shall be healed; save me, and I shall be saved.   2147
     Jeremiah 17:14

Honor a physician with the honor due unto him for the uses which ye may have of him: for the Lord hath created him. For of the most High cometh healing, and he shall receive honor of the king. The skill of the physician shall lift up his head: and in the sight of great men he shall be in admiration. The Lord hath created medicines out of the earth; and he that is wise will not abhor them.   2148
     Ecclesiasticus 38:1–4, *The Jerusalem Bible*

If thou wilt, thou canst make me clean.   2149
     Matthew 8:2

They that be whole need not a physician, but they that are sick.   2150
     Jesus in Matthew 9:12

Heal the sick, cleanse the lepers, raise the dead, cast out devils.   2151
     Matthew 10:8

The prayer of faith shall heal the sick.   2152
     James 5:15

Christian Science is so often therapeutically successful because it lays stress on the patient's believing in his or her own health rather than in Noah's Ark or the Ascension.   2153
     J. B. S. Haldane, *Possible Worlds*

Health and intellect are the two blessings of life. 2154
> Menander (c. 342– c. 292 B.C.), *Monostichoi*

We are all ill [i.e. neurotic]: but even a universal sickness implies an idea of health. 2155
> Lionel Trilling, *The Liberal Imagination*

The mere pursuit of health always leads to something unhealthy. Physical nature must not be made the direct object of obedience; it must be enjoyed, not worshiped. 2156
> G. K. Chesterton, *Orthodoxy*

O God, the Creator and Preserver of all mankind, we humbly beseech thee for all sorts and conditions of men, that thou wouldest be pleased to make thy ways known unto them, thy saving health unto all nations. 2157
> Book of Common Prayer, *A Prayer for All Conditions of Men*

If you would live in health be old early. 2158
> Spanish Proverb

A sound mind in a sound body is a short but full description of a happy state in this world. 2159
> John Locke, *Some Thoughts Concerning Education*

Health and sanity are synonyms. It is sane to talk to yourself, saner to talk with yourself; sane to sing yourself to sleep, saner to sing yourself awake. 2160
> C. E. S.

Heart

The Lord seeth not as man seeth; for man looketh upon the outward appearance, but the Lord looketh on the heart. 2161
> 1 Samuel 16:7

Give thy servants an understanding heart. 2162
> 1 Kings 3:9

Keep thy heart with all diligence; for out of it are the issues of life. 2163
> Proverbs 4:23

A sound heart is the life of the flesh. 2164
> Proverbs 14:30

Out of the abundance of the heart the mouth speaketh. 2165
> Jesus in Matthew 12:34

A good man out of the good treasure of the heart bringeth forth good things: and an evil man out of the evil treasure bringeth forth evil things. 2166
> Jesus in Matthew 12:35

The history of every country begins in the heart of a man or a woman. 2167
> Willa Cather, *O Pioneers!*

In each human heart there are a tiger, a pig, an ass, and a nightingale. Diversity of character is due to their unequal activity. 2168
> Ambrose Bierce, *The Devil's Dictionary*

There's nothing you can do about "a soft spot in your heart." Just make sure it doesn't spread to your head. 2169

> Abigail Van Buren ("Dear Abby"), syndicated column, 1976

Hearts live by being wounded. 2170

> Oscar Wilde, *A Woman of No Importance*

A lion lurks within every heart: awake him not. 2171

> Bulgarian Proverb

Heartbreak is gratuitous wreckage. It is futility. 2172

> Max Wylie, response to murder of his daughter. *Ladies Home Journal,* March 1964

A man who is right in his head and wrong in his heart is wrong all over. 2173

> C. E. S.

Heaven

And God called the firmament Heaven. 2174

> Genesis 1:8

If I ascend up into heaven, Thou art there; if I make my bed in hell, behold, thou art there. 2175

> Psalm 139:8

The heavens declare the glory of God, and the firmament showeth his handiwork. 2176

> Psalm 19:1

Lay up for yourselves treasures in heaven, where neither moth nor rust doth corrupt, and where thieves do not break through nor steal. 2177

> Jesus in Matthew 6:20

In my Father's house are many mansions. 2178

> Jesus in John 14:2

Here we have no continuing city, but we seek one to come. 2179

> Hebrews 13:14

The gates of it shall not be shut at all by day: for there shall be no night there. 2180

> Revelation 21:25

This world is peopled only to people heaven. 2181

> St. Francis de Sales, *Letters to Persons in the World*

Entrance into heaven is not at the hour of death, but at the moment of conversion. 2182

> Benjamin Whichcote, *Moral and Religious Aphorisms*

Heaven is not a cash payment for walking with God: it is where the road goes. 2183

> Austin Farrer, *Saving Belief*

Do not ask God the way to heaven: he will show you the hardest way. 2184

> Stanislaw J. Lec, *Unkempt Thoughts*

Guesses, of course, only guesses. If they are not true, something better will be. For "we know we shall be like him, for we shall see him as he is." 2185
> C. S. Lewis, *Letters to Malcolm: Chiefly on Prayer*

Heaven must be in thee before thou canst be in heaven. 2186
> George Swinnock, *The Golden Treasury of Puritan Quotations*

Heaven is large but the way to heaven must be narrow. 2187
> Henry Smith, *Ibid.*

The more we grow in grace, the more we shall flourish in glory. Though every vessel of glory shall be full, yet some vessels hold more. 2188
> Thomas Watson, *Ibid.*

We are like little children strayed from home, and God is now fetching us home; and we are ready to turn into every house, stay and play with everything in our way, and sit down on every green bank, and much ado there is to get us home. 2189
> Richard Baxter, *Ibid.*

There is a great deal of difference between the desires of heaven in a sanctified man and an unsanctified. The believer prizeth it above earth, and had rather be with God than here (though death that stands in the way, may possibly have harder thoughts from him). But to the ungodly, there is nothing seemeth more desirable than this world; and therefore he only chooseth heaven before hell, but not before earth; and therefore shall not have it upon such a choice. 2190
> Ibid.

There is no coming to heaven with dry eyes. 2191
> Thomas Adams, *Sermons*

Heaven's sunlight is Sonlight. 2192
> Peter J. Kreeft, *Everything You Ever Wanted to Know About Heaven—But Never Dreamed of Asking*

The bottom line is in heaven. 2193
> Edwin Herbert Land, in reply rejecting the view that only the bottom line of the balance sheet uses the worth of a product.

And doubtless, unto thee is given
    A life that bears immortal fruit
    In those great offices that suit
The full-grown energies of heaven. 2194
> Alfred, Lord Tennyson, *In Memoriam A. H. H.*

We say and sing that our loved ones are "with God," but they always have been. God does not dwell more fully in heaven than on earth, not even in the "highest heaven." What alters is our capacity to know, love, appreciate and indwell God. 2195
> Leslie Weatherhead, *The Christian Agnostic*

Man's first, last home. 2196
> Alfred, Lord Tennyson, *Timbuctoo*

Pardon is not over and done with once for all, but incessant contrition and incessant pardon are the compensating dainties of those in heaven who have lost the dainties of first innocence. 2197
> Coventry Patmore, *The Rod, the Root and the Flower*

I long for the Island of Songs across the heaving Sea of Shouts.   2198
Rabindranath Tagore, *Stray Birds*

Heaven is the future of world and man, which is God himself.   2199
Hans Küng, *Eternal Life?*

On the earth the broken arcs; in the heaven, a perfect round   2200
Robert Browning, *Abt Vogler*

Heaven is a metaphor for the fulfillment of life in God.   2201
Joseph Sittler, *Gravity and Grace*

Heaven is first a temper and then a place.   2202
Author unknown, identified as a Cambridge Platonist of the 17th century by W. R. Inge in *A Rustic Moralist*

In heaven we shall live truth. On earth we exist by facts and we live by myths.   2203
C. E. S.

Heaven and Hell

Are there not millions of us who would rather go sleeping to hell than sweating to heaven?   2204
Thomas Watson, *The Golden Treasury of Puritan Quotations*

We know much more about heaven than hell, for heaven is the home of humanity and therefore contains all that is implied in a glorified human life; but hell was not made for men. It is in no sense *parallel* to heaven: it is "the darkness outside," the outer rim where being fades away into nonentity.   2205
C. S. Lewis, *The Problem of Pain*

The doors of heaven and hell are adjacent, and identical: both green, both beautiful. Take care, Adam! Take care! Take care!   2206
Nikos Kazantzakis, *The Last Temptation of Christ*

The Turks tell their people of a heaven where there is a sensible pleasure, but of a hell where they shall suffer they don't know what. The Christians quite invert this order. They tell us of a hell where we shall feel sensible pain, but of a heaven where we shall enjoy we can't tell what.   2207
John Selden (1584–1654), *Table Talk*

Better to reign in Hell than serve in Heaven. *[Satan.]*   2208
John Milton, *Paradise Lost*

Hell

Thou wilt not leave my soul in hell: neither wilt thou suffer thy Holy One to see corruption.   2209
Psalm 16:10

If thine eye offend thee, pluck it out, and cast it from thee: it is better for thee to enter into life with one eye rather than having two eyes, to be cast into hell fire.   2210
Jesus in Matthew 18:9

I looked, and behold a pale horse: and his name that sat on him was Death, and Hell followed him.   2211

> Revelation 6:8

Death and hell were cast into the lake of fire. This is the second death.   2212

> Revelation 20:14

To live without feeling or exciting sympathy, to be fortunate without adding to the felicity of others, or afflicted without tasting the balm of pity, is a state more gloomy than solitude: it is not retreat, but exclusion from mankind.   2213

> Samuel Johnson, *Rasselas*

Man against Hell, without the help of God, is as a rabbit against the Russian empire.   2214

> Coventry Patmore, *The Rod, the Root and the Flower*

Even Hell is truth, known too late.   2215

> Peter J. Kreeft, *Everything You Ever Wanted to Know About Heaven—But Never Dreamed of Asking*

Hell is yourself. When you ignore other people completely, that is hell.   2216

> Tennessee Williams. *Time,* 9 March 1962

The natural penalty for being a bad man is not to be baked in an oven: it is to become a worse man, and to banish oneself from the presence of God, both here and hereafter.   2217

> William R. Inge, *A Rustic Moralist*

Hell is more bearable than nothingness.   2218

> Philip James Bailey, *Festus*

Hell is the place where the satisfied compare disappointments.   2219

> Phillip Moeller, *Madame Sand*

The safest road to Hell is the gradual one—the gentle slope, soft underfoot, without sudden turnings, without milestones, without guideposts.   2220

> C. S. Lewis, *The Screwtape Letters*

"It is a fearful thing to fall into the hands of the living God" (Heb. 10:3). Undoubtedly so; but how much more fearful must it be to fall out of them!   2221

> C. E. S.

Heresy

None save great men have been the authors of great heresies.   2222

> St. Augustine, *De trinitate*

The greatest heresy in the world is a wicked life.   2223

> John Tillotson, *Sermons*

It is the customary fate of new truths to begin as heresies and to end as superstitions.   2224

> Thomas Henry Huxley, *The Coming of Age of "The Origin of Species"*

With the Bible one becomes a heretic.   2225

> Italian Proverb

Hidebound Traditionalism

Our fathers have been Churchmen
Nineteen hundred years or so,
And to every new proposal
They have always answered NO!   2226
　　　　　　　　　　Author Unknown

History

There is no history of mankind; there are only many histories of all kinds of aspects of human life. And one of these is the history of political power. This is elevated into the history of the world.   2227
　　　　　　Sir Karl Popper, *The Open Society and Its Enemies*

History is the workshop of God.   2228
　　　　　　Gustav Aulén, quoted by Gusta Wingren in an article on Aulén in *A Handbook of Christian Theologians,* edited by Martin E. Marty and Dean G. Peerman

History does not consist of completed and crumbling ruins, rather it consists of half-built villas abandoned by a bankrupt-builder. This world is more like an unfinished suburb than a deserted cemetery.   2229
　　　　　　G. K. Chesterton, *What's Wrong with the World*

It is the wicked who make history.   2230
　　　　　　Isaac Bashevis Singer, *A Friend of Kafka*

History repeats itself in the large because human nature changes with geological leisureliness.   2231
　　　　　　Will and Ariel Durant, *The Lessons of History*

Man does not reveal himself in his history, he struggles up through it.   2232
　　　　　　Rabindranath Tagore, *Stray Birds*

History is the record of an encounter between character and circumstances. 2233
　　　　　　Donald Creighton, *Toward the Discovery* (of Canada)

Holiness

Put off the shoes from off thy feet, for the place whereon thou standest is holy ground.   2234
　　　　　　Exodus 3:5

I will be sanctified in them that come nigh me.   2235
　　　　　　Leviticus 10:3

There is none holy as the Lord: for there is none beside thee: neither is there any rock like our God.   2236
　　　　　　1 Samuel 2:2

Who shall ascend into the hill of the Lord? or who shall stand in his holy place? He that hath clean hands, and a pure heart; who hath not lifted up his soul unto vanity, nor sworn deceitfully.   2237
　　　　　　Psalm 24:3–4

191

If the root be holy, so are the branches. 2238
Romans 11:16

As he which hath called you is holy, so be ye holy. 2239
1 Peter 1:15

Holy, holy, holy, Lord God Almighty, which was, and is, and is to come. 2240
Revelation 4:8

To be holy and not happy is a contradiction. 2241
Author Unknown

Everything that lives is holy. 2242
William Blake, *The Marriage of Heaven and Hell*

Holiness appeared to me to be of a sweet, pleasant, charming, serene, calm nature; which brought an inexpressible purity, brightness, peacefulness, and ravishment to the soul. In other words, that it made the soul like a field or garden of God, with all manner of pleasant flowers. 2243
Jonathan Edwards, *Holiness*

There is nothing destroyed by sanctification but that which would destroy us. 2244
William Jenkyn, *The Golden Treasury of Puritan Quotations*

There is a beauty in holiness as well as a beauty of holiness. 2245
George Swinnock, *Ibid.*

Holy Spirit

And the Spirit of God moved upon the face of the waters. 2246
Genesis 1:2

The Spirit of the Lord God is upon me; because the Lord hath anointed me to preach good tidings. 2247
Isaiah 61:1

And Jesus, when he was baptized, went up straightway out of the water: and lo, the heavens were opened unto him, and he saw the Spirit of God descending like a dove, and lighting upon him. 2248
Matthew 3:16

Whosoever speaketh against the Holy Ghost, it shall not be forgiven him, neither in this world, neither in the world to come. 2249
Jesus in Matthew 12:32

Except a man be born of water and of the Spirit, he cannot enter into the kingdom of God. 2250
Jesus in John 3:5

It is the spirit that quickeneth; the flesh profiteth nothing. 2251
Jesus in John 6:63

These things I have spoken unto you, being yet present with you. But the Comforter, which is the Holy Ghost, whom the Father will send in my name, he shall teach you

all things, and bring all things to your remembrance, whatsoever I have said
unto you.   2252

>Jesus in John 14:25–26

As many as are led by the Spirit of God, they are the sons of God.   2253

>Romans 8:14

The kingdom of God is not meat and drink; but righteousness, and peace, and joy
in the Holy Ghost.   2254

>Romans 14:17

The fruit of the Spirit is love, joy, peace, longsuffering, gentleness, goodness, faith,
meekness, temperance.   2255

>Galatians 5:22–23

All that is true, by whomsoever it has been said, is from the Holy Ghost.   2256

>St. Thomas Aquinas, quoted in Ananda K. Coomaraswany, *Am I My Brother's Keeper?*

When the flames and hellish cries
Fright mine ears, and fright mine eyes,
And all terrors me surprise,
>Sweet Spirit, comfort me.   2257

>Robert Herrick, *Noble Numbers,* 1647

Come, Holy Ghost, our souls inspire,
And lighten with celestial fire.
Thou the anointing Spirit art,
Who dost thy sevenfold gifts impart.
Thy blessed unction from above
Is comfort, life, and fire of love.
Enable with perpetual light
The dullness of our blinded sight.
Anoint and cheer our soilèd face
With the abundance of thy grace.
Keep far our foes, give peace at home:
Where Thou art guide, no ill can come.
Teach us to know the Father, Son,
And Thee, of both, to be but One,
That through the ages all along,
This may be our endless song:
Praise to thy eternal merit,
Father, Son, and Holy Spirit.   2258

>Rabanus Maurus, *Veni, Creator Spiritus,* c. 825

Holy Trinity

Father, Son, and Holy Spirit mean that the mystery beyond us, the mystery among
us, and the mystery within us are all the same mystery. Thus the Trinity is a way of
saying something about us and the way we experience God.   2259

>Frederick Buechner, *Wishful Thinking: A Theological ABC*

On a walk together, Porson and a Trinitarian friend were discussing the nature of the Trinity. A buggy passed them with three men in it. "There," said the friend, "that's an illustration of the Trinity." "No," said Porson, "you must show me one man in three buggies—if you can." 2260

> *The Little, Brown Book of Anecdotes,* edited by Clifton Fadiman.
> Richard Porson (1759–1808) was a renowned classical scholar

The Father's is the goodwill and command. The Son executes and fabricates. The Spirit nourishes and increases. 2261

> G. L. Prestige, *God in Patristic Thought*

Home

Bury me not, I pray thee, in Egypt. 2262

> Genesis 47:29

By the rivers of Babylon, there we sat down, yea, we wept, when we remembered Zion. 2263

> Psalm 137:1

Foxes have holes, and the birds of the air have nests; but the Son of man hath not where to lay his head. 2264

> Jesus in Luke 9:58

The home is not a convent. 2265

> Jean Pierre Camus, *The Spirit of St. Francis de Sales*

In fact there was but one thing wrong with the Babbitt house: it was not a home. 2266

> Sinclair Lewis, *Babbitt*

To be happy at home is the ultimate result of all ambition, the end to which every enterprise and labor tends, and of which every desire prompts the prosecution. 2267

> Samuel Johnson, *The Rambler,* 10 November 1750

Home is the girl's prison and the woman's workhouse. 2268

> Bernard Shaw, *Maxims for Revolutionists,* 1905

Honesty

"Honesty," without compassion and understanding, is not honesty, but subtle hostility. 2269

> Rose N. Franzblau, *New York Post,* 24 August 1966

To make your children *capable of honesty* is the beginning of education. 2270

> John Ruskin, *Time and Tide*

He who tells the truth should have one foot in the stirrup. 2271

> Arab Proverb

An honest man's the noblest work of God. 2272

> Alexander Pope, *An Essay on Man*

Honor

Honor's the moral conscience of the great.   2273
> William Davenant, *Gondibert*

Hardly any of us have ethical energy enough for more than one really inflexible point of honor.   2274
> Bernard Shaw, *The Doctor's Dilemma*, Preface

The louder he talked of his honor, the faster we counted our spoons.   2275
> Ralph Waldo Emerson, *The Conduct of Life*

I had rather play cards against a man who was quite sceptical about ethics, but bred to believe that "a gentleman does not cheat," than against an irreproachable philosopher who had been brought up among sharpers.   2276
> C. S. Lewis, *The Abolition of Man*

Hope

The poor hath hope.   2277
> Job 5:16

The hypocrite's hope shall perish.   2278
> Job 8:13

The needy shall not always be forgotten: the expectation of the poor shall not perish for ever.   2279
> Psalm 9:18

Tribulation worketh patience; And patience, experience; and experience, hope.   2280
> Romans 5:3–4

We are saved by hope.   2281
> Romans 8:24

We are perplexed, but not in despair; Persecuted, but not forsaken; cast down, but not destroyed.   2282
> 2 Corinthians 4:8–9

Greet the unseen with a cheer.   2283
> Robert Browning, *Epilogue*

There are no hopeless situations, there are only hopeless men.   2284
> Clare Boothe Luce, in *Europe in the Spring,* quoting an unnamed diplomat

We are not perfectly free until we live in pure hope.   2285
> Thomas Merton, *No Man Is an Island*

Hope, like faith, is nothing if it is not courageous; it is nothing if it is not ridiculous.   2286
> Thornton Wilder, *The Eighth Day*

Hope arouses, as nothing else can arouse, a passion for the possible.   2287
> William Sloane Coffin, Jr., *Once to Every Man*

Keep a green tree in your heart and perhaps the singing bird will come.　　2288
>
> Chinese Proverb

The sunshine smiles upon the winter days of my heart, never doubting of its spring flowers.　　2289
>
> Rabindranath Tagore, *Stray Birds*

The sun has made a veil of gold
So lovely that my body aches.
Above, the heavens shriek with blue—
Convinced I've smiled by some mistake.
The world's abloom and seems to smile.
I want to fly, but where, how high.
If in barbed wire things can bloom
Why cannot I? I will not die.　　2290
>
> Author unknown. These lines appear to be an English translation of
> what a prisoner in a Nazi death camp wrote in 1944.

Human Beings

The actor is not quite a human being—but then who is?　　2291
>
> George Sanders, quoted in *The Portable Curmudgeon,* compiled and
> edited by Jon Winokur

I am simply a human being, more or less.　　2292
>
> Saul Bellow, *Herzog*

Rather than "ghosts in machines" we are more like "messages in circuitry" and the message itself transcends the means of its expression.　　2293
>
> Paul Davies, *God and the New Physics*

No man really knows about other human beings. The best he can do is to suppose that they are like himself.　　2294
>
> John Steinbeck, *The Winter of Our Discontent*

As far as we can discern, the sole purpose of human existence is to kindle a light in the darkness of mere being.　　2295
>
> Carl Gustav Jung, *Memories*

There is a great deal of unmapped country within us which would have to be taken into account in an explanation of our gusts and storms.　　2296
>
> George Eliot, *Daniel Deronda*

Every man bears the whole stamp of the human condition.　　2297
>
> Michel de Montaigne, *Essays,* III, i.

Human Completion

From Gertrude Stein's autobiography: "After a little while I murmured to Picasso that I liked his portrait of Gertrude Stein. Yes, he said, everybody says that she does not look like it but that does not make any difference, she will, he said." Is it flippant to suggest that this audacity of Picasso images in fact a power of the divine Artist? In God's mind is a picture of the fully grown-up, completed you. If you could see that picture now you would have to say that you don't look very much like it. God could reasonably reply, with cool and confident aplomb: "Don't worry—you will." Now are we the sons of God, says St. John, and it does not yet appear what we shall be—when we grow up to look like God's picture of us.   2298

C. E. S.

Human Failures

All failures—neurotics, psychotics, criminals, drunkards, problem children, suicides, perverts, and prostitutes—are failures because they are lacking in social interest.   2299

Alfred Adler, *What Life Should Mean to You*

Human Fallibility

The spirit of liberty is the spirit which is not too sure that it is right.   2300

Learned Hand, recalled on his death, 18 August 1961

Human Ignorance

The known is finite, the unknown infinite; intellectually we stand on an islet in the midst of an illimitable ocean of inexplicability. Our business in every generation is to reclaim a little more land.   2301

Thomas Henry Huxley. Quoted in Carl Sagan, *Cosmos*

Human Interest

Our interest's on the dangerous side of things.
The honest thief, the tender murderer,
The superstitious atheist, demirep
That loves and saves her soul in new French books.   2302

Robert Browning, *Bishop Bloughram's Apology*

Human Life

[There is] an immense, painful longing for a broader, more flexible, fuller, more coherent, more comprehensive account of what we human beings are, who we are and what this life is for.   2303

Saul Bellow, accepting Nobel Prize, 12 December 1976

Allons! to that which is endless as it was beginningless.   2304

Walt Whitman, *Song of the Open Road*

In one manner or the other it still remains true that, even in the view of the mere biologist, the human epic resembles nothing so much as a way of the Cross.   2305

Pierre Teilhard de Chardin, *The Phenomenon of Man*

To have contemplated human life for forty years is the same as to have contemplated it for ten thousand years. For what more wilt thou see?   2306

Marcus Aurelius, *Meditations*

Human Nature

There's nought so queer as folk.   2307

English Proverb

I do not know of a description of a devil in literature which does not leave one with some sense of sympathy. Milton's devils are admirable; Dante's devils stir our pity; Goethe's devil makes us feel what a good thing has been wasted. Human nature seems incapable of imagining that which is wholly bad, just because it is not wholly bad itself.   2308

Alan Goodier, *The School of Love*

The sun and the moon and the stars would have disappeared long ago . . . had they happened to have been within reach of predatory human hands.   2309

Havelock Ellis, *The Dance of Life*

Whenever man forgets that he is an animal, the result is always to make him less humane.   2310

Joseph Wood Krutch, *The Twelve Seasons*

I got disappointed in human nature and gave it up because I found it too much like my own.   2311

J. P. Dunleavy, *Fairy Tales of New York*

I don't like human nature, but I do like human beings.   2312

Ellen Glasgow, *In This Our Life*

Cats and monkeys—monkeys and cats—all human life is there!   2313

Henry James, *Madonna of the Future*

Human Pests

Taking hold of Jonah they threw him into the sea; and the sea grew calm again.   2314

Jonah 1:15, *The Jerusalem Bible*

Human Solidarity

Not only are we all in the same boat, but we are all seasick.   2315

G. K. Chesterton, *What's Wrong with the World*

Humanity

If you could see humanity spread out in time, as God sees it, it would not look like a lot of separate things dotted about. It would look like one single growing thing— rather like a very complicated tree. Every individual would appear connected with every other. And not only that. Individuals are not really separate from God any more than from one another. Every man, woman, and child all over the world is feeling and breathing at this moment only because God, so to speak, is "keeping him going."   2316

C. S. Lewis, *Mere Christianity*

I am a man: I consider nothing human as alien to myself. *(Homo sum: humani nil a me alienum puto.)*   2317
> Terence, *The Self-Tormentor*

The finest rivalry is in humanity. *(Humanitatis optima est certatio.)*   2318
> Publilius Syrus, *Sententiae*

We must soften into a credulity below the milkiness of infancy to think all men virtuous. We must be tainted with a malignity truly diabolical, to believe all the world to be equally corrupt.   2319
> Edmund Burke, *Thoughts on the Cause of the Present Discontents,* 1770

Mankind will not be reasoned out of all feelings of humanity.   2320
> William Blackstone, *Commentaries on the Laws of England*

I confess that any hopefulness for the future of civilization is based on the reasonable expectation that humanity is still only beginning its course.   2321
> William R. Inge, *The Church and the Age*

Everyone in the world is Christ and they are all crucified.   2322
> Sherwood Anderson, *Winesburg, Ohio,* "The Philosopher"

I hate "Humanity" and all such abstracts: but I love *people.* Lovers of "Humanity" generally hate *people* and *children,* and keep parrots and puppy dogs.   2323
> Roy Campbell, *Light on a Dark Horse*

Taking a very gloomy view of the future of the human race, let us suppose that it can only expect to survive for two thousand million years longer, a period about equal to the past age of the earth. Then, regarded as being destined to live for three-score years and ten, humanity, although it has been born in a house seventy years old, is itself only three days old.   2324
> Sir James Jeans, *Eos*

Humility

I am slow of speech, and of a slow tongue.   2325
> Exodus 4:10

Who am I, O Lord God? and what is my house, that thou hast brought me hitherto?   2326
> 2 Samuel 7:18

I am but a little child: I know not how to go out or come in.   2327
> 1 Kings 3:7

Shall any teach God knowledge?   2328
> Job 21:22

The Lord is nigh unto them that are of a broken heart; and saveth such as be of a contrite spirit.   2329
> Psalm 34:18

God is in heaven, and thou upon earth: therefore let thy words be few.   2330
> Ecclesiastes 5:2

He hath showed thee, O man, what is good; and what doth the Lord require of thee, but to do justly, and to love mercy, and to walk humbly with thy God?　　　　　　2331
>> Micah 6:8

Behold, thy King cometh unto thee: he is just, and having salvation; lowly, and riding upon an ass.　　　　　　2332
>> Zechariah 9:9

Blessed are the poor in spirit: for theirs is the kingdom of heaven.　2333
>> Jesus in Matthew 5:3

Blessed are the meek: for they shall inherit the earth.　　　2334
>> Jesus in Matthew 5:5

Whosoever will be great among you, let him be your minister.　2335
>> Jesus in Matthew 20:26

Our sufficiency is of God.　　　　　　2336
>> 2 Corinthians 3:5

Humility is the refusal to exist outside God. It is the queen of virtues. 2337
>> Simone Weil, *Gravity and Grace*

Humility must always be the portion of any man who receives acclaim earned in the blood of his followers and the sacrifices of his friends.　2338
>> Dwight D. Eisenhower, in address at Guildhall, London, 12 July 1945

Humility wrestleth with God, like Jacob, and wins by yielding.　2339
>> Thomas Adams, *The Golden Treasury of Puritan Quotations*

True humility is not submission to authority but total disregard of it when reality speaks to us.　　　　　　2340
>> John Oman, *The Natural and the Supernatural*

Those who know honor
but practice humility
will be as a valley
receiving all the world into it.　　　　　　2341
>> Kung-Fu Meditations

Bishop Clark, of Rhode Island, told of a dispute at Providence between two hot church members. One said at last, "I should like to know who *you* are." "Who I am!" cried the other,—"Who I am! I am a humble Christian, you damned old heathen, you!"　　　　　　2342
>> Ralph Waldo Emerson, *Journals,* 1861

Humor

Good jests bite like lambs, not like dogs.　　　　　　2343
>> Author Unknown

I love such mirth as does not make friends ashamed to look upon one another next morning. 2344

Izaak Walton, *The Compleat Angler*

It will not hurt a great but humorless man like St. Paul for us to laugh when he slips. I imagine that now at last, in heaven, he can laugh at himself, a thing he could never do on earth. 2345

William H. Ralston, Jr., in *The Parish Paper of St. John's Church,* Savannah, Georgia, 22 February 1987

Humor is a prelude to faith and laughter is the beginning of prayer. 2346

Reinhold Niebuhr, *Discerning the Signs of the Times*

Absolute seriousness is never without a dash of humor. 2347

Dietrich Bonhoeffer, *Letters and Papers from Prison*

Clumsy jesting is no joke. 2348

Aesop, *Fables,* "The Ass and the Lapdog"

Hunting

The English country gentleman galloping after a fox—the unspeakable in full pursuit of the uneatable. 2349

Oscar Wilde, *A Woman of No Importance*

It is very strange, and very melancholy, that the paucity of human pleasures should persuade us ever to call hunting one of them. 2350

Samuel Johnson, *Johnsonian Miscellanies,* edited by G. B. Hill

Hypocrisy

How can thou say, I love thee, when thine heart is not with me? 2351

Judges 16:15

What is the hope of the hypocrite, though he hath gained, when God taketh away his soul? 2352

Job 27:8

They bless with their mouth, but they curse inwardly. 2353

Psalm 62:4

They love to pray standing in the synagogues and in the corners of the streets, that they may be seen of men . . . They have their reward. 2354

Jesus in Matthew 6:5

No hypocrite can bear the cross. 2355

Henry Smith, *The Golden Treasury of Puritan Quotations*

Great hypocrites are the real atheists. 2356

Francis Bacon, *The Advancement of Learning*

If we must be enemies, let us be men, and fight it out as we propose to do, and not deal in hypocritical appeals to God and humanity. 2357

General William T. Sherman, USA, in letter to General J. H. Hood, CSA, Atlanta, 10 September 1864.

Let it never be forgotten that a hypocrite is a very unhappy man; he is a man who has devoted himself to a most delicate and arduous intellectual art in which he may achieve masterpieces which he must keep secret, fight thrilling battles and win hair-breadth victories for which he cannot have a whisper of praise. A really accomplished impostor is the most wretched of geniuses: he is a Napoleon on a desert island.   2358

G. K. Chesterton, *Robert Browning*

I

I and Thou

Abide in me, and I in you.   2359

> Jesus in John 15:4

In every sphere, through everything that becomes present to us, we gaze toward the train (Isaiah 6:1) of the eternal You; in each we preserve a breath of it; in every You we address the eternal You, in every sphere according to its matter.   2360

> Martin Buber, *I and Thou*

Iconoclasm

To knock a thing down, especially if it is cocked at an arrogant angle, is a deep delight of the blood.   2361

> George Santayana, quoted in Jon Winokur, *The Portable Curmudgeon*

Rough work, iconoclasm,—but the only way to get at truth.   2362

> Oliver Wendell Holmes, *The Professor at the Breakfast-Table*

When smashing monuments, save the pedestals—they always come in handy.   2363

> Stanislaw J. Lec, *Unkempt Thoughts*

Ideas

One of the greatest pains to human nature is the pain of a new idea.   2364

> Walter Bagehot, *Physics and Politics*

Good ideas may fail but they are not lost. *(Bene cogitate si excidunt non occident.)*   2365

> Publilius Syrus, *Sententiae*

A new idea is delicate. It can be killed by a sneer or a yawn; it can be stabbed to death by a quip and worried to death by a frown on the right man's brow.   2366

> Charles Brower, *Advertising Age,* 10 August 1959

Ideas are fatal to caste.   2367

> E. M. Forster, *A Passage to India*

An idea, to be suggestive, must come to the individual with the force of a revelation. 2368

William James, *Varieties of Religious Experience*

If you are possessed by an idea, you find it expressed everywhere, you even *smell* it. 2369

Thomas Mann, *Death in Venice*

If we watch ourselves honestly, we shall often find that we have begun to argue against a new idea even before it has been completely stated. 2370

Arthur Koestler, *The Act of Creation*

An idea is the most exciting thing there is. 2371

John Russell. *New York Times,* 7 January 1979

Ideals

The ideal, after all, is truer than the real: for the idea is the eternal element in perishable things: it is their type, their sun, their *raison d'être,* their formula in the book of the Creator, and therefore at once the most exact and the most condensed expression of them. 2372

Henri Frédéric Amiel. *Journal,* 20 March 1865

An ideal is never yours until it comes out of your fingertips. 2373

Florence Allshorn, a missionary teacher, quoted in William Barclay, The *Gospel of Matthew,* I

Never look down to test the ground before taking your next step: only he who keeps his eye on the far horizon will find his right road. 2374

Dag Hammarskjöld, *Markings*

Idolatry

Thou shalt have no other gods before me. 2375

Exodus 20:3

Thou shalt not make unto thee any graven image. 2376

Exodus 20:4

They that make them are like unto them; so is every one that trusteth in them. 2377

Psalm 115:8

Little children, keep yourselves from idols. 2378

1 John 5:21

Men are idolaters, and want something to look at and kiss and hug or throw themselves down before; they always did, they always will; and if you don't make it out of wood, you must make it out of words. 2379

Oliver Wendell Holmes, *The Autocrat of the Breakfast-Table*

Idolatry is the elevation of a preliminary concern to ultimacy. 2380

Paul Tillich, *Systematic Theology*

There are four classes of idols which beset the human mind . . . Idols of the Tribe, Idols of the Den, Idols of the Market, and Idols of the Theatre.   2381
> Francis Bacon, *Novum Organum*

Ignorance

They were both naked, the man and the wife, and were not ashamed.   2382
> Genesis 2:25

My people have gone into captivity, because they have no knowledge.   2383
> Isaiah 5:13

If the blind lead the blind, both shall fall into the ditch.   2384
> Jesus in Matthew 15:14

Father, forgive them; for they know not what they do.   2385
> Jesus in Luke 23:34

He was in the world, and the world was made by him, and the world knew him not.   2386
> John 1:10

Art thou a master of Israel, and knowest not these things?   2387
> John 3:10

We know in part, and we prophesy in part.   2388
> 1 Corinthians 13:9

A man only becomes wise when he begins to calculate the approximate depth of his ignorance.   2389
> Gian Carlo Menotti. *New York Times,* 14 April 1974

Ignorance is always swift to speak.   2390
> Author Unknown

We are here and it is now. Further than that all knowledge is moonshine.   2391
> Henry L. Mencken, in Robert Byrne, *The 637 Best Things Anybody Ever Said*

To know anything well involves a profound sensation of ignorance.   2392
> John Ruskin, *Modern Painters*

Nothing in all the world is more dangerous than sincere ignorance and conscientious stupidity.   2393
> Martin Luther King, Jr., *Strength to Love*

Not to know is bad; not to wish to know is worse.   2394
> Nigerian Proverb

There is no dunce like a mature dunce.   2395
> George Santayana, *Character and Opinion in the United States*

Most ignorance is vincible ignorance. We don't know because we don't want to know.   2396
> Aldous Huxley, recalled on his death, 22 November 1963

Imagination

And God saw that the wickedness of man was great in the earth, and that every imagination of the thoughts of his heart was only evil continually. 2397
Genesis 6:5

He hath showed strength with his arm; he hath scattered the proud in the imagination of their hearts. 2398
Luke 1:51

Mere imagination would indeed be mere trifling; only no imagination is *mere*. 2399
Charles Sanders Pierce, *Collected Papers*

Perhaps imagination is only intelligence having fun. 2400
George Scialabra. *Reader's Digest,* "Quotable Quotes," October 1984

How can an age which is so utterly devoid of poetic imagination as ours be truly religious? 2401
Reinhold Niebuhr, *Leaves from the Notebook of a Tamed Cynic*

The great instrument of moral good is the imagination. 2402
Percy Bysshe Shelley, *The Defense of Poetry*

"Imagination is more important than information." Einstein said that, and he should know. 2403
Robert Fulghum, *All I Really Need to Know I Learned in Kindergarten*

I am certain of nothing but the holiness of the heart's affections, and the truth of imagination—What the imagination seizes as beauty must be truth—whether it existed before or not. . . . The imagination may be compared to Adam's dream—he awoke and found it truth. 2404
John Keats. Letter to Benjamin Bailey, 22 November 1817

Immortality

See also Eternal Life; Resurrection

If a man die, shall he live again? 2405
Job 14:14

This corruptible must put on incorruption, and this mortal must put on immortality. 2406
1 Corinthians 15:53

Our Saviour Jesus Christ hath abolished death, and hath brought life and immortality to light through the gospel. 2407
2 Timothy 1:10

Nothing is real that is not eternal. 2408
Miguel de Unamuno, *Tragic Sense of Life*

This life is the crossing of a sea, where we meet in the same narrow ship. In death we reach the shore to go to different worlds. 2409
Rabindranath Tagore, *Stray Birds*

The meanest man is immortal and the mightiest movement is temporal, not to say temporary.   2410

G. K. Chesterton, in *Blackfriars,* January 1923

If something comes to life in others because of you, then you have made an approach to immortality.   2411

Norman Cousins, *Anatomy of an Illness*

I can easily overlook any present momentary sorrow when I reflect that it is in my power to be happy a thousand years hence. If it were not for this thought, I had rather be an oyster than a man.   2412

Bishop George Berkeley, in *The Guardian,* 23 June 1713

The major problem of our time is the decay of the belief in personal immortality.   2413

George Orwell, *Looking Back on the Spanish War*

To the question "Where does the soul go, when the body dies?" Jacob Boehme answered: "There is no necessity for it to go anywhere."   2414

Aldous Huxley, *The Perennial Philosophy*

It is plain that the hope of a future life arises from the feeling which exists in the breast of every man, that the temporal is inadequate to meet and satisfy the demands of his nature.   2415

Immanuel Kant, *Critique of Pure Reason,* preface to 2d edition

Incarnation

Since the Incarnation, Jesus has only one desire: to recommence the human life he lived. That's why he wants additional human natures, people who will let him start all over again.   2416

Paul Claudel, quoted in Brennan Manning, *Lion & Lamb*

I had never known the dignity of my nature, hadst thou not esteemed it; I had never seen or understood its glory, hadst thou not assumed it.   2417

Thomas Traherne, *Centuries of Meditations*

God all-bounteous, all-creative,
    Whom no ills from good dissuade,
Is incarnate, and a native
    Of the very world he made.   2418

Christopher Smart, *The Nativity of Our Lord*

The Eternal Being, who knows everything and who created the whole universe, became not only a man but (before that) a baby, and before that a fetus in a woman's body. If you want to get the hang of it, think how you would like to become a slug or a crab.   2419

C. S. Lewis, *Mere Christianity*

When Jesus came
The world was all at peace in utter wickedness.   2420

Coventry Patmore, *The Rod, the Root and the Flower*

Individualism

Every man is the center of a circle, whose fatal circumference he cannot pass. 2421

John James Ingalls, in eulogy of Benjamin Hill in U.S. Senate, 23 January 1882

The strongest man in the world is the man who stands most alone. 2422

Henrik Ibsen, *The Enemy of the People*

Except as its clown and jester, society does not encourage individuality and the State abhors it. 2423

Bernard Berenson, *Aesthetics and History*

There are no precedents: You are the first You that ever was. 2424

Christopher Morley, *Inward Ho*

If a man does not keep pace with his companions, perhaps it is because he hears a different drummer. Let him step to the music which he hears, however measured or far away. 2425

Henry David Thoreau, *Walden*

Infallibility

We are none of us Jehovahs—not even the youngest of us. 2426

Author Unknown

The Christian will believe that he has an infallible authority in the mind of Christ; but he should also know that he has no infallible means of ascertaining this in application to given circumstances. 2427

William Temple, *Nature, Man and God*

There is no infallible Bible, and there is no infallible Pope, and there is no infallible Science; and anybody who puts his fallible trust in any such creature, rather than in God only infallible, is an idolater no less than the heathen in his blindness bowing down to stocks and stones. 2428

C. E. S.

Influence

Music in the soul can be heard by the universe. 2429

Kung-Fu Meditations

The best effect of fine persons is felt after we have left their presence. 2430

Ralph Waldo Emerson, *Journals,* 1839

Half our standards come from our first masters, and the other half from our first loves. 2431

George Santayana, *The Life of Reason*

You can exert no influence if you are not susceptible to influence. 2432

Carl Gustav Jung, *Modern Man in Search of a Soul*

On faraway influences: You were certain that others disapproved of your behavior without their having expressed their disapproval. In solitude you felt a quiet sense of well-being without having known why; some faraway person thought well of you, spoke well of you. 2433

Franz Kafka, *The Diaries of Franz Kafka 1914–1923*

Innocence

And with Absalom went two hundred men out of Jerusalem, that were called; and they went in their simplicity, and they knew not any thing. 2434

2 Samuel 15:11

And David said unto God, Is it not I that commanded the people to be numbered? even I it is that have sinned and done evil indeed; but as for these sheep, what have they done? let thine hand, I pray thee, O Lord my God, be on me, and on my father's house; but not on thy people, that they should be plagued. 2435

1 Chronicles 21:17

Let me be weighed in an even balance, that God may know mine integrity. 2436

Job 31:6

A little child shall lead them. 2437

Isaiah 11:6

He is brought as a lamb to the slaughter. 2438

Isaiah 53:7

If ye were blind, ye should have no sin. 2439

Jesus in John 9:41

Unto the pure all things are pure. 2440

Titus 1:15

If we say that we have no sin, we deceive ourselves. 2441

1 John 1:8

In their mouth was found no guile: for they are without fault before the throne of God. 2442

Revelation 14:5

She fear'd no danger, for she knew no sin. 2443

John Dryden, *The Hind and the Panther*

This shall be the test of innocence—if I can hear a taunt, and look out on this friendly moon, pacing the heavens in queen-like majesty, with the accustomed yearning. 2444

Henry David Thoreau, *Journal,* 13 November 1837

Innocent actions carry their warrant with them. 2445

English Proverb

To dread no eye, and to suspect no tongue, is the greatest prerogative of innocence. 2446

Samuel Johnson, *The Rambler,* 10 November 1750

A man is not to aim at innocence, any more than he is to aim at hair; but he is to keep it. 2447

Ralph Waldo Emerson, *Journals,* 1855

Ponder the fact that few of us can speak of innocence innocently, without a rather studied cynicism calling itself sophistication. The very word makes us nervous and uncomfortable. Can it be that we are trying to conceal from others, and still more from ourselves, a festering soreness of our souls resulting from our own irreversible loss of innocence? How explain it otherwise?   2448

C. E. S.

Inspiration

Go, and I will be with thy mouth, and teach thee what thou shalt say.   2449

Exodus 4:12

The Spirit of the Lord came upon Gideon, and he blew a trumpet.   2450

Judges 6:34

Your old men shall dream dreams, your young men shall see visions.   2451

Joel 2:28

It is not ye that speak, but the Spirit of your Father which speaketh in you. 2452

Jesus in Matthew 10:20

There is something in our minds like sunshine and the weather, which is not under control. When I write, the best things come to me from I know not where.   2453

Georg Christoph Lichtenberg, *Reflections*

Something tells me needs only decent attention and confidence to tell us much more.   2454

Anonymous (Henry S. Haskins), *Meditations on Wall Street*

Almighty God, unto whom all hearts are open, all desires known, and from whom no secrets are hid: cleanse the thoughts of our hearts by the inspiration of thy Holy Spirit, that we may perfectly love thee, and worthily magnify thy holy Name; through Christ our Lord.   2455

Book of Common Prayer, *The Order for Holy Communion*

Institutions

I wonder whether the fences and taboos which used to surround institutions and the savage sanctions against anyone who laid hands on them, originated in an awareness of their vulnerability. We have seen how a scratch on an institution easily develops into a cancer.   2456

Eric Hoffer, *Before the Sabbath*

Every institution not only carries within it the seeds of its own dissolution, but prepares the way for its most hated rival.   2457

William R. Inge, *Outspoken Essays: Second Series,* "The Victorian Age"

An institution can be like a decapitated chicken—dead, but still flopping around.   2458

C. E. S.

Intelligence

Gird up the loins of your mind. 2459
> 1 Peter 1:13

The Moral Obligation to Be Intelligent 2460
> John Erskine, title of book, 1915

Life is the art of drawing sufficient conclusions from insufficient premises. 2461
> Samuel Butler, *Note Books*

The test of a first-rate intelligence is the ability to hold two opposed ideas in the mind at the same time, and still retain the ability to function. 2462
> F. Scott Fitzgerald, *The Crack-Up*

The intelligent are to the intelligentsia as a gentleman is to a gent. 2463
> Stanley Baldwin. Quoted in G. M. Young, *Stanley Baldwin*

An honest heart being the first blessing, a knowing head is the second. 2464
> Thomas Jefferson, in letter to Peter Carr, 19 August 1785

Many complain of their looks, but none of their brains. 2465
> Yiddish Proverb

Intelligence is characterized by a natural incomprehension of life. 2466
> Henri Bergson, *Creative Evolution*

Intention

A right intention aims only at a right action. 2467
> Thomas Merton, *No Man Is an Island*

If there's anything that can rightly be said to pave the way, not to hell, but to heaven—yes, heaven—not any other destination, it has got to be good intentions. I mean real intentions, of course; you cannot properly be said to intend anything until you have already begun to do it in your mind and will, with all your heart and soul and immediate engagement with it. 2468
> C. E. S.

J

Jealousy

They [Joseph's brothers] hated him yet the more for his dreams, and for his words.   2469

Genesis 37:8

They have ascribed unto David tens of thousands, and to me they have ascribed but thousands.   2470

1 Samuel 18:8

Fret not thyself because of him that prospereth.   2471

Psalm 37:7

Wrath is cruel, and anger is outrageous; but who is able to stand before envy? 2472

Proverbs 27:4

Jealousy is cruel as the grave: the coals thereof are coals of fire, which hath a most vehement flame.   2473

Song of Solomon 8:6

Charity envieth not.   2474

1 Corinthians 13:4

Jealousy is that pain which a man feels from the apprehension that he is not equally loved by the person whom he entirely loves.   2475

Joseph Addison, *The Spectator,* 1711–1712

It is not love that is blind, but jealousy.   2476

Lawrence Durrell, *Justine*

Jealousy is always born together with love, but it does not always die when love dies.   2477

François de la Rochefoucauld, *Maxims*

Jealousy is the tribute mediocrity pays to genius.   2478

Fulton J. Sheen, quoted in Daniel P. Noonan, *The Passion of Fulton Sheen*

The jealous are troublesome to others but a torment to themselves.   2479

William Penn, *Some Fruits of Solitude*

Jesus Christ

Thou shalt call his name JESUS: for he shall save his people from their sins. 2480
Matthew 1:21

What manner of man is this, that even the winds and the sea obey him! 2481
Matthew 8:27

The Son of man hath power on earth to forgive sins. 2482
Jesus in Matthew 9:6

He that taketh not his cross, and followeth after me, is not worthy of me. 2483
Jesus in Matthew 10:38

In his name shall the Gentiles trust. 2484
Matthew 12:21

Is not this the carpenter's son? 2485
Matthew 13:55

The Son of man is come to save that which was lost. 2486
Jesus in Matthew 18:11

Art thou the King of the Jews? 2487
Matthew 27:11

The Word was made flesh, and dwelt among us, (and we beheld his glory, the glory as of the only begotten of the Father,) full of grace and truth. 2488
John 1:14

Behold, the Lamb of God, which taketh away the sin of the world. 2489
John 1:29

He that believeth not the Son shall not see life; but the wrath of God abideth on him. 2490
John 3:36

He that was healed wist not who it was. 2491
John 5:13

He that eateth my flesh, and drinketh my blood, dwelleth in me, and I in him. 2492
Jesus in John 6:56

I am the door: by me if any man enters in, he shall be saved. 2493
Jesus in John 10:9

I am the resurrection, and the life. 2494
Jesus in John 11:25

Though he was rich, yet for our sakes he became poor, that ye through his poverty might be rich. 2495
2 Corinthians 8:9

He is before all things, and by him all things consist. 2496
Colossians 1:17

Jesus, the author and finisher of our faith. 2497
Hebrews 12:2

The marriage of the Lamb is come, and his wife hath made herself ready. 2498
Revelation 19:7

Jesus Christ is a God to whom we can approach without pride, and before whom we humble ourselves without despair. 2499
Blaise Pascal, *Pensées*

Jesus Christ for all, Moses for one people. 2500
Ibid.

Is it any wonder that to this day this Galilean is too much for our small hearts? 2501
H. G. Wells, *Outline of History*

By a Carpenter the world was made, and only by that Carpenter can mankind be remade. 2502
Desiderius Erasmus, attributed

His life was from the beginning a complete acceptance and embracing of insecurity. "Foxes have holes, and the birds of the air have nests, but the Son of man hath not where to lay his head." 2503
Alan W. Watts, *The Wisdom of Insecurity*

We can hardly think of Jesus without thinking of the sparrows, the grass, fig trees, sheep. 2504
Vincent McNabb, *God's Way of Mercy*

What is the use of a modern man saying that Christ is only a thing like Atys or Mithras, when the next moment he is reproaching Christianity for not following Christ? 2505
G. K. Chesterton, *The New Jerusalem*

His morality was all sympathy, just what morality should be. 2506
Oscar Wilde, *De profundis*

When Jesus came
The world was all at peace in utter wickedness. 2507
Coventry Patmore, *The Rod, the Root and the Flower*

A Jesus of history is really a contradiction in terms; like an eternity clock or an infinity tape-measure. Jesus can exist only now; and, in existing now, makes now always. 2508
Malcolm Muggeridge, *Something Beautiful for God*

"You're going contrary to the Law, Son of Mary," (the village chief) screeched. "The Law goes contrary to my heart," Jesus calmly replied. 2509
Nikos Kazantzakis, *The Last Temptation of Christ*

It was the Church, not the world, that crucified Christ. 2510
Karl Barth, *The Epistle to the Romans*

We may be suspicious of the clergy, and refuse to have anything to do with catechisms, and yet love the Holy and the Just who came to save and not to curse. Jesus will always supply us with the best criticism of Christianity, and when Christianity has

215

passed away the religion of Jesus will in all probability survive. After Jesus as God we shall come back to the God of Jesus.   2511

>   Henri Frédéric Amiel, *Journal,* 12 April 1868 (Easter Day)

We're more popular than Jesus now.   2512

>   John Lennon, speaking of the Beatles. *Time,* 12 August 1966

He outsells Jesus!   2513

>   Otto Bettman, Director of Bettman Archive, on requests for pictures of Sigmund Freud. *Time,* 23 March 1981

No man ever made more trouble than the "gentle Jesus, meek and mild."   2514

>   James M. Gillis, *This Our Day*

I'm sure this Jesus will not do
Either for Englishman or Jew.   2515

>   William Blake, *The Everlasting Gospel*

Tell me the picture of Jesus you have reached and I will tell you some important facts of your nature.   2516

>   Oscar Pfister, *Christianity and Fear*

The work of Christ is "person-forming," and the Christian Church is the people who know themselves as persons through him.   2517

>   Richard Niebuhr, expounding the theology of Friedrich Schleiermacher in *A Handbook of Theologians,* edited by Martin E. Marty and Dean J. Peerman

The moment we start to be *precise* about Jesus—anything he said, anything he did, who he is, what he is, we start to be wrong about him. And this need not shock or surprise or frustrate, for we cannot be absolutely precise about anybody or anything.   2518

>   C. E. S.

Jews

Sublimity is Hebrew by birth.   2519

>   Samuel Taylor Coleridge, *Table Talk*

What a shame it is that they should be more miserable under Christian princes than they were under Pharaoh.   2520

>   Pope Innocent IV (d. 1254), Letter in defense of the Jews

Dear Abby: I am not Jewish but I wish I were. You see, my best friend was a Jew. He loved me so much that he died for me. His name was Jesus.   2521

>   "A True Christian." Quoted in Abigail Van Buren. *The Best of Dear Abby*

I never heard of an idiot being born among them. Some admire the Jewish female physiognomy. I admire it—but with trembling. Jael had those dark inscrutable eyes.   2522

>   Charles Lamb, *Essays of Elia,* "Imperfect Sympathies"

Because I was a Jew, I found myself free from any prejudices which limited others in the use of their intellect, and being a Jew I was prepared to enter opposition and to renounce agreement with the "compact majority."　　　2523
　　　　　Sigmund Freud. Quoted in Max Dimont, *Jews, God and History*

To the Christian, the Jew is a stubborn fellow, who in an unredeemed world is waiting for the Messiah. To the Jew, the Christian is a heedless fellow who, in an unredeemed world, affirms that redemption has somehow or other taken place.　　　2524
　　　　　Martin Buber. Quoted in Reinhold Niebuhr, *Justice and Mercy*

I am a Jew. Hath not a Jew eyes? hath not a Jew hands, organs, dimensions, senses, affections, passions? fed with the same food, hurt with the same weapons, subject to the same diseases, healed by the same means, warmed and cooled by the same winter and summer, as a Christian is? [*Shylock.*]　　　2525
　　　　　William Shakespeare, *The Merchant of Venice*, III, i, 62

They are an ancient people, a famous people, an enduring people, and a people who in the end have generally attained their objects. I hope Parliament may endure for ever, and sometimes I think it will; but I cannot help remembering that the Jews have outlived Assyrian kings, Egyptian Pharaohs, Roman Caesars, and Arabian Caliphs.　　　2526
　　　　　Benjamin Disraeli. Speech in the House of Commons, 25 May 1854

Half of Christendom worships a Jew, and the other half a Jewess.　　　2527
　　　　　Author Unknown

Resurrection with us is not a miracle, but a habit. *(us: Jews.)*　　　2528
　　　　　Isaac Bashevis Singer. Interview in *New York Post*, 1 February 1972

A Jewish man with parents alive is a fifteen-year-old boy, and will remain a fifteen-year-old boy until they die.　　　2529
　　　　　Philip Roth, *Portnoy's Complaint*

Job

Job's best words are his last, "The words of Job are ended." *Then* God *appears*.　　　2530
　　　　　Peter J. Kreeft, *Love Is Stronger than Death*

Job prayed. His friends only philosophized. Job talked *to* God, his three friends talked *about* God.　　　2531
　　　　　Peter J. Kreeft, *Making Sense Out of Suffering*

Jonah

God in the Bible seldom appears as charming. But he does in Jonah, chapter four (especially in the King James Version). Jonah as a whole is the most charming book in the Bible.　　　2532
　　　　　C. E. S.

Joy

They that sow in tears shall reap in joy.　　　2533
　　　　　Psalm 126:5

With joy shall ye draw waters out of the wells of salvation. 2534
Isaiah 12:3

These things have I spoken unto you, that my joy might remain in you, and that your joy might be full. 2535
Jesus in John 15:11

Joy is the grace we say to God. 2536
Jean Ingelow, *Dominion*

Joy is not a substitute for sex; sex is very often a substitute for joy. I sometimes wonder whether all pleasures are not substitutes for joy. 2537
C. S. Lewis, *Surprised by Joy*

It is the lack of joy in Mudville, rather than the presence of sorrow, that makes the difference. 2538
Norman M. Bradburn, *In Pursuit of Happiness*

Because the road is rough and long,
Shall we despise the skylark's song? 2539
Anne Brontë, *Views of Life*

Grief can take care of itself, but to get the full value of joy you must have somebody to divide it with. 2540
Mark Twain, *Pudd'nhead Wilson's New Calendar*

Great joys weep; great sorrows laugh. 2541
Joseph Roux, *Meditations of a Parish Priest*

God is not otherwise to be enjoyed than as He is obeyed. 2542
John Howe, *The Golden Treasury of Puritan Quotations*

Joy is more divine than sorrow, for joy is bread and sorrow is medicine. 2543
Henry Ward Beecher, *Proverbs from Plymouth Pulpit*

O God, may I live to have one day of unsullied joy! 2544
Ludwig von Beethoven, *The Testament of Heiligenstadt*

Joy appears now in little things. The big themes remain tragic. But a leaf fluttered in through a window this morning, as if supported by the rays of the sun, a bird settled on the fire escape, joy was in the taste of the coffee, joy accompanied me as I walked to the press. The secret of joy is the mastery of pain. 2545
Anaïs Lin, *The Diaries of Anaïs Lin*

One joy scatters a hundred griefs. 2546
Chinese Proverb

Well, I suppose joy is a passion, and all passionate things are perhaps very close in their nature to their opposites. Joy, pain, fear—there comes a point, perhaps, where one no longer knows which is which. What people call ecstasy is more like terror than it is like contentment, isn't it? 2547
Denise Leverton, *The Craft of Poetry*

Judaism and Christianity

The Mosaic religion had been a Father religion; Christianity became a Son religion. 2548

Sigmund Freud, *Moses and Monotheism*

Judas

"I would I had never been born!" must be the cry of Judas, not because of the hell-fire around him, but because he loathes the man that betrayed his Friend, the world's Friend. 2549

George MacDonald, *Creation in Christ*

Judging Others

Judge not, that ye be not judged. 2550

Jesus in Matthew 7:1

He that is without sin among you, let him first cast a stone. 2551

Jesus in John 8:7

Every man is entitled to be valued for his best moment. 2552

Ralph Waldo Emerson, *The Conduct of Life*, "Beauty"

They have a right to censure that have a heart to help. 2553

William Penn, *Fruits of Solitude*

I do not judge men by anything they do. Their greatest deed is the impression they make upon me. 2554

Henry David Thoreau, *Journal*, 18 February 1841

In men whom men condemn as ill
I find so much of goodness still!
In men whom men pronounce divine
I find so much of sin and blot,
I do not dare to draw a line
Between the two, where God has not. 2555

Joachin Miller, *Byron*

Judgment, Divine

See God's Judgments

Judgment, Human

Judgment comes from experience, and great judgment comes from bad experience. 2556

Bob Packwood, U. S. Senator. *New York Times,* 30 May 1986

Our judgments about things vary according to the time left us to live—that we think is left us to live. 2557

André Gide, *Journals,* 19 December 1930

Knowledge is the treasure, but judgment the treasurer of a wise man. 2558

William Penn, *Some Fruits of Solitude*

The value and force of a man's judgment can be measured by his ability to think independently of his temperamental leanings.   2559

Algernon S. Logan, *Vistas from the Stream*

Most people suspend their judgment till somebody else has expressed his own and then they repeat it.   2560

Ernest Dimnet, *The Art of Thinking*

He that judges without informing himself to the utmost that he is capable, cannot acquit himself of judging amiss.   2561

John Locke, *An Essay Concerning Human Understanding*

Judgment Day

Alas for the day! for the day of the Lord is at hand.   2562

Joel 1:15

The day of the Lord is great and very terrible; and who can abide it?   2563

Joel 2:11

He shall separate them one from another, as a shepherd divideth his sheep from the goats.   2564

Jesus in Matthew 25:32

These be the days of vengeance, that all things which are written may be fulfilled.   2565

Jesus in Luke 21:22

We must all appear before the judgment seat of Christ.   2566

2 Corinthians 5:10

I saw the dead, small and great, stand before God.   2567

Revelation 20:12

The Day of Judgment is an important notion: but that Day is always with us.   2568

Alfred North Whitehead, *Adventures of Ideas*

God will not look you over for medals, degrees or diplomas, but for scars.   2569

Elbert Hubbard, *Roycroft Dictionary and Book of Epigrams*

A visitor, seeking to console the dying Thomas Hooker: "Sir, you are going to receive the reward of your labor." Thomas Hooker: "Brother, I am going to receive mercy!"   2570

Thomas Hooker, *The Golden Treasury of Puritan Quotations*

Just and Unjust

The rain it raineth on the just
And also on the unjust fella:
But chiefly on the just, because
The unjust steals the just's umbrella.   2571

Author Unknown

Justice

None calleth for justice, nor any pleadeth for truth: they trust in vanity, and speak lies; they conceive mischief, and bring forth iniquity. 2572
Isaiah 59:4

Justice being taken away, what are kingdoms but great robberies? For what are robberies but little kingdoms? 2573
St. Augustine, The *City of God*

Learn to do justice. *(Discite iustitiam.)* 2574
Virgil, *Aeneid,* vi.

I have loved justice and hated iniquity; therefore I die an exile. 2575
Pope Gregory VII, last words, 1085

Justice is a certain rectitude of mind whereby a man does what he ought to do in the circumstances confronting him. 2576
St. Thomas Aquinas, *Summa theologiae,* LXI

Rigid justice is the greatest injustice. 2577
Thomas Fuller, *Gnomologia*

Let justice be done, though the world perish. *(Fiat justitia, et pereat mundus.)* 2578
Ferdinand I, Holy Roman Emperor (1503–1564), motto

Injustice is relatively easy to bear; what stings is justice. 2579
Henry L. Mencken, *Prejudices*

The perfection of love implies charity, because we have a right to be loved. 2580
Austin O'Malley, *Keystones of Thought*

That which is above justice must be based on justice, and include justice, and be reached through justice. 2581
Henry George, *Social Problems*

Indeed, I tremble for my country when I reflect that God is just. 2582
Thomas Jefferson, *Notes on the State of Virginia,* 1781–85

It is a funny sort of justice whose limits are marked by a river: true on this side of the Pyrenees, false on the other. 2583
Blaise Pascal, *Pensées*

Justice is as much a matter of fashion as charm is. 2584
Ibid.

Justice in punishment can be defined in the same way as justice in almsgiving. It means giving our attention to the victim of affliction as to a being and not a thing; it means wishing to preserve in him the faculty of free consent. 2585
Simone Weil, *Waiting on God*

We have invented the distinction between justice and charity. It is easy to understand why. Our notion of justice dispenses him who possesses from the obligation of giving. 2586
Ibid.

Justification

By him all that believe are justified (him: Jesus.)   2587
>   Acts 13:39

A man is justified by faith without the deeds of the law.   2588
>   Romans 3:28

It is God that justifieth.   2589
>   Romans 8:33

The best things we do have somewhat in them to be pardoned. How then can we do anything meritorious, and worthy to be rewarded?   2590
>   Richard Hooker (c. 1554–1600), *A Learned Discourse on Justification*

He who created you without you will not justify you without you.   2591
>   St. Augustine, *Sermons*

K

Killing

Thou shalt not kill. 2592
Exodus 20:13

All they that take the sword shall perish with the sword. 2593
Jesus in Matthew 26:52

The worst thing that can be said of the most powerful is that they can take your life; but the same thing can be said of the most weak. 2594
Charles Caleb Colton, *Lacon*

We kill everybody, my dear. Some with bullets, some with words, and everybody with our deeds. We drive people to their graves, and neither see nor feel it. 2595
Maxim Gorki, *Enemies*

Human blood is heavy; the man who has shed it cannot run away. 2596
African Proverb

No humane being, past the thoughtless age of boyhood, will wantonly murder any creature which holds its life by the same tenure that he does. 2597
Henry David Thoreau, *Walden*

To live without killing is a thought which could electrify the world, if men were only capable of staying awake long enough to let the truth soak in. 2598
Henry Miller, *The Henry Miller Reader,* "Reunion in Brooklyn"

Kindness

The Lord deal kindly with you, as ye have dealt with the dead, and with me. 2599
Ruth 1:8

The merciful man doeth good to his own soul: but he that is cruel troubleth his own flesh. 2600
Proverbs 11:17

The unfortunate need people who will be kind to them; the prosperous need people to be kind to. 2601
Aristotle, *Nichomachean Ethics*

If thine enemy be hungry, give him bread to eat; and if he be thirsty, give him water to drink.　　　2602
　　　Proverbs 25:21

She stretcheth out her hand to the poor. . . . and in her tongue is the law of kindness. *(she: the virtuous woman.)*　　　2603
　　　Proverbs 31:20, 26

Be ye kind one to another, tenderhearted, forgiving one another, even as God for Christ's sake hath forgiven you.　　　2604
　　　Ephesians 4:32

I am sometimes asked, "Why do you spend so much of your time and money talking about kindness to animals when there is so much cruelty to man?" I answer: "I am working at the roots."　　　2605
　　　Nathaniel Altman. Quoted in The *Extended Circle: A Dictionary of Humane Thought,* edited by Jon Wynne-Tyson

Every kindness to another is a little death in the Divine Image.　　　2606
　　　William Blake, *Jerusalem*

There is no beautifier of complexion, or form, or behavior, like the wish to scatter joy and not pain around us.　　　2607
　　　Ralph Waldo Emerson, *The Conduct of Life*

Men are cruel, but Man is kind.　　　2608
　　　Rabindranath Tagore, *Stray Birds*

That best portion of a good man's life,
The little, nameless, unremembered acts
Of kindness and of love.　　　2609
　　　William Wordsworth, *Lines composed a few miles above Tintern Abbey*

The milk of human kindness is less apt to turn sour if the vessel that holds it stands steady, cool, and separate, and is not too often uncorked.　　　2610
　　　George Santayana, *Character and Opinion in the United States*

Kindness teaches us to learn, and to forget, many things.　　　2611
　　　Madame Soy Monoff Swetchine, *The Writings of Madame Swetchine*

The ministry of kindness is a ministry which may be achieved by all men, rich and poor, learned and illiterate. Brilliance of mind and capacity for deep thinking have rendered great service to humanity, but by themselves they are impotent to dry a tear or mend a broken heart.　　　2612
　　　Author Unknown

Kingdom of God/Heaven

In those days came John the Baptist, preaching in the wilderness of Judea, And saying: Repent ye, for the kingdom of heaven is at hand.　　　2613
　　　Matthew 3:1–2

I say unto you, that except your righteousness shall exceed the righteousness of the scribes and Pharisees, ye shall in no wise enter into the kingdom of heaven.　　　2614
　　　Jesus in Matthew 5:20

Verily I say unto you, Among them that are born of women there hath not risen a greater than John the Baptist: notwithstanding he that is least in the kingdom of heaven is greater than he.   2615

Jesus in Matthew 11:11

If I cast out devils by the Spirit of God, then the kingdom of God is come unto you.   2616

Jesus in Matthew 12:28

Whosoever shall not receive the kingdom of God as a little child, he shall not enter therein.   2617

Jesus in Mark 10:15

Seek ye the kingdom of God, and all these things shall be added unto you.   2618

Jesus in Luke 12:31

It is like a grain of mustard seed, which a man took, and cast into his garden; and it grew, and waxed a great tree. *(it: kingdom of God.)*   2619

Jesus in Luke 13:19

And when he was demanded of the Pharisees, when the kingdom of God should come, he answered them and said, The kingdom of God cometh not with observation: Neither shall they say, Lo here! or, lo there! for, behold, the kingdom of God is within you. *(he: Jesus.)*   2620

Luke 17:20–21

Except a man be born again, he cannot see the kingdom of God.   2621

Jesus in John 3:3

The kingdom of God is not meat and drink; but righteousness, and peace, and joy in the Holy Ghost.   2622

Romans 14:17

There is a kingdom of heaven prior to the actual passage of actual things, and there is the same kingdom finding its completion through the accomplishment of this passage.   2623

Alfred North Whitehead, *Religion in the Making*

Power in complete subordination to love—that is something like a definition of the kingdom of God.   2624

William Temple, attributed

The Kingdom of God is a society upon earth where God's will is as perfectly done as it is in heaven.   2625

William Barclay, The *Gospel of Matthew,* I

There can be a true consummation and a true happiness of mankind only when not merely the last generation, but all men, even those who suffered and bled in the past, come to share in it. Not a kingdom of man, but only the kingdom of God, is the kingdom of perfection, the kingdom of fulfilled justice, of unbroken love, of liberated freedom, of universal peace, of eternal life. *Credo in vitam venturi saeculi.*   2626

Hans Küng, *Does God Exist?*

Knowledge

Of every tree of the garden thou mayest freely eat: But of the tree of the knowledge of good and evil, thou shalt not eat.　　　2627
> Genesis 2:16–17

The Lord is a God of knowledge, and by him actions are weighed.　　　2628
> 1 Samuel 2:3

Shall any teach God knowledge?　　　2629
> Job 21:22

I understand more than the ancients, because I keep thy precepts.　　　2630
> Psalm 119:100

A wise man will hear, and will increase learning.　　　2631
> Proverbs 1:5

Knowledge is easy unto him that understandeth.　　　2632
> Proverbs 14:6

He that increaseth knowledge increaseth sorrow.　　　2633
> Ecclesiastes 1:18

Hear, and understand.　　　2634
> Jesus in Matthew 15:10

It is not for you to know the times or the seasons.　　　2635
> Jesus in Acts 1:7

I know nothing by myself.　　　2636
> 1 Corinthians 4:4

If any man think that he knoweth any thing, he knoweth nothing yet as he ought to know.　　　2637
> 1 Corinthians 8:2

Add to your faith virtue, and to virtue, knowledge.　　　2638
> 2 Peter 1:5

There is knowledge and knowledge: knowledge that resteth in the bare speculation of things, and knowledge that is accompanied with the grace of faith and love, which puts a man upon doing even the will of God from the heart.　　　2639
> John Bunyan, *The Pilgrim's Progress*

You must be above your knowledge, not under it, or it will oppress you; and the more you have of it, the greater will be the load.　　　2640
> John Henry Newman, *On the Scope and Nature of University Education*

Knowledge and timber shouldn't be much used until they are seasoned.　　　2641
> Oliver Wendell Holmes, *The Autocrat of the Breakfast-Table*

All knowledge that is divorced from justice is called cunning.　　　2642
> Plato, quoted in Cicero, *De Officiis*

Knowledge is a recognition of something absent: it is a salutation, an embrace.　　　2643
> George Santayana, *The Life of Reason*

You can know more and more about one thing but you can never know everything about one thing: It's hopeless.   2644
>
> Vladimir Nabokov, *Strong Opinions*

All knowledge is sterile which does not lead to action and end in charity.   2645
>
> Desirée Joseph Cardinal Mercier. Quoted in John A. Cade, *The Life of Cardinal Mercier*

We're drowning in information and starving for knowledge.   2646
>
> Rutherford D. Rogers, on the enormous annual number of publications of every kind. *New York Times,* 1 June 1986

The pope and the peasant know more between them than the pope alone.   2647
>
> Italian Proverb

Knowledge of God

And they shall know that I am the Lord their God, that brought them forth out of the land of Egypt.   2648
>
> Exodus 29:46

We know him not, neither can the number of his years be searched out.   2649
>
> Job 36:26

Be still, and know that I am God.   2650
>
> Psalm 46:10

The earth shall be full of the knowledge of the Lord, as the waters cover the sea.   2651
>
> Isaiah 11:9

No man knoweth the Son, but the Father; neither knoweth any man the Father, save the Son, and he to whomsoever the Son will reveal him.   2652
>
> Jesus in Matthew 11:27

If ye had known me, ye should have known my Father also.   2653
>
> Jesus in John 8:19

Grow in grace, and in the knowledge of our Lord.   2654
>
> 2 Peter 3:18

Can I explain the Friend to one for whom He is no Friend?   2655
>
> Jalaluddin Rumi. Quoted in Aldous Huxley, *The Perennial Philosophy*

You can only know God through an open mind just as you can only see the sky through an open window. You will not see the sky if you have covered the glass with blue paint.   2656
>
> Alan W. Watts, *The Wisdom of Insecurity*

Man is very precious to God, so I believe, and can be in a close and loving relationship with Him, but *intellectually* man probably knows as little of the vast, far-reaching activities of God as the ant knows about preaching, let alone about the wider life of the world.   2657
>
> Leslie Weatherhead, *The Christian Agnostic*

There is something almost ludicrous in sitting down at a desk and writing the word "God" and then being presumptuous enough to add anything.   2658

        Ibid.

What a long way it is between knowing God and loving him!   2659

        Blaise Pascal, *Pensées*. [Surely Pascal is wrong here. How can
        anybody know God *apart from* loving him? C. E. S.]

L

Labor

In the sweat of thy brow shalt thou eat bread.   2660
> Genesis 3:19

Six days shalt thou labor, and do all thy work: but the seventh day is the sabbath of the Lord thy God: in it thou shalt not do any work.   2661
> Exodus 20:9–10

Go to the ant, thou sluggard; consider her ways, and be wise.   2662
> Proverbs 6:6

In all labor there is profit: but the talk of the lips tendeth only to penury.   2663
> Proverbs 14:23

What profit hath a man of all the labor which he taketh under the sun? 2664
> Ecclesiastes 1:3

The sleep of a laboring man is sweet.   2665
> Ecclesiastes 5:12

Come unto me, all ye that labor and are heavy laden, and I will give you rest.   2666
> Jesus in Matthew 11:28

The laborer is worthy of his hire.   2667
> Jesus in Luke 10:7

If any would not work, neither should he eat.   2668
> 2 Thessalonians 3:10

Don't condescend to unskilled labor. Try it for half a day first.   2669
> Brooks Atkinson, *Once Around the Sun,* "March 27"

We put our love where we have put our labor.   2670
> Ralph Waldo Emerson, *Journals,* 1836

Thou, O God, dost sell us all good things at the price of labor.   2671
> Leonardo da Vinci, *Notebooks*

Labor without joy is base. Labor without sorrow is base. Sorrow without labor is base. Joy without labor is base.   2672
    John Ruskin, *Time and Tide*

In the things of this life, the laborer is most like God.   2673
    Ulrich Zwingli, written in 1525. Quoted in Tawney, *Religion and the Rise of Capitalism*

The labor of a human being is not a commodity or article of commerce. You can't weigh the soul of a man with a bar of pig-iron.   2674
    Samuel Gompers, *Seventy Years of Life and Labor*

Blessed is he who has found his work; let him ask no other blessedness. 2675
    Thomas Carlyle, *Past and Present*

Ah, little recks the laborer
How near his work is holding him to God,
The loving laborer through space and time!   2676
    Author Unknown

All the best work is done the way ants do things—by tiny but untiring and regular additions.   2677
    Lafcadio Hearn. Quoted in *Lafcadio Hearn: Life and Letters*, edited by Elizabeth Risland

Work is much more fun than fun.   2678
    Noel Coward, *Observer,* "Sayings of the Week," 21 June 1963

Either you have work or you have not. When you have to say, "Let us do something," then begins mischief.   2679
    Rabindranath Tagore, *Stray Birds*

Last Words

Now God be with you, my dear children: I have breakfasted with you and I shall sup with my Lord Jesus Christ.   2680
    Robert Bruce, attributed

Open the window, and let in more light!   2681
    Johann Wolfgang von Goethe, attributed

Let this be my last word, that I trust in thy love.   2682
    Rabindranath Tagore, *Stray Birds*

I shall ask leave to desist, when I am interrupted by so great an experiment as dying.   2683
    William Davenant, his apology, in his last illness, for not having finished the writing of *Gondibert*

My desire is to make what haste I may to be gone.   2684
    Oliver Cromwell

Don't let poor Nelly starve.   2685
    Charles II of England, last words, referring to his mistress Nell Gwynn

I am dying, sir, of a hundred good symptoms.   2686
    Alexander Pope, on his deathbed

A dying man can do nothing easy. 2687
>Benjamin Franklin, on his deathbed, 17 April 1790

Doctor, I die hard, but I am not afraid to go. 2688
>George Washington. Last words, 14 December 1799

I have lived an honest and useful life to mankind; my time has been spent in doing good, and I die in perfect composure and resignation to the will of my Creator. 2689
>Thomas Paine. Last will, 1809

This is the last of earth! I am content. 2690
>John Quincy Adams, on his deathbed, 23 February 1848

I am ready at any time. Do not keep me waiting. 2691
>John Brown, on the scaffold, 1859

As the last bell struck, a peculiar sweet smile shone over his face, and he lifted up his head a little, and quickly said, "Adsum!" and fell back. It was the word we used at school, when names were called, and lo, he, whose heart was that of a little child, had answered to his name, and stood in the presence of the Master. 2692
>William Makepeace Thackeray, of Colonel Newcome, in *The Newcomes*, lxxx

Laughter

Even in laughter, the heart is sorrowful. 2693
>Proverbs 14:13

I said of laughter, It is mad; and of mirth, What doeth it? 2694
>Ecclesiastes 2:2

As the crackling of thorns under a pot, so is the laughter of the fool. 2695
>Ecclesiastes 7:6

No one is more profoundly sad than he who laughs too much. 2696
>Jean Paul Richter, *Hesperus*

Laughter would be bereaved if Snobbery died. 2697
>Peter Ustinov. *Observer*, "Sayings of the Week," 13 March 1955

I hate scarce smiles. I love laughing. 2698
>William Blake, *Annotations to Lavater*

The man who cannot laugh is not only fit for treasons, stratagems, and spoils; but his whole life is already a treason and a stratagem. 2699
>Thomas Carlyle, *Sartor Resartus*

Laughter is a form of internal jogging. It moves your internal organs around. It enhances respiration. It is an igniter of great expectations. 2700
>Norman Cousins, *Anatomy of an Illness*

For me, a hearty "belly laugh" is one of the most beautiful sounds in the world. 2701
>Bennet Cerf, in Foreword to *An Encyclopedia of Modern American Humor*

Law

It may be true that the law cannot make a man love me, but it can keep him from lynching me, and I think that's pretty important.   2702
>   Martin Luther King, Jr. *Wall Street Journal,* 13 November 1962

Wrong must not win by technicalities.   2703
>   Aeschylus, *The Eumenides* (458 B.C.), translation of Richard Lattimore

In civilized life, law floats on a sea of ethics.   2704
>   Chief Justice Earl Warren. *New York Times,* 12 November 1962

All laws are an attempt to domesticate the natural ferocity of the species.   2705
>   John W. Gardner. *San Francisco Examiner & Chronicle,* 3 July 1974

One law for the lion and ox is oppression.   2706
>   William Blake, *Proverbs of Hell*

Man is an able creature, but he has made 12,647,389 laws and hasn't improved on the Ten Commandments.   2707
>   Mark Twain, attributed

There is never a deed so foul that something couldn't be said for the guy: and that's why there are lawyers.   2708
>   Melvin Belli. *Los Angeles Times,* 18 December 1981

Beware of law-abiding citizens who do not beware of themselves as law-abiding citizens.   2709
>   C. E. S.

Leadership

Can we find such a one as this, a man in whom the Spirit of God is?   2710
>   Genesis 41:38

Provide out of all the people able men, such as fear God, men of truth, hating covetousness.   2711
>   Exodus 18:21

The cause that is too hard for you, bring it unto me, and I will hear it.   2712
>   Deuteronomy 1:17

The Spirit of the Lord came upon Gideon, and he blew a trumpet.   2713
>   Judges 6:34

Because thou hast rejected the word of the Lord, he hath also rejected thee from being king.   2714
>   1 Samuel 15:23

Give therefore thy servant an understanding heart to judge thy people, that I may discern between good and bad.   2715
>   1 Kings 3:9

Where no counsel is, the people fall.   2716
>   Proverbs 11:14

Better is a poor and a wise child than an old and foolish king who will no more be admonished.   2717
>Ecclesiastes 4:13

My people have been lost sheep: their shepherds have caused them to go astray.   2718
>Jeremiah 50:6

Follow me, and I will make you fishers of men.   2719
>Jesus in Matthew 4:19

My sheep hear my voice, and I know them, and they follow me.   2720
>Jesus in John 10:27

To command is to serve, nothing more and nothing less.   2721
>André Malraux, *Man's Hope*

If an individual wants to be a leader and isn't controversial, that means he never stood for anything.   2722
>Richard M. Nixon. *Dallas Times Herald,* 10 December 1978

Leadership should be born out of the understanding of the needs of those who would be affected by it.   2723
>Marian Anderson. *New York Times,* 22 July 1951

O for a living man to lead!
That will not babble when we bleed;
O for the silent doer of the deed;
One that is happy in his height,
And one that in a nation's night
Hath solitary certitude of light.   2724
>Stephen Phillips, *A Man*

The real leader has no need to lead—he is content to point the way.   2725
>Henry Miller, *The Wisdom of the Heart*

A leader is a dealer in hope.   2726
>Napoleon Bonaparte, *Maxims* (1804–1815)

A chief is a man who assumes responsibility. He says, "I was beaten." He does not say, "My men were beaten."   2727
>Antoine de Saint-Exupéry, *Flight to Arras*

Learning

The end of learning is to repair the ruins of our first parents by regaining to know God aright, and out of that knowledge to love him, to imitate him, to be like him, as we may the nearest by possessing our souls of true virtue, which being united to the heavenly gift of faith makes up the highest perfection.   2728
>John Milton, *Tractate on Education*

It's what you learn after you know it all that counts.   2729
>John Wooden, *They Call Me Coach*

Everyone should learn to do one thing supremely well because he likes it, and one thing supremely well because he detests it. 2730

> B. W. M. Young, Headmaster of Charterhouse School, Godalming, England. *New York Times,* 12 January 1964

Learning makes the wise wiser and the fool more foolish. 2731

> English Proverb

Learning without thought is labor lost; thought without learning is perilous. 2732

> Confucius, *Analects*

Tim was so learned that he could name a horse in nine languages. So ignorant that he bought a cow to ride on. 2733

> Benjamin Franklin, *Poor Richard's Almanack,* 1750

Everywhere, we learn only from those whom we love. 2734

> Johann Wolfgang von Goethe. Quoted in *Eckermann's Conversations with Goethe*

He who is learned but does not fear God is like a woman without manners. 2735

> Jewish Proverb

Liberation

Every man must free himself of Egypt every day. 2736

> Rebbe Israel of Kozhenitz, quoted in Elie Wiesel, *Souls on Fire*

Liberty

I will walk at liberty for I seek thy precepts. 2737

> Psalm 119:45

The Spirit of the Lord God is upon me; because the Lord hath appointed me to preach good tidings unto the meek; he hath sent me to bind up the brokenhearted, to proclaim liberty to the captives, and the opening of the prison to them that are bound. 2738

> Isaiah 61:1

Take heed lest by any means this liberty of yours become a stumblingblock to them that are weak. 2739

> 1 Corinthians 8:9

Where the Spirit of the Lord is, there is liberty. 2740

> 2 Corinthians 3:17

Liberty means responsibility. That is why most men dread it. 2741

> Bernard Shaw, *Maxims for Revolutionaries*

There are inexcusable lies and consecrated lies. For instance, we are told that on the arrival of the news of the unfortunate battle of Fontenoy, every heart beat, and every eye swam in tears. Now we know that no man ate his dinner the worse, but there *should* have been all this concern; and to say there was (smiling) may be reckoned a consecrated lie. 2742

> Samuel Johnson, in Boswell's *Life of Johnson*

I love the University of Salamanca; for when the Spaniards were in doubt as to the lawfulness of their conquering America, the University of Salamanca gave it as their opinion that it was not lawful.　2743
Ibid.

Is life so dear or peace so sweet as to be purchased at the price of chains and slavery? Forbid it, almighty God! I know not what course others may take, but as for me, give me liberty or give me death.　2744
Patrick Henry. Speech, Virginia Convention, 23 March 1775

The love of liberty is the love of others; the love of power is the love of ourselves.　2745
William Hazlitt, *Political Essays,* "The 'Times' Newspaper"

Liberty is the soul's right to breathe, and, when it cannot take a long breath, laws are girdled too tight.　2746
Henry Ward Beecher, *Proverbs from Plymouth Pulpit*

How is it that we hear the loudest yelps for liberty among the drivers of Negroes?　2747
Samuel Johnson, *Taxation No Tyranny*

The hungry and the homeless don't care about liberty any more than they care about cultural heritage. To pretend that they do care is cant.　2748
E. M. Forster, *Abinger Harvest*

O liberty, what crimes are committed in thy name!　2749
Jeanne Manon Roland. Last words before dying on the guillotine

O Liberty! can man resign thee,
Once having felt thy generous flame?
Can dungeon bolts and bars confine thee,
Or whips thy noble spirit tame?　2750
Author unknown, a free translation of *La Marseillaise*

Lies

I said in my haste, All men are liars.　2751
Psalm 116:11

These six things doth the Lord hate: yea, seven are an abomination unto him: A proud look, a lying tongue, and hands that shed innocent blood, An heart that deviseth wicked imaginations, feet that be swift in running to mischief, A false witness that speaketh lies, and he that soweth discord among brethren.　2752
Proverbs 6:16–19

The wicked is snared by the transgression of his lips.　2753
Proverbs 12:13

A lying tongue is but for a moment.　2754
Proverbs 12:19

Woe unto them that call evil, good, and good, evil; that put darkness for light, and light for darkness; that put bitter for sweet, and sweet for bitter!　2755
Isaiah 5:20

He is a liar, and the father of it. *(He: Satan.)*   2756
     Jesus in John 8:44

There are 869 different forms of lying, but only one of them has been squarely forbidden. Thou shalt not bear false witness against thy neighbor.   2757
     Mark Twain, *Pudd'nhead Wilson's Calendar*

A mixture of a lie doth ever add pleasure.   2758
     Francis Bacon, *Essays,* "Of Truth"

It is not the lie that passeth through the mind, but the lie that sinketh in, and settleth in it, that doth the hurt.   2759
     Ibid.

Sin has many tools, but a lie is the handle which fits them all.   2760
     Oliver Wendell Holmes, *The Autocrat of the Breakfast-Table*

The cruelest lies are often told in silence.   2761
     Robert Louis Stevenson, *Virginibus Puerisque*

Repetition does not transform a lie into a truth.   2762
     Franklin D. Roosevelt. Speech, 26 October 1939

Life

The Lord God formed man of the dust of the ground, and breathed into his nostrils the breath of life.   2763
     Genesis 2:7

Wherefore is light given to him that is in misery, and life unto the bitter in soul?   2764
     Job 3:20

What is mine end, that I should prolong my life?   2765
     Job 6:11

Man that is born of a woman is of few days, and full of trouble.   2766
     Job 14:1

Give me understanding, and I shall live.   2767
     Psalm 119:144

A pleasant thing it is for the eyes to behold the sun.   2768
     Ecclesiastes 11:7

Seek ye the Lord, and ye shall live.   2769
     Amos 5:6

In him was life; and the life was the light of men.   2770
     John 1:4

In him we live, and move, and have our being.   2771
     Acts 17:28

He that hath the Son hath life.   2772
     1 John 5:12

Life is a long lesson in humility.   2773
     James Barrie, *The Little Minister*

Life can be explained only after it has been lived, just as Christ only began to interpret the Scriptures and show how they applied to him—after his resurrection.   2774

Søren Kierkegaard, *Journals,* 14 April 1838

Life is like an onion, which one peels crying   2775

French Proverb

Life is like playing a violin in public and learning the instrument as one goes on.   2776

Samuel Butler, *Note Books*

To keep a lamp burning we have to keep putting oil in it.   2777

Mother Teresa of Calcutta. *Time,* 29 December 1975

Life is too short to be little.   2778

Benjamin Disraeli, attributed

Life is God's novel. Let him write it.   2779

Isaac Bashevis Singer, quoted in *Voices for Life,* edited by Dom Moraes

The life of every man is a diary in which he means to write one story, and writes another; and his humblest hour is when he compares the volume as it is with what he vowed to make it.   2780

James Barrie, *The Little Minister*

I don't understand life at all, but I don't say it is impossible that God may understand it a little.   2781

Jules Renard, *Journal,* March 1910

Cheerless is the day, the light under frowning clouds is like a punished child with traces of tears on its pale cheeks, and the cry of the wind is like the cry of a wounded world. But I know I am travelling to meet my Friend.   2782

Rabindranath Tagore, *Stray Birds*

After lecturing learnedly on miracles, a great theologian was asked to give a specific example of one. "There is only one miracle," he answered. "It is life."   2783

Frederick Buechner, *Wishful Thinking: A Theological ABC*

Listening

Speak, Lord; for thy servant heareth.   2784

1 Samuel 3:9

Hold thy peace, and I shall teach thee wisdom.   2785

Job 33:33

A wise man will hear, and will increase learning.   2786

Proverbs 1:5

I spake unto thee in thy prosperity, but thou saidst, I will not hear.   2787

Jeremiah 22:21

We have piped unto you, and ye have not danced; we have mourned unto you, and ye have not lamented. 2788

Jesus in Matthew 11:17

Who hath ears to hear, let him hear. 2789

Jesus in Matthew 13:9

Let every man be swift to hear, slow to speak, slow to wrath. 2790

James 1:19

Love depends upon listening. 2791

Morton Kelsey, *Afterlife*

People ought to listen more slowly! 2792

Jean Sparks, librarian, on confused requests such as "Do you have the wrath of grapes?" and "I want a book about the Abdominal Snowman." Christian Science Monitor, 9 December 1986

There is only one cardinal rule: One must always *listen* to the patient. 2793

Oliver Sacks, British neurologist. *Newsweek*, 20 August 1984

Overheard at Stonehenge: "What a story these old stones would tell if only they could speak!" *Responsio:* What a story these old stones are telling—if only we could listen! 2794

C. E. S.

Logic

Logic is only Cigol spelled backward. 2795

Frederick Buechner, *Wishful Thinking: A Theological ABC*

Loneliness

The thing that makes you exceptional, if you are at all, is inevitably that which makes you lonely. 2796

Lorraine Hansberry, *To Be Young, Gifted, and Black*

It is not good that the man should be alone; I will make him an help meet for him. 2797

Genesis 2:18

My kinsfolk have failed, and my familiar friends have forgotten me. 2798

Job 19:14

I am a brother to dragons, and a companion to owls. 2799

Job 30:29

How long wilt thou forget me, O Lord? for ever? how long wilt thou hide thy face from me? 2800

Psalm 13:1

I am forgotten as a dead man out of mind: I am like a broken vessel. 2801

Psalm 31:12

Woe to him that is alone when he falleth; for he hath not another to help him up.   2802
> Ecclesiastes 4:10

I am not alone, because the Father is with me.   2803
> Jesus in John 16:32

Didst Thou give me this inescapable loneliness so that it would be easier to give Thee all?   2804
> Dag Hammarskjöld, *Markings*

Real loneliness consists not in being alone, but in being with the wrong person, in the suffocating darkness of a room in which no real communication is possible.   2805
> Sydney J. Harris, *Strictly Personal*

Whom the heart of man shuts out,
Sometimes the heart of God takes in,
And fences them all round about
With silence mid the world's loud din.   2806
> James Russell Lowell, *The Forlorn*

Lord's Prayer

The third clause of the Lord's Prayer is repeated daily by millions, who have not the slightest intention of letting any will be done except their own.   2807
> Aldous Huxley, *The Perennial Philosophy*

Jesus teaches us to pray *Thy will be done,* not *Thy will be changed.*   2808
> William Barclay, attributed

Suggested emendation in the Lord's Prayer: Take out "Thy Kingdom come" and substitute "Give us time!"   2809
> Thomas Merton, *Conjectures of a Guilty Bystander*

Lostness

All is not gold that glitters; not all that wander are lost.   2810
> J. R. R. Tolkien, *The Fellowship of the Ring*

Love

See also Charity

Jacob served seven years for Rachel; and they seemed unto him but a few days, for the love he had to her.   2811
> Genesis 29:20

Now let me die, since I have seen thy face, because thou art yet alive.   2812
> Genesis 46:30

Thou shalt not avenge, nor bear any grudge against the children of thy people, but thou shalt love thy neighbor as thyself: I am the Lord.   2813
> Leviticus 19:18

239

Hatred stirreth up strifes: but love covereth all sins.   2814
> Proverbs 10:12

Better is a dinner of herbs where love is, than a stalled ox and hatred therewith.   2815
> Proverbs 15:17

In the broad ways will I seek him whom my soul loveth.   2816
> Song of Solomon 3:2

Many waters cannot quench love, neither can the floods drown it.   2817
> Song of Solomon 8:7

If ye love them which love you, what reward have ye? do not even the publicans the same?   2818
> Jesus in Matthew 5:46

How alike are the groans of love to the groans of the dying.   2819
> Malcolm Lowry, *Under the Volcano*

He that loveth father or mother more than me is not worthy of me: and he that loveth son or daughter more than me is not worthy of me.   2820
> Jesus in Matthew 10:37

By this shall all men know that ye are my disciples, if ye have love one to another.   2821
> Jesus in John 13:35

We know that we have passed from death unto life, because we love the brethren. He that loveth not his brother abideth in death.   2822
> 1 John 3:14

In true love it is not we who love the afflicted but it is God in us who loves them.   2823
> Simone Weil, *Waiting on God*

To love a thing means wanting it to live.   2824
> Confucius, *Analects*

The love that lasts longest is the love that is never returned.   2825
> W. Somerset Maugham, recalled on his death, 16 December 1965

Love as a substitute for justice is odious, but love as a complement to justice is an absolute necessity.   2826
> Reinhold Niebuhr. *The Christian Century,* January 1958

Witness—that is the word for love.   2827
> Peter J. Kreeft, *Making Sense Out of Suffering*

Where Love administers physic, its tenderness is observed in balms and cordials.   2828
> Thomas Traherne, *Centuries*

Where there is no extravagance there is no love, and where there is no love there is no understanding.   2829
> Oscar Wilde. Quoted in Richard Ellmann, *Oscar Wilde*

You can love a person deeply and sincerely whom you do not like. You can like a person passionately whom you do not love.   2830

                  Robert Hugh Benson, *Spiritual Letters of Monsignor R. Hugh*
                  Benson to One of His Converts

They have invented a new phrase, a phrase that is a black-and-white contradiction in two words—"free love"—as if a lover ever had been, or ever could be, free. It is the nature of love to bind itself, and the institution of marriage merely paid the average man the compliment of taking him at his word.   2831

                  G. K. Chesterton, *The Defendant*

M

Madness

Sanity is very rare; every man almost, and every woman, has a dash of madness.   2832
> Ralph Waldo Emerson, *Journal*, 1836

Madness need not be all breakdown. It may also be breakthrough. It is potential liberation and renewal as well as enslavement and existential death.   2833
> R. D. Laing, *The Politics of Experience*

Malice

He that scattereth thorns must not go barefoot.   2834
> Thomas Fuller, *Gnomologia*

I am convinced that we have a degree of delight, and that no small one, in the real misfortunes and pains of others.   2835
> Edmund Burke, *A Philosophical Inquiry into the Origin of our Ideas of the Sublime and Beautiful*

One likes people much better when they're battered down by a prodigious sea of misfortune than when they triumph.   2836
> Virginia Woolf, *A Writer's Diary*, 13 August 1921

Mammonism

Mammon, n. The god of the world's leading religion.   2837
> Ambrose Bierce, *The Devil's Dictionary*

Some people will touch their crowns to Carnegie in heaven.   2838
> H. M. Tomlinson, *The Sea and the Jungle*

Man (Humankind)

God created man in his own image, in the image of God created he him; male and female created he them.   2839
> Genesis 1:27

Be fruitful, and multiply, and replenish the earth, and subdue it.   2840
> Genesis 1:28

It repented the Lord that he had made man on the earth. 2841
> Genesis 6:6

Shall mortal man be more just than God? shall a man be more pure than his maker? 2842
> Job 4:17

I will praise thee; for I am fearfully and wonderfully made. 2843
> Psalm 139:14

We are the clay, and thou our potter. 2844
> Isaiah 64:8

Man is a fallen god who remembers the heavens. 2845
> Alphonse de Lamartine, *Nouvelles meditations poetiques*

Man is a great deep, Lord. You number his very hairs and they are not lost in your sight; but the hairs of his head are easier to number than the attractions and movements of his heart. 2846
> St. Augustine, *Confessions*

Man *becomes* man only by the intelligence, but he *is* man only by the heart. 2847
> Henri Frédéric Amiel, *Journal In Time,* 7 December 1851

Man is the language of God. 2848
> Menahem-Mendl of Vitebsk, quoted in Elie Wiesel, *Souls on Fire*

Man partly is, and wholly hopes to be. 2849
> Robert Browning, *A Death in the Desert*

That man alone is affected by tickling is due firstly to the delicacy of his skin, and secondly to his being the only animal that laughs. 2850
> Aristotle, *Parts of Animals*

Man is the shepherd of being. 2851
> Martin Heidegger, *Being and Time*

Man is all ready to become a god, and instead he appears at times to be a zombie. 2852
> Thomas Merton, *Through the Year with Thomas Merton,* January 7

Man is not the center of the universe as once we thought in our simplicity, but something much more wonderful—the arrow pointing the way to the final unification of life. Man alone constitutes the last-born, the freshest, the most complicated, the most subtle of all the successive layers of life. 2853
> Pierre Teilhard de Chardin, *The Phenomenon of Man*

Man is certainly crazy. He could not make a mite, but he makes gods by the dozen. 2854
> Michel de Montaigne, *Essays*

All men that are ruined are ruined on the side of their natural propensities. 2855
> Edmund Burke, *Letters on a Regicide Peace*

Man's unhappiness, as I construe, comes of his greatness; it is because there is an Infinite in him, which with all his cunning he cannot quite bury under the Finite. 2856

Thomas Carlyle, *Sartor Resartus*

The fish in the water is silent, the animal on the earth is noisy, the bird in the air is singing. But Man has in him the silence of the sea, the noise of the earth and the music of the air. 2857

Rabindranath Tagore, *Stray Birds*

Man is so the universe will have something to talk through, so God will have somebody to talk with, and so the rest of us will have something to talk about. 2858

Frederick Buechner, *Wishful Thinking: A Theological ABC*

Man's Bellicosity

If you want an audience, start a fight. 2859

Irish Proverb

Man's Complexity

I condemn equally those who choose to praise man, those who choose to condemn him and those who choose to divert themselves, and I can only approve those who seek with groans. 2860

Blaise Pascal, *Unclassified Papers*

We think playing upon man is like playing upon an ordinary organ. It is indeed an organ, but strange, shifting, and changeable. Those who only know how to play an ordinary organ would never be in tune with this one. You have to know where the keys are. 2861

Blaise Pascal, *Pensées*

Man's Dominion

The word *dominion* is a direct English effort to translate the Latin. In English *dominion* suggests *domination,* but that is an incorrect translation. The Hebrew statement (Gen. 1:28) is, rather, "And God said, You are to exercise care over the earth and hold it in its proper place." 2862

Joseph Sittler, *Gravity and Grace*

Look at the old myth of Genesis—I know you don't believe in it, of course, but you can look at it anyway—nowhere does it say that God appoints the Adamic couple the absolute, unlimited, arbitrary masters of the earth or the garden, that destiny requires them to exploit it to death. On the contrary, they are placed at the summit of creation so that it may be respected. They are its guardians; that is, they must safeguard it and keep it beautiful and well, in accordance with God's plan. Humankind is responsible for—that is, they will have to answer to God for—what happens on earth. And God can always ask them: what have you done with the world's beauty, its harmony, its perfection? 2863

Jacques Ellul, *Living Faith*

Man's Fallenness

We are all kings in exile. 2864

G. K. Chesterton, *The Thing: Why I Am a Catholic*

Man's Meaning

If a man is happy and content selling cheeses or prattling in an evening dress, it is that a greater uses him: the meaning that is not in him is without, and his gyration or his placid movement on the set path tells of a great wind blowing. 2865

Stephen Mackenna, *Journal*, 27 January 1907

Man's Mulishness

It is not the ape, nor the tiger in man that I fear, but the donkey. 2866

William Temple, attributed

Man's Potentialities

The fact that the Matthew Passion, for example, the Hammerklavier Sonata, had human authors was a source of hope. It was just conceivable that humanity might someday and somehow be made a little more John-Sebastianlike. 2867

Aldous Huxley, *Eyeless in Gaza*

Man's Reason for Being

Man only of a softer mould was made
Not for his fellows' ruin but their aid:
Created kind, beneficent and free,
The noble image of the Deity. 2868

John Dryden, *The Hind and the Panther*

Man's Restlessness

You have made us toward Yourself *(ad te)*, and our heart is restless until it finds its rest in You. 2869

St. Augustine, *Confessions*

How tiresome it is to give up pursuits to which we have become attached. A man enjoying a happy home life has only to see a woman who attracts him, or spend five or six pleasant days gambling, and he will be very sorry to go back to what he was doing before. It happens every day. 2870

Blaise Pascal, *Pensées*

Man's Self-Transcendence

Man transcends himself. 2871

Blaise Pascal, *Pensées*

Man's Spirit

Man's spirit is like a kite, which rises by means of those very forces which seem to oppose its rise; the tie that joins it to the earth, the opposing winds of temptations, and the weight of earth-born affections which it carries with it into the sky.   2872

Coventry Patmore, *The Rod, the Root and the Flower*

Man's Theologies

The Ethiopians say that their gods are snub-nosed and black, the Thracians that theirs have light blue eyes and red hair. But if cattle and horses, or lions had hands, or were able to draw with their feet and produce the works that men can do, horses would draw the forms of the gods like horses, and cattle like cattle, and they would make their bodies such as they each had themselves.   2873

Xenophanes of Colophon, 6th cent. B.C., fragment. Cited in G. S. Kirk & J. E. Raven, *The Presocratic Philosophers*

Man and Nature

In nature a repulsive caterpillar turns into a lovely butterfly. But with human beings it is the other way round: a lovely butterfly turns into a repulsive caterpillar.   2874

Anton Chekhov. *The Viking Book of Aphorisms,* selected by W. H. Auden and Louis Kronenberger

Man and the Universe

With deep Self-realization, a person influences the universe with his subtle vibrations, and is less affected by the flow of events.   2875

Kung-Fu Meditations

The only universe capable of containing the human person is an irreversibly "personalizing" universe.   2876

Pierre Teilhard de Chardin, *The Phenomenon of Man*

Man and Woman

The woman preserves: she is tradition as the man is progress. And if there is no family and no humanity without the two sexes, without these two forces there is no history.   2877

Henri Frédéric Amiel, *Journal,* 6 May 1852

Man that is born of woman has short days and full of misery; but nobody can picture the obscenity and bestial tragedy that would belong to such a monster as man that was born of a man.   2878

G. K. Chesterton, *What's Wrong with the World*

Individually men may present a more or less rational appearance, eating, sleeping, and scheming. But humanity as a whole is changeful, mystical, fickle, delightful. Men are men, but Man is a woman.   2879

G. K. Chesterton, *The Napoleon of Notting Hill*

247

Men come of age at sixty, women at fifteen. 2880

James Stephens. *Observer*, "Sayings of the Week," 1 October 1944

In politics if you want anything said, ask a man. If you want anything done, ask a woman. 2881

Margaret Thatcher. *People*, 15 September 1975

Women are not men's equals in anything except responsibility. We are not their inferiors either, or even their superiors. We are quite simply different races. 2882

Phyllis McGinley, *The Province of the Heart*

Man under God

Man is the ark of God. The mercy seat is above the ark, cherubims guard it on either side, and in the midst is the holy law. Man is either the ark of God or a phantom of the earth and of the water. If thou seekest by human policy to guide this ark, remember Uzzah. 2883

William Blake, *Annotations to Lavater*

Marriage

And they shall be one flesh. 2884

Genesis 2:24

Thy desire shall be to thy husband, and he shall rule over thee. 2885

Genesis 3:16

A virtuous woman is a crown to her husband. 2886

Proverbs 12:4

It is better to dwell in the corner of a housetop, than with a brawling woman in a wide house. 2887

Proverbs 21:9

Let none deal treacherously against the wife of his youth. 2888

Malachi 2:15

What therefore God hath joined together, let no man put asunder. 2889

Jesus in Matthew 19:6

To avoid fornication, let every man have his own wife, and let every woman have her own husband. 2890

1 Corinthians 7:2

Let the husband render unto the wife due benevolence: and likewise the wife unto the husband. 2891

1 Corinthians 7:3

It is better to marry than to burn. 2892

1 Corinthians 7:9

The husband is the head of the wife, even as Christ is the head of the church. 2893

Ephesians 5:23

Husbands, love your wives, even as Christ also loved the church. 2894

Ephesians 5:25

He that loveth his wife loveth himself.   2895
　　　　Ephesians 5:28

. . . an honorable estate, instituted of God, signifying unto us the mystical union
that is betwixt Christ and his Church. . . .   2896
　　　　Book of Common Prayer, *The Form of Solemnization of Matrimony*

Marriage is a fine institution; no home should be without one.   2897
　　　　Author Unknown

Marriage is both honourable and onerable.   2898
　　　　George Swinnock, *The Golden Treasury of Puritan Quotations*

Woman takes her being from man, man takes his well-being from woman. 2899
　　　　Thomas Adams, *ibid.*

First, he must choose his love, and then he must love his choice.   2900
　　　　Henry Smith, *ibid.*

Marriage is tough, because it is woven of all these various elements, the weak and
the strong. "In loveness" is fragile for it is woven only with the gossamer threads of
beauty. It seems to me absurd to talk about "happy" and "unhappy" marriages. 2901
　　　　Anne Morrow Lindbergh, *Within and Without*

When marrying, one should ask himself this question: Do you believe that you will
be able to discourse with this woman into your old age? Everything else in marriage is
transitory, but the most time during the association belongs to conversation.   2902
　　　　Friedrich Wilhelm Nietzsche, *Human, All-Too-Human*

The life of a wife and husband who love each other is never at rest. Whether the
marriage is true or false, the marriage portion is the same: elemental discord. 2903
　　　　Jean Giraudoux, *Duel of Engels*

If Americans can be divorced for "incompatibility" I cannot conceive why they are
not all divorced. I have known many happy marriages, but never a compatible one. The
whole aim of marriage is to fight through and survive the instant when incompatibility becomes unquestionable. For a man and woman, as such, are incompatible. 2904
　　　　G. K. Chesterton, *What's Wrong with the World*

Marriage does not change people; it merely unmasks them.   2905
　　　　Sydney J. Harris, *Pieces of Eight*

Martyrs

Let me die the death of the righteous, and let my last end be like his!   2906
　　　　Numbers 23:10

For thy sake we are killed all the day long; we are counted as sheep for the
slaughter.   2907
　　　　Psalm 44:22

Precious in the sight of the Lord is the death of his saints.   2908
　　　　Psalm 116:15

The Lord hath laid on him the iniquity of us all.   2909
　　　　Isaiah 53:6

Blessed are they which are persecuted for righteousness' sake: for theirs is the kingdom of heaven.   2910

Jesus in Matthew 5:10

Whosoever will lose his life for my sake and the gospel's, the same shall save it.   2911

Jesus in Mark 8:35

Behold, I see the heavens opened, and the Son of man standing on the right hand of God.   2912

Acts 7:56

I am ready not to be bound only, but also to die at Jerusalem for the name of the Lord Jesus.   2913

Acts 21:13

And though I bestow all my goods to feed the poor, and though I give my body to be burned, and have not charity, it profiteth me nothing.   2914

1 Corinthians 13:3

All that will live godly in Christ Jesus will suffer persecution.   2915

2 Timothy 3:12

These are they which came out of great tribulation, and have washed their robes, and made them white in the blood of the Lamb. Therefore are they before the throne of God, and serve him day and night in his temple: and he that sitteth on the throne shall dwell among them. They shall hunger no more, neither thirst any more; neither shall the sun light on them, nor any heat. For the Lamb which is in the midst of the throne shall feed them, and shall lead them unto living fountains of waters: and God shall wipe away all tears from their eyes.   2916

Revelation 7:14-17

The martyrs were bound, imprisoned, scourged, racked, burnt, rent, butchered— and they multiplied.   2917

St. Augustine, *The City of God*

Lloyd George could have a better rating in British mythology if he had suffered the fate of Abraham Lincoln.   2918

John Grigg. *Observer,* "Sayings of the Week," 7 April 1963

The noble army of martyrs praise thee.   2919

The Book of Common Prayer, *Te Deum Laudamus*

Men reject their prophets and slay them, but they love their martyrs and honor those whom they have slain.   2920

Fyodor Dostoyevski, *The Brothers Karamazov,* Pt. XI, Bk. Vi, ch. 3

The martyr cannot be dishonored. Every lash inflicted is a tongue of fame; every prison a more illustrious abode; every burned book or house enlightens the world; every suppressed or expunged word reverberates through the earth from side to side. Hours of sanity and consideration are always arriving to communities, as to individuals, when the truth is seen and the martyrs are justified.   2921

Ralph Waldo Emerson, *Essays,* "Compensation"

Materialism

Man doth not live by bread only, but by every word that proceedeth out of the mouth of the Lord. 2922

Deuteronomy 8:3

Lay not up for yourselves treasures upon earth, where moth and rust doth corrupt, and where thieves break through and steal: But lay up for yourselves treasures in heaven, where neither moth nor rust doth corrupt, and where thieves do not break through nor steal: For where your treasure is, there will your heart be also. 2923

Jesus in Matthew 6:19–21

Ye cannot serve God and mammon. 2924

Jesus in Matthew 6:24

What shall it profit a man, if he shall gain the whole world, and lose his own soul? 2925

Jesus in Mark 8:36

A man's life consisteth not in the abundance of things which he possesseth. 2926

Jesus in Luke 12:15

The materialist is a Calvinist without a God. 2927

Edward Bernstein, *Evolutionary Socialism*

Materialism is decadent and degenerate only if the spirit of the nation has withered and if individual people are so unimaginative that they wallow in it. 2928

Brooks Atkinson, *Once Around the Sun*, "January 22"

Matter oozes mind, body oozes thought, says the philosophical materialist with splendid audacity. But may not some nonmaterialist like myself say with equally splendid audacity: Mind oozes matter, thought oozes body? In either case, that is the thing to be demonstrated; and demonstration in either case is not nearly so easy as audacious assertion. 2929

C. E. S.

Matter

Christ proposed the docility of matter to us as a model when he told us to consider the lilies of the field which neither toil nor spin. 2930

Simone Weil, *Waiting on God*

Matter is not beautiful when it obeys man, but only when it obeys God. 2931

Ibid.

We stood talking for some time together of Bishop Berkeley's ingenious sophistry to prove the non-existence of matter, and that everything in the universe is merely ideal. . . . I shall never forget the alacrity with which Johnson answered, striking his foot with mighty force against a large stone, till he rebounded from it,—"I refute it thus." 2932

James Boswell, *Life of Johnson*, 6 August 1763

Blessed be you, harsh matter, barren soil, violent sea, stubborn rock: you who yield only to violence, you who force us to work if we would eat.

251

Without you, without your onslaughts, without your uprootings of us, we
    should remain all our lives inert, stagnant, puerile,
ignorant both of ourselves and of God.
You who batter us and then dress our wounds,
you who resist us and yield to us,
you who wreck and build,
you who shackle and liberate,
the sap of our souls,
the hand of God,
the flesh of Christ:
it is you, matter, that I bless. . . .   2933

        Pierre Teilhard de Chardin, *Hymn of the Universe,* "Hymn to
        Matter"

Maturity

When I was a child, I spake as a child, I understood as a child, I thought as a child:
but when I became a man, I put away childish things.   2934
        1 Corinthians 13:11

In malice be ye children, but in understanding be men.   2935
        1 Corinthians 14:20

Flee also youthful lusts: but follow righteousness, faith, charity, peace.   2936
        2 Timothy 2:22

Grow in grace, and in the knowledge of our Lord.   2937
        2 Peter 3:18

Maturity is coming to terms with that other part of yourself.   2938
        Dr. Ruth Tiffany Barnhouse. News summaries, 1 March 1962

Maturity: among other things, the unclouded happiness of the child at play, who
takes it for granted that he is at one with his play-mates.   2939
        Dag Hammarskjöld, *Markings*

The Peace Corps is a kind of Howard Johnson's on the main drag to
maturity.   2940
        Paul Theroux, *Sunrise with Seamonsters*

When I was ten, I read fairy tales in secret and would have been ashamed if I had
been found doing so. Now that I am fifty I read them openly. When I became a man I
put away childish things, including the fear of childishness and the desire to be very
grown up.   2941
        C. S. Lewis, *Of Other Worlds*

The turning point in the process of growing up is when you discover the core of
strength within you that survives all hurt.   2942
        Max Lerner, *The Unfinished Country*

Who of us is mature enough for offspring before the offspring themselves arrive?
The value of marriage is not that adults produce children but that children produce
adults.   2943
        Peter de Vries, *Tunnel of Love*

Meaning

Everything's got a meaning, if you can find it. 2944
> Lewis Carroll, *Alice's Adventures in Wonderland*

This world's no blot for us,
Nor blank—it means intensely, and means good:
To find its meaning is my meat and drink. 2945
> Robert Browning, *Fra Lippo Lippi*

Means and Ends

Food is for nourishment, with gastronomy an incidental. Likewise, fornication is for procreation, with eroticism as an incidental. In the same sort of way, Truth is for enlightenment, with meaning as an incidental. Change this round, and make gastronomy the end and nourishment the incidental, eroticism the end and procreation the incidental, and sickness ensues—in the one case, satiety, in the other impotence; in both cases, the ultimate outcome is the vomitorium. As for the quest for truth—it gets lost in the quicksand of history, the jungle of fact, the slough of meaning or consensus. To make all this clear to us, God has adopted His usual device of *reductio ad absurdum,* providing so much food that the prevention of obesity becomes a cult, so much and so varied eroticism that desire itself falters and dies, and finally, along comes this computer, the ultimate farce of fact. 2946
> Malcolm Muggeridge, *Confessions of a Twentieth-Century Pilgrim*

Meeting and Parting

Ships that pass in the night, and speak each other in passing,
Only a signal shown and a distant voice in the darkness;
So on the ocean of life we pass and speak one another,
Only a look and a voice; then darkness again and a silence. 2947
> Henry Wadsworth Longfellow, *Tales of a Wayside Inn,* "The Theologian's Tale"

Like the meeting of the seagulls and the waves we meet and come near.
The seagulls fly off, the waves roll away and we depart. 2948
> Rabindranath Tagore, *Stray Birds*

Memory

Remember this day, in which ye came out from Egypt, out of the house of bondage. 2949
> Exodus 13:3

If I forget thee, O Jerusalem, let my right hand forget her cunning. 2950
> Psalm 137:5

This is my body, which is broken for you: this do in remembrance of me. 2951
> Jesus in 1 Corinthians 11:24

How vast a memory has Love! 2952
> Alexander Pope, *Sappho to Phaon*

Memory is the power to gather roses in winter.   2953
Author Unknown

The mystic chords of memory, stretching from every battlefield and patriot grave to every living heart and hearthstone all over this broad land, will yet swell the chorus of the Union when again touched, as surely they will be, by the better angels of our nature.   2954
Abraham Lincoln. First Inaugural Address, 4 March 1861

I think it is all a matter of love; the more you love a memory, the stronger and stranger it is.   2955
Vladimir Nabokov, *Strong Opinions*

In the cellars of the night, when the mind starts moving around old trunks of bad times, the pain of this and the shame of that, the memory of a small boldness is a hand to hold.   2956
John Leonard. *New York Times,* 2 February 1977

What was hard to bear is sweet to remember.   2957
Portuguese Proverb

We do not remember days, we remember moments.   2958
Cesare Pavese, *The Burning Brand*

Mercy

The Lord thy God is a merciful God.   2959
Deuteronomy 4:31

Let me fall now into the hand of the Lord, for great are his mercies: but let me not fall into the hand of man.   2960
1 Chronicles 21:13

God has punished us less than our iniquities deserve.   2961
Ezra 9:13

Have mercy upon me, O Lord, for I am weak.   2962
Psalm 6:2

Though he cause grief, yet will he have compassion.   2963
Lamentations 3:32

I will spare them, as a man spareth his own son that serveth him.   2964
Malachi 3:17

Blessed are the merciful: for they shall obtain mercy.   2965
Jesus in Matthew 5:7

Be ye therefore merciful, as your Father also is merciful.   2966
Jesus in Luke 6:36

Only the man who has had to face despair is really convinced that he needs mercy.   2967
Thomas Merton, *No Man Is an Island*

The mercies of God make a sinner proud, but a saint humble.   2968
Thomas Watson, *The Golden Treasury of Puritan Quotations*

There's a wideness in God's mercy
Like the wideness of the sea.
There's a kindness in his justice,
Which is more than liberty.   2969

Frederick William Faber, Hymns

The quality of mercy is not strain'd,
It droppeth as the gentle rain from heaven
Upon the place beneath: it is twice blest,
It blesseth him that gives and him that takes:
'Tis mightiest in the mightiest: it becomes
The throned monarch better than his crown,
It is enthroned in the hearts of kings,
It is an attribute of God himself.   2970

William Shakespeare, The Merchant of Venice, IV, i, 184

Mind

As they did not like to retain God in their knowledge, God gave them over to a reprobate mind.   2971

Romans 1:28

God hath not given us the spirit of fear; but of power, and of love, and of a sound mind.   2972

2 Timothy 1:7

He [H. G. Wells] thought that the object of opening the mind is simply opening the mind. Whereas I am incurably convinced that the object of opening the mind, as of opening the mouth, is to close it again on something solid.   2973

G. K. Chesterton, Autobiography of G. K. Chesterton

All the choir of heaven and furniture of earth—in a word, all those bodies which compose the frame of the world—have not any subsistence without a mind.   2974

George Berkeley, Principles of Human Knowledge

There are no chaste minds. Minds copulate wherever they meet.   2975

Eric Hoffer, Reflections on the Human Condition

The brain is wider than the sky,
For, put them side by side,
The one the other will contain
With ease—and you beside.

The brain is deeper than the sea,
For hold them—blue to blue—
The one the other will absorb
As sponges, buckets, do.

The brain is just the weight of God:
For heft them—pound for pound—
And they will differ (if they do)
As syllable from sound.   2976

Emily Dickinson, Poems, "The mind is wider than the sky"

The highest function of *mind* is its function of messenger. 2977
> D. H. Lawrence, *Kangaroo*

My mind to me a kingdom is,
   Such perfect joy therein I find
As far exceeds all earthly bliss
   That God or nature hath assigned. 2978
> Edward Dyer, *My Mind to Me a Kingdom Is*

What is mind? No matter. What is matter? Never mind. 2979
> Author Unknown

Ministry

See Clergy

Minorities

The drums of Africa still beat in my heart. They will not let me rest while there is a single Negro boy or girl without a chance to prove his worth. 2980
> Mary McCloud Bethune. News summaries, 19 May 1955

Being a minority never makes you right. Being right always makes you a minority. 2981
> C. E. S.

When great changes occur in history, when great principles are involved, as a rule the majority are wrong. The minority are right. 2982
> Eugene V. Debs. Speech in Federal Court, Cleveland,
> 11 September 1919

Miracle

Behold, the bush burned with fire, and the bush was not consumed. 2983
> Exodus 3:2

Speak ye unto the rock before their eyes, and it shall give forth his water. 2984
> Numbers 20:8

Your eyes have seen what I have done in Egypt. 2985
> Joshua 24:7

An evil and adulterous generation seeketh after a sign; and there shall no sign be given to it, but the sign of the prophet Jonas. 2986
> Jesus in Matthew 12:39

In my name shall they cast out devils. 2987
> Jesus in Mark 16:17

He laid his hands on every one of them, and healed them. 2988
> Luke 4:40

No man can do these miracles that thou doest, except God be with him. 2989
> John 3:2

Whether he be a sinner or no, I know not: one thing I know, that, whereas I was blind, now I see. 2990

John 9:25

He who says "God" says "miracle." 2991

Karl Barth, *The Epistle to the Romans*

Men talk about miracles because there is no miracle in their lives. Cease to gnaw that crust. There is ripe fruit over your head. 2992

Henry David Thoreau, *Journal,* June 1850

A scientist who airily dismisses "miracles" will yet unquestioningly accept the postulate of quantum physics that a "particle" (which no one has ever seen) moves from one place to another without going through any intervening space. 2993

Sydney J. Harris. Syndicated column, 8 March 1985

A miracle means only the liberty of God. 2994

G. K. Chesterton, *Orthodoxy*

The Age of Miracles is forever here! 2995

Thomas Carlyle, *Heroes and Hero-Worship*

Miracles are not the proofs, but the necessary results, of revelation. 2996

Samuel Taylor Coleridge, *Omniana*

I have never seen a greater monster or miracle in the world than myself. 2997

Michel de Montaigne, *Essays,* II, 2

Mission

Whom shall I send, and who will go for us? Then said I, Here am I: send me. 2998

Isaiah 6:8

I will also give thee for a light to the Gentiles. 2999

Isaiah 49:6

To proclaim liberty to the captives, and the opening of the prison to them that are bound. 3000

Isaiah 61:1

Now the word of the Lord came unto Jonah the son of Amittai, saying, Arise, go to Nineveh, that great city, and cry against it: for their wickedness is come up before me. 3001

Jonah 1:1–2

Heal the sick, cleanse the lepers, raise the dead, cast out devils. 3002

Jesus in Matthew 10:8

My meat is to do the will of him that sent me, and to finish his work. 3003

Jesus in John 4:34

As my Father hath sent me, even so send I you. 3004

Jesus in John 20:21

And a vision appeared to Paul in the night; there stood a man of Macedonia, and prayed him, saying, Come over into Macedonia, and help us. 3005

Acts 16:9

If he have faith, the believer cannot be restrained. He betrays himself. He breaks out. He confesses and teaches this gospel to the people at the risk of life itself. 3006

Martin Luther, in preface to his translation of the New Testament, 1522

Here is the test to find whether your mission on earth is finished: if you're alive, it isn't. 3007

Richard Bach. *365 Quotes, Maxims & Proverbs Calendar 1990*, compiled by Debby Roth

You have the Gospel because missionaries came your way. 3008

Author Unknown

The only people who don't believe in missions are they who don't believe in the religion they profess. 3009

C. E. S.

Moderation

Let your moderation be known unto all men. The Lord is at hand. 3010

Philippians 4:5

It is very possible to practise moderation in some things, in drink and the like—to restrain the appetites—but can a man restrain the affections of his mind, and tell them, so far shall you go, and no farther? 3011

George Borrow, *Lavengro*

A thing moderately good is not so good as it ought to be. Moderation in temper is always a virtue, but moderation in virtue is always a vice. 3012

Thomas Paine, *The Rights of Man*

Modernism

There is a species of person called a "Modern Churchman" who draws the full salary of a beneficed clergyman and need not commit himself to any religious belief. 3013

Evelyn Waugh, *Decline and Fall*

Modern Man

Our experience is that man today can cope with everything possible—except himself. 3014

Hans Küng, *Does God Exist?*

It must be clearly understood that the mere fact of living in the present does not make a man modern, for in that case everyone at present alive would be so. He alone is modern who is fully conscious of the present. 3015

Carl Gustav Jung, *Psychological Reflections*

Perhaps this is an age when men think bravely of the human spirit, for surely they have a strange lust to lay it bare. 3016
Christopher Morley, *Inward Ho*

It is only the modern that ever becomes old-fashioned. 3017
Oscar Wilde, *Intentions,* "The Decay of Lying"

Modesty

Let another man praise thee, and not thine own mouth. 3018
Proverbs 27:2

When thou doest thine alms, do not sound a trumpet before thee, as the hypocrites do. 3019
Jesus in Matthew 6:2

He must increase, but I must decrease. 3020
John 3:30

True modesty does not consist in an ignorance of our merits, but in a due estimate of them. 3021
J. C. Hare and A. W. Hare, *Guesses at Truth*

Loquacity storms the ear, but modesty takes the heart. 3022
Thomas Fuller, *Gnomologia*

I have done one braver thing
  Than all the Worthies did;
And yet a braver thence doth spring,
  Which is, to keep that hid. 3023
John Donne, *The Undertaking*

I take it to be the highest instance of a noble mind to bear great qualities without discovering in a man's behavior any consciousness that he is superior to the rest of the world. 3024
Richard Steele, *The Spectator,* 31 March 1712

Moments

Every moment comes to us pregnant with a command from God, only to pass on and plunge into eternity, there to remain forever what we have made of it. 3025
St. Francis de Sales. Quoted in Aelred Graham, *Zen Catholicism*

Every minute life begins all over again. 3026
Thomas Merton, *The Sign of Jonas*

Seize from every moment its unique novelty and do not prepare your joys. 3027
André Gide, *The Fruits of the Earth*

Florence Farr once said to me, "If we could say to ourselves, with sincerity, 'this passing moment is as good as any I shall ever know,' we could die upon the instant, and be united with God." 3028
William Butler Yeats, *Autobiography*

God works in moments. 3029
French Proverb

Obey the spur of the moment. . . . Let the spurs of constant moments goad us incessantly into life.   3030

> Henry David Thoreau, *Journals,* 26 January 1852

Never be afraid of the moments—thus sings the voice of the everlasting.   3031

> Rabindranath Tagore, *Stray Birds*

I have a feeling it's the in-between times, the times that narratives like this leave out and that memory in general loses track of, which are the times when souls are saved or lost.   3032

> Frederick Buechner, *The Book of Bebb*

Money

Money answereth all things.   3033

> Ecclesiastes 10:19

Thy money perish with thee, because thou hast thought that the gift of God may be purchased with money.   3034

> Acts 8:20

The love of money is the root of all evil.   3035

> 1 Timothy 6:10

I have no time to make money. I am searching for truth.   3036

> Jean Louis Agassiz, refusing the offer of a lucrative lecture course

Money can't bring you friends, but it can bring you a better class of enemies.   3037

> *The Milwaukee Journal,* 22 June 1977

Money ranks with love as man's greatest joy. And it ranks with death as his greatest source of anxiety.   3038

> John Kenneth Galbraith, *The Age of Uncertainty*

Bags of old, tattered bills were being returned to the U. S. Treasury. A one-dollar bill and a twenty-dollar bill in the same bag started talking. "Gee, I went to nice stores, good restaurants, country clubs and exotic places," the twenty-dollar bill said. "How about you?" Replied the one-dollar bill glumly, "all I ever did was go to church, go to church, go to church."   3039

> Author Unknown

Money is like a sixth sense without which you cannot make a complete use of the other five.   3040

> W. Somerset Maugham, *Of Human Bondage*

The love of money grows as the money itself grows. *(Crescit amor nummi quantum ipsa pecunia crescit.)*   3041

> Juvenal, *Satires*

Anybody who thinks money is everything has never been sick. Or is.   3042

> Malcolm S. Forbes, quoted by Dear Abby, 20 July 1989

Monotony

Monotony is only bearable if it is lit up by the divine. But for this very reason a monotonous life is much more propitious for salvation.   3043

Simone Weil, *Gateway to God*

Moral Action

The three hardest tasks in the world are neither physical facts nor intellectual achievements, but moral acts: to return love for hate, to include the excluded, and to say "I was wrong."   3044

Sydney J. Harris, *Pieces of Eight*

Moral Education

Moral education is impossible apart from the habitual vision of greatness.   3045

Alfred North Whitehead, *The Aims of Education*

Moral Freedom

If some great Power would agree to make me always think what is true and do what is right on condition of being turned into a sort of clock and wound up every morning before I got out of bed, I should instantly close with the offer.   3046

Thomas Henry Huxley, *On Descartes' Discourse on Method*

Morality

One should not destroy an insect, one should not quarrel with a dog, without a reason to vindicate one through all the courts of morality.   3047

William Shenstone, *Of Men and Manners*

The passions need the rein and curb, but moral sentiments need the spur.   3048

Henry Ward Beecher, *Proverbs from Plymouth Pulpit*

Somebody should do for morals what that old Pecksniff Bacon has obtained the credit for doing for science.   3049

Samuel Butler, *The Way of All Flesh*

The young man in the Gospel might have been a better man if he had not been so good.   3050

William Gurnall, The *Golden Treasury of Puritan Quotations*

Works make not the heart good, but a good heart makes the works good.   3051

Stephen Charnock, *Ibid.*

The Moral Law tells us the tune we have to play: our instincts are merely the keys.   3052

C. S. Lewis, *Mere Christianity*

Morals is not preaching, it is beauty of a rare kind.   3053

Ernest Dimnet, *What We Live By*

Morality, said Jesus, is kindness to the weak; morality, said Nietzsche, is the bravery of the strong; morality, said Plato, is the effective harmony of the whole. Probably all

261

three doctrines must be combined for a perfect ethic; but can we doubt which of the elements is fundamental? 3054

Will Durant, *The Story of Philosophy*

Morality and Religion

Morality did not begin by one man saying to another, "I will not hit you if you will not hit me"; there is no trace of such a transaction. There *is* a trace of both men having said, "We must not hit each other in the holy place." They gained their morality by guarding their religion. 3055

G. K. Chesterton, *Orthodoxy*

Mortality

Dust thou art, and unto dust shalt thou return. 3056

Genesis 3:19

My days are swifter than a weaver's shuttle and are spent without hope. 3057

Job 7:6

Lord, make me to know mine end, and the measure of my days, what it is, that I may know how frail I am. 3058

Psalm 39:4

It is better to go to the house of mourning than to go to the house of feasting: for that is the end of all men; and the living will lay it to his heart. 3059

Ecclesiastes 7:2

His is the breath that is in us, and at His own good pleasure will He take it away. 3060

St. Clement of Rome, in *Early Christian Writings* (Penguin edition)

Don't hurry, don't worry,
You're only here for a short visit.
So be sure to smell the flowers along the way. 3061

Walter Hagen. *The Little, Brown Book of Anecdotes,* compiled by Clifton Fadiman

The fall of a leaf is a whisper to the living. 3062

English Proverb

Mortality has its compensations: one is that all evils are transitory, another that better times may come. 3063

George Santayana, *The Life of Reason*

It is said an Eastern monarch once charged his wise men to invent him a sentence to be ever in view, and which should be true and appropriate in all times and situations. They presented him the words: "And this, too, shall pass away." How much it expresses! How chastening in the hour of pride! How consoling in the depths of affliction! 3064

Abraham Lincoln. Address to the Wisconsin State Agricultural Society, Milwaukee, 30 September 1859

We are such stuff
As dreams are made of, and our little life
Is rounded with a sleep. 3065
William Shakespeare, The Tempest, IV, i, 156

Moses

Moses was a merciful, meek man, and yet with what fury did he run through the camp, and cut the throats of three-and-thirty thousand of his dear Israelites that were fallen into idolatry. 3066
Daniel Defoe, The Shortest Way with Dissenters

Mothers

Mother is the name of God in the lips and hearts of little children. 3067
William Makepeace Thackeray, Vanity Fair

He that wipes the child's nose kisses the mother's cheek. 3068
George Herbert, Outlandish Proverbs

A mother is not a person to lean on, but a person to make leaning unnecessary. 3069
Dorothy Canfield Fisher, Her Son's Wife

What the mother sings to the cradle goes all the way down to the coffin. 3070
Henry Ward Beecher, Proverbs from Plymouth Pulpit

Our [women]s] bodies are shaped to bear children, and our lives are a working out of the processes of creation. All our ambitions and intelligence are beside that great elementary point. 3071
Phyllis McGinley, The Province of the Heart

A mother never realizes that her children are no longer children. 3072
Holbrook Jackson, All Manner of Folk

Motherhood is neither a duty nor a privilege, but simply the way that humanity can satisfy the desire for physical immortality and triumph over the fear of death. 3073
Rebecca West, New York Times, 8 May 1960

Every mother is like Moses. She does not enter the promised land. She prepares a world she will not see. 3074
Pope Paul VI. Jean Guitton, Conversations with Pope Paul

Motive

Motives, like eggs, lose their fertility when hard-boiled. 3075
Anonymous (Henry S. Haskins), Meditations in Wall Street

Mouth-Shutting

Never pass up a chance to keep your mouth shut. 3076
Author Unknown

A shut mouth gathers no foot. 3077
Author Unknown

Music

Praise him upon the loud cymbals: praise him upon the high sounding cymbals.   3078
> Psalm 150:5

Music is a higher revelation than philosophy.   3079
> Ludwig von Beethoven. Letter to Mettina von Arnim, 1810

All music is only a sweet striving to express character.   3080
> Henry David Thoreau, *Journals,* 12 December 1841

It is a year now since I have heard a hymn sung. But it is strange how the music that we hear inwardly can almost surpass, if we really concentrate on it, what we hear physically. It has a greater purity, the dross falls away, and in a way the music acquires a "new body."   3081
> Dietrich Bonhoeffer, *Letters and Papers from Prison,* 27 March 1944

If you think deep enough you think musically.   3082
> Thomas Carlyle. Quoted in Robert Frost, *Poetry and Prose*

When people hear good music, it makes them homesick for something they never had, and never will have.   3083
> Edgar Watson Howe, *Country Town Sayings*

All music is folk music; I ain't never heard no horse sing a song.   3084
> Louis Armstrong, in *New York Times,* 7 July 1971

Mutuality

Men aspiring to heights must reach for them through others, with their help and helping them. If all of Israel's children joined hands, they would form a chain and reach the celestial throne.   3085
> Rebbe Maggid of Kozhenitch. Quoted in Elie Wiesel, *Souls on Fire*

God has so ordained things that we grow in faith only through the frail instrumentality of one another.   3086
> St. John of the Cross, *The Dark Night of the Soul*

Mystery

The atoms of Democritus
And Newton's particles of light
Are sands upon the Red Sea Shore
Where Israel's tents do shine so bright.   3087
> William Blake, *Songs and Ballads*

Everything that is incomprehensible does not cease to exist.   3088
> Blaise Pascal, *Pensées*

Mystery, which most certainly exists, has nothing to do with the little game of questions and answers. You don't put it in the catechism. To declare "It's a mystery" is to talk nonsense; mystery should be met with silence and adoration.   3089
> Jacques Ellul, *Living Faith*

Mysticism

The whole secret of mysticism is this: that man can understand everything by the help of what he does not understand. 3090
> G.K. Chesterton, *Orthodoxy*

The mystic can live happy in the droning consciousness of his own heartbeats and those of the universe. 3091
> George Santayana, *Winds of Doctrine*

Myth

Myth embodies the nearest approach to absolute truth that can be put into words. 3092
> Ananda Coomaraswamy, *Hinduism and Buddhism*

It has been well said that mythology is the penultimate truth—penultimate because the ultimate cannot be put into words. It is beyond words, beyond images, beyond that bounding rim of the Buddhist Wheel of Becoming. Mythology pitches the mind beyond that rim, to what can be known but not told. So this is the penultimate truth. 3093
> Joseph Campbell, *The Power of Myth*

N

Names

Whatsoever Adam called every living creature, that was the name thereof.　3094
> Genesis 2:19

That which hath been is named already.　3095
> Ecclesiastes 6:10

He called his own sheep by name.　3096
> John 10:3

God also hath highly exalted him, and given him a name which is above every name: that at the name of Jesus every knee should bow, of things in earth, and things under the earth; and that every tongue should confess that Jesus Christ is Lord, to the glory of God the Father.　3097
> Philippians 2:9–11

Giving a name, indeed, is a poetic art; all poetry, if we go to that with it, is but giving of names.　3098
> Thomas Carlyle, *Journal*, 18 May 1832

The Ancient Mariner would not have taken so well if it had been called *The Old Sailor*.　3099
> Samuel Butler, *Note Books*

Here lies one whose name was writ in water.　3100
> John Keats, his epitaph

Our names are the light that glows on the sea waves at night and then dies without leaving its signature.　3101
> Author Unknown

The name of a man is a numbing blow from which he never recovers.　3102
> Marshal Mc Luhan, *Understanding Media*

Nations

And God said unto Abraham, As for Sarai thy wife, thou shalt not call her name Sarai, but Sarah shall her name be. And I will bless her . . . and she shall be a mother of nations; kings of people shall be of her.　3103
> Genesis 17:15–16

The kingdom is the Lord's; and he is the governor among the nations.   3104
> Psalm 22:28

All the gods of the nations are idols: but the Lord made the heavens.   3105
> Psalm 96:5

All nations before him are as nothing; and they are counted to him less than nothing, and vanity.   3106
> Isaiah 40:17

Thus saith the Lord of hosts; In those days it shall come to pass, that ten men shall take hold out of all languages of the nations, even shall take hold of the skirt of him that is a Jew, saying, We will go with you: for we have heard that God is with you.   3107
> Zechariah 8:23

When the Son of man shall come in his glory, and all the holy angels with him, then shall he sit upon the throne of his glory: And before him shall be gathered all nations: and he shall separate them one from another, as a shepherd divideth his sheep from the goats.   3108
> Jesus in Matthew 25:31–32

[God] hath made of one blood all nations of men for to dwell on the face of the earth.   3109
> Acts 17:26

Rome fell; Babylon fell; Scarsdale's turn will come.   3110
> Bernard Shaw, *Misalliance*. (The original in Shaw's play reads
> "Hindhead's turn will come." Hindhead was a jibe at the stockbroker
> township south of London.) Quoted in Paul Kennedy, *The Rise and
> Fall of the Great Powers*

The ruin of a nation begins in the homes of its people.   3111
> Ashanti Proverb

Nations die of softening of the brain, which, for a long time, passes for softening of the heart.   3112
> Coventry Patmore, *The Rod, the Root and the Flower*

The great nations have always acted like gangsters, and the small nations like prostitutes.   3113
> Stanley Kubrick. *The Guardian,* 5 June 1963

All the great things have been done by little nations.   3114
> Benjamin Disraeli, *Tancred*

You can tell the ideals of a nation by its advertisements.   3115
> Norman Douglas, *South Wind*

A nation without dregs and malcontents is orderly, decent, peaceful and pleasant, but perhaps without the seed of things to come.   3116
> Eric Hoffer, The *True Believer*

A nation never falls but by suicide.   3117
> Ralph Waldo Emerson, *Journal,* 1861

It is a maxim founded on the universal experience of mankind that no nation is to be trusted farther than it is bound by its interest.　　　　3118

George Washington. Letter to Henry Laurens, 1778

Nationalism

Patriotism is a lively sense of responsibility. Nationalism is a silly cock crowing on its own dunghill.　　　　3119

Richard Aldington, *The Colonel's Daughter*

Patriotism makes a man a gentleman. Nationalism makes him a cad.　　　3120

Author Unknown

The nationalist has a broad hatred and a narrow love.　　　　3121

André Gide, *Journals*, 1918

Nationalism is an infantile disease. It is the measles of mankind.　　　3122

Albert Einstein, to G. S. Viereck, 1921

Nationality

All places, all airs, make unto me one country; I am in England, everywhere, and under any meridian.　　　　3123

Sir Thomas Browne, *Religio Medici*

Natural Law

The natural law may be described briefly as a force working in history to keep human beings human.　　　　3124

Julian V. Langmead-Casserly, *The Fate of Modern Culture*

Natural Man

The natural man receiveth not the things of the Spirit of God, for they are foolishness unto him: neither can he know them, because they are spiritually discerned.　　　　3125

1 Corinthians 2:14

Natural man has only two primal passions: to get and to beget.　　　3126

Sir William Osler, *Science and Immortality*

Nature

And God made two great lights; the greater light to rule the day, and the lesser light to rule the night.　　　　3127

Genesis 1:16

Ye shall not pollute the land wherein ye are.　　　　3128

Numbers 35:33

The tree of the field is man's life.　　　　3129

Deuteronomy 20:19

Speak to the earth, and it shall teach thee: and the fishes of the sea shall declare unto thee.   3130
>> Job 12:8

Stand still, and consider the wondrous works of God.   3131
>> Job 37:14

The sun also ariseth.   3132
>> Ecclesiastes 1:5

A time to be born, and a time to die; a time to plant, and a time to pluck up that which is planted.   3133
>> Ecclesiastes 3:2

The Lord hath his way in the whirlwind and in the storm, and the clouds are the dust of his feet.   3134
>> Nahum 1:3

That man can interrogate as well as observe nature was a lesson slowly learned in his evolution.   3135
>> Sir William Osler, *Aphorisms*

Consider the lilies of the field, how they grow; they toil not, neither do they spin: And yet I say unto you, that even Solomon in all his glory was not arrayed like one of these.   3136
>> Jesus in Matthew 6:28–29

The grass withereth, and the flower thereof falleth away: But the word of the Lord endureth forever.   3137
>> 1 Peter 1:24–25

Nature has some perfections to show that she is the image of God, and some defects to show that she is only His image.   3138
>> Blaise Pascal, *Pensées*

Nature hath meal and bran, contempt and grace.   3139
>> William Shakespeare, *Cymbeline*, IV, ii, 27

What a book a devil's chaplain might write on the clumsy, wasteful, blundering, low, and horribly cruel works of nature!   3140
>> Charles Darwin. Letter to J. D. Hooker, 11 July 1856

To him who in the love of Nature holds
Communion with her visible forms, she speaks
A various language.   3141
>> William Cullen Bryant, *Thanatopsis*

"Sail!" quoth the king; "Hold!" saith the wind.   3142
>> English Proverb

All Nature wears one universal grin.   3143
>> Henry Fielding, *Tom Thumb the Great*

There are no penalties for breaking the laws of Nature, because there are no crimes: Nature is self-regulating and merely arranges things so that its prohibitions are impossible to transgress.   3144
>> Carl Sagan, *Cosmos*

Nature [is] that lovely lady to whom we owe polio, leprosy, smallpox, syphilis, tuberculosis, cancer. 3145

Stanley N. Cohen, geneticist at Stanford University; quoted by David N. Leff in letter to the editor, *New York Times,* 15 March 1987

There must be a streak of real beastliness in the Dutch—they use the cut flowers for *manure.* Nature in her harshest and most dreadful mood has never equalled that, has she? 3146

Evelyn Underhill, *The Letters of Evelyn Underhill.* (As a warm admirer and deep-in debtor to E. H. I must break in here to express my total dissent and my astonishment at her remark. *Of course* Nature uses cut flowers for manure when we who cut them have had our pleasures of them. What is so cruel and uncouth about this? So used, the flowers are given opportunity to help other lovely things to live and grow. Now that I've said this I feel better. C. E. S.)

The only words that ever satisfied me as describing Nature are the terms used in fairy books, "charm," "spell," "enchantment." They express the arbitrariness of the fact and its mystery. 3147

G. K. Chesterton, *Orthodoxy*

Nature is rather like a wise old bitch. She will heal herself by licking her own sores, if you give her a chance. 3148

C. E. S.

Nature and Grace

Nature fulfilled by grace is not less natural, but is supernaturally natural. 3149

Coventry Patmore, *The Rod, the Root and the Flower*

Need

If there be among you a poor man of one of the brethren within any of thy gates in the land which the Lord thy God giveth thee, thou shalt not harden thine heart, nor shut thine hand from thy poor brother: But thou shalt open thine hand wide unto him, and shall surely lend him sufficient for his need, in that which he wanteth. 3150

Deuteronomy 15:7–8

Your Father knoweth what things ye have need of, before ye ask him. 3151

Jesus in Matthew 6:8

Have ye never read what David did, when he had need, and was an hungred, he, and they that were with him? How he went into the house of God in the days of Abiathar, the high priest, and did eat the shewbread, which is not lawful to eat but for the priests, and gave also to them which were with him? And he said unto them, The sabbath was made for man, and not man for the sabbath. 3152

Mark 2:25–27

And all that believed were together, and had all things common; And sold their possessions and goods, and parted them to all men, as every man had need. 3153

Acts 2:44–45

If any one has the world's goods and sees his brother in need, yet closes his heart against him, how does God's love abide in him?   3154

1 John 3:17, *Revised Standard Version*

The finest poems in the world have been expedients to get bread.   3155

Ralph Waldo Emerson, *Journals,* 1834

Need and struggle are what inspire us; our hour of triumph is what brings the void. Not the Jews of the captivity, but those of the days of Solomon's glory are those from whom the pessimistic utterances in our Bible come.   3156

William James, *The Will to Believe*

Neighbor

Thou shalt not covet thy neighbor's house, thou shalt not covet thy neighbor's wife, nor his manservant, nor his maidservant, nor his ox, nor his ass, nor anything that is thy neighbor's.   3157

Exodus 20:17

Let none of you imagine evil in your hearts against his neighbor.   3158

Zechariah 8:17

Love worketh no ill to his neighbor.   3159

Romans 13:10

A man must not choose his neighbor: he must take the neighbor God sends him. The neighbor is just the man who is next to you at the moment, the man with whom any business has brought you into contact.   3160

George MacDonald, *Unspoken Sermons,* "Love thy neighbor"

My neighbor: someone who needs me but by whom I am not enchanted.   3161

W. H. Auden, *A Certain World*

Sometimes a neighbor whom we have disliked a lifetime for his arrogance and conceit lets fall a single commonplace remark that shows us another side, another man, really; a man uncertain, and puzzled, and in the dark like ourselves.   3162

Willa Cather, *Shadows on the Rock,* Epilogue

There is no central machinery to provide a substitute for a good neighbor.   3163

Edward VIII, in 1932. *Observer,* "Sayings of the Week," 31 May 1953

Next to the Blessed Sacrament itself, your neighbor is the holiest object presented to your senses. If he is your Christian neighbor he is holy in almost the same way, for in him also Christ *vere latitat*—the glorifier and the glorified—Glory himself, is truly hidden.   3164

C. S. Lewis, *The Weight of Glory*

Nobility

To be nobly wrong is more manly than to be meanly right.   3165

Thomas Paine, *The American Spirit*

Nonattachment

Nonattachment means that we be not taken in by the world and its ways, and that we physically renounce them.   3166

Aelred Graham, *Zen Catholicism*

Noninvolvement

People who insist on keeping their hands clean are likely to find themselves without hands.   3167

Charles Péguy. Quoted in William Sloane Coffin, Jr., *Once to Every Man*

Nonreturn

You can't go back home to your family—
    to a young man's dream of fame and glory
    to the country cottage away from strife and conflict
    to the father you have lost
    to the old forms and systems of things which seemed
    everlasting but are changing all the time.   3168

Thomas Wolfe, *You Can't Go Home Again*

Nonviolence

This is the word of the Lord unto Zerubbabel, saying, Not by might nor by power, but by my spirit, saith the Lord of hosts.   3169

Zechariah 4:6

I say unto you, that ye resist not evil: but whosoever shall smite thee on thy right cheek, turn to him the other also. And if any man will sue thee at the law, and take away thy coat, let him have thy cloak also. And whosoever shall compel thee to go a mile, go with him twain.   3170

Jesus in Matthew 5:39–41

Nonviolence is a powerful and just weapon . . . which cuts without wounding and ennobles the man who wields it. It is a sword that heals.   3171

Martin Luther King, Jr., *Why We Can't Wait*

Nothingness

Nothingness is capacity, and night the opportunity of light.   3172

Coventry Patmore, *The Rod, the Root and the Flower*

Now

I have heard thee in a time accepted, and in the day of salvation have I succoured thee: behold, Now is the accepted time; behold, now is the day of salvation.   3173

2 Corinthians 6:2

Almighty God, give us grace that we may cast away the works of darkness, and put upon us the armor of light, now in the time of this mortal life, in which thy Son Jesus Christ came to visit us in great humility; that in the last day, when he shall come again in his glorious majesty to judge both the quick and the dead, we may rise to the life immortal.   3174

Book of Common Prayer, *Collect for Advent*

O

Obedience

Of every tree of the garden mayest thou freely eat: but of the tree of the knowledge of good and evil, thou shalt not eat. 3175
Genesis 2:16–17

Walk before me, and be thou perfect. 3176
Genesis 17:1

In thy seed shall all the nations of the earth be blessed; because thou hast obeyed my voice. 3177
Genesis 22:18

If ye walk in my statutes, and keep my commandments, and do them, Then I will give you rain in due season, and the land shall yield her increase, and the trees of the field shall yield their fruit. 3178
Leviticus 26:3–4

Behold, I set before you this day a blessing and a curse: A blessing, if ye obey the commandments of the Lord your God, which I command you this day, And a curse if ye will not obey. 3179
Deuteronomy 11:26–28

Hath the Lord as great delight in burnt offerings and sacrifices as in obeying the voice of the Lord? 3180
1 Samuel 15:22

He did that which was right in the sight of the Lord. 3181
2 Kings 14:3

All the paths of the Lord are mercy and truth unto such as keep his covenant. 3182
Psalm 25:10

He that keepeth the law, happy is he. 3183
Proverbs 29:18

Fear God, and keep his commandments: for this is the whole duty of man. 3184
Ecclesiastes 12:13

Whosoever heareth these words of mine, and doeth them, I will liken him unto a wise man, which built his house upon a rock.   3185

Jesus in Matthew 7:24

Whosoever shall do the will of my Father, which is in heaven, the same is my brother, and sister, and mother.   3186

Jesus in Matthew 12:50

Not my will, but thine, be done.   3187

Jesus in Luke 22:42

If a man keep my saying, he shall never see death.   3188

Jesus in John 8:51

We ought to obey God rather than men.   3189

Acts 5:29

Though he were a Son, yet learned he obedience by the things which he suffered.   3190

Hebrews 5:8

Blessed are they that do his commandments, that they may have right to the tree of life.   3191

Revelation 22:14

Sacrifice without obedience is sacrilege.   3192

William Gurnall, *The Golden Treasury of Puritan Quotations*

Judas heard all Christ's sermons.   3193

Thomas Goodwin, *Ibid.*

To say that blind custom of obedience should be a surer obligation than duty taught and understood . . . is to affirm that a blind man may tread surer by a guide than a seeing man by a light.   3194

Francis Bacon, *Advancement of Learning*

God sets the soul long, weary, impossible tasks, yet is satisfied by the first sincere proof that obedience is intended, and takes the burden away forthwith. "Could ye not watch with me one hour?"   3195

Coventry Patmore, *The Rod, the Root and the Flower*

On one occasion a woman in the crowd shouted out to Jesus, "Blessed is the womb that bore you, and the breasts that you sucked!" Jesus responded, "Blessed rather are those who hear the word of God and keep it!" (Lk. 11:27–28). It is a more blessed thing to live in obedience than to have been the mother of the Messiah!   3196

Richard J. Foster, *Celebration of Discipline*

Obscurity

And some there be, which have no memorial; who are perished as though they had never been, and are become as though they had never been born, and their children after them. But these were righteous men, whose righteousness hath not been forgotten.   3197

Ecclesiasticus 44:9–10, *The Jerusalem Bible*

Let not ambition mock their useful toil,
Their homely joys, and destiny obscure;
Nor grandeur hear with a disdainful smile,
The short and simple annals of the poor.   3198

Thomas Gray, *Elegy Written in a Country Churchyard*

If the bridge fall, it won't crush the minnows.   3199
Chinese Proverb

The greater part [of mankind] must be content to be as though they had not been, to be found in the register of God, not in the record of man.   3200
Sir Thomas Browne, *Urn Burial*

He is happiest of whom the world says least, good or bad.   3201
Thomas Jefferson. Letter to John Adams, 1786

Not a day passes over the earth, but men and women of no note do great deeds, speak great words and suffer noble sorrows.   3202
Charles Reade, *The Cloister and the Hearth*

Obstacles

The way of the wicked is as darkness: they know not at what they stumble. 3203
Proverbs 4:19

I will lay stumblingblocks before this people, and the fathers and the sons together shall fall upon them.   3204
Jeremiah 6:21

Every valley shall be exalted, and every mountain and hill shall be made low; and the crooked shall be made straight, and the rough places plain.   3205
Isaiah 40:4

Men trip not on mountains, they stumble on stones.   3206
Hindustani Proverb

Obstinacy

The difference between perseverance and obstinacy is that the one often comes from a strong will and the other from a strong won't.   3207
Henry Ward Beecher, *Proverbs from Plymouth Pulpit*

No man is good for anything who has not some particle of obstinacy to use upon occasion.   3208
Ibid.

Is there anything so assured, so resolute, so disdainful, so contemplative, so serious and so grave as the ass?   3209
Michel de Montaigne, *Essays,* III, "Of the art of conference"

A man will do more for his stubbornness than for his religion or his country.   3210
Edgar Watson Howe, *Country Town Sayings*

Offering

All things come of thee, O Lord, and of thine own have we given thee.   3211

1 Chronicles 29:14

I will offer to thee the sacrifice of thanksgiving, and will call upon the name of the Lord.   3212

Psalm 116:17

We cannot offer to God the service of angels; we cannot obey Him as man in a state of perfection could; but fallen men can do their best, and this is the perfection that is required of us. It is only the perfection of our best endeavors, a careful labor to be as perfect as we can.   3213

William Law, *A Serious Call to a Devout and Holy Life*

God waits to win back his own flowers as gifts from man's hands.   3214

Rabindranath Tagore, *Stray Birds*

Opinion

The man who never alters his opinion is like standing water, and breeds reptiles of the mind.   3215

William Blake, *Proverbs of Hell*

Loyalty to petrified opinion never yet broke a chain or freed a human soul. 3216

Mark Twain. Inscription beneath his bust in the Hall of Fame

First learn, then form opinions.   3217

Babylonian Talmud

Opinion in good men is but knowledge in the making.   3218

John Milton, *Tractate of Education*

I could never divide myself from any man upon a difference of opinion, or be angry with his judgment for not agreeing with me in that from which perhaps within a few days I should dissent myself.   3219

Sir Thomas Browne, *Religio Medici*

Truth is one forever absolute, but opinion is truth filtered through the moods, the blood, the disposition of the spectator.   3220

Wendell Phillips. *Idols,* 4 October 1859

How far would Moses have gone if he had taken an opinion poll in Egypt?   3221

Harry S. Truman, attributed

It were not best that we should all think alike; it is difference of opinion that makes horse-sense.   3222

Mark Twain, *Pudd'nhead Wilson*

Opportunity

The Lord thy God hath set the land before thee: go up and possess it.   3223
Deuteronomy 1:21

Curse ye Meroz, said the angel of the Lord, curse ye bitterly the inhabitants thereof; because they came not to the help of the Lord, to the help of the Lord against the mighty.   3224
Judges 5:23

Seek ye the Lord while he may be found, call ye upon him while he is near. 3225
Isaiah 55:6

Seek, and ye shall find.   3226
Jesus in Matthew 7:7

Lift up your eyes, and look on the fields; for they are white already to harvest.   3227
Jesus in John 4:35

This sickness is not unto death, but for the glory of God.   3228
Jesus in John 11:4

Walk while ye have the light, lest darkness come upon you.   3229
Jesus in John 12:35

The time is short.   3230
1 Corinthians 7:29

Thou strong seducer, opportunity!   3231
John Dryden, *The Conquest of Granada*

My name is Might-have-been:
I am also called No-more, Too-late, Farewell.   3232
Dante Gabriel Rossetti, *Sonnets from the House of Life*, "A Superscription"

The opportunity that God sends does not wake up him who is asleep.   3233
Senegalese Proverb

Oppression

Ye shall no more give the people straw to make brick.   3234
Exodus 5:7

My father hath chastised you with whips, but I will chastise you with scorpions.   3235
1 Kings 12:11

Deliver me from the oppression of man.   3236
Psalm 119:134

He that oppresseth the poor reproacheth his Maker.   3237
Proverbs 14:31

He looked for judgment, but behold oppression; for righteousness, but behold a cry.   3238
Isaiah 5:7

What mean ye that ye beat my people to pieces, and grind the faces of the poor? saith the Lord God of hosts. 3239

Isaiah 3:15

You can't hold a man down without staying down with him. 3240

Booker T. Washington, attributed

Time is on the side of the oppressed today, it's against the oppressor. Truth is on the side of the oppressed today, it's against the oppressor. You don't need anything else. 3241

Malcolm X, *Malcolm X Speaks*

Optimism and Pessimism

See also Pessimism

There is an optimism which nobly anticipates the triumph of the great moral laws, and there is an optimism which cheerfully tolerates unworthiness. 3242

Agnes Repplier, *Under Dispute,* "Are Americans Timid?"

Everybody, my friend, everybody lives for something better to come. That's why we want to be considerate of every man—Who knows what's in him, why he was born and what he can do? 3243

Maxim Gorki, *The Lower Depths*

The optimist proclaims that we live in the best of all possible worlds, and the pessimist fears this is true. 3244

James Branch Cabell, *The Silver Stallion*

If you will be a pessimist with me over the next ten years I will be an optimist with you over the next hundred years. 3245

Reinhold Niebuhr, attributed

The difference between an optimist and a Christian is that the optimist says "Life is good" and the Christian says "God is good." 3246

C. E. S.

Ordinary People

There are no ordinary people. You have never talked to a mere mortal. Nations, cultures, arts, civilizations—these are mortal, and their life is to ours as the life of a gnat. But it is immortals whom we joke with, work with, marry, snub, and exploit—immortal horrors or everlasting splendors. 3247

C. S. Lewis, *The Weight of Glory*

Original Sin

Original sin *is* unfair, just as a baby inheriting heroin addiction is unfair. 3248

Peter J. Kreeft, *Making Sense Out of Suffering*

What distinguishes true civilizations from their mass-fabricated substitutes except that taproot to the Unconscious, the sense of original sin? What artist-philosophers except Voltaire and Dante have been without it? 3249

Cyril Connolly, *The Unquiet Grave*

We are not merely imperfect creatures who need to be improved; we are, as Newman said, rebels who must lay down their arms.   3250

C. S. Lewis, *The Problem of Pain*

"Original Sin" means we all originate out of a sinful world that taints us from the word go. We all tend to make ourselves the center of the universe, pushing away centrifugally from that center anything that seems to impede its freewheeling. More even than hunger, poverty, or disease, it is what Jesus said he came to save the world from.   3251

Frederick Buechner, *Wishful Thinking: A Theological ABC*

Carlyle said that men were mostly fools. Christianity, with its surer and more reverent realism, says that they are all fools. This doctrine is sometimes called the doctrine of original sin. It may also be described as the doctrine of the equality of man.   3252

G. K. Chesterton, *Heretics*

Orthodoxy

Orthodoxy is reticence.   3253

Author Unknown

The test of fundamental truth is its power to produce superior manhood; and the test of an orthodox church is its power to produce the most men of the largest caliber from generation to generation, transforming society and bringing up averages.   3254

Henry Ward Beecher, *Proverbs from Plymouth Pulpit*

Otherworldliness

There's not much practical Christianity in the man who lives on better terms with angels and seraphs than with his children, servants, and neighbors.   3255

Henry Ward Beecher, *Proverbs from Plymouth Pulpit*

Aim at heaven and you will get earth "thrown in"; aim at earth and you will get neither.   3256

C. S. Lewis, *Mere Christianity*

P

Pacifism

See also Peace

A bayonet is a weapon with a worker at each end.   3257
British pacifist slogan, 1946

The peace of the man who has forsworn the use of the bullet seems to me not quite peace, but a canting impotence.   3258
Ralph Waldo Emerson, *Journals,* 1839

I have always been against the Pacifists during the quarrel, and against the Jingoes at its close.   3259
Winston Churchill, *My Early Years*

I am an absolute pacifist . . . It is an instinctive feeling. It is a feeling that possesses me, because the murder of men is disgusting.   3260
Albert Einstein, in interview with Paul Hutchinson. *The Christian Century,* 28 August 1929

Paganism

The pagan determined with admirable sense to enjoy himself. But by the end of his civilization he had discovered that a man cannot enjoy himself and continue to enjoy anything else.   3261
G. K. Chesterton, *Heretics*

Pain

See also Suffering

Lay down this book and reflect for five minutes on the fact that all the great religions were first preached and long practiced, in a world without chloroform.   3262
C. S. Lewis, *The Problem of Pain*

God whispers to us in our pleasures, speaks in our conscience, but shouts in our pains: it is His metaphor to rouse a deaf world.   3263
Ibid.

Those who do not feel pain seldom think that it is felt. 3264

Samuel Johnson, *The Rambler,* 1 September 1750

Nothing begins and nothing ends,
That is not paid with moan;
For we are born in other's pain,
And perish in our own. 3265

Francis Thompson, *Daisy*

I cannot but think that he who finds a certain proportion of pain and evil inseparably woven up in the life of the very worms will bear his own share with more courage and endurance. 3266

Thomas Henry Huxley, *On the Educational Value of the Natural Sciences*

Illness is the doctor to whom we pay the most heed: to kindness, to knowledge, we make promises only; pain we obey. 3267

Marcel Proust, *Cities of the Plain*

To render ourselves insensible to pain we must forfeit also the possibility of happiness. 3268

John Lubbock, *The Pleasures of Life*

Pain is life—the sharper, the more evidence of life. 3269

Charles Lamb. Letter to Bernard Barton, 9 January 1824

Man endures pain as an undeserved punishment, woman accepts it as a natural heritage. 3270

Author Unknown

Pain makes man think. Thought makes man wise. Wisdom makes life endurable. 3271

John Patrick, *The Teahouse of the August Moon*

Pantheism

Every path in life has its potentiality of greatness, and as it is impossible to be outside God, the best is consciously to dwell in Him. 3272

Henri Frédéric Amiel, *Journal,* 16 July 1848

Parables

With parables and jokes both: if you've got to have it explained, don't bother. 3273

Frederick Buechner, *Wishful Thinking: A Theological ABC*

Pardon

Pardon is not over and done with once for all, but incessant contrition and incessant pardon are the compensating dainties of those in heaven who have lost the dainties of first innocence. 3274

Coventry Patmore, *The Rod, the Root and the Flower*

Parents

I am Joseph; doth my father yet live?   3275
> Genesis 45:3

Honor thy father and thy mother.   3276
> Exodus 20:12

Would God I had died for thee, O Absalom, my son, my son!   3277
> 2 Samuel 18:33

Ask on, my mother: for I will not say thee nay.   3278
> 1 Kings 2:20

O my lord, give her the living child, and in no wise slay it.   3279
> 1 Kings 3:26. The whole episode in which these words are spoken
> must be read to explain them: 1 Kings 3:16–27.

When my father and my mother forsake me, then the Lord will take me up. 3280
> Psalm 27:10

Hearken unto thy father that begat thee, and despise not thy mother when she is
old.   3281
> Proverbs 23:22

Can a woman forget her sucking child, that she should not have compassion on the
son of her womb?   3282
> Isaiah 49:15

What man is there of you, whom, if his son ask bread, will he give him a
stone?   3283
> Jesus in Matthew 7:9

Honor your father and your mother even as you honor God; for all three were part-
ners in your creation.   3284
> The Zohar

How sharper than a serpent's tooth it is
To have a thankless child!   3285
> William Shakespeare, *King Lear*, II, iv, 312

There are times when parenthood seems nothing but feeding the mouth that bites
you.   3286
> Peter de Vries, *Comfort Me with Apples*

Parenthood remains the greatest single preserve of the amateur.   3287
> Alvin Toffler, *Future Shock*

There are no illegitimate children—only illegitimate parents.   3288
> Judge Leon R. Yankwich, in a decision in State District Court for the
> Southern District of California, 1928

When a child is born into the world, God draws his hand out from near his own
heart, and lends something of himself to the parent, and says, "Keep it till I
come."   3289
> Henry Ward Beecher, *Proverbs from Plymouth Pulpit*

The value of marriage is not that adults produce children but that children produce adults.　　3290

Peter de Vries, *Tunnel of Love*

You can sort of be married, you can sort of be divorced, you can sort of be living together, but you can't sort of have a baby.　　3291

David Shire. *Time,* 2 January 1984

This is a moment that I deeply wish my parents could have lived to share. My father would have enjoyed what you have so generously said of me—and my mother would have believed it.　　3292

Lyndon B. Johnson. Commencement address, Baylor University, 28 May 1965

Parting

Every parting gives a foretaste of death; every coming together again a foretaste of resurrection.　　3293

Arthur Schopenhauer, *Further Psychological Observations*

To part is always to die a little.　　3294

French Proverb

Parting is all we know of heaven,
And all we need of hell.　　3295

Emily Dickinson, *Poems,* "My life closed twice before it closed"

It takes two to make even a parting.　　3296

William Cowper, *Scenes from Provincial Life*

For ever, and for ever, farewell, Cassius!
If we do meet again, why, we shall smile;
If not, why then, this parting was well made. [*Brutus.*]　　3297

William Shakespeare, *Julius Caesar,* V, i, 117

When (C. S. Lewis) died, I remembered his great shout across the Oxford High Street: "Christians NEVER say goodbye!" In eternity there will be "time enough." And as Jack said, "We must talk of 1000 things when you come." [*Jack: C. S. Lewis.*]　　3298

Sheldon Vanauken, *A Severe Mercy*

Passion

The power of the Soul for good is in proportion to the strength of its passions. Sanctity is not the negation of passion but its order. (See *Confessions of St. Augustine* and the Letter of St. Bernard on the death of his brother.) Hence great Saints have often been great sinners.　　3299

Coventry Patmore, *The Rod, the Root and the Flower*

Is the devil to have all the passions as well as the good tunes?　　3300

Bernard Shaw, *Man and Superman*

Without passion man is a mere latent force and possibility, like the flint which awaits the shock of the iron before it can give forth its spark.　　3301

Henri Frédéric Amiel, *Journal,* 17 December 1856

The church combats passion by excision; its remedy is castration. It never inquires how desire can be spiritualized, beautified, deified.   3302

> Frederich Wilhelm Nietzsche, *The Twilight of the Idols*

Past, Present, and Future

It will be a great thing for the human soul when it finally stops worshiping backwards.   3303

> Charlotte Perkins Gilman, *The Home*

It is futile to talk too much about the past—something like trying to make birth control retroactive.   3304

> Charles E. Wilson. News summaries, 22 May 1955

The past has revealed to me the structure of the future.   3305

> Pierre Teilhard de Chardin, *Letters from a Traveller*

No man who is correctly informed as to the past will be disposed to take a morose or desponding view of the present.   3306

> Thomas Babington Macauley, *History of England*

I am not afraid of tomorrow, for I have seen yesterday and I love today.   3307

> William Allen White. Quoted in *Reader's Digest,* June 1938

Patience

How long shall I bear with this evil congregation, which murmur against me? 3308

> Numbers 14:27

Our soul waiteth for the Lord: he is our help and our shield.   3309

> Psalm 33:20

He that is slow to wrath is of great understanding.   3310

> Proverbs 14:29

The patient in spirit is better than the proud in spirit.   3311

> Ecclesiastes 7:8

Shall a nation be born at once?   3312

> Isaiah 66:8

It is good that a man should both hope and quietly wait for the salvation of the Lord.   3313

> Lamentations 3:26

The end is not yet.   3314

> Jesus in Matthew 24:6

Tribulation worketh patience; And patience, experience; and experience, hope.   3315

> Romans 5:3-4

One day is with the Lord as a thousand years, and a thousand years as one day.   3316

> 2 Peter 3:8

The longsuffering of our Lord is salvation. 3317
2 Peter 3:15

I knew a wise man that had it for a byword, when he saw men hasten to a conclusion: "Stay a little, that we make an end the sooner." 3318
Francis Bacon, *Essays,* "Of Dispatch"

Patience will do wonders, but it was not much help to the man who planted an orange grove in Maine. 3319
Author Unknown

The strongest of all warriors are these two—Time and Patience. 3320
Leo Tolstoy, *War and Peace*

If it takes nine months to make a natural baby, would it be very surprising if it took nine years to make a supernatural baby? Tarry thou the Lord's leisure. 3321
Evelyn Underhill, *The Fruits of the Spirit*

One moment of patience may ward off great disaster, one moment of patience may ruin a whole life. 3322
Chinese Proverb

Patriotism

O Jerusalem, Jerusalem, thou that killest the prophets, and stonest them which are sent unto thee, how often would I have gathered thy children together, even as a hen gathereth her chickens under her wings, and ye would not! 3323
Jesus in Matthew 23:37

I'd rather see America save her soul than save her face. 3324
Norman Thomas. Speech at antiwar protest meeting,
Washington, D.C., 27 November 1965

"My country, right or wrong," is a thing that no patriot should think of saying except in a desperate case. It is like saying, "My mother, drunk or sober." 3325
G. K. Chesterton, *The Defendant*

To strike freedom of the mind with the first of patriotism is an old and ugly subtlety. 3326
Adlai E. Stevenson. Speech, New York City, 27 August 1952

It was a Roman who said it is sweet and proper to die for one's country. The Greeks never said it is sweet to die for anything. They had no vital lies. 3327
Edith Hamilton, *The Greek Way*

When a whole nation is roaring Patriotism at the top of its voice, I am fain to explore the cleanness of its hands and the purity of its heart. 3328
Ralph Waldo Emerson, *Journals,* 1824

Patriotism is when love of your own people comes first; nationalism, when hate for people other than your own comes first. 3329
Charles de Gaulle, recalled on his leaving the presidency of France.
Life, 9 May 1969

England, with all thy faults I love thee still—my country! 3330
William Cowper, *The Task*

Standing, as I do, in the view of God and eternity, I realize that patriotism is not enough. I must have no hatred or bitterness towards anyone. 3331
> Edith Cavell, British army nurse, spoken to her chaplain before her execution by a German firing squad, 12 October 1915

You'll never have a quiet world till you knock the patriotism out of the human race. 3332
> Bernard Shaw, *O'Flaherty V. C.*

Paul

Let us not underline Paul too much; he is the first of our own cataclysmic converts—do take him, for Heaven's sake, *"cum grano"!* 3333
> Friederich von Hügel, from remarks made at a conference in 1917

If the twelve were a team, Paul came close to being a one-man band: passionate, sometimes harsh and unfair, a monomaniac thruster but also and singularly a man capable of lofty thought, not a ranter. 3334
> Peter Calvocoressi, *Who's Who in the Bible*

Peace, Peacemaking

The right is more precious than peace. 3335
> Woodrow Wilson. Speech to Congress, 2 April 1917

Mark the perfect man, and behold the upright: for the end of that man is peace. 3336
> Psalm 37:37

They shall beat their swords into plowshares, and their spears into pruninghooks: nation shall not lift up sword against nation, neither shall they learn war any more. 3337
> Isaiah 2:4

Blessed are the peacemakers: for they shall be called the children of God. 3338
> Jesus in Matthew 5:9

Peace I leave with you, my peace I give unto you. 3339
> Jesus in John 14:27

Out of the strain of the doing,
Into the peace of the done. 3340
> Julia Louise Woodruff, *Harvest Home*

The deliberate aim at Peace very easily passes into its bastard substitute, Anesthesia. 3341
> Alfred North Whitehead, *Adventures of Ideas*

You cannot shake hands with a clenched fist. 3342
> Indira Gandhi. *Christian Science Monitor,* 17 May 1982

Sometimes, when you stand face to face with someone, you cannot see his face. 3343
> Mikhail S. Gorbachev, following summit meeting with Ronald Reagan in Iceland. *Time,* 12 October 1986

Delight is pleasanter than pleasure; peace more delightful than delight. "Seek peace and ensue it." 3344

> Coventry Patmore, *The Rod, the Root and the Flower*

The note of the perfect personality is not rebellion, but peace. 3345

> Oscar Wilde, *The Soul of Man under Socialism*

The real equation is not Peace = satisfied feeling, but Peace = willed abandonment. 3346

> Evelyn Underhill, *The Letters of Evelyn Underhill*

We must be patient—making peace is harder than making war. 3347

> Adlai E. Stevenson. Speech to Chicago Council on Foreign Relations, 21 March 1946

Peace of God

Thou wilt keep him in perfect peace, whose mind is stayed on thee: because he trusteth in thee. 3348

> Isaiah 26:3

In His will is our peace. 3349

> Dante Alighieri, *Divine Comedy*, "Paradiso"

People

And Job answered and said, No doubt but ye are the people, and wisdom shall die with you. But I have understanding as well as you; I am not inferior to you: yea, who knoweth not such things as these? 3350

> Job 12:1–3

The immense majority of our species are candidates for humanity, and nothing more. Virtually we are men; we might be, we ought to be, men; but practically we do not succeed in realizing the type of our race. 3351

> Henri Frédéric Amiel, *Journal*, 6 November 1877

'Tis but a toss-up whether they cry
Hosanna, or Crucify! 3352

> Coventry Patmore, *The Rod, the Root and the Flower*

Don't put no constrictions on da people. Leave 'em to hell alone. 3353

> Jimmy Durante, attributed (no doubt correctly)

The voice of the people is the kettledrum of God. 3354

> Hindu Proverb

The instinct of the people is right. 3355

> Ralph Waldo Emerson, *The Conduct of Life*, "Power"

Every country is renewed out of the unknown ranks, and not out of the ranks of those already famous and powerful and in control. 3356

> Woodrow Wilson. Speech, Chester, Pa., 28 October 1912

Perfection

If thou wilt be perfect, go and sell that thou hast, and give to the poor, and thou shalt have treasure in heaven; and come and follow me.   3357

Matthew 19:21

The indefatigable pursuit of an unattainable perfection, even though it consist of nothing more than the pounding of an old piano, alone gives a meaning to our life on this unavailing star.   3358

Logan Pearsall Smith, *Apothegms*

Not a having and a resting, but a growing and a becoming, is the character of perfection as culture conceives it.   3359

Matthew Arnold, *Culture and Anarchy,* "Sweetness and Light"

Perseverance

A professional writer is an amateur who didn't quit.   3360

Richard Bach, *A Gift of Wings*

Patience and perSEverance
Made a bishop of his Reverence.   3361

Author Unknown

Persons

The making of a personality, like that of an omelet, requires the breaking of eggs, and the first egg to be broken is a man's own heart.   3362

A. E. Taylor, *The Faith of a Moralist*

People today understand the term "person" not ontologically, as formerly, but psychologically.   3363

Hans Küng, *Does God Exist?*

As a teacher, as a propagandist, Mr. Shaw is no good at all, even in his own generation. But as a personality he is immortal.   3364

Max Beerbohm, *G.B.S.*

I pretended to be somebody I wanted to be until finally I became that person. Or he became me.   3365

Cary Grant, on shaping his personality early in his career. *Parade,* 22 September 1985

Pessimism

Pessimism is essentially a religious disease.   3366

William James, *The Will to Believe*

He that hopes no good fears no ill.   3367

Thomas Fuller, *Gnomologia*

The pessimist is what he is largely because of the taxes the optimists put upon him.   3368

Author Unknown

The originator of a depressing mental view, mood, or idea is less permanently affected by its contemplation than are those who imbibe it from him at second hand. Jeremiah probably retired to rest at night and slept soundly long before his listeners to his fearful words closed their eyes, even though the miseries he spoke of would affect him no less than themselves.   3369

Thomas Hardy, *Thomas Hardy's Notebooks*

Philosophy

Philosophy will clip an angel's wings.   3370

John Keats, *Endymion*

Philosophy is not a theory but an activity.   3371

Ludwig Wittgenstein, *Tractatus Logico-Philosophicus*

Philosophy is language idling.   3372

Ibid.

I have a simple philosophy. Fill what's empty. Empty what's full. Scratch where it itches.   3373

Alice Roosevelt Longworth. *The 637 Best Things Anybody Ever Said,* compiled by Robert Byrne

Vain is the word of a philosopher who does not heal any suffering of man.   3374

Author unknown, quoted by W. Somerset Maugham, *A Writer's Notebook,* 1933–1944

All true philosophers make dying their profession.   3375

Socrates, in Plato's *Phaedo*

Piety

I had rather be a doorkeeper in the house of my God, than to dwell in the tents of wickedness.   3376

Psalm 84:10

Piety, in its nobler and Roman sense, may be said to mean man's reverent attachment to the sources of his being and the steadying of his life by that attachment.   3377

George Santayana, *The Life of Reason*

True piety, which flourishes only when the spirit spontaneously strives to grow in charity, withers when the spirit sluggishly reposes in external ceremonies chosen for it by others.   3378

Erasmus. Quoted by Thomas Merton, *Conjectures of a Guilty Bystander*

Experience makes us see an enormous difference between piety and goodness.   3379

Blaise Pascal, *Pensées*

The strength of a man consists in finding out the way in which God is going, and going that way too.   3380

Henry Ward Beecher, *Proverbs from Plymouth Pulpit*

If your neighbor has made one pilgrimage to Mecca, watch him; if two, avoid him; if three, move to another street.   3381

Arab Proverb

The pious man is ever alert to see beyond the appearance of things a trace of the divine, and thus his attitude toward life is one of expectant reverence. Because of this attitude the pious man is at peace with life, in spite of its conflicts. He patiently acquiesces in life's vicissitudes, because he glimpses spiritually their potential meaning. Every experience opens the door into a temple of new light, although the vestibule be dark and dismal.   3382

Abraham Heschel, The Wisdom of Heschel

Divine contemplation must not be made an excuse for material carelessness.   3383

Chinese Proverb

Pleasure

Can that which is unsavory be eaten without salt?   3384

Job 6:6

Every man should eat and drink, and enjoy the good of all his labor, it is the gift of God.   3385

Ecclesiastes 3:13

To torture a man you have to know his pleasures.   3386

Stanislaw J. Lec. Holiday, September 1963

One way of getting an idea of our fellow-countrymen's miseries is to go and look at their pleasures.   3387

George Eliot, Felix Holt

A fool bolts pleasure, then complains of moral indigestion.   3388

Minna Antrim, Naked Truth and Veiled Allusions

I can sympathize with people's pains, but not with their pleasures. There is something curiously boring about somebody else's happiness.   3389

Aldous Huxley, Limbo

Politics

The sad duty of politics is to establish justice in a sinful world.   3390

Reinhold Niebuhr. Quoted by Jimmy Carter, Why Not the Best?

Ideas are great arrows, but there has to be a bow. And politics is the bow of idealism.   3391

Bill Moyers. Time, 29 October 1965

I am not made for politics because I am incapable of wishing for or accepting the death of my adversary.   3392

Albert Camus, The Fall

Politics I supposed to be the second-oldest profession. I have come to realize that it bears a very close resemblance to the first.   3393

Ronald Reagan. Los Angeles Herald-Examiner, 3 March 1978

To do evil that good may come of it is for the bungler in politics as well as morals. 3394

William Penn, *Fruits of Solitude*

Although he's regularly asked to do so, God does not take sides in American politics. 3395

Senator George J. Mitchell, to Lt. Col. Oliver North, before the Iran-Contra Committee, 13 July 1987

Everybody is always in favor of general economy and particular expenditure. 3396

Anthony Eden. *Observer,* "Sayings of the Week," 17 June 1956

I always admired Mrs. Grote's saying that politics and theology were the only two great subjects. 3397

William E. Gladstone. Letter to Lord Rosebery, 15 September 1880

Pollution

If you want to clear the stream get the hog out of the spring. 3398

American Proverb

Poverty

The poor shall never cease out of the land. 3399

Deuteronomy 15:11

He raiseth up the poor out of the dust, and lifteth up the beggar from the dunghill. 3400

1 Samuel 2:8

Naked came I out of my mother's womb, and naked shall I return thither. 3401

Job 1:21

The needy shall not always be forgotten: the expectation of the poor shall not perish forever. 3402

Psalm 9:18

Blessed is he that considereth the poor: the Lord will deliver him in time of trouble. 3403

Psalm 41:1

The destruction of the poor is their poverty. 3404

Proverbs 10:15

Having nothing, and yet possessing all things. 3405

2 Corinthians 6:10

It has always been a recommendation to me to know that a man has ever been poor, has been regularly born into this world, knows the language. I require to be assured of certain philosophers that they have once been barefooted, footsore, have eaten a crust because they had nothing better, and know what sweetness resides in it. 3406

Henry David Thoreau, *Journal,* 20 October 1855

Half an hour spent with Christ's poor is worth far more than half a million spent on them. 3407

Evelyn Underhill, *The Letters of Evelyn Underhill*

Nothing and nobody down here frightens me; not even an angel, not even the angel of fear. But the moaning of a beggar makes me shudder.   3408

>   Rebbe Hune of Kolochitz, quoted in Elie Wiesel, *Souls on Fire*

A decent provision for the poor is the true test of civilization.   3409

>   Samuel Johnson. Boswell's *Life,* 1770

The greatest man in the world was the poorest.   3410

>   Ralph Waldo Emerson, *Domestic Life*

One must be poor to know the luxury of giving.   3411

>   George Eliot, *Middlemarch*

People who are much too sensitive to demand of cripples that they run races ask of the poor that they get up and act just like everyone else in the society.   3412

>   Michael Harrington, *The Other America*

Power

He will take your fields, and your vineyards, and your olive yards, even the best of them, and give them to his servants. *(He: a king.)*   3413

>   1 Samuel 8:14

Power belongeth unto God.   3414

>   Psalm 62:11

What manner of man is this, that even the winds and the sea obey him!   3415

>   Matthew 8:27

Thou couldest have no power at all against me, except it were given thee from above.   3416

>   John 19:11

Hath not the potter power over the clay?   3417

>   Romans 9:21

The kingdom of God is not in word, but in power.   3418

>   1 Corinthians 4:20

If a rhinoceros were to enter this restaurant now, there is no denying he would have great power here. But I should be the first to rise and assure him that he had no authority whatever.   3419

>   G. K. Chesterton, in conversation with Alexander Woolcott in London restaurant. Quoted in Clifton Fadiman, *The Little, Brown Book of Anecdotes*

I thank thee that I am not one of the wheels of power but I am one with the living creatures that are crushed by it.   3420

>   Rabindranath Tagore, *Stray Birds*

The false can never grow into truth by growing in power.   3421

>   Ibid.

Goodness, armed with power, is corrupted; and pure love without power is destroyed.   3422

>   Reinhold Niebuhr, *Beyond Tragedy*

Our sense of power is more vivid when we break a man's spirit than when we win his heart. 3423

Eric Hoffer, *The Passionate State of Mind*

The only prize much cared for by the powerful is power. The prize of the general is not a bigger tent, but command. 3424

Oliver Wendell Holmes, Jr. *Law and the Court,* 1913

Prayer

God usually answers our prayers according rather to the measure of His own magnificence than to that of our asking; so that we often do not know His boons to be those for which we besought Him. 3425

Coventry Patmore, *The Rod, the Root and the Flower*

The most eloquent prayer is the prayer through hands that heal and bless. The highest form of worship is the worship of unselfish Christian service. The greatest form of praise is the sound of consecrated feet seeking out the lost and helpless. 3426

Billy Graham. *The Chicago American,* 16 April 1967

Kneeling is the proper posture for putting seeds into the ground. 3427

Brooks Atkinson, *Once Around the Sun,* "May 14"

I believe that God prays in us and through us, whether we are praying or not (and whether we believe in God or not). So, any prayer on my part is a conscious response to what God is already doing in my life. 3428

Malcolm Boyd. *Saturday Evening Post,* 27 August 1966

The right relation between prayer and conduct is not that conduct is supremely important and prayer may help it, but that prayer is supremely important and conduct tests it. 3429

William Temple. Quoted in Aldous Huxley, *The Perennial Philosophy*

God never does anything for us except as we are willing for him to do it through us. 3430

C. E. S.

Remember me, I pray thee, and strengthen me, I pray thee, only this once, O God. 3431

Judges 16:28

God forbid that I should sin against the Lord by ceasing to pray for you. 3432

1 Samuel 12:23

Think upon me, my God, for good. 3433

Nehemiah 5:19

He heareth the cry of the afflicted. 3434

Job 34:28

Let the words of my mouth, and the meditation of my heart, be acceptable in thy sight, O Lord, my strength, and my redeemer. 3435

Psalm 19:14

Ye shall seek me, and find me, when ye shall search for me with all your
heart.   3436

> Jeremiah 29:13

Whatsoever ye shall ask in prayer, believing, ye shall receive.   3437

> Jesus in Matthew 21:22

God is prayer.   3438

> Rebbe Pinhas of Koretz. Quoted in Elie Wiesel, *Souls on Fire*

Work as if you were to live 100 years; pray as if you were to die tomorrow.   3439

> Benjamin Franklin, *Poor Richard's Almanack*, May 1757

A place is reserved in heaven for those who weep, and cannot pray.   3440

> Jewish Proverb

Words are but the body, the garment, of prayer; sighs are nearer the heart work. A
dumb beggar getteth an alms at Christ's gates, even by making signs, when his tongue
cannot plead for him; and the rather, because he is dumb. . . . Tears have a tongue, and
grammar, and language, that our Father knoweth. Babes have no prayer for the breast,
but weeping: the mother can read hunger in weeping.   3441

> Samuel Rutherford, *The Golden Treasury of Puritan Quotations*

Prayer is the soul's breathing itself into the bosom of its heavenly Father.   3442

> Thomas Watson, *Ibid.*

Prayers

God, thou art my God: early will I seek thee.   3443

> Psalm 63:1

Into thy hands I commend my spirit: for thou hast redeemed me, O Lord, thou God
of truth.   3444

> Psalm 31:5

Lord, what wilt thou have me to do? *[Paul.]*   3445

> Acts 9:6

Lord, I believe, help thou mine unbelief.   3446

> Mark 9:24

Dearest good Lord, teach us to be generous.
Teach us to serve Thee as Thou deservest;
To give and not to count the cost,
To fight and not to heed the wounds,
To toil and not to seek for rest,
To labor and not to seek reward
Save that of knowing that I do Thy will.   3447

> St. Ignatius Loyola (1491–1556). *The Oxford Book of Prayer,* edited
> by George Appleton

Lord, make me according to thy heart.   3448

> Brother Lawrence (1611–1691), *Ibid.*

O Jesus
Be the canoe that holds me in the sea of life.

Be the steer that keeps me straight.
Be the outrigger that supports me in times of great temptations.
Let thy spirit be my sail that carries me through each day.
Keep my body strong
so that I can paddle steadfastly on,
in the long voyage of life.   3449

A New Hebridean Prayer, *Ibid.*

I live in this little world of mine and am afraid to make it the least less. Lift me into
thy world and let me have the freedom gladly to lose my all.   3450

Rabindranath Tagore, *Stray Birds*

I have learnt the simple meaning of thy whispers in flowers and sunshine—teach
me to know thy words in pain and death.   3451

Ibid.

Ah, great, sweet Lord, make Thou of little me
Only a soft reciprocal of Thee.   3452

Coventry Patmore, *The Rod, the Root, and the Flower*

Good morning, Guvnor, and thank You.   3453

Author Unknown, a London hospital porter. *The Oxford Book of
Prayer*

Preaching

It pleased God by the foolishness of preaching to save them that believe.   3454
1 Corinthians 1:21

People must be charmed into righteousness. The language of aspiration rather
than of criticism and command is the proper pulpit language.   3455

Reinhold Niebuhr, *Leaves from the Notebook of a Tamed Cynic*

A sermon is always like a bucketful of water dashed over rows of narrow-necked
vessels.   3456

William R. Inge, *Mysticism in Religion*

Three things make a preacher—reading, prayer and temptation.   3457

John Trapp, *The Golden Treasury of Puritan Quotations*

Politics and preaching are terms that have little agreement. No sound ought to be
heard in the church but the healing voice of Christian charity.   3458

Edmund Burke, *Reflections on the Revolution in France*

No man can at one and the same time prove that he is clever and that Christ is
wonderful.   3459

James Denney. Quoted in William Barclay, *The Gospel of Matthew*

I believe in preaching to the converted; for I have generally found that the converted do not understand their own religion.   3460

G. K. Chesterton, *Tremendous Trifles*

If I had only one sermon to preach, it would be a sermon against Pride. The more I
see of existence, and especially of modern and experimental existence, the more I am
convinced of the reality of the old religious thesis: that all evil began with some

attempt at superiority; some moment when, as we might say, the very skies were cracked across like a mirror, because there was a sneer in Heaven.   3461

G. K. Chesterton, "If I had only one sermon to preach." Quoted in *As I Was Saying . . . A Chesterton Reader,* edited by Robert Knille

Prejudice

Prejudice, n. A vagrant opinion without visible means of support.   3462

Ambrose Bierce, *The Devil's Dictionary*

Some men, under the notion of weeding out prejudices, eradicate virtue, honesty, and religion.   3463

Jonathan Swift, *Thoughts on Various Subjects*

Sometimes we feel the loss of a prejudice as a loss of vigor.   3464

Eric Hoffer, *Reflections on the Human Condition*

The most difficult subjects can be explained to the most slow-witted man if he has not formed any idea of them already; but the simplest thing cannot be made clear to the most intelligent man if he is firmly persuaded that he knows already, without a shadow of doubt, what is laid before him.   3465

Leo Tolstoy, *The Kingdom of God Is Within You*

The mind that has no prejudices at the outset is empty.   3466

Allan Bloom, *The Closing of the American Mind*

The Catholic and the Communist are alike in assuming that an opponent cannot be both honest and intelligent.   3467

George Orwell, *Selected Essays,* "The Prevention of Literature"

We believe an old apple-woman when she says that she ate an apple; but when she says she saw a ghost we say, "But she's only an old apple-woman."   3468

G. K. Chesterton, *Orthodoxy*

Pride

The beauty of Israel is slain upon thy high places: how are the mighty fallen!   3469

2 Samuel 1:19

Pride compasseth them about as a chain; violence covereth them as a garment. *(them: the wicked.)*   3470

Psalm 73:6

When pride cometh, then cometh shame.   3471

Proverbs 11:2

Pride goeth before destruction, and an haughty spirit before a fall.   3472

Proverbs 16:18

Let him that glorieth glory in this, that he understandeth and knoweth me, that I am the Lord.   3473

Jeremiah 9:24

Whosoever shall exalt himself shall be abased; and he that shall humble himself shall be exalted.   3474

                    Jesus in Matthew 23:12

A man who is eating or lying with his wife or preparing to go to sleep in humility, thankfulness and temperance is, by Christian standards, in an infinitely *higher* state than one who is listening to Bach or reading Plato in a state of pride.   3475

                    C. S. Lewis, to undergraduates at Oxford. *Letters of C. S. Lewis,*
                    edited by W. H. Lewis

Pride grows in the human heart like lard in a pig.   3476

                    Alexandr I. Solzhenitsyn, *The Gulag Archipelago*

Pride gives no food unless he can a feast:
The quality of grace is goodness in the least.   3477

                    Coventry Patmore, *The Rod, the Root and the Flower*

Pride does much and ill,
Love does little and well.   3478

                    Ibid.

The devil never tempts us with more success than when he tempts us with the sight of our own good actions.   3479

                    Thomas Wilson, *Maxims of Piety and Christianity*

There are two sorts of pride: one in which we approve ourselves, the other in which we cannot accept ourselves.   3480

                    Henri Frédéric Amiel, *Journal,* 27 October 1853

In pride, in reas'ning pride our error lies;
All quit their sphere, and rush into the skies!
Pride still is aiming at the blest abodes,
Men would be Angels, angels would be Gods.   3481

                    Alexander Pope, *An Essay on Man*

Priesthood

And the Lord spake unto Moses, saying, Command the children of Israel, that they bring unto thee pure oil beaten for the light, to cause the lamps to burn continually. Without the veil of the testimony, in the tabernacle of the congregation, shall Aaron order it from the evening unto the morning before the Lord continually: it shall be a statute for ever in your congregations. He shall order the lamps upon the pure candlestick before the Lord continually.   3482

                    Leviticus 24:1–4

Ye also, as lively stones, are built up a spiritual house, an holy priesthood, to offer up spiritual sacrifices, acceptable to God by Jesus Christ.   3483

                    1 Peter 2:5

Jesus Christ. . . . hath made us kings and priests unto God.   3484

                    Revelation 1:5–6

Each of you has liberating and healing power over someone to whom you are a priest. We are all called to be priests to each other; and if priests, also physicians. And if physicians, also counsellors. And if counsellors, also liberators.   3485

Paul Tillich, *The Eternal Now*

Every man is a priest, even involuntarily; his conduct is an unspoken sermon, which is forever preaching to others; but there are priests of Baal, of Moloch, and of all the false gods. Such is the high importance of example. Thence comes the terrible responsibility which weighs upon us all. An evil example is a spiritual poison: it is the proclamation of a sacrilegious faith, of an impure God.   3486

Henri Frédéric Amiel, *Journal*, 2 May 1852

Principles

"Principle" is an even duller word than "Religion."   3487

Frederick Buechner, *Wishful Thinking: A Theological ABC*

Prisons

Prisons are built with stones of law, brothels with bricks of religion.   3488

William Blake, *The Marriage of Heaven and Hell*

This metallic world that is society's outrageous attempt to imitate a wrathful god.   3489

Jack Kroll. *Newsweek,* 19 January 1976

America has the longest prison sentences in the West, yet the only condition long sentences demonstrably cure is heterosexuality.   3490

Bruce Jackson. *New York Times,* 12 September 1968

While we have prisons it matters little which of us occupy the cells.   3491

Bernard Shaw, *Maxims for Revolutionists*

We must have a program to "learn the way out of prison."   3492

Warren E. Burger, Chief Justice, calling for program to teach convicts how to read and write; to American Bar Association, Houston, 8 February 1981

A prison is a house of care, a place where none can thrive;
A touchstone true to find a friend, a grave for one alive.
Sometimes a place of right, sometimes a place of wrong,
Sometimes a place of rogues and thieves, and honest men among.   3493

Author unknown. Inscription on Edinburgh's old Tolbooth prison, demolished in 1817

Progress

All progress is based upon a universal innate desire on the part of every organism to live beyond its income.   3494

Samuel Butler, *Note Books*

Progress is Providence without God.   3495

G. K. Chesterton, *What I Saw in America*

What we call progress is the exchange of one nuisance for another.   3496

> Havelock Ellis. Quoted in Sagittarius and George, *The Perpetual Pessimist*

Progress, man's distinctive mark alone,
Not God's, and not the beasts': God is, they are;
Man partly is, and wholly hopes to be.   3497

> Robert Browning, *A Death in the Desert*

Is it progress if a cannibal uses a knife and fork?   3498

> Stanislaw J. Lec, *Unkempt Thoughts*

The greatest obstacle to progress is not man's inherited pugnacity, but his incorrigible tendency to parasitism.   3499

> William R. Inge, *Outspoken Essays: First Series*, "Patriotism"

The march of the human mind is slow.   3500

> Edmund Burke. *Speech on Conciliation with America*, 22 March 1776

All progress is hindsight forward.   3501

> C. E. S.

Property

Where your treasure is, there will your heart be also.   3502

> Jesus in Matthew 6:21

Property is merely the art of democracy. It means that every man should have something that he can shape in his own image, as he is shaped in the image of heaven.   3503

> G. K. Chesterton, *What's Wrong with the World*

A pot that belongs to many is ill stirred and worse boiled.   3504

> Thomas Fuller, *Gnomologia*

What we call real estate—the solid ground to build a house on—is the broad foundation on which nearly all the guilt of this world rests.   3505

> Nathaniel Hawthorne, *The House of Seven Gables*

We must not forget that property has duties even if other people forget that it has rights.   3506

> Samuel Johnson, *Lives of the Poets*

Prophets

Would God that all the Lord's people were prophets, and that the Lord would put his spirit upon them!   3507

> Numbers 11:29

I hate him; for he doth not prophesy good concerning me, but evil.   3508

> 1 Kings 22:8

A prophet is not without honor, save in his own country, and in his own house.   3509

> Jesus in Matthew 13:57

The prophet is appointed to oppose the king, and even more: history. 3510
Martin Buber, *On History*

A member of that unfortunate fraternity to whom the world has never listened, because they have not prophesied acceptable things. 3511
Rupert T. Gould, *Oddities*, "The Wizard of Mauritius"

A prophet is one who, when everyone else despairs, hopes. And when everyone else hopes, he despairs. You'll ask me why. It's because he has mastered the Great Secret: that the Wheel turns. 3512
Nikos Kazantzakis, *The Last Temptation of Christ*

It has not pleased God to build either the congregation of Israel or the fellowship of the Church on prophets. They are the warning, the correction, the voice in the wilderness. 3513
Charles Williams, *He Came Down From Heaven*

Prosperity

In the day of prosperity be joyful, but in the day of adversity consider. 3514
Ecclesiastes 7:14

In prosperous times no altars smoke. 3515
Italian Proverb

We need greater virtues to sustain good fortune than bad. 3516
François de la Rochefoucauld, *Maxims*

It is the curse of prosperity that it takes work away from us, and shuts that door to hope and health of spirit. 3517
William Dean Howells, *The Rise of Silas Lapham*

Hardship is vanishing, but so is style, and the two are more closely connected than the present generation supposes. 3518
E. M. Forster, Two *Cheers for Democracy*

Punishment

Each man suffers his own hell. *(Quisquis suos patimur manis.)* 3519
Virgil, *The Aeneid*

Distrust all in whom the impulse to punish is powerful. 3520
Friedrich Wilhelm Nietzsche, *Thus Spake Zarathustra*

Only the man who has enough good in him to feel the justice of the penalty can be punished; the others can only be hurt. 3521
William E. Hocking, *The Coming World Civilization*

Whipping and abuse are like laudanum; you have to double the dose as the sensibilities decline. 3522
Harriet Beecher Stowe, *Uncle Tom's Cabin*

Purity

It is the privilege of the simple and pure in heart to know God when they see Him. All men have seen God, but nearly all call Him by a different name. The light shineth in darkness, but the darkness comprehendeth it not.   3523

> Coventry Patmore, *The Rod, the Root and the Flower*

Purity is the ability to contemplate defilement.   3524

> Simone Weil, *Gravity and Grace*

The pure heart is pure alike of good and evil, it belongs exclusively to Christ and looks only to him who goes on before.   3525

> Dietrich Bonhoeffer, *The Cost of Discipleship*

Q

Quality

Good things cost less than bad ones.   3526
  Italian Proverb

I suspect that the present chatter about quality of life is an attempt to mask the fact that to the new generation the good life is a life of little effort.   3527
  Eric Hoffer, *Before the Sabbath*

Quarrels

I object to a quarrel because it always interrupts an argument.   3528
  G. K. Chesterton, *Magic*

Looking at God instantly reduces our disposition to dissent from our brother. 3529
  Ralph Waldo Emerson, *Journals,* 1831

For souls in growth, great quarrels are great emancipations.   3530
  Logan Pearsall Smith, *Afterthoughts*

It takes in reality only one to make a quarrel. It is useless for the sheep to pass resolutions in favor of vegetarianism, while the wolf remains of a different opinion.   3531
  William R. Inge, *Outspoken Essays: First Series,* "Patriotism"

Questions and Answers

Can a mortal ask questions which God finds unanswerable? Quite easily, I should think. All nonsense questions are unanswerable. How many hours are there in a mile? Is yellow square or round? Probably half the questions we ask—half our great theological and metaphysical problems—are like that.   3532
  C. S. Lewis, *A Grief Observed*

The Socratic manner is not a game at which two can play. Please answer my question to the best of your ability.   3533
  Max Beerbohm, *Zuleika Dobson*

A school girl answered the question "In what countries are elephants found?" "Elephants are very large and intelligent animals. And are seldom lost."   3534
  James Agate. *The Penguin Dictionary of Modern Quotations*

It is better to know some of the questions than all of the answers.   3535

> James Thurber, in Robert Byrne: *The 637 Best Things Anybody Ever Said*

I don't need to know all the answers, or any of them, so long as I know Him who has them all. But I can't help thinking that He wants me to keep on asking the questions in a spirit of asking rather than demanding, because it is while I am asking that I am open to His instruction in ultimate reality: Himself.   3536

> C. E. S.

Quietness

Be still, and know that I am God.   3537

> Psalm 46:10

Better is an handful with quietness, than both the hands full with travail and vexation of spirit.   3538

> Ecclesiastes 4:6

Thus saith the Lord God, the Holy One of Israel: In returning and rest ye shall be saved, in quietness and in confidence shall be your strength.   3539

> Isaiah 30:15

Study to be quiet.   3540

> 1 Thessalonians 4:11

Quiet persons are welcome everywhere.   3541

> Thomas Fuller, *Gnomologia*

Quiet, to quick bosoms, is a hell.   3542

> George Gordon, Lord Byron, *Childe Harold*

Drop Thy still dews of quietness
   Till all our strivings cease:
Take from our souls the strain and stress,
And let our ordered lives confess
   The beauty of Thy peace.   3543

> John Greenleaf Whittier, hymn, "Dear Lord and Father of Mankind"

R

Race

[God] hath made of one blood all nations of men.   3544
    Acts 17:26

The world is white no longer, and it will never be white again.   3545
    James Baldwin, *Notes of a Native Son*

The so-called white races are really pinko-gray.   3546
    E. M. Forster, *A Passage to India*

The black man who cannot let love and sympathy go out to the white man is but half-free. The white man who retards his own development by opposing the black man is but half-free.   3547
    Booker T. Washington. Address, Boston, 31 May 1897

The race to which we belong is the most arrogant and rapacious, the most exclusive and indomitable in history. It is the conquering and the unconquerable race, through which alone man has taken possession of the physical and moral world. All other races have been its enemies or its victims.   3548
    John James Ingalls. Speech in the U. S. Senate, 23 January 1890

There is a tendency to judge a race, a nation, or any distinct group by its least worthy members.   3549
    Eric Hoffer, *The True Believer*

There are no "white" or "colored" signs on the foxholes or graveyards of battle.   3550
    John F. Kennedy. Message to Congress on civil rights, 19 June 1963

I have a dream that my four little children will one day live in a nation where they will not be judged by the color of their skin but by the content of their character.   3551
    Martin Luther King, Jr. Speech, Washington, D.C., 15 June 1963

Realism

Let us replace sentimentalism with realism, and dare to cover those simple and terrible laws which, be they seen or unseen, pervade and govern.   3552
    Ralph Waldo Emerson, *The Conduct of Life*

Pants get shiny even on a throne. 3553
Stanislaw J. Lec, Unkempt Thoughts

Mud sometimes gives the illusion of depth. 3554
Ibid.

I would be bold and bear
To look into the swarthiest face of things
For God's sake who had made them. 3555
Elizabeth Barrett Browning, Aurora Leigh

An idealist believes the short run doesn't count. A cynic believes the long run doesn't matter. A realist believes that what is done or left undone in the short run determines the long run. 3556
Sydney J. Harris. Reader's Digest, May 1979

Reality

We must prefer real hell to an imaginary paradise. 3557
Simone Weil, Gravity and Grace

Reality is a condition of unrest. 3558
Heraclitus (6th-5th cent. B.C.), Fragments

In all things there is a Within, co-extensive with their Without. 3559
Pierre Teilhard de Chardin, Hymn of the Universe

The real with its meaning read wrong and emphasis misplaced is the unreal. 3560
Rabindranath Tagore, Stray Birds

I like reality. It tastes of bread. 3561
Jean Anouilh, Catch as Catch Can

If it were possible to talk to the unborn, one could never explain to them how it feels to be alive, for life is washed in the speechless real. 3562
Jaques Barzun, The House of Intellect

Facts as facts do not always create a spirit of reality, because reality is a spirit. 3563
G. K. Chesterton, Come to Think of It

Reality is the best possible cure for dreams. 3564
Roger Starr, The Rise and Fall of New York City

Reason

Come now, and let us reason together, saith the Lord. 3565
Isaiah 1:18

Reason in man is rather like God in the world. 3566
St. Thomas Aquinas, Opuscula, "De Regno"

The world was made to be inhabited by beasts, but studied and contemplated by man: 'tis the debt of our reason we owe to God, and the homage we pay for not being beasts. 3567
Sir Thomas Browne, Religion Medici

We distrust our heart too much, and our head not enough. 3568
> Joseph Roux, *Meditations of a Parish Priest*

The last function of reason is to recognize that there are an infinity of things which surpass it. 3569
> Blaise Pascal, *Pensées*

Language is a form of reason and has its reasons which are unknown to man. 3570
> Claude Levi-Strauss, *The Savage Mind*

Let any man look back upon his own life, and see what use he has made of his reason, how little he has consulted it, and how less he has followed it. 3571
> William Law, *A Serious Call to a Devout and Holy Life*

I call it reason because in my philosophy reason is only a harmony among irrational impulses. 3572
> George Santayana, *The Middle Span*

He who will not reason, is a bigot; he who cannot is a fool; and he who dares not is a slave. 3573
> William Drummond of Hawthornden (1584–1649), *Academical Questions*

We may take Fancy for a companion, but must follow Reason as our guide. 3574
> Samuel Johnson. Letter to James Boswell, 1774

Reconciliation

Saul and Jonathan were lovely and pleasant in their lives, and in their death they were not divided. 3575
> 2 Samuel 1:23

If thou bring thy gift to the altar, and there rememberest that thy brother hath ought against thee; Leave there thy gift before the altar, and go thy way; first be reconciled to thy brother, and then come and offer thy gift. 3576
> Jesus in Matthew 5:23–24

Be ye reconciled to God. 3577
> 2 Corinthians 5:20

Love can forbear, and Love can forgive . . . but Love can never be reconciled to an unlovely object. He can never therefore be reconciled to your sin, because sin itself is incapable of being altered; but he may be reconciled to your person, because that may be restored. 3578
> Thomas Traherne, *Centuries*

Word over all, beautiful as the sky,
Beautiful that war and all its deeds of carnage must in time be utterly lost,
That the hands of the sisters Death and Night incessantly wash again, and ever
    again, this soiled world;
For my enemy is dead, a man divine as myself is dead,
I look where he lies white-faced and still in the coffin—I draw near,
Bend down and touch lightly with my lips the white face in the coffin. 3579
> Walt Whitman, *Drum-Taps*, "Reconciliation"

Religion

If any man among you seem to be religious, and bridleth not his tongue, but deceiveth his own heart, that man's religion is vain. True religion and undefiled before God and the Father is this, To visit the fatherless and widows in their affliction, and to keep himself unspotted from the world.   3580
James 1:26–27

The lovers of God have no religion but God alone.   3581
Jalaluddin Rumi. Quoted in Dag Hammarskjöld, *Markings*

It is a mistake to think that God is only, or even chiefly, concerned with religion.   3582
William Temple. Quoted in R.V.C. Bodley, *In Search of Serenity*

Another world to live in—whether we expect ever to pass wholly into it or not—is what we mean by having a religion.   3583
George Santayana, *The Life of Reason*

Being religious means asking passionately the question of the meaning of our existence and being willing to receive answers, even if the answers hurt.   3584
Paul Tillich. *Saturday Evening Post,* 14 June 1954

Religion is the relation of the soul to God, and therefore the progress of Sectarianism marks the decline of religion. For, looking at God instantly reduces our disposition to dissent from our brother. A man may die of a fever as well as by consumption, and religion is as effectually destroyed by bigotry as by indifference.   3585
Ralph Waldo Emerson, *Journals,* 1831

Religious talk is a very feast to self-deceit.   3586
Frederick W. Faber, *Spiritual Conferences*

Sooner or later souls will end by giving themselves to the religion which activates them most as human beings.   3587
Pierre Teilhard de Chardin, *Christianity and Evolution*

For religion all men are equal, as all pennies are equal, because the only value of any of them is that they bear the image of the king.   3588
G. K. Chesterton, *Charles Dickens*

It has often been said, very truly, that religion is the thing that makes the ordinary man extraordinary; it is an equally important truth that religion is the thing that makes the extraordinary man feel ordinary.   3589
G. K. Chesterton, *Ibid.*

A man can no more possess a private religion than he can possess a private sun and moon.   3590
G. K. Chesterton. Introduction to *The Book of Job*

It is the root of all religion that a man knows that he is nothing in order to thank God that he is something.   3591
G. K. Chesterton, *The Resurrection of Rome*

Must "religion" always remain a synonym for "hatred"?   3592
Alfred North Whitehead, *Adventures of Ideas*

The task of organized religion is not to prove that God was in the first century, but that he is in the 20th.   3593

Golda Meir. *Quote,* 14 November 1965

We do not need to prove religion to men but to prove to them that they are religious   3594

George Tyrrell, attributed

What excellent fools religion makes of men!   3595

Ben Jonson, *Fall of Sejanus*

I read in a religious paper, "Nothing is more important than to teach children to use the Sign of the Cross." Nothing? Not compassion, nor veracity, nor justice? *Voila l'ennemi.*   3596

C. S. Lewis, *Letters to Malcolm: Chiefly on Prayer*

I am so profoundly religious that the religious often make me furious.   3597

Lin Yutang, *From Pagan to Christian*

In religion our exclusions are nearly always wrong, and our inclusions, however inconsistent, nearly always right.   3598

Evelyn Underhill, *The Letters of Evelyn Underhill*

No man's Religion survives his Morals.   3599

Thomas Fuller, *Gnomologia*

Religion and Science

The conflict between science and religion, which reached its peak toward the end of the last century, is like the conflict between a podiatrist and a poet. One says that Susie Smith has fallen arches. The other says she walks in beauty like the night. In his own way each is speaking the truth. What is at issue is the kind of truth they're after.   3600

Frederick Buechner, *Wishful Thinking: A Theological ABC*

Repentance

Turn ye from your evil ways, and keep my commandments and my statutes. 3601

2 Kings 17:13

The Lord your God is gracious and merciful, and will not turn his face from you if you return unto him.   3602

2 Chronicles 30:9

To depart from evil is understanding.   3603

Job 28:28

I abhor myself, and repent in dust and ashes.   3604

Job 42:6

When he slew them, then they sought him.   3605

Psalm 78:34

Is not this the fast that I have chosen? to loose the bands of wickedness, to undo the heavy burdens, and to let the oppressed go free?   3606

Isaiah 58:6

If the wicked will turn from all the sins that he hath committed, and keep all my statutes, and do that which is lawful and right, he shall surely live.   3607
Ezekiel 18:21

I am not come to call the righteous, but sinners to repentance.   3608
Jesus in Matthew 9:13

Rejoice with me; for I have found my sheep which was lost.   3609
Jesus in Luke 15:6

The goodness of God leadeth thee to repentance.   3610
Romans 2:4

"Oh God, if I was sure I were to die tonight, I would repent at once." It is the commonest prayer in all languages.   3611
Sir James Barrie, *Sentimental Tommy*

Fractures well cur'd make us more strong.   3612
George Herbert, *The Temple*

Amendment is repentance.   3613
Thomas Fuller, *Gnomologia*

He that repents is angry with himself; I need not be angry with him.   3614
Benjamin Whichcote, *Moral and Religious Aphorisms*

Repentance is possible only from God and is seen only by him.   3615
Karl Barth, *The Epistle to the Romans*

The repentant say never a brave word. Their resolves should be mumbled in silence.   3616
Henry David Thoreau, *Journal,* 28 February 1842

Everything can be taken up again and re-cast in God, even one's faults.   3617
Pierre Teilhard de Chardin, *The Divine Milieu*

Resolves

All day for God to work or fight,
And be within His arms all night.   3618
Coventry Patmore, *The Rod, the Root and the Flower*

From me, thine altar, let no strange fire hiss.   3619
Ibid.

Responsibility

Am I my brother's keeper?   3620
Genesis 4:9

If thou meet thine enemy's ox or his ass going astray, thou shalt surely bring it back to him again.   3621
Exodus 23:4

Wherefore have I not found favor in thy sight, that thou layest the burden of all this people upon me?   3622
Numbers 11:11

The cause that is too hard for you, bring it unto me and I will hear it.   3623
Deuteronomy 1:17

He took water, and washed his hands. *(He: Pilate.)*   3624
Matthew 27:24

Unto whomsoever much is given, of him shall be much required.   3625
Jesus in Luke 12:48

He that is faithful in that which is least is faithful also in much.   3626
Jesus in Luke 16:10

Every one of us shall give account of himself to God.   3627
Romans 14:12

America has no-fault automobile accidents, no-fault divorces, and it is moving with the aid of modern philosophy toward no-fault choices.   3628
Allan Bloom, *The Closing of the American Mind*

Basically, love means that life has no meaning except in terms of responsibility; responsibility toward our family, toward our nation, toward our civilization, and now, by the pressures of history, toward the universe of mankind which includes our enemies.   3629
Reinhold Niebuhr, *Justice and Mercy*

Everybody's business is nobody's business.   3630
English Proverb

Resurrection

Though after my skin worms destroy this body, yet in my flesh shall I see God.   3631
Job 19:26

He will swallow up death in victory.   3632
Isaiah 25:8

Awake and sing, ye that dwell in dust.   3633
Isaiah 26:19

Many of them that sleep in the dust of the earth shall awake, some to everlasting life and some to shame and everlasting contempt.   3634
Daniel 12:2

The third day he shall rise again.   3635
Jesus in Matthew 20:19

God is not the God of the dead, but of the living.   3636
Jesus in Matthew 22:32

They shall mock him, and shall scourge him, and shall spit upon him, and shall kill him: and the third day he shall rise again.   3637
Jesus in Mark 10:34

I am the resurrection and the life.   3638
Jesus in John 11:25

Lazarus, come forth. 3639
> Jesus in John 11:43

Why should it be thought a thing incredible with you, that God should raise the dead? 3640
> Acts 26:8

As in Adam all die, even so in Christ shall all be made alive. 3641
> 1 Corinthians 15:22

I am alive for evermore. 3642
> Jesus in Revelation 1:18

How are we to imagine the resurrection? The answer is: Not at all. 3643
> Hans Küng. *Eternal Life?*

"Resurrection" means a life that bursts through the dimensions of space in God's invisible, imperishable, incomprehensible domain. This is what is meant by "heaven"—not the heaven of the astronauts, but God's heaven. It means going into God's reality, not going out. 3644
> Ibid.

There is no fragment or particle of the world, which, in the grip of its present misery, does not hope for resurrection. 3645
> John Calvin. Quoted in Karl Barth, *The Epistle to the Romans*

Our Lord has written the promise of the resurrection not in books alone, but in every leaf in springtime. 3646
> Martin Luther, *Table Talk*

The New Testament never simply says "Remember Jesus Christ." That is a half-finished sentence. It says "Jesus Christ is risen from the dead." 3647
> Robert Runcie, Archbishop of Canterbury. Easter sermon, 1980

Only the person of Jesus gives meaning and authority to his words. His word is creative because he rose again. 3648
> Jacques Ellul, *Living Faith*

A man really ought to say, "The Resurrection happened two thousand years ago" in the same spirit in which he says, "I saw a crocus yesterday." Because we know what is coming behind the crocus. The spring comes slowly down this way; but the great thing is that the corner has been turned. 3649
> C. S. Lewis, *God in the Dock*, "The Grand Miracle"

God knows to what part of the world every grain of every man's dust lies; and *sibilat populum suum* (as his Prophet speaks in another case), He whispers, He hisses, He beckons for the bodies of His saints, and in the twinkling of an eye, that body that was scattered over all the elements is sate down at the right hand of God, in glorious resurrection. 3650
> John Donne, *Sermons*

Retribution

Whoso sheddeth man's blood, by man shall his blood be shed. 3651
> Genesis 9:6

Eye for eye, tooth for tooth, hand for hand, foot for foot.   3652
  Exodus 21:24

Why hast thou troubled us? the Lord shall trouble thee this day.   3653
  Joshua 7:25

The dead which he slew at his death were more than that which he slew in his life. *(he: Samson.)*   3654
  Judges 16:30

In the place where dogs licked the blood of Naboth shall dogs lick thy blood, even thine. *(thy: Ahab.)*   3655
  1 Kings 21:19

They hanged Haman on the gallows that he had prepared for Mordecai.   3656
  Esther 7:10

As he loved cursing, so let it come unto him: as he delighted not in blessing, so let it be far from him.   3657
  Psalm 109:17

He that diggeth a pit shall fall into it.   3658
  Ecclesiastes 10:8

Whatever a man soweth, that shall he reap.   3659
  Galatians 6:7

Retribution often means that we eventually do to ourselves what we have done to others.   3660
  Eric Hoffer, *Reflections on the Human Condition*

For every false word or unrighteous deed, for cruelty and oppression, for lust or vanity, the price has to be paid at last, not always by the chief offenders, but paid by someone.   3661
  James Anthony Froude. Lecture, 5 February 1864

Revelation

Stand thou still a while, that I may shew thee the word of God.   3662
  1 Samuel 9:27

No man knoweth the Son, but the Father; neither knoweth any man the Father, save the Son, and he to whomsoever the Son will reveal him.   3663
  Jesus in Matthew 11:27

Flesh and blood hath not revealed it unto thee, but my Father which is in heaven.   3664
  Jesus in Matthew 16:17

I speak to the world those things which I have heard of him.   3665
  Jesus in John 8:26

He that hath seen me hath seen the Father.   3666
  Jesus in John 14:9

I looked, and behold, a door was opened in heaven; and the first voice which I heard was . . . as a trumpet talking with me; which said, come up hither, and I will shew thee things which must be hereafter.   3667
>> Revelation 4:1

Belshazzar had a letter,—
He never had but one.
Belshazzar's correspondence
Concluded and begun
In that immortal copy
The conscious of us all
Can read without its glasses
On revelation's wall.   3668
>> Emily Dickinson, *Poems,* "Belshazzar had a letter"

If God has spoken, why is the world not convinced?   3669
>> Percy Bysshe Shelley, *Queen Mab*

A revelation is not made for the purpose of showing to indolent men that which, by faculties already given to them, they may show to themselves; no: but for the purpose of showing that which the moral darkness of man will not, without supernatural light, allow him to perceive.   3670
>> Thomas de Quincy, *The True Relations of the Bible to Merely Human Science*

Revelation is reason in ecstasy.   3671
>> Paul Tillich, *A History of Christian Thought*

Revelation is the manifestation of that which concerns us ultimately.   3672
>> Paul Tillich, *Systematic Theology*

I do not "see his blood upon the rose" or "in the stars the glory of his eyes" until I have seen God's love more intimately than it can be revealed in nature's public glance.   3673
>> Geddes MacGregor, *The Nicene Creed*

Reverence

Put off thy shoes from off thy feet, for the place whereon thou standest is holy ground.   3674
>> Exodus 3:5

Thou shalt fear the Lord thy God; him shalt thou serve, and to him shalt thou cleave, and swear by his name.   3675
>> Deuteronomy 10:20

God is in heaven, and thou upon earth: therefore let thy words be few.   3676
>> Ecclesiastes 5:2

And when I saw him, I fell at his feet as dead.   3677
>> Revelation 1:17

Much talk is heard in our time about building a new human race. How are we to build a new humanity? Only by leading men toward a true, inalienable ethic of our own, which is capable of further development. But this goal cannot be reached unless countless individuals will transform themselves from blind men into seeing ones and begin to spell out the great commandment which is: Reverence for Life. Existence depends more on reverence for life than the Law and the Prophets. Reverence for life comprises the whole ethic of love in its deepest and highest sense. It is the source of constant renewal for the individual and for mankind.   3678

Albert Schweitzer. Sermon, 10 February 1010

> Let knowledge grow from more to more,
>   But more of reverence in us dwell;
>   That mind and soul, according well,
> May make one music as before,
> But vaster. . . .   3679

Alfred, Lord Tennyson, *In Memoriam, A. H. H.*

Riches

See Wealth

Rich and Poor

Laws grind the poor, and rich men rule the law.   3680

Oliver Goldsmith, *She Stoops to Conquer*

Religion is what keeps the poor from murdering the rich.   3681

Napoleon Bonaparte. Quoted in Robert Byrne, *The Other 637 Best Things Anybody Ever Said*

Who has little shall receive. Who has much shall be embarrassed.   3682

Kung-Fu Meditations

For rich people, the sky is just an extra, a gift of nature. The poor, on the other hand, see it as it really is: an infinite grace.   3683

Albert Camus, *Notebooks, 1935–1942*

Poor people have more fun than rich people, they say; and I notice it's the rich people who keep saying it.   3684

Jack Paar, *Three on a Toothbrush*

Add to the New Beatitudes: Lucky are the rich, and blessed are the poor.   3685

C. E. S.

Righteousness

Can we find such a one as this is, a man in whom the Spirit of God is?   3686

Genesis 41:38

In righteousness shalt thou judge thy neighbor.   3687

Leviticus 19:15

Thou art more righteous than I: for thou hast rewarded me good, whereas I have rewarded thee evil.   3688

1 Samuel 24:17

One that feared God, and eschewed evil.   3689

Job 1:1

How should man be just with God?   3690
> Job 9:2

I was eyes to the blind, and feet was I to the lame.   3691
> Job 29:15

Shout for joy, all ye that are upright in heart.   3692
> Psalm 32:11

Light is sown for the righteous, and gladness for the upright in heart. 3693
> Psalm 97:11

Blessed are they which do hunger and thirst after righteousness: for they shall be
filled.   3694
> Jesus in Matthew 5:6

But there remains the question: what righteousness really is. The sweet reason-
ableness of Jesus.   3695
> Matthew Arnold, *Literature and Dogma*

Men are righteous, only in the secret of God: that is, they are righteous undeserv-
edly and non-historically. They cannot convince themselves of righteousness. 3696
> Karl Barth, *The Epistle to the Romans*

Righteousness goes beyond justice. Justice is strict and exact, giving each person his due. Righteousness implies benevolence, kindness, generosity. . . . Justice
may be legal; righteousness is associated with a burning compassion for the
oppressed.   3697
> Abraham Heschel, *The Wisdom of Heschel*

May God prevent us from becoming "right-thinking men"—that is to say men who
agree perfectly with their own police.   3698
> Thomas Merton. Quoted in his obituary, *New York Times*,
> 11 December 1968

Today does not always belong to the righteous, but tomorrow always does (though
the tomorrow may not be strictly by the calendar).   3699
> C. E. S.

S

Sacrifice

He that loseth his life for my sake shall find it.   3700
        Jesus in Matthew 10:39

The Son of man came not to be ministered unto, but to minister, and to give his life a ransom for many.   3701
        Jesus in Matthew 20:28

For God so loved the world, that he gave his only begotten Son, that whosoever believeth in him should not perish, but have everlasting life.   3702
        John 3:16

The good shepherd giveth his life for the sheep.   3703
        Jesus in John 10:11

Greater love hath no man than this, that a man lay down his life for his friends.   3704
        Jesus in John 15:13

Christ died for the ungodly.   3705
        Romans 5:6

This is my body, which is broken for you: this do in remembrance of me.   3706
        Jesus in 1 Corinthians 11:24

To do good and to communicate forget not: for with such sacrifices God is well pleased.   3707
        Hebrews 13:16

All men are led to Heaven by their own loves; but these must first be sacrificed.   3708
        Coventry Patmore, *The Rod, the Root and the Flower*

To sacrifice something is to make it holy by giving it away for love.   3709
        Frederick Buechner, *Wishful Thinking: A Theological ABC*

In the last analysis, what does the word "sacrifice" mean? Or even the word "gift"? He who has nothing can give nothing. The gift is God's—to God.   3710
        Dag Hammarskjöld, *Markings*

Ernest felt now that the turning point of his life had come. He would give up all for Christ—even his tobacco. 3711

Samuel Butler, *The Way of All Flesh*

A true sacrifice is every work which is done that we may be united to God in holy fellowship, and which has a reference to that supreme good and end in which alone we can be truly blessed. 3712

St. Augustine, *The City of God*

Nothing so enhances a good as to make sacrifices for it. 3713

George Santayana, *The Sense of Beauty*

Nothing is costly to one who does not count the cost. 3714

Antonin G. Sertillanges, *Rectitude*

Saints

He will keep the feet of his saints, and the wicked shall be silent in darkness; for by strength shall no man prevail. 3715

1 Samuel 2:9

Precious in the sight of the Lord is the death of his saints. 3716

Psalm 116:15

To most, even good people, God is a belief. To the saints he is an embrace. 3717

Francis Thompson. *Works,* Vol. VIII.

To all that be in Rome, beloved of God, called to be saints: Grace to you and peace from God our Father, and the Lord Jesus Christ. 3718

Romans 1:7

Do ye not know that the saints shall judge the world? 3719

1 Corinthians 6:2

Here is the patience of the saints: here are they that keep the commandments of God, and the faith of Jesus. 3720

Revelation 14:12

Saint, n. A dead sinner revised and edited. 3721

Ambrose Bierce, *The Devil's Dictionary*

In his holy flirtation with the world, God occasionally drops a handkerchief. These handkerchiefs are called saints. 3722

Frederick Buechner, *Wishful Thinking: A Theological Handbook*

Can one be a saint if God doesn't exist? That is the only concrete problem I know today. 3723

Albert Camus, *The Plague*

The wonderful thing about saints is that they were human. They lost their tempers, scolded God, were egotistical or testy or impatient in their turns, made mistakes and regretted them. Still they went on doggedly blundering their way toward heaven. 3724

Phyllis McGinley. Quoted in *365 Quotes, Maxims & Proverbs Calendar 1990,* compiled by Debby Roth

We are content to place a statue of Francis of Assisi in the middle of a birdbath and let the whole business of the saints go at that.   3725

C. Kiler Myers. *New York Times,* 19 March 1962

I might compare Simone Weil with Mother Teresa, who likewise gives God's universal love a homely and familiar face. They are both pilgrims of the absolute— Simone of absolute truth, and Mother Teresa of absolute love: the two, of course, amounting to the same thing.   3726

Malcolm Muggeridge. Introduction to Simone Weil, *Gateway to God*

If we may credit certain hints contained in the lives of the Saints, love raises the Spirit above the sphere of reverence and worship into one of laughter and dalliance; a sphere in which the soul says
Shall I, the gnat, that dances in thy ray,
Dare to be reverent?   3727

Coventry Patmore, *The Rod, the Root and the Flower*

The most ardent love is rather epigrammatical than lyrical. The Saints, above all St. Augustine, abound in epigrams.   3728

Ibid.

Secret saints, unstained with human honor.   3729

Ibid.

It is always the saints who insist that they are the worst of sinners. When we see a Hitler we say, like the Pharisee, "God, I thank thee that I am not like other men." The saint says, "There but for the grace of God go I."   3730

Peter J. Kreeft, *Everything You Ever Wanted to Know About Heaven—But Never Dreamed of Asking*

Salt of the Earth

It is to be noted that Jesus calls not himself but his disciples salt of the earth, for he entrusts his work on earth to them.   3731

Dietrich Bonhoeffer, *The Cost of Discipleship*

Salvation

The Lord is my strength and song, and he is become my salvation.   3732

Exodus 15:2

They that dwell in the land of the shadow of death, upon them hath the light shined.   3733

Isaiah 9:2

Heal me, O Lord, and I shall be healed; save me, and I shall be saved.   3734

Jeremiah 17:14

Unto you that fear My name shall the Sun of righteousness arise with healing in his wings.   3735

Malachi 4:2

Strait is the gate, and narrow is the way, which leadeth unto life, and few there be that find it.   3736

Jesus in Matthew 7:14

The kingdom of heaven is at hand.   3737
    Jesus in Matthew 10:7

The Son of man is come to save that which was lost.   3738
    Jesus in Matthew 18:11

He that shall endure unto the end, the same shall be saved.   3739
    Jesus in Matthew 24:13

God sent not his Son into the world to condemn the world, but that the world through him might be saved.   3740
    Jesus in John 3:17

Salvation is of the Jews.   3741
    Jesus in John 4:22

If thou shalt confess with thy mouth the Lord Jesus, and shalt believe in thine heart that God hath raised him from the dead, thou shalt be saved.   3742
    Romans 10:9

Now is our salvation nearer than when we believed.   3743
    Romans 13:11

By grace are ye saved through faith.   3744
    Ephesians 2:8

The longsuffering of our Lord is salvation.   3745
    2 Peter 3:15

Salvation is free for you because Someone Else paid.   3746
    Author Unknown

If a man born among infidels and barbarians does what lies in his power God will reveal to him what is necessary to salvation, either by inward inspiration or by sending to him a preacher of the faith.   3747
    St. Thomas Aquinas, *Summa Theologica,* ii

Salvation is healing in the ultimate sense; it is final cosmic and individual healing.   3748
    Paul Tillich, *The Protestant Era*

What is most contrary to salvation is not sin but habit.   3749
    Charles Péguy, *Basic Verities,* "Sinners and Saints"

When we meet in heaven, don't be surprised if after embracing each other we'll be saying things like "I'd know you anywhere, and you look wonderful. But merciful heaven, how you've changed!" "Merciful heaven" will be the exactly right exclamation. It will all have been done by the Mercy who came down from heaven and for our salvation was made man.   3750
    C. E. S.

Sanctity

Sanctity does not consist merely in *doing* the will of God. It consists in *willing* the will of God.   3751
    Thomas Merton, *No Man Is an Island*

Sanctity and genius are as rebellious as vice. 3752

> George Santayana, *Little Essays,* edited by Logan Pearsall Smith

Sanity

Who then *is* sane? *(Quisnam igitur sanus?)* 3753

> Horace, *Satires*

Sanity is a madness put to good uses; waking life is a dream controlled. 3754

> George Santayana, *Interpretations of Poetry and Religion*

Sanity means health. It is sane to talk to yourself, saner to talk with yourself; sane to sing yourself to sleep, saner to sing yourself awake. 3755

> C. E. S.

Satisfaction

It is better to be a human being dissatisfied than a pig satisfied; better to be a Socrates dissatisfied than a fool satisfied. And if the fool, or the pig, be of a different opinion, it is because they know only one side of the question. The other party to the comparison knows both sides. 3756

> John Stuart Mill, *Utilitarianism*

The sovereign source of melancholy is repletion. Need and struggle are what excite and inspire us; our hour of triumph is what brings the void. 3757

> William James, *The Will to Believe*

In the world there are only two tragedies. One is not getting what one wants, and the other is getting it. 3758

> Oscar Wilde, *Lady Windermere's Fan*

Scars

You know what happens to scar tissue. It's the strongest part of your skin. 3759

> Michael R. Mantell, San Diego police psychiatrist, on the psychological recovery of disaster victims. *New York Daily News,* 14 December 1986

Most things break, including hearts. The lessons of life amount not to wisdom, but to scar tissue and callus. 3760

> Wallace Stegner, *The Spectator Bird*

Those dear tokens of his passion
  Still his dazzling body bears,
Cause of endless exultation
  To his ransomed worshippers:
With what rapture, with what rapture
Gaze we on those glorious scars! 3761

> Charles Wesley, hymn, "Lo! he comes, with clouds descending"

Science

Science never saw a ghost, nor does it look for any, but it sees everywhere the traces, and it is itself, the agent of a Universal Intelligence.   3762
> Henry David Thoreau, *Journal*, 2 December 1853

True science teaches, above all, to doubt and be ignorant.   3763
> Miguel de Unamuno, *Tragic Sense of Life*

Science should leave off making pronouncements; the river of knowledge has too often turned back on itself.   3764
> Sir James Jeans, The *Mysterious Universe*

A modern poet has characterized the personality of art and the impersonality of science as follows: Art is I: Science is We.   3765
> Claude Bernard. Quoted in *New York Bulletin of Medicine,* vol. iv
> (1928)

To argue whether the date of the Creation was 4004 B.C. or 10,000 B.C. is irrelevant if scientific measurements reveal a 4-1/2 billion-year-old Earth. No religion that bases its belief on demonstrably incorrect assumptions can expect to survive very long.   3766
> Paul Davies, *God and the New Physics*

Extinguished theologians lie about the cradle of every science as the strangled snakes beside that of Hercules.   3767
> Thomas Henry Huxley, *Darwinism, The Origin of the Species*

"Faith" is a fine invention
When gentlemen can see;
But microscopes are prudent
In an emergency.   3768
> Emily Dickinson, *Poems,* "'Faith' is a fine invention"

Self

The self is given to me far more that it is formed in me.   3769
> Pierre Teilhard de Chardin, *The Divine Milieu*

We possess nothing in the world—a mere chance can strip us of everything—except the power to say "I." That is what we have to give to God, in other words, to destroy. There is absolutely no other free act which is given to us to accomplish, only the destruction of the "I."   3770
> Simone Weil, *Gravity and Grace*

People often say that this or that person has not yet found himself. But the self is not something that one finds. It is something that one creates.   3771
> Thomas Szasz, *The Secret Sin*

One may understand the cosmos, but never the ego; the self is more distant than any star.   3772
> G. K. Chesterton, *Orthodoxy*

We are all serving a life-sentence in the dungeon of self.   3773
> Cyril Connolly, *The Unquiet Grave*

The only man I have to fear is James A. Garfield.   3774
James A. Garfield, attributed

Self-Absorption

If thou couldst empty all thyself of self
   Like to a shell dishabited,
Then might He find thee on an ocean shelf
   And say, this is not dead,
And fill thee with Himself instead.

But thou art all replete with very thou
   And hast such shrewd activity
That when He comes He says, this is enow
   Unto itself; 'twere better let it be,
So small and full, there is no room for Me.   3775
Author Unknown

Self-Acceptance

We experience moments in which we accept ourselves, because we feel that we have been accepted by that which is greater than we. If only more such moments were given us! For it is such moments that make us love our life, that make us accept ourselves, not in our goodness and self-complacency, but in our certainty of the eternal meaning of our life.   3776
Paul Tillich, The Shaking of the Foundations

Self-Affliction

But human bodies are sic fools
For a' their colleges and schools,
That when nae real ills perplex them
They mak enow themsels to vex them.   3777
Robert Burns, The Twa Dogs

Self-Assertion

The perfection preached in the Gospels never yet built an empire. Every man of action has a strong dose of egotism, pride, hardness, and cunning.   3778
Charles de Gaulle. Quoted in The New York Times Magazine,
12 May 1968

Self-Assurance

I may have my faults, but being wrong ain't one of them.   3779
Jimmy Hoffa, attributed

Self-Being

Before Rebbe Zusia died, he said: "When I shall face the celestial tribunal, I shall not be asked why I was not Abraham, Jacob or Moses. I shall be asked why I was not Zusia."   3780

Elie Wiesel, *Souls on Fire*

Self-Concern

When I have talked of myself, I am presently punished by a sense of emptyness, and, as it were, flatulency, that I have lost all the solemnity and majesty of being.   3781

Ralph Waldo Emerson, *Journals,* 1840

Self-Confidence

We are not interested in the possibilities of defeat.   3782

Queen Victoria, during Boer War; to A. J. Balfour, December 1899

Self-Conflict

I cannot understand my own behaviour. I fail to carry out the things I want to do, and I find myself doing the very things I hate. When I act against my own will, that means I have a self that acknowledges that the Law is good, and so the thing behaving in that way is not my self but sin living in me. . . . In my inmost self I dearly love God's Law, but I can see that my body follows a different law that battles against the law which my reason dictates. . . . What a wretched man I am! Who will rescue me from this body doomed to death?   3783

Romans 7:15–18, 22–24, *The Jerusalem Bible*

Inside every Little Nell there is a Lady Macbeth trying to get out.   3784

James Thurber. Quoted in Sister Margaret Magdalen, *Jesus—Man of Prayer*

Self-Conquest

And Jacob was left alone; and there wrestled a man with him until the breaking of the day.   3785

Genesis 32:24

No when the fight begins within himself
A man's worth something.   3786

Robert Browning, *Bishop Bloughram's Apology*

Self-Contempt

Who can justify a man who runs himself down, or respect a man who despises himself?   3787

Ecclesiasticus 10:29, *The Jerusalem Bible*

By despising himself too much a man comes to be worthy of his own contempt.   3788

Henri Frédéric Amiel, *Journal,* 6 December 1870

He who despises himself esteems himself as a self-despiser. 3789

Susan Sontag, *Death Kit*

Self-Contradiction

Do I contradict myself?
Very well then I contradict myself,
(I am large, I contain multitudes). 3790

Walt Whitman, *Song of Myself*

Self-Control

He that is slow to anger is better than the mighty; and he that ruleth his spirit than he that taketh a city. 3791

Proverbs 16:32

What it lies in our power to do, it lies in our power not to do. 3792

Aristotle, *Nichomachean Ethics*

There is a raging tiger inside every man whom God put on this earth. Every man worthy of the respect of his children spends his life building inside himself a cage to pen that tiger in. 3793

Murray Kempton, *America Comes of Middle Age*

Self-Criticism

The motto of Levi-Yitzhak of Berditchev was: "Man must criticize himself and praise his fellow man." He pushed this line of thought to the point of holding himself responsible if mankind was in bad straits. 3794

Elie Wiesel, *Souls on Fire*

How shall we expect charity towards others, when we are uncharitable to ourselves? 3795

Sir Thomas Browne, *Religio Medici*

There is a luxury of self-dispraise,
And inward self-disparagement affords
To meditative spleen a grateful feast. 3796

William Wordsworth, *The Excursion*

Self-Deception

If we say that we have no sin, we deceive ourselves, and the truth is not in us. If we confess our sins, God is faithful and just to forgive us our sins and to cleanse us from all unrighteousness. 3797

1 John 1:8–9

Things oppress us not because of an objective world, but because of a self-deceiving mind. 3798

Kuo-An, Chinese Zen master. Quoted in Alan Watts, *Nature, Man and Woman*

It is as easy to deceive oneself without perceiving as it is difficult to deceive other people without their perceiving it.　　　　　3799

　　　François de la Rochefoucauld, *Maxims*

We lie loudest when we lie to ourselves.　　　　　3800

　　　Eric Hoffer, *The Passionate State of Mind*

Self-Denial

The sweetness even of self-denial wears with time, and becomes tediously easy.　　　　　3801

　　　Coventry Patmore, *The Rod, the Root and the Flower*

Self-Discipline

Perhaps the most valuable result of all education is the ability to make yourself do the thing you have to do, when it ought to be done, whether you like it or not; it is the first lesson that ought to be learned; and however early a man's training begins, it is probably the last lesson that he learns thoroughly.　　　　　3802

　　　Thomas Henry Huxley, *Technical Education*

Self-Discovery

Young man, the secret of my success is that at an early age I discovered that I was not God.　　　　　3803

　　　Oliver Wendell Holmes, Jr., reply to a reporter on his 90th birthday,
　　　8 March 1931

Self-Evangelization

One is Christianized to the extent that he is a Christianizer. One is evangelized to the extent that he is an evangelist.　　　　　3804

　　　Leon Joseph Cardinal Suenens, Archbishop of Mechlin-Brussels,
　　　Belgium. *Catholic Digest,* June 1964

Self-Fixation

In spite of the honestest efforts to annihilate my *I-ity,* or merge it in with what the world doubtless considers my better half, I still find myself a self-subsisting and, alas! self-seeking *me.*　　　　　3805

　　　Jane Welsh Carlyle. Letter to John Sterling, 15 June 1835

Selfishness

We all know that our good works are better to the degree that there is less of self in them. The *I, me,* and *mine* render worthless over half of what we do. They are like an ugly cobweb clinging to a beehive and spoiling all the honey.　　　　　3806

　　　St. Francis de Sales. Quoted in Jean Pierre Camus, *The Spirit of St.
　　　Francis de Sales*

No man is more cheated than the selfish man.　　　　　3807

　　　Henry Ward Beecher, *Proverbs from Plymouth Pulpit*

Selfish people are incapable of loving others, but they are not capable of loving themselves either. 3808

Erich Fromm, *Man for Himself*

The world has been controlled by two parties: those who have ruled by "love of self to the contempt of God" and those who have governed by "love of God to the contempt of self." 3809

St. Augustine, *The City of God*

Selfishness, Love's cousin. 3810

John Keats, *Isabella*

We are all serving a life-sentence in the dungeon of self. 3811

Cyril Connolly, *The Unquiet Grave*

Self-Knowledge

He who knows others is wise.
He who knows himself is enlightened. 3812

Kung-Fu Meditations

I am I plus my circumstances. 3813

José Ortega y Gasset. *Time,* 31 October 1955

We can know ourselves only through knowing others. 3814

Sydney J. Harris, *Pieces of Eight*

I do not know myself, and God forbid that I should. 3815

Johann Wolfgang von Goethe. *Conversations with Eckermann,* 10 April 1829

O wad some pow'r the giftie gie us
To see oursels as ithers see us!
It wad frae mony a blunder free us,
   An' foolish notion. 3816

Robert Burns, *To a Louse*

The folly of that impossible precept, "Know thyself," till it be translated into this particularly possible one, "Know what thou canst work at." 3817

Thomas Carlyle, *Sartor Resartus*

I am not at all the kind of person you and I took me for. 3818

Jane Welsh Carlyle. Letter to Thomas Carlyle, 7 May 1822

Self-knowledge is an everlasting task. 3819

Christopher Hardy, *Scholar Cordis*

One reason, I'm afraid, why some of us have so much trouble finding our real selves is that we are afraid of what we might find. 3820

C. E. S.

Self-Love

Self-love or pride is a sin when, instead of leading you to share with others the self you love, it leads you to keep yourself in perpetual self-deposit. You not only don't accrue any interest that way but become less and less interesting every day. 3821

Frederick Buechner, *Wishful Thinking: A Theological ABC*

Self-Righteousness

Why beholdest thou the mote that is in thy brother's eye, but considerest not the beam that is in thine own eye? 3822

Jesus in Matthew 7:3

It needs some intelligence to be truly selfish. The unintelligent can only be self-righteous. 3823

Eric Hoffer, *Reflections on the Human Condition*

I am much more afraid of my good deeds that please me than of my bad deeds that repel me. 3824

Nahum of Tchernobil. Quoted in Elie Wiesel, *Souls on Fire*

Sensibility

Nothing is little to him that feels it with great sensibility. 3825

Samuel Johnson. Boswell's *Life,* 20 July 1762

A great man is not a man so strong that he feels less than other men; he is a man so strong that he feels more. And when Nietzsche says, "A new commandment I give to you, *be hard,*" he is really saying, "A new commandment I give to you, *be dead.*" Sensibility is the definition of life. 3826

G. K. Chesterton, *Heretics*

If we had keen vision and feeling of all human life, it would be like hearing the grass grow and the squirrel's heart beat, and we should die of that which lies on the other side of silence. 3827

George Eliot, *Middlemarch*

Laughter and tears are meant to turn the wheels of the same machinery of sensibility; one is wind-power, and the other water-power; that is all. 3828

Oliver Wendell Holmes, *The Autocrat of the Breakfast-Table*

Serenity

No one can achieve Serenity until the glare of passion is past the meridian. 3829

Cyril Connolly, *The Unquiet Grave*

It is important to understand that serenity of spirit has no connection whatever with serendipity of fortune. 3830

C. E. S.

Service

If any man serve me, him will my Father honor. 3831

Jesus in John 12:26

Freely ye have received, freely give.   3832
> Jesus in Matthew 10:8

And there was also a strife among them, which of them should be accounted the greatest. And he said unto them, The kings of the Gentiles exercise lordship over them; and they that exercise authority upon them are called benefactors. But ye shall not be so: but he that is greatest among you, let him be as the younger; and he that is chief, as he that doth serve.   3833
> Jesus in Luke 22:24–26

Christ will thank the people who give in the way they eat.   3834
> Simone Weil, *Pensées sans ordre,* "On Science, Necessity, and the Love of God"

Life is like a crossword puzzle,
You must make the letters fit.
Working on it is a pleasure—
You can do it while you sit.

Those who say "Be up and doing"
Haven't learned the Christian charm:
We *are* serving while we're sitting
Moving only brain and arm.   3835
> L. H., to C. E. S. convalescing

There is something better, if possible, that a man can give than his life. That is his living spirit to a service that is not easy, to resist counsels that are hard to resist, to stand against purposes that are difficult to stand against.   3836
> Woodrow Wilson. Speech, 20 May 1919

Small service is true service while it lasts:
Of humblest friends, bright creature! scorn not one:
The daisy, by the shadow that it casts,
Protects the lingering dewdrop from the sun.   3837
> William Wordsworth, *To a Child, Written in Her Album*

Sex

In the day that God created man, in the likeness of God created he him; Male and female created he them; and blessed them, and called their name Adam, in the day when they were created.   3838
> Genesis 5:1–2

Sex is the Tabasco sauce which an adolescent national palate sprinkles on every course on the menu.   3839
> Mary Day Winn, *Adam's Rib*

The moderns have achieved the feat, which I should have thought impossible, of making the whole subject (of sex) a bore.   3840
> C. S. Lewis, *Letters to Malcolm: Chiefly on Prayer*

The sexual embrace can only be compared with music and with prayer.   3841
> Havelock Ellis, *On Life and Sex: Essays of Love and Virtue*

I consider promiscuity immoral. Not because sex is evil, but because sex is too good and too important. 3842

Ayn Rand. *Playboy*, March 1964

I am still of the opinion that only two topics can be of the least interest to a serious and studious mind—sex and the dead. 3843

William Butler Yeats. Letter to Olivia Shakespeare, 2 October 1927

Contrary to Mrs. Grundy, sex is not a sin. Contrary to Hugh Hefner, it's not salvation either. Like nitroglycerin, it can be used either to blow up bridges or to heal hearts. 3844

Frederick Buechner, *Wishful Thinking: A Theological ABC*

Traditionally, sex has been a very private, secretive activity. Herein perhaps lies its powerful force for uniting people in a strong bond. As we make sex less secretive, we may rob it of its power to hold men and women together. 3845

Thomas Szasz, *The Second Sin*

Shame

And they were both naked, the man and his wife, and were not ashamed. 3846

Genesis 2:25

Bodily shame symbolizes anxiety about a broken relationship with God. 3847

Revised Standard Version of the Bible, annotation on *Genesis 3:7*

There is a shame that leads to sin,
as well as a shame that is honorable and gracious. 3848

Ecclesiasticus 4:21, *The Jerusalem Bible*

In trying to extirpate Shame we have broken down one of the ramparts of the human spirit, madly exulting in the work as the Trojans exulted when they broke down their walls and pulled the Horse into Troy. 3849

C. S. Lewis, *The Problem of Pain*

Better a red face than a black heart. 3850

Portuguese Proverb

Man is the only animal that blushes. Or needs to. 3851

Mark Twain, *Pudd'nhead Wilson's New Calendar*

Sharing

Rejoice with them that do rejoice, and weep with them that weep. 3852

Romans 12:15

The Holy Supper is kept, indeed,
In whatso we share with another's need;
Not what we give, but what we share,
For the gift without the giver is bare. 3853

James Russell Lowell, *The Vision of Sir Launfal*

Sickness

Sickness tells us where we are. 3854

Thomas Fuller, *Gnomologia*

Sickness is civil war. 3855

Henry David Thoreau, *Winter,* 19 January 1841

Rheumatism has kept many people on the right path of life. 3856

Author Unknown

We are so fond of one another because our ailments are the same. 3857

Jonathan Swift, *Journal to Stella,* 1 February 1711

One should not miss the flavor of being sick, nor the experience of being destitute. 3858

Chinese Proverb

Can there be worse sickness, than to know
That we are never well, nor can be so? 3859

John Donne, *An Anatomy of the World*

We forget ourselves and our destinies in health, and the chief use of temporary sickness is to remind us of these concerns. 3860

Ralph Waldo Emerson, *Journals,* 1821

One pleasant little thing about a sickbed is that from its hardships one's daily burdens come to look like pleasures; one never dreamed they could look so cheerful. 3861

Oscar Firkins. *Oscar Firkins: Memoirs and Letters,* edited by Ida Ten Eyck

Silence

If a fool can hold his tongue, even he can pass for wise,
and pass for clever if he keeps his lips tight shut. 3862

Proverbs 17:28, *The Jerusalem Bible*

Into a shut mouth flies fly not. 3863

George Herbert, *Outlandish Proverbs*

As we must account for every idle word, so must we account for every idle silence. 3864

Benjamin Franklin, *Poor Richard's Almanacks,* September 1738

If a word is worth one shekel, a silence is worth two. 3865

Jewish Proverb

Sometimes you have to be silent to be heard. 3866

Stanislaw J. Lec, *Unkempt Thoughts*

It takes a man to make a room silent. 3867

Henry David Thoreau, *Journal,* 3 February 1839

Silence is not a thing we make: it is something into which we enter. It is always there. We talk about keeping silence. We keep only that which is precious. Silence is precious, for it is of God. In silence all God's acts are done; in silence alone can his voice be heard and his word spoken.   3868

> Mother Maribel, CSMV. Quoted by Sister Janet, CSMV, in *Mother Maribel of Wantage*

Better that we remain silent and allow our soul, that is always longing for solitude, to sigh without words to God.   3869

> Paul Tillich, *The Eternal Now*

Be silent about great things, let these grow inside you. Never discuss them: discussion is so limiting and distracting. It makes things grow smaller. You think you swallow things when they ought to swallow you. Before all greatness, be silent—in art, in music, in religion: be silent.   3870

> Friedrich von Hügel, *Letters to a Niece*

Simplicity

If you try to simplify or pare off the superfluities from the minds and speech of most men, you will find that nothing is left. There is no simplicity in them, for there is no truth: truth and simplicity being, as Aquinas says, the same thing.   3871

> Coventry Patmore, *The Rod, the Root and the Flower*

There is a certain majesty in simplicity which is far above all quaintness of wit.   3872

> Alexander Pope. Letter to George Walsh, 1706

Perfect simplicity is unconsciously audacious.   3873

> George Meredith, *The Ordeal of Richard Feverel*

The more simple an idea, the more fertile it is in variations.   3874

> G. K. Chesterton, *All Things Considered*

I explained to him I had simple tastes and didn't want anything ostentatious, no matter what it cost me.   3875

> Art Buchwald, *I Chose Caviar*

For every problem there is a solution that is simple, neat, and wrong.   3876

> Henry L. Mencken. Quoted in *MacNeil/Lehrer Report*, PBS, 17 December 1975

There is a simplicity born of shallowness, and falsely so-called; and there is a simplicity which is the costly outcome of the discipline of mind and heart and will. Simplicity in preaching is properly the simplicity of the knowledge of God and of human beings. To say of someone "he preaches simply" is to say "he walks with God." 3877

> Arthur Michael Ramsey, Archbishop of Canterbury. Quoted in James B. Simpson, *The Hundredth Archbishop of Canterbury*

Simplicity, simplicity, simplicity! I say, let your affairs be as two or three, not a hundred or a thousand; instead of a million count half a dozen, and keep your accounts on your thumbnail.   3878

> Henry David Thoreau, *Walden*

Sin

She took of the fruit thereof, and did eat. 3879
Genesis 3:6

Be sure your sin will find you out. 3880
Numbers 32:23

Who can bring a clean thing out of an unclean? Not one. 3881
Job 14:4

There is none that doeth good, no, not one. 3882
Psalm 14:3

Against thee, thee only, have I sinned, and done this evil in thy sight. 3883
Psalm 51:4

If we say that we have no sin, we deceive ourselves. 3884
1 John 1:8

Stolen waters are sweet, and bread eaten in secret is pleasant. 3885
Proverbs 9:17

Righteousness exalteth a nation: but sin is a reproach to any people. 3886
Proverbs 14:34

He was wounded for our transgressions, he was bruised for our iniquities. 3887
Isaiah 53:5

Not that which goeth into the mouth defileth a man; but that which cometh out of the mouth, this defileth a man. 3888
Jesus in Matthew 15:11

He that is without sin among you, let him first cast a stone. 3889
Jesus in John 8:7

All have sinned, and come short of the glory of God. 3890
Romans 3:23

What I hate, that do I. 3891
Romans 7:15

Whatsoever is not of faith is sin. 3892
Romans 14:23

All sins are attempts to fill voids. 3893
Simone Weil. Quoted by W. H. Auden in *A Certain World*

The basic formula of all sin is frustrated or neglected love. 3894
Franz Werfel, *Between Heaven and Earth*

Sin, by which Heaven obtained the exquisite edge of sorrow. 3895
Coventry Patmore, *The Rod, the Root and the Flower*

Sin has many forms, but the work of all is the same—the preference of an immediately satisfying experience of things to the believed pattern of the universe: one may even say, the pattern of the glory. 3896
Charles Williams, *He Came Down from Heaven*

People are no longer sinful, they are only immature or underprivileged or frightened or, more particularly, sick. 3897

Phyllis McGinley, *The Province of the Heart*

I never cut my neighbor's throat;
My neighbor's gold I never stole;
I never spoiled his house and land:
But God have mercy on my soul!
For I am haunted night and day
By all the deeds I have not done;
O unattempted loveliness!
O costly valor never won! 3898

Marguerite Wilkinson, *Guilty*

Sin is a refusal to grow bigger. 3899

Author Unknown

There is nothing interesting about sin, or about evil as evil. 3900

Thomas Merton, *The Seeds of Contemplation*

If it be true that men are miserable because they are wicked it is likewise true that they are wicked because they are miserable. 3901

Samuel Taylor Coleridge, *Aids to Reflection*

Sins cannot be undone, only forgiven. 3902

Igor Stravinsky, *Conversations with Igor Stravinsky*

She (the Catholic Church) holds that it were better for sun and moon to drop from heaven, for the earth to fall, and for all the millions who are upon it to die of starvation in extremest agony, as far as temporal affliction goes, than that one soul, I will not say, should be lost, but should commit one single venial sin, should tell one willful untruth, or steal one poor farthing without excuse. 3903

John Henry Newman, *Lectures on Anglican Difficulties*

Pope's famous phrase to the contrary notwithstanding, to err is not human if it is moral error, sin, that is in question. To err is one or more of these adjectives: *inhuman, subhuman, prehuman*. It is always inhuman in that it is always bad for all people and never good for anybody. It is subhuman in that it is refusal to abide by the moral standard of simple human decency and dignity. You must call it prehuman if you see sin as the product of undevelopment and immaturity rather than of willful perversity and rebellion. To err is to fail to be authentically human. No matter that we all do it: we are all, at times, either inhuman or subhuman or prehuman, or all together at once. 3904

C. E. S.

Solitude

A solitude is the audience-chamber of God. 3905

Walter Savage Landor, *Lord Brooke and Sir P. Sidney*

When is man strong, until he feels alone? 3906

Robert Browning, *Colomba's Birthday*

The great ones of earth have been those who have struggled to share their solitude. The sign of their success has lain in the conviction of others that they were less solitary because of these struggles. The way of this sharing has been love.　　3907
Jessamyn West, *Love Is Not What You Think*

One hour of solitude may bring us closer to those we love than many hours of communication. We can take them with us to the hills of eternity.　　3908
Paul Tillich, *The Eternal Now*

True solitude is the home of the person, false solitude the refuge of the individualist.　　3909
Thomas Merton, *New Seeds of Contemplation*

Whosoever delighteth in solitude is either a beast or a god.　　3910
Francis Bacon, paraphrasing Aristotle. Quoted in George Seldes, *The Great Thoughts*

The worst solitude is to have no true friendships.　　3911
Francis Bacon, *The Advancement of Learning*

Solitude vivifies; isolation kills.　　3912
Joseph Roux, *Meditations of a Parish Priest*

Sorrow

By the rivers of Babylon, there we sat down, yea, we wept, when we remembered Zion.　　3913
Psalm 137:1

Even in laughter the heart is sorrowful.　　3914
Proverbs 14:13

A time to weep, and a time to laugh; a time to mourn, and a time to dance. 3915
Ecclesiastes 3:4

He is despised and rejected of men; a man of sorrows, and acquainted with grief.　　3916
Isaiah 53:3

Ye shall be sorrowful, but your sorrow shall be turned into joy.　　3917
Jesus in John 16:20

Every man is a solitary in his griefs. One soon finds that out.　　3918
Norman Douglas, *South Wind*

There shall be no more death, neither sorrow, nor crying, neither shall there be any more pain: for the former things are passed away.　　3919
Revelation 21:4

Where there is sorrow there is holy ground. Some day people will realize what that means. They will know nothing of life until they do.　　3920
Oscar Wilde, *De Profundis*

Sorrow makes us all children again.　　3921
Ralph Waldo Emerson, *Journals,* 1842

Who never ate his bread in sorrow,
Who never spent the midnight hours

Weeping and wailing for the morrow,
He knows you not, ye heavenly powers.   3922
> Johann Wolfgang von Goethe, translated by Oscar Wilde. Quoted in
> Richard Ellmann, *Oscar Wilde*

Pure and complete sorrow is as impossible as pure and complete joy.   3923
> Leo Tolstoy, *War and Peace*

Great sorrows are silent.   3924
> Italian Proverb

There is something pleasurable in calm remembrance of a past sorrow.   3925
> Cicero, *Ad Familiares*

Not until each loom is silent
And the shuttles cease to fly,
Will God unroll the pattern
And explain the reason why
The dark threads are as needful
In the Weaver's skillful hand
As the threads of gold and silver
For the pattern which He planned.   3926
> Author Unknown

Blessed to us is the night, for it reveals the stars.   3927
> Author Unknown

Soul

Thou wilt not leave my soul in hell; neither wilt thou suffer thy Holy One to see corruption.   3928
> Psalm 16:10

It is with the soul that we grasp the essence of another human being, not with the mind, not even with the heart.   3929
> Henry Miller, *The Books in My Life*

None can keep alive his own soul.   3930
> Psalm 22:29

Fear not them which kill the body, but are not able to kill the soul.   3931
> Jesus in Matthew 10:28

The soul is but a hollow which God fills.   3932
> C. S. Lewis, *The Problem of Pain*

No writer, sacred or profane, ever uses the word "he" or "him" of the soul. It is always "she" or "her"; so universal is the intuitive knowledge that the soul, with regard to God who is her life, is feminine.   3933
> Coventry Patmore, *The Rod, the Root and the Flower*

The human soul develops up to death.   3934
> Hippocrates, attributed

We are not the captains but the stokers of our souls.   3935
> John Lodwick, *Running to Paradise*

God gave thy soul brave wings, put not those feathers
Into a bed to sleep out all ill weathers. 3936

George Herbert, *The Temple*, "The Church Porch"

Man is one name belonging to every nation upon earth. In them all is one soul
though many tongues. Every country has its own language, yet the subjects of which
the untutored soul speaks are the same everywhere. 3937

Tertullian, *Testimony of the Soul*, c. A.D. 200

Call the world if you please "The vale of soul-making." 3938

John Keats. Letter to George and Georgiana Keats, 21 April 1819

What profits now to understand
The merits of a spotless shirt—
a dapper boot—a little hand—
If half the little soul is dirt? 3939

Alfred, Lord Tennyson, *The New Timon and the Poets*

As the flower turns to the sun, or the dog to his master, so the soul turns to
God. 3940

William Temple, *Nature, Man and God*

Build thee more stately mansions, O my soul,
As the swift seasons roll!
Leave thy low-vaulted past!
Let each new temple, nobler than the last,
Shut thee from heaven with a dome more vast
Till thou at length art free,
Leaving thine outworn shell by life's unresting sea! 3941

Oliver Wendell Holmes, *The Autocrat of the Breakfast-Table*, "The
Chambered Nautilus"

Davy and I, after a journey in which we had seen some old friends that we hadn't
seen for a decade or longer, observed and discussed a curious thing. On first remeeting
someone not seen for years, one may feel: Who is this stranger grown so fat, so cynical,
so something? But in a few minutes, whatever the change, one finds the person we
knew. The unique person abides. Always. The peculiar quality of "John-ness" in John
or "Mary-ness" in Mary. And we decided that that unchanging "John-ness" is
the soul. 3942

Sheldon Vanauken, *A Severe Mercy*

Speech

A kindly turn of speech multiplies a man's friends,
and a courteous way of speaking invites many a friendly reply. 3943

Ecclesiasticus 6:5, *The Jerusalem Bible*

Let your speech be alway with grace, seasoned with salt. 3944

Colossians 4:6

The spoken word's function is to humanize thought. 3945

Rebbe Wolfe of Zhitomar. Quoted in Elie Wiesel, *Souls in Fire*

Human speech is like a cracked kettle on which we tap crude rhythms for bears to dance to, while we long to make music that will melt the stars.　　　3946
Gustave Flaubert, Madame Bovary

The sound of tireless voices is the price we pay for the right to hear the music of our own opinions.　　　3947
Adlai E. Stevenson. Speech, New York City, 28 August 1952

Speech is the small change of Silence.　　　3948
George Meredith, The Ordeal of Richard Feverel

Grant me the power of saying things
Too simple and too sweet for words.　　　3949
Coventry Patmore, The Angel in the House

Speech is the mother, not the handmaid, of thought.　　　3950
Karl Krause. Quoted in W. H. Auden, A Certain World

I like people who refuse to speak until they are ready to speak.　　　3951
Lillian Hellman, An Unfinished Woman

Spermatozoa

Behind every spermatozoon lies the whole history of the universe: locked within it is no small part of the world's future.　　　3952
C. S. Lewis, God in the Dock, "Miracles"

Spinelessness

Cannibals prefer those who have no spines.　　　3953
Stanislaw J. Lec, Unkempt Thoughts

Spirit

We wrestle not against flesh and blood, but against principalities, against powers, against the rulers of the darkness of this world, against spiritual wickedness in high places.　　　3954
Ephesians 6:12

Speak to Him thou for He hears, and Spirit with Spirit can meet—
Closer is He than breathing, nearer than hands and feet.　　　3955
Alfred, Lord Tennyson, The Higher Pantheism

Spirit is not in the I but between I and You. It is not like the blood that circulates in you but like the air in which you breathe. Man lives in the spirit when he is able to respond to his You.　　　3956
Martin Buber, I and Thou

During a sabbatical year in Paris I was walking on a street in an old, very poor section of the city, a working people's section. And there came down the street on her way from school a little French girl whose shoes were broken down and who was dressed in a frock that looked like it had been made from a sewed-up flour sack. She was poor, obviously, but she swung along the avenue with a flower stuck in her black hair and the grace of a princess, as if to say, "Here is a little French girl, and don't you forget it."

There is a kind of *élan* in the French spirit that we are all aware of. But when we try to nail the word down, we're in trouble. 3957

Joseph Sittler, *Gravity & Grace*

Spirituality

I am certainly convinced that it is one of the greatest impulses of mankind to arrive at something higher than a natural state. 3958

James Baldwin, *Nobody Knows My Name*

The natural inheritance of everyone who is capable of spiritual life is an unsubdued forest where the wolf howls and the obscene bird of night chatters. 3959

Henry James, Sr. Letter to William James and Henry James, Jr., date unknown.

It is not by meticulous care in avoiding all contaminations that we can keep our spirit clean and give it grace, but by urging it to give vigorous expression to its inner life in the very midst of all the dust and heat. 3960

Rabindranath Tagore, *Letters to a Friend*

Compare the sudden change in the religious life at maturity to the sudden autumnal infusion of sweet juices into the sour and bitter fruit of summer. 3961

Coventry Patmore, *The Rod, the Root and the Flower*

Sticking the Neck Out

Consider the turtle. He makes progress only when he sticks his neck out. 3962

Author Unknown. When James B. Conant was president of Harvard he had on his desk a little model of a turtle, under which was this inscription

Submission

Make sure that you let God's grace work in your souls by accepting whatever he gives you, and giving him whatever he takes from you. True holiness consists of doing God's work with a smile. 3963

Mother Teresa of Calcutta. Quoted in Malcolm Muggeridge, *Something Beautiful for God*

Success

Every man has a right to be conceited until he is successful. 3964

Benjamin Disraeli, attributed

If I have been of service, if I have glimpsed more of the nature and essence of ultimate good, if I am inspired to reach wider horizons of thought and action, if I am at peace with myself, it has been a successful day. 3965

Alex Noble. *Christian Science Monitor,* 6 March 1979

I do not pray for success. I pray for faithfulness. 3966

Mother Teresa of Calcutta. *New York Times,* 18 June 1980

The moral flabbiness born of the exclusive worship of the bitch-goddess Success. That—with the squalid cash interpretation put on the word success—is our national disease. 3967

William James. Letter to H. G. Wells, 11 September 1906

Deification of success is truly commensurate with human meanness. 3968

Friedrich Wilhelm Nietzsche, *Notes* (1873)

All you need in this life is ignorance and confidence, then success is sure. 3969

Mark Twain. Letter to Mrs. Foster, 3 December 1887

Success is more a function of consistent common sense than it is of genius. 3970

An Wang. *Boston Magazine,* December 1986

Suffering

Lord, wherefore hast thou so evil entreated this people? 3971

Exodus 5:22

For Thy sake are we killed all the day long; we are counted as sheep for the slaughter. 3972

Psalm 44:22

Thou feedest them with the bread of tears. 3973

Psalm 80:5

I praised the dead which are already dead more than the living which are yet alive. 3974

Ecclesiastes 4:2

I have chosen thee in the furnace of affliction. 3975

Isaiah 48:10

He was oppressed, and he was afflicted, yet he opened not his mouth. 3976

Isaiah 53:7

My sighs are many, and my heart is faint. 3977

Lamentations 1:22

Let this cup pass from me. 3978

Jesus in Matthew 26:39

We must through much tribulation enter into the kingdom of God. 3979

Acts 14:22

Tribulation worketh patience; And patience, experience; and experience hope. 3980

Romans 5:3–4

If in this life only we have hope in Christ, we are of all men most miserable. 3981

1 Corinthians 15:19

A thorn in the flesh, the messenger of Satan to buffet me. 3982

2 Corinthians 12:7

We count them happy which endure. 3983

James 5:11

Rejoice, inasmuch as ye are partakers of Christ's sufferings; that, when his glory shall be revealed, ye may be glad also with exceeding joy.   3984

1 Peter 4:13

Three Passions, simple but overwhelmingly strong, have governed my life: the longing for love, the search for knowledge, and unbearable pity for the suffering of mankind.   3985

Bertrand Russell, *Autobiography*

No pain, no palm; no thorns, no throne; no gall, no glory; no cross, no crown.   3986

William Penn, *No Cross, No Crown*

The piece of pagan anthropomorphism: the belief that, in order to educate us, God wishes us to suffer. How far from this is the assent to suffering when it strikes us *because* we have obeyed what we have seen to be God's will.   3987

Dag Hammarskjöld, *Markings*

Sufferings are but as little chips of the cross.   3988

Joseph Church, *The Golden Treasury of Puritan Quotations*

This is Daddy's bedtime secret for today: Man is born broken. He lives by mending. The grace of God is glue.   3989

Eugene O'Neill, *The Great God Brown*

Suffering is the sole origin of consciousness.   3990

Fyodor Dostoyevski, *Letters from the Underworld*

Man's grandeur stems from his knowledge of his own misery. A tree does not know itself to be miserable.   3991

Blaise Pascal, *Pensées*

Suicide

I have a hundred times wished that one could resign life as an officer resigns a commission.   3992

Robert Burns. Letter to Mrs. Dunlop, 21 January 1788

As the lights in the penitentiary grow dim when the current is switched on for the electric chair, so we quiver in our hearts at a suicide, for there is no suicide for which all society is not responsible.   3993

Cyril Connolly, *The Unquiet Grave*

Yet there are many who dare not kill themselves for fear of what the neighbors will say.   3994

Ibid.

Obviously a suicide is the opposite of a martyr. A martyr is a man who cares so much for something outside him that he forgets his own personal life. A suicide is a man who cares so little for anything outside him that he wants to see the last of everything.   3995

G. K. Chesterton, *Orthodoxy*

As we cannot live without a *permittis,* so we must not die without a *dimittis.* 3996

Thomas Adams, *The Golden Treasury of Puritan Quotations*

Suicide is the worst form of murder, because it leaves no opportunity for repentance. 3997

John Churton Collins, *Maxims and Reflections*

One does not commit suicide in the middle of a sentence. 3998

Elie Wiesel, *The Oath*

Suicide seems to me to be a flight by which man hopes to capture Paradise Lost instead of trying to deserve Heaven. 3999

Paul Louis Landsberg, *The Experience of Death and the Moral Problem of Suicide.* Quoted in *The Oxford Book of Death,* edited by D. J. Enright

Suicide is not abominable because God forbids it. God forbids it because it is abominable. 4000

Immanuel Kant, *Lectures*

Supernatural

Take away the supernatural, and what remains is the unnatural. 4001

G. K. Chesterton, *Heretics*

Seeing angels in a vision may make a man a supernaturalist to excess. But merely seeing snakes in *delirium tremens* does not make him a naturalist. 4002

Ibid.

There are more things in heaven and earth, Horatio,
Than are dreamt of in your philosophy. *[Hamlet.]* 4003

William Shakespeare, *Hamlet,* I, v, 166

Survival

Fear is an emotion indispensable for survival. 4004

Hannah Arendt. *The New Yorker,* 21 November 1977

The human race's prospects of survival were considerably better when we were defenseless against tigers than they are today when we have become defenseless against ourselves. 4005

Arnold Toynbee. *Observer,* "Sayings of the Year," 1963

Concern about one's own survival, or the whole world's, strictly speaking, is never a Christian concern. The integral Christian concern is for God's survival. 4006

C. E. S.

Survival of the Fittest

Nature's stern discipline enjoins mutual help at least as often as warfare. The fittest may also be the gentlest. 4007

Theodosius Dobzhansky, *Mankind Evolving*

Sympathy

See also Compassion

Jesus wept.   4008
John 11:35

Remember them that are in bonds, as bound with them; and them which are in adversity, as being yourselves also in the body.   4009
Hebrews 13:3

Our sympathy is cold to the relation of distant misery.   4010
Edward Gibbon, *Decline and Fall of the Roman Empire*

Teach me to feel another's woe,
   To hide the fault I see:
That mercy I to others show,
   That mercy show to me.   4011
Alexander Pope, *The Universal Prayer*

T

Tact

Tact is the intelligence of the heart. 4012

> Author Unknown

You never know till you try to reach them how accessible men are; we must approach each man by the right door. 4013

> Henry Ward Beecher, *Proverbs from Plymouth Pulpit*

Everything is pardoned save want of tact. 4014

> French Proverb

Tact, n. From *tangere,* to touch. You are tactful when by intuitive empathy you feel the sore spots in another person before you touch them—if you touch them at all. 4015

> C. E. S.

Talent

Woe to the man who receives a talent and ties it in a napkin. 4016

> St. Jerome, *Letters*

Talents are best nurtured in solitude; but character is best formed in the strong billows of the world. 4017

> Johann Wolfgang von Goethe, *Among My Books*

Where talent is a dwarf, self-esteem is a giant. 4018

> J. Petit-Senn, *Conceits and Caprices*

Talk

Should a wise man utter vain knowledge, and fill his belly with the east wind? 4019

> Job 15:2

Many have fallen by the edge of the sword, but many more have fallen by the tongue. 4020

> Ecclesiasticus 28:18, *The Jerusalem Bible*

Talking is like playing the harp; there is as much in laying the hands on the strings to stop the vibrations as in twanging them to bring out their music. 4021

Oliver Wendell Holmes, *The Autocrat of the Breakfast-Table*

Talk low, talk slow, and don't say too much. 4022

John Wayne. *365 Quotes, Maxims & Proverbs Calendar 1990*, compiled by Debby Roth

I tell my tongue to repeat what my ears are hearing, and it all sounds absurd. 4023

Rebbe Shmelke of Nicolsburg. Quoted in Elie Wiesel, *Souls on Fire*

The worst of Warburton is that he has a rage for saying something when there's nothing to be said. 4024

Samuel Johnson, in Boswell's *Life of Johnson*

Talking with Ourselves

A man who has the ability to converse with himself does not feel the slightest need for anyone else's conversation. 4025

Cicero, *Discussions at Tusculum*

The end comes when we no longer talk with ourselves. It is the end of genuine thinking and the beginning of the final loneliness. The remarkable thing is that the cessation of the inner dialogue marks also the end of our concern with the world around us. It is as if we note the world and think about it only when we have to report to ourselves. 4026

Eric Hoffer, *Reflections on the Human Condition*

If you never talk with yourself, what gives you any reason to believe that you have anything worth saying to anybody else? And the same applies to laughing at your own jokes. 4027

C. E. S.

Tao

The Tao of heaven is this: to take from those who have more than enough and give to those who do not have enough. Man's way is different. It is this: to take from those who do not have enough, to give to those who already have too much. Is there a man who has more than enough and gives it away? Only the man of Tao. 4028

Kung-Fu Meditations

Taste

O taste and see that the Lord is good: blessed is the man that trusteth in him. 4029

Psalm 34:8

As our character deteriorates, so does our taste. 4030

François de la Rochefoucauld, *Maxims*

I say whatever tastes sweet to the most perfect persons, that is finally right. 4031

Walt Whitman, a line among verses excluded from *Leaves of Grass*

A bee upon a briar-rose hung
And wild with pleasure suck'd and kiss'd;
A flesh-fly near, with snout in dung,
Sneer'd, "what a Transcendentalist!" 4032
Coventry Patmore, *The Rod, the Root and the Flower*

"'Taste and see that the Lord is sweet." 'Taste or touch discerns substance. "It is,'"
says Aristotle, "a sort of sight," with this difference that it is infallible. 4033
Ibid.

Good taste belongs to the beatitudes. 4034
Anonymous (Henry S. Haskins), *Meditations in Wall Street*

What one relishes, nourishes. 4035
Benjamin Franklin, *Poor Richard's Almanack,* 1734

Taste is not only a part and an index of morality—it is the only morality. The first,
and last, and closest trial question to any living creature is, "What do you like?" Tell
me what you like, and I'll tell you what you are. 4036
John Ruskin, *The Crown of Wild Olive*

Teaching

Be gentle unto all men, apt to teach, patient. 4037
2 Timothy 2:24

Only a few of you, my brothers, should be teachers, bearing in mind that those of
us who teach can expect a stricter judgment. 4038
James 3:1, *The Jerusalem Bible*

Speak thou the things which become sound doctrine. 4039
Titus 2:1

We teachers can only help the work going on, as servants wait upon a
master. 4040
Maria Montessori, *The Absorbent Mind*

Give me a log hut, with only a simple bench, Mark Hopkins on one end and I on the
other, and you may have all the buildings, apparatus and libraries without
him. 4041
James A. Garfield. Address to Williams College alumni,
New York City, 28 December 1871

I have only one rule—attention. They give me theirs and I give them mine. 4042
Sister Evangelist RSM, on teaching high school students. *Billings
(MT) Gazette,* 4 May 1980

It should be the chief aim of a university professor to exhibit himself in his own
true character—that is, as an ignorant man thinking, actively utilizing his small share
of knowledge. 4043
Alfred North Whitehead, *The Aims of Education*

I am quite sure that in the hereafter she will take me by the hand and lead me to
my proper seat. 4044
Bernard Baruch, on one of his early teachers. News summaries,
29 August 1955

Tears

Weeping may endure for a night, but joy cometh in the morning. 4045
Psalm 30:5

They that sow in tears shall reap in joy. 4046
Psalm 126:5

A time to weep, and a time to laugh. 4047
Ecclesiastes 3:4

Blessed are ye that weep now: for ye shall laugh. 4048
Jesus in Luke 6:21

God shall wipe away all tears from their eyes. 4049
Revelation 7:17

The gift of tears is (as has been said) the best gift of God to suffering man. 4050
John Keble, *Lectures on Poetry*

The sorrow which has no vent in tears may make other organs weep. 4051
Francis J. Hartland, psychiatrist, on psychosomatic disorders.
National Observer, 28 December 1964

For a tear is an intellectual thing,
And a sigh is the sword of an Angel King.
And the bitter groan of the martyr's woe
Is an arrow from the Almighty's bow. 4052
William Blake, *Jerusalem*

I am very sorry indeed to hear that anxieties again assail you. (By the way, don't "weep inwardly" and get a sore throat. If you must weep, weep; a good honest howl. I suspect we—and especially my sex—don't cry enough nowadays. Aeneas and Hector and Beowulf, Roland and Lancelot blubbered like schoolgirls, so why shouldn't we?) 4053
C. S. Lewis, *Letters to an American Lady*

When I consider life and its few years—
A wisp of fog between us and the sun;
A call to battle, and the battle done
Ere the last echo dies within our ears;
A rose choked in the grass; an hour of fears;
The gusts that past a darkening shore do beat;
The burst of music down an unlistening street—
I wonder at the idleness of tears.
Ye old, old dead, and ye of yesternight,
Shepherds and bards and keepers of the sheep:
By every cup of sorrow that you had,
Loose me from tears, and make me see aright
How each hath back what once he stayed to weep:
Homer his sight; David his little lad. 4054
Lizette Woodworth Reese, "Tears." *Scribner's,* November 1899

Tears of Things (*Lacrimae Rerum*)

The phrase is borrowed from Virgil, who speaks of the *lacrimae rerum* (*Aeneid* I, 462) to describe the bittersweet character of much human experience.

Even in laughter the heart is sorrowful.   4055
> Proverbs 14:13

In any really good subject one has only to probe deep enough to come to tears. 4056
> Edith Wharton, *The Writing of Fiction*

The heartbreak in the heart of things.   4057
> Wilfred Gibson, *Lament*

Cosmic upheaval is not so moving as a little child pondering the death of a sparrow in the corner of a barn.   4058
> Thomas Savage, *Her Side of It*

Everything human is pathetic. The secret source of Humor itself is not joy but sorrow. There is no humor in heaven.   4059
> Mark Twain, *Pudd'nhead Wilson's Calendar*

Life is a tragedy full of joy.   4060
> Bernard Malamud. *New York Times,* 29 January 1978

Through the sadness of all things I hear the crooning of the Eternal Mother.   4061
> Rabindranath Tagore, *Stray Birds*

It is the tears of the earth that keep her smiles in bloom.   4062
> Ibid.

A patient complaining of melancholy consulted Dr. (John) Abernathy (1764–1831). After an examination the doctor pronounced, "You need amusement. Go and hear the comedian Grimaldi; he will make you laugh and that will be better for you than any drugs." Said the patient, "I am Grimaldi."   4063
> Clifton Fadiman, *The Little, Brown Book of Anecdotes*

Why does the most joyful music, as much as the saddest, make me choke up?   4064
> C. E. S.

Temperance

Put a knife to thy throat, if thou be a man given to appetite.   4065
> Proverbs 23:2

Every man that striveth for the mastery is temperate in all things.   4066
> 1 Corinthians 9:25

Temperance is simply a disposition of the mind which sets bounds to the passions.   4067
> St. Thomas Aquinas, *Summa theologiae*, LVII

Temptation

And the serpent said to the woman, Ye shall not surely die. 4068
Genesis 3:4

The serpent beguiled me, and I did eat. 4069
Genesis 3:13

Take heed to yourselves, that your heart be not deceived. 4070
Deuteronomy 11:16

Can a man take fire in his bosom, and his clothes not be burned? 4071
Proverbs 6:27

Look not thou upon the wine when it is red. 4072
Proverbs 23:31

If thou be the Son of God, command that these stones be made bread. 4073
Matthew 4:3

Wide is the gate, and broad is the way, that leadeth to destruction. 4074
Jesus in Matthew 7:13

Woe to that man by whom the offence cometh! 4075
Jesus in Matthew 18:7

The spirit indeed is willing, but the flesh is weak. 4076
Jesus in Matthew 26:41

Resist the devil, and he will flee from you. 4077
James 4:7

An open door may tempt any saint. 4078
John Heywood, *Proverbs*

It is easy to keep a castle that was never assaulted. 4079
Thomas Fuller, *Gnomologia*

Has it ever struck you that the trouts bite best on the Sabbath? God's critters tempting decent men. 4080
Sir James Barrie, *The Little Minister*

No man knows how bad he is until he has tried to be good. There is a silly idea about that good people don't know what temptation means. 4081
C. S. Lewis, *The Screwtape Letters*

My temptations have been my masters in divinity. 4082
Martin Luther, *Table Talk*

The tempter or the tempted, who sins most? 4083
William Shakespeare, *Measure for Measure*, II, ii, 163

Learn to say no; it will be of more use to you than to be able to read Latin. 4084
Charles Spurgeon, *Sermons*

Ten Commandments

Begin where we will, we are pretty sure in a short space to be mumbling our ten commandments. 4085

Ralph Waldo Emerson, *Essays,* "Prudence"

A businessman notorious for his ruthlessness announced to Mark Twain, "Before I die I mean to make a pilgrimage to the Holy Land. I will climb Mount Sinai and read the Ten Commandments aloud at the top." "I have a better idea," said Twain. "You could stay home in Boston and keep them." 4086

Clifton Fadiman, *The Little, Brown Book of Anecdotes*

No mere man, since the Fall, is able in this life perfectly to keep the commandments. 4087

Book of Common Prayer, 1662 edition, *Shorter Catechism*

In vain we call old notions fudge
And bend our conscience to our dealing.
The Ten Commandments will not budge,
And stealing will continue stealing. 4088

James Russell Lowell, *International Copyright* (motto of American Copyright League)

I stand by the Ten Commandments. They are bully. 4089

Theodore Roosevelt, attributed

Tenderness

An infinitude of tenderness is the chief gift and inheritance of all great men. 4090

John Ruskin, *The Two Paths*

No society can be considered civilized unless tenderness is viewed as an integral part of manliness, and not alien to it. 4091

Sydney J. Harris, *Clearing the Ground*

Thanksgiving

See Gratitude

Thanksgiving Daily

The first five minutes of a Jewish daily morning service contain blessings in which I thank God for the fact that:

My mind works and I know it is morning,
My eyes work,
My arms and legs function,
My spinal column works and I can stand upright,
I have clothes to wear,
I have things to look forward to during the day.

353

Without these prescribed blessings, it might not occur to me to be grateful for all these things. I might have to wait until I encountered a blind man or a cripple, and then my gratitude would be mixed with a large dose of pity.　　4092

Harold Kushner, *Who Needs God*

Theology

Theology is belief in a supremely attractive centre which has personality.　4093

Pierre Teilhard de Chardin, *The Phenomenon of Man*

Theology is the study of God and his ways. For all we know, dung beetles may study man and his ways and call it humanology. If so, we would probably be more touched and amused than irritated. One hopes that God feels likewise.　　4094

Frederick Buechner, *Wishful Thinking: A Theological ABC*

You will, perhaps, wish to ask, what study I would recommend. I shall not speak of theology, because it ought not to be considered as a question whether you shall endeavor to know the will of God.　　4095

Samuel Johnson, in a letter to James Boswell planning to study in Utrecht, 8 December 1763

Put into heaven a despot, and the earth will swarm with despots.　　4096

Henry Ward Beecher, *Proverbs from Plymouth Pulpit*

We must not confound religion with theology, any more than we must confound the music of an organ with the notes from which it is played.　　4097

Ibid.

The most tedious of all discourses are on the subject of the Supreme Being. 4098

Ralph Waldo Emerson, *Journals,* 1836

Before theology comes doxology.　　4099

Author Unknown

Our theology is not a fixed system we must accept but a gracious experience we must declare.　　4100

Peter Taylor Forsythe. Quoted by Robert McAfee Brown in *A Handbook of Christian Theologians,* edited by Martin E. Marty and Dean Peerman

What soul ever perished for believing that God the Father really has a beard?　　4101

C. S. Lewis, *Letters to Malcolm: Chiefly on Prayer*

As for those wingy mysteries in divinity, and airy subtleties in religion, which have unhinged the brains of better heads, they never stretched the pia mater of mine.　　4102

Sir Thomas Browne, *Religio Medici*

Theological ideas are created on the Continent, corrected in England, and corrupted in America.　　4103

Author Unknown

The living God is related to the categories and formal arguments of our abstract thinking as fire is related to paper.　　4104

Arthur Vogel, *The Christian Person*

A theologian is born by living, nay dying and being damned, not by thinking, reading, or speculating. 4105

> Martin Luther, *Table Talk*

Men are better than their theology. 4106

> Ralph Waldo Emerson, *Essays,* "Compensation"

So far as concerns religious problems, simple solutions are bogus solutions. 4107

> Alfred North Whitehead, *Adventures of Ideas*

Theology is that part of religion that requires brains. 4108

> G. K. Chesterton. Quoted in *New York Times,* 1 September 1985

Theology is rather a divine life than a divine knowledge. In heaven, indeed, we must first see and then love; but here, on earth, we must first love, and love will open our eyes as well as our hearts; and we shall then see, and perceive and understand. 4109

> Jeremy Taylor (1613–1667). Sermon preached late in his life at the University of Dublin

It is rashness to search, godliness to believe, safeness to preach, and eternal blessedness to know the Trinity. 4110

> Thomas Adams, *The Golden Treasury of Puritan Quotations*

Thinking

The Lord knoweth the thoughts of man, that they are vanity. 4111

> Psalm 94:11

My thoughts are not your thoughts, neither are your ways my ways, saith the Lord. 4112

> Isaiah 55:8

I know the things that come into your mind, every one of them. 4113

> Ezekiel 11:5

Think soberly. 4114

> Romans 12:3

Gird up the loins of your mind. 4115

> 1 Peter 1:13

Beware when the great God lets loose a thinker on this planet. 4116

> Ralph Waldo Emerson, *Essays,* "Circles"

There are no dangerous thoughts; thinking itself is dangerous. 4117

> Hannah Arendt. *The New Yorker,* 5 December 1977

To think well is to serve God in the interior court. 4118

> Thomas Traherne, *Centuries*

The grinding of the intellect is for most people as painful as a dentist's drill. 4119

> Leonard Woolf. *Observer,* "Sayings of the Week," 28 June 1959

Thinking is when your mouth stays shut and your head keeps talking to itself. 4120

> Hank Ketcham, through his cartoon character "Dennis the Menace," 1987

We must dare to think about "unthinkable things," because when things become "unthinkable," thinking stops and action becomes mindless. 4121

J. William Fulbright. Speech in U. S. Senate, 25 March 1964

Man is a thought-adventurer. But by thought we mean, of course, discovery. We don't mean this telling himself stale facts and drawing false conclusions, which usually passes for thought. Thought is an adventure, not a trick. 4122

D. H. Lawrence, *Selected Essays*

Man is but a reed, the feeblest thing in nature; but he is a thinking reed. 4123

Blaise Pascal, *Pensées*

This Life and World

See also World

This may not be the best of all possible worlds, but to say that it is the worst is mere petulant nonsense. 4124

Thomas Henry Huxley, *Struggle for Existence in Human Society*

A brave world, Sir, full of religion, knavery, and change: we shall soon see better days. 4125

Alpha Behn (1640–1689), *The Roundheads*

Whoso enjoys not this life, I count him but an apparition, though he wear about him the sensible affections of flesh. In these moral acceptions, the way to be immortal is to die daily. 4126

Sir Thomas Browne, *Religio Medici*

This life is a hospital in which every patient is possessed with a desire to change his bed. 4127

Charles Baudelaire, *Le Spleen de Paris*

This is a puzzling world, and Old Harry's got a finger in it. 4128

George Eliot, *The Mill on the Floss*

It's a lousy home, but it's a fine gymnasium. 4129

Peter J. Kreeft, *Making Sense Out of Suffering*

Many times man lives and dies
Between his two eternities. 4130

William Butler Yeats, *Under Ben Bulben*

I have often said and oftener think, that this world is a comedy for those who think, and a tragedy for those who feel. 4131

Horace Walpole. Letter to Sir Horace Mann, 31 December 1769

We often mistake our own sweet childhood for the old time, which, had we lived in it, we should have found almost as intolerable as our own. The world has always been the dunghill it is now, and it only exists to nourish, here and there, the roots of some rare, unknown, and immortal flowers of individual humanity. 4132

Coventry Patmore, *The Rod, the Root and the Flower*

We live in this world when we love it. 4133

Rabindranath Tagore, *Stray Birds*

Time

To everything there is a season, and a time to every purpose under heaven. 4134
Ecclesiastes 3:1

Time deals gently only with those who take it gently. 4135
Anatole France, *The Crime of Sylvestre Bonnard*

We must use time as a tool, not as a couch. 4136
John F. Kennedy. *Observer,* "Sayings of the Week,"
10 December 1961

Time does not become sacred to us until we have lived it. 4137
John Burroughs, *The Spell of the Past*

When you are deeply absorbed in what you are doing, time gives itself to you like a woman and a willing lover. 4138
Brendan Francis. Quoted in *The Crown Treasury of Relevant Quotations,* edited by Edward E. Murphy

Time wounds all heels. 4139
Author Unknown

Where does discontent start? You are warm enough, but you shiver. You are fed, yet hunger gnaws you. You have been loved, but your yearning wanders in new fields. And to prod all there's time, the Bastard Time. 4140
John Steinbeck, *Sweet Thursday*

Everything we feel is made of Time. All the beauties of life are shaped by it. 4141
Peter Shaffer, *The Royal Hunt of the Sun*

Time is a dressmaker specializing in alterations. 4142
Faith Baldwin, *Face Toward the Spring*

Time is our natural environment. We live in time as we live in the air we breathe. And we love the air—who has not taken breaths of pure country air, just for the pleasure of it? How strange that we cannot love time. It spoils our loveliest moments. Nothing quite comes up to expectations because of it. We alone: animals, so far as we can see, are unaware of time, untroubled. Time is their natural environment. Why do we sense that it is not ours? 4143
Sheldon Vanauken, *A Severe Mercy*

Every moment and every event of every man's life on earth plants something in his soul. 4144
Thomas Merton, *Through the Year with Thomas Merton,* January 14

Time is a storm in which we are all lost. 4145
William Carlos Williams, *Selected Essays*

Time is but the stream I go a-fishing in. I drink of it; but while I drink I see the sandy bottom and detect how shallow it is. Its thin current slides away, but eternity remains. 4146
Henry David Thoreau, *Walden*

Tributes

—Churchill to Roosevelt

Meeting Franklin Roosevelt was like opening your first bottle of champagne: knowing him was like drinking it. 4147

Winston Churchill, recalled on his death, 24 January 1965

—Bagehot to Gladstone

He believes, with all his heart and soul and strength, that there *is* such a thing as truth; he has the soul of a martyr with the intellect of an advocate. 4148

Walter Bagehot, *Historical Essays,* "Mr. Gladstone"

—Muggeridge to Weil

They are both pilgrims of the absolute—Simone of absolute truth, and Mother Teresa of absolute love; the two, of course, amounting to the same thing. 4149

Malcolm Muggeridge. Introduction to Simone Weil, *Gateway to God*

—Arnold to Wordsworth

Time may restore us in his course
Goethe's sage mind and Byron's force:
But where will Europe's latter hour
Again find Wordsworth's healing power? 4150

Matthew Arnold, *Memorial Verses*

—Bragg to Cleveland

They love him most for the enemies he has made. 4151

Edward S. Bragg. Speech seconding the nomination of Grover Cleveland for the presidency, 9 July 1884

—Jefferson to John Adams

He is vain, irritable, and a bad calculator of the force and probable effect of the motives which govern men. This is all the ill which can possibly be said of him. He is as disinterested as the Being who made him. 4152

Thomas Jefferson. Letter to James Madison, 1787

—John Quincy Adams to Abigail Adams

There is not a virtue that can abide in the female heart but it was the ornament of hers. She had been fifty-four years the delight of my father's heart, the sweetener of all his toils, the comforter of all his sorrows, the sharer and heightener of all his joys. 4153

John Quincy Adams. *Diary,* 2 November 1818

—Oliver Wendell Holmes to Robert Burns

We praise him not for gifts divine,
His muse was born of woman,
His manhood breathes in every line,
Was ever heart more human? 4154

Oliver Wendell Holmes, for the Burns Centennial Celebration

—Pope to Newton

Nature and nature's laws lay hid in night;
God said, "Let Newton be!" 4155

Alexander Pope, *Epistles,* "On Sir I. Newton"

—Chesterton to Lincoln

He was not always right; but he always tried to be reasonable, and that is the exact sense which his special admirers have never understood from that day to this. He tried to be reasonable. It is not surprising that his life was a martyrdom, and that he was murdered.   4156

G. K. Chesterton, *Come to Think of It*

—Johnson to Goldsmith

He touched nothing that he did not adorn. *(Nullum quod tetigit non ornavit.)*   4157

James Boswell, *Life of Johnson,* 22 June 1776

—Macauley to John Hampden

A great man who neither sought nor shunned greatness, who found glory only because glory lay in the plain path of duty.   4158

Thomas B. Macauley, *Critical and Historical Studies,*
"John Hampden"

—Bertrand Russell of George Edward Moore

I have never but once succeeded in making him tell a lie, and that was by a subterfuge. "Moore," I said, "do you *always* tell the truth?" "No," he replied. I believe this to be the only lie he ever told.   4159

Bertrand Russell, of his friend. Clifton Fadiman, *The Little, Brown Book of Anecdotes*

—Austin Farrer of C. S. Lewis

He had more actuality of soul than the common breed of men. He took in more, he felt more, he remembered more, he invented more.   4160

Austin Farrer. James T. Como, *C. S. Lewis at the Breakfast Table, and Other Reminiscences*

The life that Lewis lived with zest he surrendered with composure.   4161

Ibid.

—Thoreau to John Brown

He did not go to the college called Harvard, good old Alma Mater as she is. He was not fed on the pap there furnished. As he phrased it, "I know no more of your grammar than one of your calves." But he went to the great university of the West, where he sedulously pursued the study of Liberty, for which he had early betrayed a fondness, and having taken many degrees he finally commenced the public practice of humanity in Kansas, as you all know. Such were *his humanities,* and not any study of grammar. He would have left a Greek accent slanting the wrong way, and righted up a falling man.   4162

Henry David Thoreau, *A Plea for John Brown*

He is not Old Brown any longer; he is an angel of light.   4163

Ibid.

—Phyllis McGinley to St. Ignatius Loyola

He died in 1556, so suddenly that there was no time even for the last rites. Few men could have needed them less. And he must have died content to see most of his sons so obedient, his work so flourishing, yet still at hand the hardships he welcomed. One cannot bring oneself to write after his name, "Rest in peace." He who had loved struggle one can only hope is now being given in heaven the most difficult, the most demanding, the most quixotic assignments that an obliging God can invent for His saints.   4164

Phyllis McGinley, *Saint-Watching*

Trouble

Man is born unto trouble as the sparks fly upward.   4165

Job 5:7

The Lord also will be a refuge for the oppressed, a refuge in times of trouble.   4166

Psalm 9:9

Give us help from trouble: for vain is the help of man.   4167

Psalm 60:11

If thou faint in the day of adversity, thy strength is small.   4168

Proverbs 24:10

The harvest is past, the summer is ended, and we are not saved.   4169

Jeremiah 8:20

Sufficient unto the day is the evil thereof.   4170

Jesus in Matthew 6:34

This sickness is not unto death, but for the glory of God.   4171

Jesus in John 11:4

Last night I dreamed of a consolation enjoyed *only* by the blind: Nobody knows the trouble I've *not* seen!   4172

James Thurber, on his failing eyesight. *Newsweek,* 16 June 1958

I believe in getting into hot water. It helps keep you clean.   4173

G. K. Chesterton, in speech c. 1900. Maisie Ward,
Gilbert Keith Chesterton

Troubles are often the tools by which God fashions us for better things.   4174

Henry Ward Beecher, *Proverbs from Plymouth Pulpit*

There are many troubles which you cannot cure by the Bible or the hymnbook, but which you can cure by a good perspiration and a breath of fresh air.   4175

Ibid.

The whole trouble is that we won't let God help us.   4176

George MacDonald, *The Marquis of Lossie*

True Holiness

Make sure that you let God's grace work in your souls by accepting whatever he gives you, and giving him whatever he takes from you. True holiness consists in doing God's will with a smile.   4177

Mother Teresa of Calcutta. Malcolm Muggeridge, *Something Beautiful for God*

True Men

Remember that Hitler positively backed down before Martin Niemöller, that Martin Luther King Jr. through his presence and his policy of nonviolence achieved more than all the Black Panthers and Black Muslims combined. They were an expression of destiny; they were the incarnation of true men. It's a matter of being men like these for others. "Be men," said Isaiah and Paul—there we have what is for nowadays an essential job for faith.　　　　　　　　　　　　　　　　　　　　　　　4178

　　　　　　　Jacques Ellul, *Living Faith*

Trust

I prefer to have too much confidence, and thereby be deceived, than to be always mistrustful. For, in the first case, I suffer for a moment at being deceived and, in the second, I suffer constantly.　　　　　　　　　　　　　　　　　　　4179

　　　　　　　Paul Gauguin. Quoted in Henri Perruchot, *Gauguin*

Let him do to me as seemeth good unto him.　　　　　　　　　　4180

　　　　　　　2 Samuel 15:26

Blessed are all they that put their trust in him.　　　　　　　　4181

　　　　　　　Psalm 2:12

Some trust in chariots, and some in horses: but we will remember the name of the Lord our God.　　　　　　　　　　　　　　　　　　　　　　　　4182

　　　　　　　Psalm 20:7

Into thine hand I commit my spirit.　　　　　　　　　　　　　4183

　　　　　　　Psalm 31:5

He knoweth them that trusteth him.　　　　　　　　　　　　　4184

　　　　　　　Nahum 1:7

Although the fig tree shall not blossom, neither shall fruit be in the vines; the labor of the olive shall fall, and the fields shall yield no meat; the flock shall be cut off from the fold, and there shall be no herd in the stalls: Yet I will rejoice in the Lord, I will joy in the God of my salvation.　　　　　　　　　　　　　　　　　4185

　　　　　　　Habakkuk 3:17–18

Though he slay me, yet will I trust in him: but I will maintain mine own ways before him.　　　　　　　　　　　　　　　　　　　　　　　4186

　　　　　　　Job 13:15

The Christian must trust in a withdrawing God.　　　　　　　　4187

　　　　　　　William Gurnall, *The Golden Treasury of Puritan Quotations*

The only way to make a man trustworthy is to trust him.　　　　　4188

　　　　　　　Henry L. Stimson. Recalled at his death, 20 October 1950

Little love, little trust.　　　　　　　　　　　　　　　　　4189

　　　　　　　English Proverb

A man who trusts nobody is apt to be the kind of man whom nobody trusts. 4190

　　　　　　　Harold MacMillan. *New York Herald Tribune*

Anxiety in human life is what squeaking and grinding are in machinery that is not oiled. In life, trust is the oil.   4191

> Henry Ward Beecher, *Proverbs from Plymouth Pulpit*

Do not trust the man who tells you all his troubles but keeps you from his joys.   4192

> Jewish Proverb

Truth

His truth endureth to all generations.   4193

> Psalm 100:5

The works of his hands are verity and judgment; all his commandments are sure.   4194

> Psalm 111:7

Great is Truth, and mighty above all things. (Vulgate: *Magna est veritas, et praevalebit.*)   4195

> 1 Esdras 4:41

Heaven and earth shall pass away, but my words shall not pass away.   4196

> Jesus in Matthew 24:35

The law was given by Moses, but grace and truth came by Jesus Christ.   4197

> John 1:17

Ye shall know the truth, and the truth shall make you free.   4198

> Jesus in John 8:32

I am the way, the truth, and the life: no man cometh unto the Father, but by me.   4199

> Jesus in John 14:6

Every one that is of the truth heareth my voice.   4200

> Jesus in John 18:37

To this end was I born, and for this cause came I into the world, that I should bear witness unto the truth.   4201

> Jesus in John 18:37

Truth is as old as God—
His twin identity,
And will endure as long as he,
A co-eternity,

And perish on the day
Himself is borne away
From mansion of the universe,
A lifeless deity.   4202

> Emily Dickinson, *Poems,* "Truth is as old as God"

Truth is just itself, and it is nonsense to ask whether it be true or false. Truth is the conformation of Appearance to Reality.   4203

> Alfred North Whitehead, *Adventures of Ideas*

When we can't handle truth we handle facts. 4204
> Peter J. Kreeft, *Love Is Stronger than Death*

The truth that makes men free is for the most part the truth which men prefer not to hear. 4205
> Herbert Agar, *A Time for Greatness*

Man can embody truth but he cannot know it. 4206
> Author uncertain, variously ascribed to W. B. Yeats and Archibald MacLeish

Craft must have clothes, but truth loves to go naked. 4207
> Thomas Fuller, *Gnomoloyia*

Truth is truth, whether from the lips of Jesus or Balaam. 4208
> George MacDonald, *Unspoken Sermons, First Series,* "The New Name"

Truth is the radiant manifestation of reality. 4209
> Simone Weil, *The Need for Roots*

Truth is within ourselves: it takes no rise
From outward things, whate'er you may believe.
There is an inmost centre in us all,
Where truth abides in fulness. 4210
> Robert Browning, *Paracelsus*

Between truth, and the search for truth, I opt for the second. 4211
> Bernard Berenson, *Essays in Appreciation*

If all men spoke the truth, there would be no further need to wait for the Messiah; he would have come long ago. 4212
> Rebbe Pinhas of Koretz. Elie Wiesel, *Souls on Fire*

The stream of truth flows through its channels of mistakes. 4213
> Rabindranath Tagore, *Stray Birds*

To love the truth is to refuse to let oneself be saddened by it. 4214
> Andre Gíde, *Journal,* 14 October 1940

Tyranny

Envy thou not the oppressor, and choose none of his ways. 4215
> Proverbs 3:31

Woe unto them that decree unrighteous decrees. 4216
> Isaiah 10:1

How art thou fallen from heaven, O Lucifer, son of the morning! 4217
> Isaiah 14:12

They that spoil thee shall be a spoil, and all that prey upon thee will I give for a prey. 4218
> Jeremiah 30:16

He shall come to his end, and none shall help him. 4219
> Daniel 11:45

Many must he fear whom many fear. *(Multos timere debet quem multi timent.)*   4220
Publilius Syrus, *Sententiae*

Nature has left this tincture in the blood,
That all men would be tyrants if they could.   4221
Daniel Defoe, *The Kentish Petition, Addenda*

The worst tyrant is not the man who rules by fear; the worst tyrant is he who rules by love and plays on it as on a harp.   4222
G. K. Chesterton, *Robert Browning*

U

Ugliness

Ugliness is a sin. 4223
>Frank Lloyd Wright. Interview, 1951

The secret of ugliness consists not in irregularity, but in being uninteresting. 4224
>Ralph Waldo Emerson, *The Conduct of Life*

A thing of ugliness is potent for evil. It deforms the taste of the thoughtless; it frets the man who knows how bad it is. 4225
>Sir Arthur Helps, *Friends in Council*

Ugliness is a point of view: an ulcer is wonderful to a pathologist. 4226
>Austin O'Malley, *Keystones of Thought*

Ultimate Union (platonically conceived)

And there's an end, I think, of kissing,
When our mouths are one with Mouth. 4227
>Rupert Brooke, *Tiare Tahiti*

Unbelief

And he did not many mighty works there because of their unbelief. (he: Jesus.) 4228
>Matthew 13:58

And straightway the father of the child cried out with tears, Lord, I believe; help thou mine unbelief. 4229
>Mark 9:24

Blind unbelief is sure to err,
   And scan His work in vain;
God is his own interpreter,
   And He will make it plain. 4230
>William Cowper, hymn, "God moves in a mysterious way"

If we love God while thinking that he does not exist, he will manifest his presence. 4231
>Simone Weil, *Gravity and Grace*

Understanding

Give thy servant an understanding heart to judge thy people, that I may discern between good and bad: for who is able to judge this so great people? 4232
1 Kings 3:9

Wisdom is the principal thing; therefore get wisdom: but with all thy getting get understanding. 4233
Proverbs 4:7

I would rather understand one cause than to be King of Persia. 4234
Democritus of Abdera. Quoted in Carl Sagan, *Cosmos*

I have tried sedulously not to laugh at the acts of men, nor to lament them, nor to detest them, but to understand them. 4235
Baruch Spinoza, *Tractatus theologico-politicus*

All the glory of greatness has no lustre for people who are in search of understanding. 4236
Blaise Pascal, *Pensées*

Of course, *understanding* of our fellow beings is important. But this understanding becomes fruitful only when it is sustained by sympathetic feeling in joy and sorrow. 4237
Albert Einstein, *Ideas and Opinions*

To me, if I can see things through and through, I get uneasy—I feel it's a fake. I know I have left something out, I've made some mistake. 4238
Friedrich von Hügel, *Letters to a Niece*

When you want to recognize and understand what takes place in the minds of others, you have first to look into yourself. 4239
Theodore Reik, *Listening with the Third Ear*

Union

Union differentiates. 4240
Pierre Teilhard de Chardin, *The Phenomenon of Man*

None can be eternally united who have not died for each other. 4241
Coventry Patmore, *The Rod, the Root and the Flower*

Union must precede conjunction. Conjunction is the fruition, or consciousness, of union. 4242
Ibid.

There are three unions in this world: Christ and the Church, husband and wife, spirit and flesh. 4243
St. Augustine, *Of Continence*

Unity

Behold how good and how pleasant it is for brethren to dwell together in unity! 4244
Psalm 133:1

When spider webs unite, they can tie up a lion. 4245
       Ethiopian Proverb

In necessary things, unity; in doubtful things, liberty; in all things, charity. 4246
       Richard Baxter, motto

Unity is plural and, at minimum, is two. 4247
       R. Buckminster Fuller, *Synergetics*, "Moral of the Work"

In the Word is involved the unity of humanity, the wholeness of the human problem, which permits nobody to separate the intellectual and artistic from the political and social, and to isolate himself within the ivory tower of the "cultural" proper. 4248
       Thomas Mann. Letter to the dean of the Philosophical Faculty, Bonn University, January 1937

Universe

It is not impossible that to some infinitely superior being the whole universe may be as one plain, the distance between planet and planet being only as the pores in a grain of sand, and the spaces between system and system no greater than the intervals between one grain and the grain adjacent. 4249
       Samuel Taylor Coleridge, *Omniana*

A man said to the universe,
"Sir, I exist!"
"However," replied the universe,
"The fact has not created in me
A sense of obligation." 4250
       Stephen Crane, *War Is Kind*

The conclusion forced upon me in the course of a life devoted to natural science is that the universe as it is assumed to be in physical science is a spiritual universe in which spiritual values count for everything. 4251
       J. B. S. Haldane, *The Sciences and Philosophy*

The universe is the language of God. 4252
       Lorenz Oken, *Elements of Physiophilosophy*

The only universe capable of containing the human person is an irreversibly "personalizing" universe. 4253
       Pierre Teilhard de Chardin, *The Phenomenon of Man*

All things by immortal power,
Near and far,
Hiddenly
To each other linked are,
That thou canst not stir a flower without troubling of a star. 4254
       Francis Thompson, *The Mistress of Vision*

The entire universe pre-exists in the Godhead, which is its primordial cause. Father, Son, and Holy Ghost are all in all, because in their divinity every other thing is anticipated and possessed. 4255
       St. Thomas Aquinas, *The Divine Names*

Unselfishness

To reach perfection, we must all pass, one by one, through the death of self-effacement.   4256

Dag Hammarskjöld, *Markings*

The small share of happiness attainable by man exists only insofar as he is able to cease to think of himself.   4257

Theodore Reik, *Of Love and Lust*

If you asked twenty good men today what they thought the highest of the virtues, nineteen of them would reply, Unselfishness. But if you asked almost any of the great Christians of old he would have replied, Love. Do you see what has happened? A negative term has been substituted for a positive and this is of more than philological importance. The negative ideal of Unselfishness carries with it the suggestion not primarily of securing good things for others, but of going without them ourselves, as if our abstinence and not their happiness was the important point. I do not think this is the Christian idea of love.   4258

C. S. Lewis, *The Weight of Glory*

Usefulness

Make yourself necessary to somebody.   4259

Ralph Waldo Emerson, *The Conduct of Life*

All men know the utility of useful things; but they do not know the utility of futility.   4260

Chuang-Tzu, *This Human World*

What is the use of a newborn child?   4261

Benjamin Franklin, when asked the use of a new invention

Utopia

Ideal society is a drama enacted exclusively to the imagination.   4262

George Santayana, *The Life of Reason*

I have searched vainly among the words of the wise for a single respectful one spoken for utopians, so here is one from the unwise, spoken with conviction: no great prophet or pioneer has ever arisen among our species who was not motivated to a considerable degree by that itch that allows its victim no rest—the goading charisma of utopianism. Of that nobly eccentric tribe of dreamers it is written that "they desire a better country . . . wherefore God is not ashamed to be called their God: for he hath prepared for them a city" (Heb. 11:16).   4263

C. E. S.

V

Value

There is no such thing as mere value. Value is the word I use for the intrinsic reality of an event. 4264
> Alfred North Whitehead, *Science in the Modern World*

The term "value," meaning the radical subjectivity of all belief about good and evil, serves the easygoing quest for comfortable self-preservation. 4265
> Allan Bloom, *The Closing of the American Mind*

All good things are cheap; all bad are very dear. 4266
> Henry David Thoreau, *Journal,* 3 March 1841

Vanity

Behold, thou hast made my days as an handbreadth; and my age is as nothing before thee: verily every man at his best state is altogether vanity. 4267
> Psalm 39:5

Vanity of vanities, saith the Preacher, vanity of vanities, all is vanity. 4268
> Ecclesiastes 1:2

Those who write against vanity wish to have the glory of having written well, and those who read them wish to have the glory of reading well, and I who write this have the same desire, and maybe also those who read this. 4269
> Blaise Pascal, *Pensées*

To say that a man is vain means merely that he is pleased with the effect he produces on other people. A conceited man is pleased with the effect he produces on himself. 4270
> Max Beerbohm, *Quia Imperfectum*

Violence

He that smiteth his father, or his mother, shall be surely put to death. 4271
> Exodus 21:15

The Lord trieth the righteous: but the wicked and him that loveth violence his soul hateth. 4272
> Psalm 11:5

Evil shall hunt the violent man to overthrow him.   4273
Psalm 140:11

Woe to him that buildeth a town with blood.   4274
Habakkuk 2:12

All they that take the sword shall perish by the sword.   4275
Jesus in Matthew 26:52

Do violence to no man, neither accuse any falsely.   4276
Luke 3:14

With violence shall that great city, Babylon, be thrown down.   4277
Revelation 18:21

Kicks only raise dust and not crops from the earth.   4278
Rabindranath Tagore, *Stray Birds*

We are all shot through with enough motives to make a massacre, any day of the week when we want to give them their head.   4279
Jacob Bronowski, *The Face of Violence*

The limitation of riots, moral questions aside, is that they cannot win it and their participants know it. Hence, rioting is not revolutionary but reactionary because it invites defeat. It involves an emotional catharsis, but it must be followed by a sense of futility.   4280
Martin Luther King, Jr., *The Trumpet of Conscience*

Most Americans would say that they disapproved of violence. But what they really mean is that they believe it should be the monopoly of the state.   4281
Edgar Z. Friedenburg, *New York Review of Books,* 20 October 1966

In violence, we forget who we are, just as we forget who we are when we are engaged in sheer perception.   4282
Mary McCarthy, *On the Contrary*

Virginity

Virginity can be lost even by a thought.   4283
St. Jerome, *Epistles,* "The Virgin's Confession"

No evil thing that walks by night
In fog or fire, by lake or moorish fen,
Blue meager hag, or stubborn unlaid ghost
That breaks his magic chains at curfew time,
No goblin, or swart faery of the mine,
Hath hurtful power o'er true virginity.   4284
John Milton, *Comus*

Virtue

I hold virtue to be nothing other than perfect love of God.   4285
St. Augustine, *De Moribus Ecclesiae Catholicae*

Virtue is not hereditary.   4286
Thomas Paine, *Common Sense.* Letter to William Johnson, 1823

Virtue lives after the funeral. *(Vivit post funera virtus.)*   4287
> Author unknown. Epitaph of Thomas Linacre, St. Paul's, London, c. 1555

Virtue is like a rich stone—best plain set.   4288
> Francis Bacon, *Essays,* "Of Beauty"

Virtue is not always amiable.   4289
> John Adams, *Diary,* 9 February 1779

Every virtue is a *habitus*—i.e. a good stock response.   4290
> C. S. Lewis, *Christian Reflections*

Virtue is bold, and goodness never fearful.   4291
> William Shakespeare, *Measure for Measure,* III, i, 209

The chief assertion of religious morality is that white is a color. Virtue is not the absence of vices or the avoidance of moral dangers; virtue is a vivid and separate thing, like pain or a particular smell.   4292
> G. K. Chesterton, *Tremendous Trifles*

Vision

Where there is no vision, the people perish.   4293
> Proverbs 29:18

And the child Samuel ministered unto the Lord before Eli. And the word of the Lord was precious in those days; there was no open vision.   4294
> 1 Samuel 3:1

Your old men shall dream dreams, your young men shall see visions.   4295
> Joel 2:28

Behold, I see the heavens opened, and the Son of man standing on the right hand of God.   4296
> Acts 7:56

We are as much as we see. Faith is sight and knowledge. The hands only serve the eyes.   4297
> Henry David Thoreau, *Journal,* 9 April 1841

Vision is the art of seeing things invisible.   4298
> Jonathan Swift, *Thoughts on Various Subjects, Moral and Diverting*

Great is his faith who dares to believe his own eyes.   4299
> Coventry Patmore, *The Rod, the Root and the Flower*

By this you may know vision: that it is not what you expected, or even what you could have imagined, and that it is never repeated.   4300
> Ibid.

Earth's crammed with heaven,
And every common bush aflame with God;
But only he who sees, takes off his shoes;
The rest sit round it and pick blackberries.   4301
> Elizabeth Barrett Browning, *Aurora Leigh*

One sees great things from the valley; only small things from the peak.   4302

G. K. Chesterton, *The Hammer of God*

Who is narrow of vision cannot be big of heart.   4303

Chinese Proverb

Vision of God

Blessed are the pure in heart: for they shall see God.   4304

Jesus in Matthew 5:8

And they shall see his face; and his name shall be in their foreheads.   4305

Revelation 22:4

I have *seen* that which makes all that I have previously taught and written seem as chaff to me.   4306

St. Thomas Aquinas, after he had completed all his monumental theologizing

Men oft see God,

But never know 'tis He till He has passed.   4307

Coventry Patmore, *The Rod, the Root and the Flower*

You may see the disc of divinity quite clearly through the smoked glass of humanity, but not otherwise.   4308

Ibid.

They alone will see God who prefer to recognize the truth and die, instead of living a long and happy existence in a state of illusion. One must want to go towards reality; then, when one thinks one has found a corpse, one meets an angel who says: "He is risen."   4309

Simone Weil, *Gateway to God*

Vivisection

You do not settle whether an experiment is justified or not by showing that it is of some use. The distinction is not between useful and useless experiments, but between barbarous and civilized behavior. Vivisection is a social evil because if it advances human knowledge it does so at the expense of human behavior.   4310

George Bernard Shaw. Quoted by "Dear Abby"

in syndicated column, 9 April 1985

Vocation

Ye see your calling, brethren, how that not many wise men after the flesh, not many mighty, not many noble, are called: But God hath chosen the foolish things of the world to confound the wise; and God hath chosen the weak things of the world to confound the things which are mighty. . . . that no flesh should glory in his presence.   4311

1 Corinthians 1:26–27, 29

Let every man abide in the same calling wherein he was called.   4312

1 Corinthians 7:20

I therefore, the prisoner of the Lord, beseech you that ye walk worthy of the vocation wherewith ye are called, With all lowliness and meekness, with longsuffering, forbearing one another in love; endeavoring to keep the unity of the Spirit in the bond of peace. 4313

Ephesians 4:1–3

Many people mistake our work for our vocation. Our vocation is the love of Jesus. 4314

Mother Teresa of Calcutta. Quoted from documentary film, *Mother Teresa*

Only God knows what is one's real work. 4315

Anton Chekhov, *Uncle Vanya*

God leads every soul by a separate path. 4316

St. John of the Cross, *Living Flame of Love*

It is not the religious act that makes the Christian, but participation in the sufferings of God in the secular life. 4317

Dietrich Bonhoeffer, *Letters and Papers from Prison*

A good vocation is simply a firm and constant will in which the called person has to serve God in the way and in the places to which almighty God has called him. 4318

St. Francis de Sales, *Letters to Persons in Religion*

The place God calls you to is the place where your deep gladness and the world's deep hunger meet. 4319

Frederick Buechner, *Wishful Thinking: A Theological ABC*

Vulgarity

A coarse-grained man is like an indiscreet story endlessly retold by the ignorant. 4320

Ecclesiasticus 20:20, *The Jerusalem Bible*

The vulgar man is always the most distinguished, for the very desire to be distinguished is vulgar. 4321

G. K. Chesterton, *All Things Considered*

It is disgusting to pick your teeth; what is vulgar is to use a gold toothpick. 4322

Louis Kronenberger, *The Cart and the Horse*

W

Waiting

Rest in the Lord, and wait patiently for him: fret not thyself because of him who prospereth in his way, because of the man who bringeth wicked devices to pass.   4323

Psalm 37:7

I wait for the Lord, my soul doth wait, and in his word do I hope.   4324

Psalm 130:5

They that wait upon the Lord shall renew their strength; they shall mount up with wings as eagles; they shall run, and not be weary; and they shall walk, and not faint.   4325

Isaiah 40:31

It is good that a man should both hope and quietly wait for the salvation of the Lord.   4326

Lamentations 3:26

Serene, I fold my hands and wait,
Nor care for wind, nor tide, nor sea;
I rave no more 'gainst time or fate,
For lo! my own shall come to me.   4327

John Burroughs, *Waiting*

The philosophy of waiting is sustained by all the oracles of the universe.   4328

Ralph Waldo Emerson, *Journals,* 1847

For a good dinner and a gentle wife you can afford to wait.   4329

Danish Proverb

They also serve who only stand and wait.   4330

John Milton, *Sonnet on his Blindness*

"If the Lord tarry wait for Him, and He will not tarry but come quickly." The impatience of the Soul for vision is one of the last faults that can be cured. Only to those who watch and wait, with absolute indifference to the season of revelation, do all things reveal themselves.   4331

Coventry Patmore, *The Rod, the Root and the Flower*

War and Peace

Either war is obsolete, or men are.   4332
> R. Buckminster Fuller, *I Seem to Be a Verb*

A great war always creates more scoundrels than it kills.   4333
> Author Unknown

There is no such thing as a *little war* for a great nation.   4334
> Duke of Wellington (Arthur Wellesley). House of Lords,
> 16 January 1838

Patriots always talk of dying for their country, and never of killing for their country.   4335
> Bertrand Russell, attributed

It is forbidden to kill, therefore all murderers are punished unless they kill in large numbers and to the sound of trumpets.   4336
> Voltaire, *Philosophical Dictionary,* "War"

Among the calamities of war may justly be numbered the diminution of the love of truth.   4337
> Samuel Johnson, *The Idler,* no. 30

If we do not abolish war on this earth, then surely one day war will abolish us from the earth.   4338
> Harry S. Truman. Speech, Independence, Mo., 1966

How good bad music and bad reasons sound when one marches against an enemy!   4339
> Friedrich Wilhelm Nietzsche, *The Dawn*

War will never cease until babies come into the world with larger cerebrums and smaller adrenal glands.   4340
> Henry L. Mencken, *Minority Report*

There are no warlike people—just warlike leaders.   4341
> Ralph J. Bunche. Address to United Nations, date unknown

Every gun that is made, every warship launched, every rocket fired, signifies in the final sense a theft from those who hunger and are not fed, those who are cold and not clothed.   4342
> Dwight D. Eisenhower. Speech to American Society of Newspaper
> Editors, 16 April 1953

Way

I am the way, the truth, and the life: no man cometh unto the Father, but by me.   4343
> Jesus in John 14:6

Even if Epictetus did see the way quite clearly, he only told men: "You are on the wrong track." He shows that there is another, but he does not lead us there. The right way is to want what God wants. Christ alone leads to it. *Via veritas.*   4344
> Blaise Pascal, *Pensées*

It is not by eating the fruit of a certain tree, as Adam thought, that one becomes the equal of God, but by going the way of the cross. 4345

Simone Weil, *Notebooks*

We

It may be hard for an egg to turn into a bird: it would be a jolly sight harder for it to learn to fly while remaining an egg. We are like eggs at present. And you cannot go on indefinitely being just an ordinary decent egg. We must be hatched or go bad. 4346

C. S. Lewis, *Mere Christianity*

We and Others

Your Honor, years ago I recognized my kinship with all living things, and I made up my mind that I was not one whit better than the meanest of earth. I said then, and I say now, that while there is a lower class, I am in it; while there is a criminal element, I am of it; while there is a soul in prison I am not free. 4347

Eugene V. Debs, when convicted of conspiring against civil order in September 1919

Strange is our situation here upon earth. Each of us comes for a short visit, not knowing why, yet sometimes seeming to divine a purpose.

From the standpoint of daily life, however, there is one thing we do know: that man is here for the sake of other men—above all for those upon whose smile and well-being our own happiness depends, and also for the countless unknown souls with whose fate we are connected by a bond of sympathy. Many times a day I realize how much my own inner and outer life is built upon the labors of my fellow men, both living and dead, and how earnestly I must exert myself in order to give in return as much as I have received. My peace of mind is often troubled by the depressing sense that I have borrowed too heavily from the work of other men. 4348

Albert Einstein. *Living Philosophies* (Pelican), "Strange Is Our Situation Here upon Earth"

When first you unite yourself by charity to the whole human race, then shall you indeed perceive that Christ died for you. 4349

Coventry Patmore, *The Rod, the Root and the Flower*

Wealth

It is only when the rich are sick that they fully feel the impotence of wealth. 4350

Charles Caleb Colton, *Lacon*

The greater the wealth the thicker will be the dirt. This indubitably describes the tendency of our time. 4351

John Kenneth Galbraith, *The Affluent Society*

Wealth is the relentless enemy of understanding. 4352

Ibid.

Wealth is a good servant, a very bad mistress. 4353

Francis Bacon, *Exempla Antithetorum,* "Divitiae"

No one has yet had the courage to memorialize his wealth on his tombstone. It would not look well there.   4354

> Corra May Harris, *A Circuit Rider's Wife*

Wealth infatuates as well as beauty.   4355

> Chinese Proverb

A man who has a million dollars is as well off as if he were rich.   4356

> John Jacob Astor III, attributed

So long as all the increased wealth which modern progress brings goes but to build up great fortunes, to increase luxury and make sharper the contrast between the House of Have and the House of Want, progress is not real and cannot be permanent.   4357

> Henry George, *Progress and Poverty,* introduction

What Might Have Been

I would have made a good Pope.   4358

> Richard M. Nixon. Robert Byrne, *The 637 Best Things Anybody Ever Said*

For of all sad words of tongue or pen,
The saddest are these: "It might have been!"   4359

> John Greenleaf Whittier, *Maud Muller*

Whither?

Every cradle asks us, "Whence?" and every coffin, "Whither?" The poor barbarian, weeping above his dead, can answer these questions as intelligently as the rabid priest of the most authentic creed.   4360

> Robert G. Ingersoll. Address at a child's grave

Wickedness

The wicked flee when no man pursueth: but the righteous are bold as a lion.   4361

> Proverbs 28:1

There is no peace, saith the Lord, unto the wicked.   4362

> Isaiah 48:22

All wickedness is weakness.   4363

> John Milton, *Samson Agonistes*

No man ever became wicked all at once.   4364

> Juvenal, *Satires*

A wicked man is his own Hell.   4365

> Thomas Fuller, *Gnomologia*

There are wicked people who would be much less dangerous if they were wholly without goodness.   4366

> François de la Rochefoucauld, *Maxims*

Wisdom

Wisdom is a loving spirit. 4367
Wisdom of Solomon 1:6, *The Jerusalem Bible*

Her ways are ways of pleasantness, and all her paths are peace. (Her: wisdom's.) 4368
Proverbs 3:17

Will and wisdom are both mighty leaders. Our times worship Will. 4369
Clarence Day, *The Crow's Nest*

Wisdom is the way in which knowledge is held. 4370
Alfred North Whitehead, *The Aims of Education*

The chief end of wisdom is to enable one to bear with the stupidity of the ignorant. 4371
Pope Sixtus I, *The Ring*

Proverbs contradict each other. That is the wisdom of a nation. 4372
Stanislaw J. Lec, *Unkempt Thoughts*

For only by unlearning Wisdom comes. 4373
James Russell Lowell, *The Parting of the Ways*

Wisdom has its roots in goodness, and not goodness its roots in wisdom. 4374
Ralph Waldo Emerson, *Journal,* 1857

Wisdom doesn't always speak in Greek and Latin. 4375
Thomas Fuller, *Gnomologia*

It is the province of knowledge to speak and it is the privilege of wisdom to listen. 4376
Oliver Wendell Holmes, *The Poet at the Breakfast-Table*

God waits for man to regain his childhood in wisdom. 4377
Rabindranath Tagore, *Stray Birds*

Withdrawal and Return

To go up alone into the mountain and come back as an ambassador to the world has ever been the method of humanity's best friends. 4378
Evelyn Underhill, *Mysticism*

Woman

It wasn't a woman who betrayed Jesus with a kiss. 4379
Catherine Carswell, *The Savage Pilgrimage*

The woman who is known only through a man is known wrong. 4380
Henry Adams, *The Education of Henry Adams*

Women prefer poverty with love to luxury without it. 4381
Haggadah, *Palestinian Talmud*

The entire being of a woman is a secret which should be kept. 4382
Isak Dinesen, *Last Tales,* "Of Hidden Thoughts and of Heaven"

One is not born, but rather becomes, a woman. 4383
Simone de Beauvoir, *The Second Sex*

To conclude that women are unfitted to the task of our historic society seems to me the equivalent of closing male eyes to female facts. 4384
Lyndon B. Johnson, at White House swearing-in ceremony of
women appointees, 13 April 1964

The endearing elegance of female friendship. 4385
Samuel Johnson, *Rasselas*

One woman reads another's character without the tedious trouble of deciphering. 4386
Ben Jonson, *The New Inn,* IV

Since women have been outside the system for so many centuries, it would be odd if they had not worked out an inner language that permitted them to puncture the pomposities. 4387
Leta Clark. *New York Times,* 26 November 1977

Wonder

There be three things which are too wonderful for me, yea, four which I know not: the way of an eagle in the air; the way of a serpent upon a rock; the way of a ship in the midst of the sea; and the way of a man with a maid. 4388
Proverbs 30:18–19

That I exist is a perpetual surprise which is life. 4389
Rabindranath Tagore, *Stray Birds*

Worship is transcendent wonder. 4390
Thomas Carlyle, *Heroes and Hero-Worship*

Words

Man does not live by words alone, despite the fact that sometimes he has to eat them. 4391
Adlai E. Stevenson. Speech, Denver, 5 September 1952

Words not only affect us temporarily; they change us, they socialize or unsocialize us. 4392
David Riesman, *The Lonely Crowd*

Fine words butter no parsnips. 4393
English Proverb

Woord is but wynd; leave woord and take the dede. 4394
John Lydgate (c. 1370–c. 1450), *Secreta Secretorum*

Words are less needful to sorrow than to joy. 4395
Helen Hunt Jackson, *Romona*

Words are wise men's counters, they do but reckon with them; but they are the money of fools. 4396
Thomas Hobbes, *Leviathan*

I sometimes hold it half a sin
  To put in words the grief I feel;
  For words, like nature, half reveal
And half conceal the soul within.   4397
        Alfred, Lord Tennyson, *In Memoriam, A. H. H.*

"Every idle word that men shall speak, they shall give account thereof in the day of judgment" *(Matt. 12:36).* O my God! Who—*me?*   4398
        C. E. S.

Work

See Labor

World

See also This Life and World

Listen, my heart, to the whispers of the world with which it makes love to you.   4399
        Rabindranath Tagore, *Stray Birds*

We read the world wrong and say that it deceives us.   4400
        Ibid.

The world is both a paradise and a prison to different persons.   4401
        Thomas Traherne, *Centuries*

The world is a dance in which good, descending from God, is disturbed by evil arising from the creatures, and the resulting conflict is resolved by God's own assumption of the suffering nature which evil produces.   4402
        C. S. Lewis, *The Problem of Pain*

No cradle for an emperor's child was ever prepared with so much magnificence as this world has been made for man. But it is only his cradle.   4403
        Henry Ward Beecher, *Proverbs from Plymouth Pulpit*

The world is not a "prison house" but a kind of spiritual kindergarten where millions of bewildered infants are trying to spell God with the wrong blocks.   4404
        Edward Arlington Robinson. Letter to *The Bookman,* March 1897

Worship

The submission of man's nothing-perfect to God's all-complete.   4405
        Robert Browning, *Saul*

O sweeter than the marriage-feast,
'Tis sweeter far to me,
To walk together to the kirk
With a goodly company!
To walk together to the kirk,
And all together pray,
While each to his great Father bends,

Old men, and babes, and loving friends
And youths and maidens gay! 4406
Samuel Taylor Coleridge, *The Rime of the Ancient Mariner*

God, if I worship thee in fear of hell, burn me in hell. And if I worship thee in hope of paradise, exclude me from paradise. But if I worship thee for thine own sake, withhold not thine everlasting beauty. 4407
Rabi'a. Quoted in Aldous Huxley, *The Perennial Philosophy*

A man's worship counts for naught, except his dog and cat are better for it. 4408
Shaker Saying

True piety, which flourishes only when the spirit spontaneously strives to grow in charity, withers when the spirit sluggishly reposes on external ceremonies chosen for it by others. 4409
Desiderius Erasmus. Quoted in Thomas Merton, *Conjectures of a Guilty Bystander*

Y

Years

A thousand years in thy sight are but as yesterday when it is past, and as a watch in the night.   4410
> Psalm 90:4

I will restore to you the years that the locust hath eaten.   4411
> Joel 2:25

The years teach much which the days can never know.   4412
> Ralph Waldo Emerson, *Essays,* "Experience"

They shall grow not old, as we that are left grow old:
Age shall not weary them, nor the years condemn.   4413
> Laurence Binyon, *For the Fallen*

Yes and No

When you do say Yes, say it quickly. But always take a half hour to say No, so you can understand the other fellow's side.   4414
> Francis Cardinal Spellman, advice to his successor Terence Cooke;
> recalled on Cooke's death, 6 October 1983

Yesterday, Today, Tomorrow

Let us not bankrupt our todays by paying interest on the regrets of yesterday and borrowing in advance the troubles of tomorrow.   4415
> Ralph W. Sockman. Radio sermon, NBC, 12 January 1958

Youth

See Age, Youth

Index of Sources

Unless otherwise noted, numerical references are to entries, not page numbers.

Scripture Index

Subject Index

All numerical references are to entries, not page numbers. Italicized numbers refer to main entries and appear first. Those in roman type are ancillary.